Laboring Women

→ role of rape? – neglected

power not exerted over
whites/Gauks?

? In one way or another state
authors explore how African
either accomodate/assimilated,
resisted,
or a mixture
↳ created new cultures

D0165651

EARLY AMERICAN STUDIES

Daniel K. Richter and Kathleen M. Brown, Series Editors

Exploring neglected aspects of our colonial, revolutionary, and early national history and culture, Early American Studies reinterprets familiar themes and events in fresh ways. Interdisciplinary in character, and with a special emphasis on the period from about 1600 to 1850, the series is published in partnership with the McNeil Center for Early American Studies.

A complete list of books in the series is available from the publisher.

Laboring Women

Reproduction and Gender in New World Slavery

Jennifer L. Morgan

PENN

University of Pennsylvania Press
Philadelphia

Copyright © 2004 University of Pennsylvania Press
All rights reserved
Printed in the United States of America on acid-free paper

10   9   8   7   6   5   4

Published by
University of Pennsylvania Press
Philadelphia, Pennsylvania 19104-4112

Library of Congress Cataloging-in-Publication Data

Morgan, Jennifer L. (Jennifer Lyle)
    Laboring women : reproduction and gender in New World slavery / Jennifer L. Morgan.
       p.   cm. (Early American Studies)
    ISBN-13: 978-0-8122-1873-2
    ISBN-10: 0-8122-1873-6 (pbk. : acid-free paper)
    Includes bibliographical references and index.
    1. Women slaves—North America—Social conditions.   2. Women slaves—West Indies,
British—Social conditions.   3. Sex role—North America—History.   4. Sex role—West Indies,
British—History.   5. Human reproduction—Social aspects—North America—History.
6. Human reproduction—Social aspects—West Indies, British—History.   7. Slavery—North
America—History.   8. Slavery—West Indies, British—History.   9. North America—Race
relations.   10. West Indies, British—Race relations.
HT1048 .M67   2004
306.3'62/082097—dc22   2003066597

For Herman

Contents

List of Illustrations   ix

Note on Sources   xi

Introduction   1

1   "Some Could Suckle over Their Shoulder": Male Travelers, Female Bodies, and the Gendering of Racial Ideology   12

2   "The Number of Women Doeth Much Disparayes the Whole Cargoe": The Trans-Atlantic Slave Trade and West African Gender Roles   50

3   "The Breedings Shall Goe with Their Mothers": Gender and Evolving Practices of Slaveownership in the English American Colonies   69

4   "Hannah and Hir Children": Reproduction and Creolization Among Enslaved Women   107

5   "Women's Sweat": Gender and Agricultural Labor in the Atlantic World   144

6   "Deluders and Seducers of Each Other": Gender and the Changing Nature of Resistance   166

Epilogue   196

Notes   203

Bibliography   251

Index   273

Acknowledgments   277

Illustrations

1. Young virgin covering her breast   22
2. Woman suckling child   23
3. Native American woman with child, two views   24
4. Woman holding leg   25
5. Women on map of Tierra del Fuego   26
6. Woman breastfeeding over her shoulder   32
7. Women in Africa   33
8. Hottentot woman suckling over her shoulder   34
9. High-breasted women illustrating America   37
10. Native American woman suckling over her shoulder on map of Granada   38
11. Native American woman with sagging breasts on map of Guiana   39
12. Native American woman suckling over her shoulder in Chile   39
13. Hottentot woman suckling over her shoulder while smoking marijuana   43
14. "Description of the Habits of Most Countries in the World"   44
15. Men and women, Barbados plantations, 1650–59   117
16. Men and women, Barbados plantations, 1660–69   118

Note on Sources

The Barbados Department of Archives contains some 3,000 wills and inventories recorded in the second half of the seventeenth century. I examined all extant wills recorded between 1640 and 1685 and all inventories from the 1650s and 1660s. I examined all the extant wills (approximately 1,500) in the South Carolina Department of Archives and History for the decades between 1690 and 1750; and approximately 500 estate inventories from 1735 to 1745. The tables in this study are derived from the total number of those wills and inventories that identified persons of African descent.

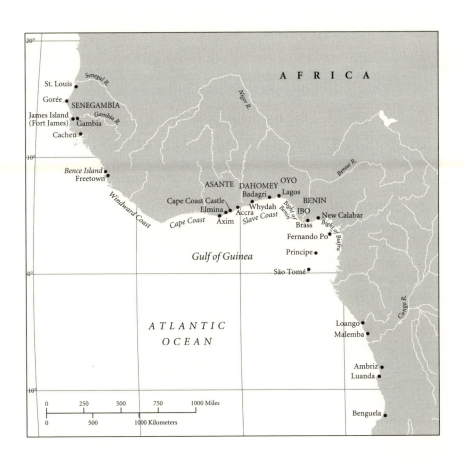

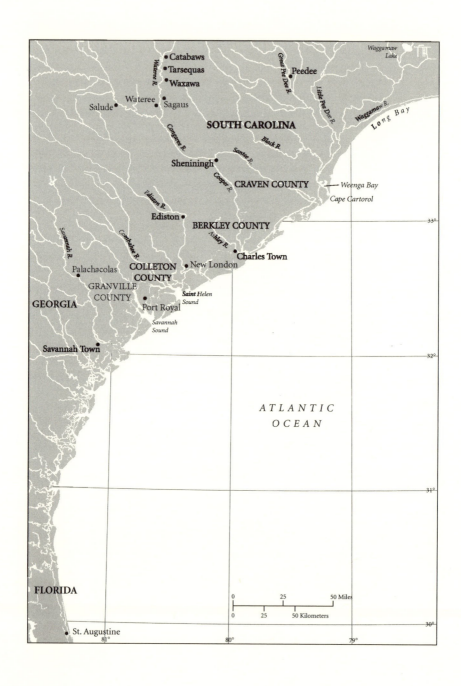

Catabaws
Tarsequas
Waxawa

Wateree *R.*

Peedee

Great Pee Dee R.

Little Pee Dee R.

Waggamaw Lake

Salude
Wateree
Sagaus

Waggamaw R.

Long Bay

SOUTH CAROLINA

Congaree R.

Black R.

Sheniningh

Santee R.

Cooper R.

CRAVEN COUNTY

Weenga Bay

Cape Cartorol

Edisto R.

Ediston

BERKLEY COUNTY

Ashley R.

33°

Savannah R.

Combahee R.

Charles Town

Palachacolas

COLLETON COUNTY

New London

GRANVILLE COUNTY

Saint Helen Sound

GEORGIA

Port Royal

Savannah Sound

Savannah Town

32°

ATLANTIC OCEAN

31°

FLORIDA

0   25   50 Miles

0   25   50 Kilometers

30°

St. Augustine
81°

80°

79°

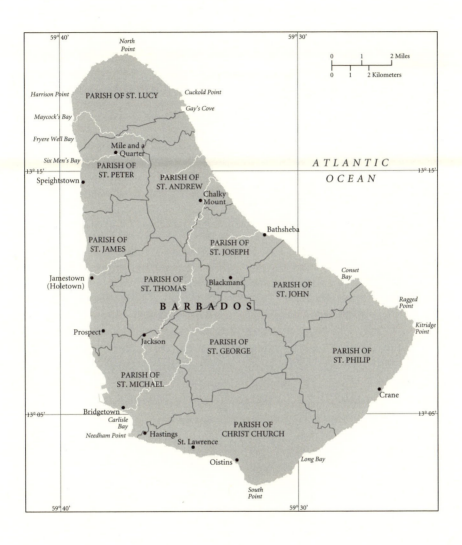

North
Point

0   1   2 Miles

0   1   2 Kilometers

Harrison Point

PARISH OF ST. LUCY

Cuckold Point

Gay's Cove

Maycock's Bay

Fryere Well Bay

Six Men's Bay

Mile and a
Quarter

ATLANTIC

OCEAN

13° 15'

PARISH OF
ST. PETER

13° 15'

Speightstown

PARISH OF
ST. ANDREW

Chalky
Mount

Bathsheba

PARISH OF
ST. JAMES

PARISH OF
ST. JOSEPH

Conset
Bay

Jamestown
(Holetown)

PARISH OF
ST. THOMAS

Blackmans

PARISH OF
ST. JOHN

Ragged
Point

B A R B A D O S

Kitridge
Point

Prospect

Jackson

PARISH OF
ST. GEORGE

PARISH OF
ST. PHILIP

PARISH OF
ST. MICHAEL

13° 05'

Bridgetown

Crane

13° 05'

Carlisle
Bay

Needham Point

Hastings

St. Lawrence

PARISH OF
CHRIST CHURCH

Oistins

Long Bay

South
Point

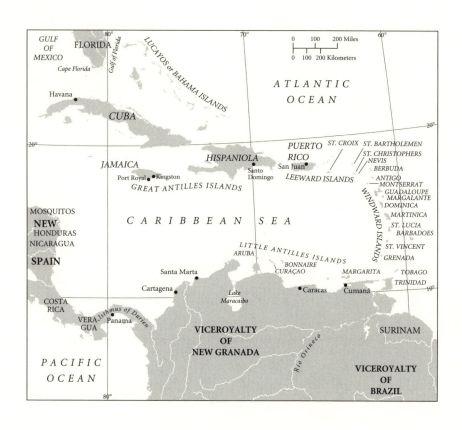

Introduction

Slaveowners in the early English colonies depended upon and exploited African women. They required women's physical labors in order to reap the profits of the colonies and they required women's symbolic value in order to make sense of racial slavery. Women were enslaved in large numbers, they performed critical hard labor, and they served an essential ideological function. Slaveowners appropriated their reproductive lives by claiming children as property, by rewriting centuries-old European laws of descent, and by defining a biologically driven perpetual racial slavery through the real and imaginary reproductive potential of women whose "blackness" was produced by and produced their enslavability.

African women were to be found throughout the early Atlantic world, as forced and free laborers, as wives of traders and settlers, and as traders and travelers in their own right. A narrowly proscriptive religious doctrine and an ultimate turn toward settler societies based on family migration on the part of the English (late starters in the scramble for New World possessions) tend to hide or obscure the extent to which black women figured in colonial settlements. Loudly voiced colonial complaints about too few (white) women on the one hand and the desirability of (black) male laborers on the other illustrate the problems of primary sources whose authors were concerned with social and political issues and were uninterested in revealing the lives on which so much depended. But ultimately the archive will give voice to not only the presence of these women but also the ways in which their lives explicate some of the connections and mobility that have come to drive historical studies of the early Atlantic. This book explores the ways in which enslaved women lived their lives in the crux of slaveowners' vision of themselves as successful white men and thus shouldered burdens connected to but distinct from those borne by enslaved men.

This book examines colonies in both the English West Indies and on the North American mainland. The connections between the two are myriad. Ties of family and commerce supported by a vibrant maritime presence meant that the exchange of goods and information brought settlers and merchants in Jamaica and, say, Philadelphia into close proximity.[1] These exchanges facilitated shared ideologies of race and racial slavery among those who were becoming slaveowners and thus provided the basis for a common set of experiences on the part of the enslaved. The tension between the unifying reality of racial slavery and the wide-ranging, divergent, and complicated experiences of labor that fell under the rubric of "slavery" has been a central force driving scholarship on forced labor in the Americas for more than forty years. Historians studying men and women caught in the crosscurrents of English colonial ambitions, have often understood geography as paramount. Ira Berlin and Philip Morgan are not alone in demanding that historians pay careful attention to the nuances of time and space when exploring the history of American slavery.[2] Distinctive labor regimes, shaped in crucial ways by the particularities of different crops and the always-waning frontier, defined the lives of enslaved Africans in ways that do not always progress singularly and steadily toward racism. Power is negotiated; mutual respect, affection, and even intimacy across cultures was possible and, in the context of a shared environment, transformed "blacks" and "whites" into trading partners, shipmates, servants, allies, and lovers. Such relationships belied fixed racial categories even as those racial identities came firmly and irrevocably into being. It is precisely the sense of "what could have been" that has shaped some of the most important studies of early American slave societies.[3] In other words, as scholarship about colonial encounters has revealed the contradictory expectations, situational ethics, and slowly evolving legal parameters of racial identity and racial slavery, it has become more than clear that those encounters embodied a wide range of possible outcomes and were shaped by the particularities of an evolving colonial landscape. This sense of possibility, however, must always be balanced by its existence inside a rubric in which "Negro" equals "Slave," with all the false simplicity that such a formulation engenders. One of the projects of this book is to look at women's lives across time and space, to grapple with the ways in which ideologies of race and gender under English colonialism contributed to a set of common experiences for enslaved women that interrupt the specificities of place. In many ways, this book is concerned with a question about the body under slavery: Does the significance of reproductive potential, embedded as it is in women's lived experience, transcend the significance of New World commodities and territories?

Enslavement on the basis of racial heredity forced a social and juridical identity upon men and women of African descent that also defined the parameters of slavery in the American colonies. Moreover, the crucial matter of heredity and the permanent mark of racial inferiority situated enslaved women's reproductive identity at the heart of the matter in ways not always explicated by slaveowners and their visible archives. Women's lives under slavery in the Americas always included the possibilities of their wombs. Whether laboring among sugar cane, coffee bushes, or rice swamps, the cost-benefit calculations of colonial slaveowners included the speculative value of a reproducing labor force. We know that the demographic realities of high infant mortality and low fertility meant that for many Caribbean slaveowners that value remained entirely speculative or was eventually abandoned in favor of replacing those they worked to death with newly purchased laborers. And indeed, the absence of natural increase across the Caribbean and much of the eighteenth-century American South has meant that scholars of slavery have tended to omit the consequences of women's reproductive capacity from their equations. But women's work and women's bodies are inseparable from the landscape of colonial slavery. The same attention to demography that removes women's reproductive lives from the picture indicates that women were enslaved in large numbers throughout slave societies in the seventeenth and early eighteenth centuries. Recent economic and demographic histories of the trans-Atlantic slave trade correct the assumption that African men greatly outnumbered African women in the trade. Particularly in the period prior to the eighteenth century, women and men arrived in near-balanced numbers to many parts of the Americas, and as slave traders shifted toward the import of children in the waning years of the trade, adult men ultimately constituted a minority of all those transported.[4] Taking these numbers of women into account forces reproduction into view and raises questions about the possibilities of comparative studies of slavery across time and space.

By situating this study of slavery and reproduction in both the Caribbean and the American South, I intend to suggest that women's reproductive identity—and by that I mean both the experience of childbirth and, perhaps more important, the web of expectations about childbirth held both by black women and men and those who enslaved them—itself provides the comparative frame rather than the crop being cultivated or the size of the household in which one labored. I do not mean to suggest that such things as work or slaveholdings are inconsequential. However, I do argue that the underlying realities of reproductive lives shape the encounter with work, community, and culture. In the context of a coercive labor system predicated upon a fictive biological marker conveyed by the mother, how could it be otherwise?

This, then, is a study of African women enslaved in the early English colonies, of the impact of slavery on women's lives and the impact of women on the development of slavery. Women's labor was at the heart of monoculture export economies in both the Caribbean and the American South, and their reproductive lives were at the heart of the entire venture of racial slavery. For women of African descent, life in the Americas unfolded in ways that implicated their bodily integrity and simultaneously provided material and ideological support to European slaveowners. English slave-owning settlers purchased women to work their fields, and they did so in significant numbers. During the early decades of most colonies in the Caribbean and the American mainland, African women and men were enslaved in relatively equal proportions. While domestic work may have characterized the lives of women in the port cities, rural slaveowners put the vast majority of enslaved women to work clearing, sowing, and reaping their fields. A clear sense of the proportional presence of enslaved women in early English slave societies requires a reassessment of women's role in these developing economies, an understanding of the degree to which women carved out the wealth that supported the English empire, and a careful appreciation of the social and cultural realities that informed both women's and men's experience of enslavement.

As I have constructed the parameters for this study, I have of necessity drawn on a wide range of disciplines. My debts to scholars of African American history, women's history, and colonial American history are obvious, as is the extent to which I have benefited from the work of feminist theory and cultural studies. Grateful acknowledgment of these debts also raises a source of frustration that itself has fueled the work of this project. Surprising gaps in these literatures generate equally startling omissions. In the 1970s interdisciplinary anthologies on African-American women's lives were published that ranged chronologically from slavery through the twentieth century. Angela Davis's 1971 work on women in slave communities inaugurated a wide range of scholarship on African American women organized around the nexus of family, sexuality, and resistance.[5] Studies generated around the larger questions of slave community and family as a whole, such as those of John Blassingame and Herbert Gutman propelled scholars such as Deborah Gray White to explore women's lives under slavery. And indeed, in the 1980s, historical work on black women's lives moved from margin to center. With the publication of White's work on the American

South and Hilary Beckles's work on enslaved women in Barbados, Barbara Bush's study of gender in the British West Indies, Marietta Morrisey's sociological work on the same topic, and a surge of work coming from scholars in other disciplines such as Hazel Carby, Henry Louis Gates Jr., Deborah McDowell, and Hortense Spillars, studies on women in slavery seemed destined to move, as the field does, in the direction of the particular—toward increasingly specific and less literary monographs in which the lives of these women moved irrevocably out of obscurity and stereotype. But by the end of the 1980s, Evelyn Brooks Higgenbotham could still lament that "black woman's voice[s] go largely unheard" in African American history, a lament that continues to resonate into the new millennium.[6] Among historical monographs concerned primarily with enslaved women, there are currently only four full-length studies: Deborah Gray White's *Ar'n't I a Woman? Female Slaves in the Plantation South*, Marietta Morrissey's *Slave Women in the New World: Gender Stratification in the New World*, Barbara Bush's *Slave Women in Caribbean Society, 1650–1838*, and, most recently, Bernard Moitt's *Women and Slavery in the French Antilles, 1635–1848*.[7] Studies that treat gender and race in the context of emerging American colonies are more widespread, but are primarily offered in either women's history or colonial history and thus do not center the problem of slavery. While initially constricted by a framework that focused primarily on the lives of white women, the fields of early American history, African American history and women's history now inform one another as they always should have and intersect in studies such as Kathleen Brown's 1996 *Good Wives, Nasty Wenches, and Anxious Patriarchs*, a work that has set the stage for early American histories that follow.[8] As historians have become increasingly committed to the ideas of intersectionality and the construction of social/racial identities—a commitment that flows equally from the literary turn and the work of racial theorists and feminist scholars—early Americanists have used the colonial and early modern period to explore the process through which colonial subjects come into being. Kirsten Fischer's study of sex and race in colonial North Carolina exemplifies work that takes colonial identity formation seriously and explores the complicated ways in which social and juridical categories were called into being in early America.[9]

This study is heavily indebted to works that model the exploration of identity and identity formation, and in this regard I have moved outside the boundaries of colonial American history. My hope is that this book will contribute to a larger process in which the very groundings of historical inquiry are reassessed in the light of race and racism's role in developing Western models of critical thinking. As Hazel Carby noted in 1982, we need to rethink, if not dismantle the very category of reproduction when we apply it to the labor of black women.[10] The connections between commodification, production, and reproduction are nowhere as clear, nor as unexplored, as in African American history. It is a source of creative frustration to me that so few scholars of reproduction have explored them. Elaborately theorized studies of the body, of reproduction, or of childbirth are notable for the persistence with which they mobilize the category of "woman" unmodified by race. In other words, all the women are still white.

The earliest slave ships to the Americas unloaded both women and men. Planter demands for labor fell equally upon the shoulders of women and men. Once in the Americas, women and men together faced questions of their spiritual, cultural, and physical survival and reproduction. At its most utilitarian level, African women's presence among the enslaved—the presence or absence of enough women to make natural increase possible—affected the rate at which slaveowners needed African imports to maintain the enslaved population. The very different cultural outcomes in the Caribbean and the American mainland reflect the centrality of women, reproduction, and racial slavery in the creation of cultural landscapes. To note and to complicate our understanding of sex ratios and birth rates under various American slave societies might seem a relatively simple endeavor. But the simplicity is deceptive because these numbers fundamentally shaped the experience of enslavement and carried with them complexities of identity, family formation, political culture, and emotional wholeness. Ultimately, to write about slave societies with a fictive neutrality that conceals a universal enslaved male, runs the risk of missing the very essence of what constituted the experience of enslavement for both men and women. The demographic relationship between the number of women and the number of men enslaved shaped every level of a slave society, and culture and creolization are profoundly shaped by demography. For slaveowners anxious to either locate evidence of placability among "island-born" slaves or identify dangerous sites of cultural and social miscegenation, creolization (or its absence) became a central, albeit malleable, category. For the enslaved, the possibility of intimacy at the heart of creolization challenged the narrow and contradictory racialized categories to which early modern slaveowners confined them. For historians, the entire endeavor of comparative slavery rests firmly upon the apparatus of creolization as a means of interrogating cultural change and challenging static or monolithic understandings of "the" institution of slavery. That is why we need to understand women's experiences.

Nonetheless, placing women's lives at the center of social-historical studies of slavery only partly explicates gender in early American slave societies. Gender functioned as a set of power relationships through which early slaveowning settlers and those they enslaved defined, understood, and adjusted the confines of racial slavery. The interplay between slaveowners' conceptualization of African women's bodies and the development of racial slavery illuminates the evolving relationship between slaveowners' expectations and the realities of enslavement for black women in the seventeenth and eighteenth centuries. Ideas about black sexuality and misconceptions about black female sexual behavior formed the cornerstone of Europeans' and Euro-Americans' general attitudes toward slavery.[11] Arguably, the sexual stereotypes levied against African-American women in the nineteenth and twentieth centuries were so powerful because of the depth and utility of their roots. Before they came into contact with enslaved women either in West Africa or on American plantations, slaveowners' images and beliefs about race and savagery were indelibly marked on the women's bodies. Tracing the emergence of such ideology through to its more pragmatic application in the economic transactions and deathbed fantasies of colonial slaveowners allows us to reconsider the importance of both gendered ideologies of race and the (until recently underestimated) numbers of African women enslaved in the Americas. Images of black women's reproductive potential, as well as images of their voracious sexuality, were crucial to slaveowners faced with female laborers. The act of forcing black women to work in fields both required and resulted in work and sex becoming intrinsic to one another. This book argues that as slaveowners contemplated women's reproductive potential with greed and opportunism, they utilized both outrageous images and callously indifferent strategies to ultimately inscribe enslaved women as racially and culturally different while creating an economic and moral environment in which the appropriation of a woman's children as well as her childbearing potential became rational and, indeed, natural.

I begin, in Chapter 1, by exploring the interplay between European writers' notions of African women's sexual identities and the development of racialist ideology. The willingness to exploit African women's labor became intimately tied to ideas about reproduction. For European travelers, both those who settled in the Americas and those who did not, the enslavement of African laborers required a sense of moral and social distance over those they would enslave. They acquired that distance in part through manipulating symbolic representations of African women's sexuality. In so doing, European men gradually brought African women into focus—women whose pain-free reproduction (at least to European men) indicated that they did not descend from Eve and who illustrated their proclivity for hard work through their ability to simultaneously till the soil and birth a child. Such imaginary women suggested an immutable difference between Africans and Europeans, a difference ultimately codified as race. As slavery took root in North American and Caribbean colonies, the interplay between inherited beliefs about gender, race, and civility coalesced to shape slaveowners' implicit expectations that their wealth and, indeed, that of entire colonial empires, derived from the reproductive potential of African women.

The interdependence of the developing languages of gender and race provides the antecedents for the development of a trans-Atlantic slave trade. Women's value and centrality as agricultural producers and as markers of wealth in West and West Central Africa had an important impact on the numbers of women made available to the trans-Atlantic slave trade.[12] There are also important shifts in the demography of the trade over time such that women's proportional presence is greater in the seventeenth-century trade than it would be later. Chapter 2 is an exploration of these factors and an attempt to integrate demographic and social-historical evidence of West African societies in order to suggest the worlds that enslaved African women might have left behind. The experience of the Middle Passage and the cultural legacy of birth, social space, and work that West African women brought with them across the Atlantic are difficult matters to identify firmly. Since before the sixteenth century, European travelers recorded their observations of familial and cultural institutions of the West African coast. I use this rich, albeit problematic, travel literature to discuss reproduction and childbearing in some West African societies. I do so with caution; early modern European writers on Africa and Africans already were part of a polemic literature about race, culture, and European superiority. Nonetheless, to abandon early written references on African cultures would be short sighted. These commentaries provide valuable glimpses of reproductive rituals, the context of male/female social space, and the parameters of women's labor. In combination with a discussion of the demography of women in the trans-Atlantic slave trade, I use the travel literature to suggest the points of social and cultural commonality and difference that women from areas of the West African coast would contend with in the Americas.

As they worked to overcome linguistic and cultural differences, women enslaved in the Americas would find their points of connection to one another highlighted both by their biology and by the intrusions of slaveowners into their reproductive lives. Chapter 3 explores slaveowners' appropriation of enslaved women's reproductive lives and argues that speculation about women's childbearing capacity was a natural outgrowth of slaveownership. Women enslaved in early American colonies would find that familiarity did not breed autonomy, not even in the first generations of settlement and slaveownership, a "frontier" period characterized by close, often intimate, proximity between slaveowner and enslaved and a mutual dependency buttressed by racial fluidity.[13] Faced with the elusive nature of economic success, even small-scale slaveowners appropriated enslaved women's reproductive legacies to augment their own. Enslaved women and their reproductive capacities and potentials thus become part of the equation of slaveownership quite early in the settlement process, despite the fact that the experience of childbirth, for both black and white women, was delineated by excessive mortality rates. In the face of a devastating disease environment, taxing work regimes, and inadequate diets, enslaved men and women maintained only a tenuous hold upon their own lives. Inadequate nutrition combined with overwork to endanger women's fertility and thus accord reproduction—both biological and cultural—new meaning in the New World. Birth rates in early English American slave societies were low, and the proportion of children who survived their childhood was even lower. But high mortality rates and decreased fertility rates did not remove childbirth from the equation for either slaveowners or enslaved women in early American slave societies. If anything, the rarity of surviving infant births may have further highlighted the pragmatic and symbolic value of African women's reproductive potential.

Chapter 4 is a discussion of the ways in which enslaved women experienced the explicit and implicit claims upon their wombs. Through a discussion of the material realities of reproduction (the frequency of births on small and large plantations, for example) and the dangers of familial disruption for those women and men whose children survived infancy only to be identified as tokens of affection bestowed by slaveowners upon their kin, I probe the consequences of reproduction for women enslaved in societies newly dependent upon slave labor. This is not a study of "motherhood" with all its attendant emotional and psychological touchstones. Any discussion of women's lives must tread carefully through the maze of cultural meaning ascribed to childbirth. The "natural" reproductive function of the female body lends itself to ahistorical readings of reproductive experience. Moreover, the connections that have been made between race and gender have shaped cultural assumptions about black women's reproductive lives that are equally ahistorical and profoundly racist.[14] My intention in this chapter is to suggest the many ways in which childbirth itself is situational and demands historicity. Historical evidence, for example, of the ways in which adults in areas affected by high rates of infant mortality delay connection with children until they reach an age at which survival is more probable should provide a corrective to the impulse to assign transparent tragedy to childbirth under slavery.[15] Childbirth under slavery must be couched in both the historical parameters of the slave trade, the physical and emotional violence of racial slavery, and an interrogation of the multiple meanings of women's reproductive lives.

The ways in which reproduction became a kind of symbolic work for enslaved women should not obscure the physical toil slaveowners subjected them to. Enslaved women worked, and they labored without illusions about the likelihood of being able, as some enslaved men did, to use their skills to ascend out of fieldwork. In the world of skilled labor, African women were incredibly rare. The narrow confines of domestic labor admitted a tiny percentage of African women to the homes of slaveowners, which with its physical and psychological closeness to the slaveowning family offered little in the way of mobility and autonomy—perquisites of many skilled occupations that were open to enslaved men. Chapter 5 establishes women's ubiquitous presence in the fields and explores the ways in which the restrictions of fieldwork shaped enslaved women's daily lives.

Throughout this study, I explore the ways in which slavery changes the meaning of reproduction for the enslaved and the ways in which reproduction changes the experience of enslavement. A child born under slavery became part of the slaveowners' profit margin, and women's voluntary or involuntary complicity in their own commodification and that of their children might be seen as the ultimate sign of resignation and accommodation. But even as that child literally enriched the slaveowner with its birth, she could be an assertion of humanity and autonomy on the part of her parent. The meanings of childbirth for the women and men who parented children, watched infants die, or raised children born of parents who were dead or had been sold away are not historically transparent. Given my focus throughout the text on the question of autonomy as it related to parenting and reproduction, a final chapter on resistance is called for. The notion that enslaved women withheld reproductive capacities—engaging in a "gyneco-logical revolt"—to damage the wealth and power of the slaveowner has gained currency among historians of the Caribbean, and the idea of repro-duction as resistance needs further discussion.[16] To treat resistance as a fac-tor integral to any aspect of the institution of slavery, as many current historians of slavery have done, is to demand a focus on the personhood of the enslaved and to resist the dehumanizing legacy of enslavement. In the context of a study that argues for the integral role of reproduction to the institution of slavery, a distinct chapter on resistance allows me to interro-gate the ways in which women's reproductive potential shaped the form and the meaning of their opposition to slavery.

Initially I conceived this book as a way to revise what I saw as a fairly significant obfuscation in the historiography of slave societies—namely, that "slave" equaled "man." I wanted to explore the consequences of the presence of women in early slave societies and the ways in which their expe-rience of enslavement differed from that of men. While I was originally loath to confine an examination of female laborers to their reproductive identities, the sources drew me into a subject matter that I found more complex and meaningful than I had previously supposed. I do not intend to argue that the experience of enslaved women should be approached only through their biological capacity to reproduce. However, the expectations and experience of reproduction significantly influenced both the violence done to enslaved African women in the Americas and their ability to survive it. In my effort to depict the broad sweep of reproduction over time and space I mean to evoke the contradictory consequences of childbirth under slavery, the ways in which slaveowners both relied upon and ignored the physiological realities of women's bodies, the slaveowners' desire to obfus-cate and exploit African women's sexual identity and the humanity they so obviously shared, and the simultaneity of violation and creativity mani-fested in creolization for enslaved women and men. In the process, I argue that the entire framework of slavery as an institution rested upon these con-tradictory assumptions and that centering the lives of enslaved women in the colonial period is not simply an exercise of inclusion but is rather a foundational methodology in writing the history of early America.

Chapter 1
"Some Could Suckle over Their Shoulder": Male Travelers, Female Bodies, and the Gendering of Racial Ideology

Prior to their entry onto the stage of New World conquests, women of African descent lived in bodies unmarked by what would emerge as Europe's preoccupation with physiognomy—skin color, hair texture, and facial features presumed to be evidence of cultural deficiency. Not until the gaze of European travelers fell upon them would African women see themselves, or indeed one another, as defined by "racial" characteristics. In a sense, European racial ideology developed in isolation from those who became the objects of racial scrutiny, but ideologies about race would soon come to be as important to the victims of racial violence as it was to the perpetrators. For English slaveowners in the Americas, neither the decision to embrace the system of slavery nor the racialized notion of perpetual hereditary slavery was natural. During the decades after European arrival to the Americas, as various nations gained and lost footholds, followed fairy-tale rivers of gold, traded with and decimated Native inhabitants, and ignored and mobilized Christian notions of conversion and just wars, English settlers constructed an elaborate edifice of forced labor on the foundation of emerging categories of race and reproduction. The process of calling blackness into being and causing it to become inextricable from brute labor took place in legislative acts, laws, wills, bills of sale, and plantation inventories just as it did in journals and adventurers' tales of travels. Indeed, the gap between intimate experience (the Africans with whom one lived and worked) and ideology (monstrous, barely human savages) would be bridged in the hearts and minds of prosaic settlers rather than in the tales of worldly adventurers.[1] It was the settlers whose ideas and praxis African women and men would have to scrutinize and navigate in order to survive. Nonetheless, I turn here to travel narratives to explore developing categories of race and racial slavery and to provide a grounding for the discussion of behaviors and materialities that follow. The process by which "Africans" became "blacks" who became "slaves" was initiated—on the European side at least—through a series of encounters made manifest in literary descriptions and only later expanded by the quotidian dimensions of slaveownership and settlement. The publication of images fueled the imaginations of settlers and would-be colonists alike and constituted an essential component of the ideological arsenal that European settlers brought to bear against African laborers.

The connections between forced labor and race became increasingly important during the life of the transatlantic slave trade as the enormity of the changes wrought by the settlement of the Americas and the mass enslavement of Africans slowly came into focus for Europeans. Despite real contemporary issues of race and racism, however, the link between what race has come to mean and the wide range of emerging ideas about difference in the early modern period must not be overdetermined. A concept of "race" rooted firmly in biology is primarily a late eighteenth- and early nineteenth-century phenomenon.[2] Nonetheless, the fact that a biologically driven explanation for differences borne on the body owes considerable debt to the science of the Enlightenment should not erase the connection between the body and socially inscribed categories of difference in the early modern period. As travelers and men of letters thought through the thorny entanglements of skin color, complexion, features, and hair texture, they constructed weighty notions of civility, nationhood, citizenship, and manliness on the foundation of the amalgam of nature and culture. Given the ways in which appearance became a trope for civility and morality, it is no surprise to find gender located at the heart of Europeans' encounter with and musings over the connection between bodies and Atlantic economies.

In June 1647, Englishman Richard Ligon left London on the ship *Achilles* to establish himself as a planter in the newly settled colony of Barbados. En route, Ligon's ship stopped in the Cape Verde islands for provisions and trade. There Ligon saw a black woman for the first time. He recorded the encounter in his *True and Exact History of Barbadoes*: she was a "Negro of the greatest beauty and majesty together: that ever I saw in one woman. Her stature large, and excellently shap'd, well favour'd, full eye'd, and admirably grac'd . . . [I] awaited her comming out, which was with far greater Majesty and gracefulness, than I have seen Queen Anne, descend from the Chaire of State."[3] Ligon's rhetoric must have surprised his English readers, for seventeenth-century images of black women did not usually evoke the monarchy as the referent.

Early modern English writers did, however, conventionally set the black female figure against one that was white—and thus beautiful. Scholars of early modern England have noted the discursive place of black women: Peter Erickson calls the image of the black woman a trope for disrupted harmony; Lynda Boose sees black women in early modern English writing as symbolically "unrepresentable," embodying a deep threat to patriarchy; Kim Hall finds early modern English literature and material culture fully involved with a gendered racial discourse committed to constructing stable categories of whiteness and blackness.[4] As these and other scholars have shown, male travelers to Africa and the Americas contributed to a European discourse about women that was already fully active by the time Barbados became England's first colony wholly committed to slave labor in the mid-seventeenth century. While descriptions of naked native females evoked desire, travelers depicted black women as simultaneously unwomanly and marked by a reproductive value that was both dependent on their sex and evidence of their lack of femininity. Writers mobilized femaleness alongside an unwillingness to allow African women to embody "proper" female space, which in turn produced a focus for the notion of racial difference. And thus, over the course of his journey, Richard Ligon came to another view of black women. He wrote that their breasts "hang down below their Navels, so that when they stoop at their common work of weeding, they hang almost to the ground, that at a distance you would think they had six legs." In this context, black women's monstrous bodies symbolized their sole utility—the ability to produce both crops and other laborers.[5] It is this dual value, sometimes explicit and sometimes lurking in the background of slaveowners' decision-making processes, that would come to define women's experience of enslavement most critically.

Seemingly because of his appraisal of beauty on Cape Verde, Ligon's attitude toward the enslaved has been characterized by modern historians as "more liberal and humane than [that] of the generality of planters."[6] Nevertheless, his text indicates the kind of symbolic work required of black women in early modern English discourse. As Ligon penned his manuscript while in debtors prison in 1653, he constructed a layered narrative in which the discovery of African women's monstrosity helped to assure the work's success. Taking the female body as a symbol of the deceptive beauty and ultimate savagery of blackness, Ligon allowed his readers to dally with him among beautiful black women, only to seductively disclose their monstrosity over the course of the narrative. Ligon's narrative is a microcosm of a much larger ideological maneuver that juxtaposed the familiar with the unfamiliar—the beautiful woman who is also the monstrous laboring beast. As the tenacious and historically deep roots of racialist ideology become more evident, it becomes clear also that, through the rubric of monstrously "raced" African women, Europeans found a way to articulate shifting perceptions of themselves as religiously, culturally, and phenotypically superior to the black or brown persons they sought to define. In the discourse used to justify the slave trade, Ligon's beautiful Negro woman was as important as her "six-legged" counterpart. Both imaginary women marked a gendered and, as Kim Hall has argued, a stabilized whiteness on which European colonial expansionism depended.[7]

Well before the mid-seventeenth-century publication of Ligon's work, New World and African narratives had been published in England and Europe that used gender to convey an emerging notion of racialized difference. By the time English colonists arrived in the Americas, they already possessed the ethno-historiographical tradition of depicting imaginary "natives" in which Ligon's account is firmly situated.[8] Travel accounts, which had proved their popularity by the time Ligon's *History of Barbados* appeared, relied on gendered notions of European social order to project African cultural disorder. Gender did not operate as a more profound category of difference than race; instead racialist discourse was deeply imbued with ideas about gender and sexual difference that, indeed, became manifest only in contact with each other. White men who laid the discursive groundwork on which the "theft of bodies" could be justified relied on mutually constitutive ideologies of race and gender to affirm Europe's legitimate access to African labor.[9]

Travel accounts produced in Europe and available in England provided a corpus from which subsequent writers borrowed freely, reproducing images of Native American and African women that resonated with readers. Over the course of the second half of the seventeenth century, some eighteen new collections with descriptions of Africa and the West Indies were published and reissued in England; by the eighteenth century, more than fifty new synthetic works, reissued again and again, found audiences in England.[10] Both the writers and the readers of these texts learned to dismiss the idea that women in the Americas and Africa might be innocuous or unremarkable. Rather, indigenous women bore an enormous symbolic burden, as writers from Walter Ralegh to Edward Long used them to mark metaphorically the symbiotic boundaries of European national identities and white supremacy. The conflict between perceptions of beauty and assertions of monstrosity such as Ligon's exemplified a much larger process through which the familiar became unfamiliar as beauty became beastliness and mothers became monstrous, all of which ultimately buttressed racial distinctions. Writers who articulated religious and moral justifications for the slave trade simultaneously grappled with the character of a contradictory female African body—a body both desirable and repulsive, available and untouchable, productive and reproductive, beautiful and black. By the time an eighteenth-century Carolina slaveowner could look at an African woman with the detached gaze of an investor, travelers and philosophers had already subjected her to a host of taxonomic calculations. The meanings attached to the female African body were inscribed well before the establishment of England's colonial American plantations, and the intellectual work necessary to naturalize African enslavement—that is, the development of racialist discourse—was deeply implicated by gendered notions of difference and human hierarchy.

Europe had a long tradition of identifying Others through the monstrous physiognomy or sexual behavior of women. Armchair adventurers might shelve Pliny the Elder's ancient collection of monstrous races, *Historia Naturalis*, which catalogued the long-breasted wild woman, alongside Herodotus's *History*, in which Indian and Ethiopian tribal women bore only one child in a lifetime.[11] They may have read Julian's arguments with Augustine in which he wrote that "barbarian and nomadic women give birth with ease, scarcely interrupting their travels to bear children," or have pondered over Aristotle's belief that Egyptian women had too many children and were therefore inclined to give birth to monsters.[12] Images of female devils included sagging breasts as part of the iconography of danger and monstrosity. The medieval wild woman, whose breasts dragged on the ground when she walked and could be thrown over her shoulder, was believed to disguise herself with youth and beauty in order to enact seductions that would satisfy her "obsessed . . . craving for the love of mortal men."[13] The shape of her body marked her deviant sexuality and both shape and sexuality evidenced her savagery.

Writers commonly looked to socio-sexual deviance to indicate savagery in Europe and easily applied similar modifiers to Others in Africa and the Americas in order to mark European boundaries. According to *The Travels of Sir John Mandeville*, "in Ethiopia and in many other countries [in Africa] the folk lie all naked . . . and the women have no shame of the men." Furthermore, "they wed there no wives, for all the women there be common . . . and when [women] have children they may give them to what man they will that hath companied with them."[14] Deviant sexual behavior reflected the breakdown of natural laws—the absence of shame, the inability to identify lines of heredity and descent. This concern with deviant sexuality, articulated almost always through descriptions of women, is a constant theme in the travel writings of early modern Europe. Explorers and travelers to the New World and Africa brought expectations of distended breasts and dangerous sexuality with them. Indeed, Columbus used his reliance on the female body to articulate the colonial venture at the very outset of his voyage when he wrote that the earth was shaped like a breast with the Indies composing the nipple; his urge for discovery of new lands was inextricable from the language of sexual conquest.[15]

Richard Eden's 1553 English translation of Sebastian Münster's *A Treatyse of the Newe India* presented Amerigo Vespucci's 1502 voyage to English readers for the first time. Vespucci did not use color to mark the difference of the people he encountered; rather, he described them in terms of their lack of social institutions ("they fight not for the enlargeing of theyr dominion for asmuch as they have no Magistrates") and social niceties ("at theyr meate they use rude and barberous fashions, lying on the ground without any table clothe or coverlet"). Nonetheless, his descriptions are not without positive attributes, and when he turned his attention to women his language bristled with illuminating contradiction:

Theyr bodies are verye smothe and clene by reason of theyr often washinge. They are in other thinges fylthy and withoute shame. Thei use no lawful coniunccion of mariage, and but every one hath as many women as him liketh, and leaveth them agayn at his pleasure. The women are very fruiteful, and refuse no laboure al the whyle they are with childe. They travayle in maner withoute payne, so that the nexte day they are cherefull and able to walke. Neyther have they theyr bellies wimpeled or loose, and hanginge pappes, by reason of bearinge manye chyldren.[16]

The passage conveys admiration for indigenous women's strength in pregnancy and their ability to maintain aesthetically pleasing bodies, but it also illustrates the conflict at the heart of European discourse on gender and difference. It hinges on both a veiled critique of European female weakness and a dismissal of Amerindian women's pain. Once English men and women were firmly settled in New World colonies, they too would struggle with the notion of female weakness; they needed both white and black women for hard manual labor, but they also needed to preserve a notion of white gentlewomen's unsuitability for physical labor.

Vespucci's familiarity with icons of difference led him to expect American women whose hanging breasts, along with their efficient labors, would mark their difference; thus, he registers surprise that women's bodies and breasts were neither "wimpeled" nor "hanginge." And indeed the icon of sagging breasts is mobilized incompletely in relation to Native American women who, ultimately, escaped an iconographical association designed to cement female bodies with manual labor. This does not preclude Vespucci's impulse to linger over the notion of savage women's pain-free childbearing, and his surprise at Native women's pert breasts is inextricable from his description of their reproductive labors, which in turn became a central component of descriptions of Africa and Africans. Vespucci presented a preliminary, ambiguously laudatory account of Amerindian women. Sixteenth-century European writers had not arrived at any kind of consensus about the significance of Amerindian difference. Potentially either Christian or heathen, Native Americans would for some time present something of a conundrum to the European imagination. Vespucci, then, offered an analysis of Native culture that depended on female physiognomy to chart the way toward clear cultural categories. He mobilized the place of women in society as a cultural referent that evoked the "fylth" and shamelessness of all indigenous people. Thus the passage exposes early modern English readers' sometimes-ambivalent encounters with narratives that used women's behavior and physiognomy to mark European national identities and inscribe racial hierarchy.[17]

That ambivalence is conveyed in Münster's narration of Columbus's voyage, where he situated women both as intermediaries between the intrusive and indigenous peoples and as animal-like reproductive units.[18] On arriving at Hispaniola, Columbus's men "pursewing [the women and men who had come down to the shore] toke a womanne whom they brought to theyr shyppe . . . fyllinge her with delicate meates and wyne, and clothing her in fayre apparel, & so let her depart . . . to her companie."[19] This woman figured as a pliable emissary who could be returned to her people as a sign of Spanish generosity (in the form of food and wine) and civility (in the form of clothes). She could be improved by the experience. Indeed, her ability to receive European goods—to be made familiar through European intervention—served as evidence of her own people's savagery, disorder, and distance from civility.[20] In a passage that closely follows, Münster considered another role for indigenous women and children, one whose contradiction evokes the complicated assessment of Native women and their bodies. Describing the behavior of so-called cannibals, Münster avowed that "such children as they take, they geld to make them fat as we doo cocke chikyns and younge hogges. . . . Such younge women as they take, they keepe for increase, as we doo hennes to laye egges."[21] The metaphor of domesticated livestock introduced a notion that became a recurrent theme concerning indigenous and enslaved women's twofold value to the European project of expansion and extraction. This metaphor, however, did not fully encompass the complexity of dangers indigenous women presented for Europe. Despite his respect for female reproductive hardiness, at the end of the volume Vespucci fixed the indigenous woman as a dangerous cannibal:

There came sodeynly a woman downe from a mountayne, bringing with her secretly a great stake with which she [killed a Spaniard.] The other wommene foorthwith toke him by the legges, and drewe him to the mountayne. . . . The women also which had slayne the yong man, cut him in pieces even in the sight of the Spaniardes, shewinge them the pieces, and rosting them at a greate fyre.[22]

Vespucci later made manifest the latent sexualized danger inherent in the man-slaying woman in a letter in which he wrote of women biting off the penises of their sexual partners, thus linking cannibalism—an absolute indicator of savagery and distance from European norms—to female sexual insatiability.[23]

The label "savage" was not uniformly applied to Amerindian people. Indeed, in the context of European national rivalries, the indigenous woman became somewhat less savage. In the mid to late sixteenth century, the bodies of women figured at the borders of national identities more often than at the edges of a larger European identity. The Italian traveler Girolamo Benzoni, in his *History of the New World* (a 1572 narrative that appeared in multiple translations), used sexualized indigenous women both as markers of difference and indicators of Spanish immorality. His first description of a person in the Americas (in Venezuela in 1541) occurs at the very beginning of his story:

Then came an Indian woman . . . such a woman as I have never before nor since seen the like of; so that my eyes could not be satisfied with looking at her for wonder. . . . She was quite naked, except where modesty forbids, such being the custom throughout all this country; she was old, and painted black, with long hair down to her waist, and her ear-rings had so weighed her ears down, as to make them reach her shoulders, a thing wonderful to see . . . her teeth were black, her mouth large, and she had a ring in her nostrils . . . so that she appeared like a monster to us, rather than a human being.[24]

Benzoni's description draws upon a sizable catalogue of cultural distance packed with meaning made visible by early modern conventions of gendered difference. His inability to satisfy his gaze speaks to an obfuscation Ligon enacted 100 years later and one that Stephen Greenblatt argues is the defining metaphor of the colonial encounter. His "wonder" created distance.[25] In the context of a society concerned with the deception of cosmetics, as Hall argues, her black-faced body was both cause for alarm and evidence of a dangerous inversion of norms. Her nakedness, her ears, and her nose—all oddities that were accentuated by willful adornment—irrevocably placed her outside the realm of the familiar. Her blackened teeth and large mouth evoked a sexualized danger that, as Benzoni himself explicitly states, linked her and, by implication, her people to an inhuman monstrosity.[26]

In evoking this singular woman—the like of whom he had never seen—Benzoni departed from his contemporaries. He used his description of her to open his narrative and, through her, placed his reader in the realm of the exotic. This "wonderful" woman alerted readers to the distance Benzoni had traveled, but he deployed another, more familiar set of female images to level a sustained critique of Spanish colonial expansion and thereby to insist on the indigenous woman's connection, or nearness, to a familiar European femininity.

Capt. Pedro de Calize arrived with upwards of 4000 slaves. . . . It was really a most distressing thing to see the way in which these wretched creatures naked, tired, and lame were treated [by the Spaniards]; exhausted with hunger, sick, and despairing. The *unfortunate mothers*, with two or three children on their shoulders or clinging round their necks, [were] overwhelmed with tears and grief, all tied with cords or with iron chains. . . . Nor was there a girl but had been violated by the depredators; wherefore, from too much indulgence, many Spaniards entirely lost their health.[27]

Benzoni used the pathetic figures of the fecund mother and the sexually violated young girl to condemn the Spaniards. Such a move was common in the aftermath of Las Casas's *In Defense of the Indians* (circa 1550) and amid the intensified resentment among European nations about Spain's control of access to the Americas. In "Discoverie of the . . . Empire of Guiana" (1598), Ralegh stated that he "suffered not any man to . . . touch any of [the natives'] wives or daughters: which course so contrary to the Spaniards (who tyrannize over them in all things) drewe them to admire her [English] majestie."[28] Although he permitted himself and his men to gaze upon naked Indian women, Ralegh accentuated the restraint they exercised. In doing so, he used the untouched bodies of Native American women to mark national boundaries and signal the civility and superiority of English colonizers in contrast to the sexually violent Spaniards. Moreover, in linking the eroticism of indigenous women to the sexual attention of Spanish men, Ralegh signaled the Spaniards' "lapse into savagery."[29] Benzoni, too, inscribed the negative consequences of too-close associations with indigenous women. For him, sexual proximity to local women depleted Spanish strength. As he prepared to abandon the topic of Indian slavery for a lengthy discussion of Columbus's travels, he again invoked motherhood to prove Spanish depravity: "All the slaves that the Spaniards catch in these provinces are sent [to the Caribbean] . . . and even when *some of the Indian women are pregnant by these same Spaniards*, they sell them without any consciences."[30]

This rhetorical flourish, through female bodies, highlighted the contradictions of the familiar and unfamiliar in the Americas. Because of her nakedness and her monstrous adornments, the woman who opened Benzoni's narrative could not be familiar to conquistadors and colonizers, yet in her role as mother, sexual victim, or even sexually arousing female she evoked the familiar. Benzoni sidestepped the tension inherent in the savage and violated mother by using her to publicize Spanish atrocity. In effect, the "Black Legend" created (among other things) this confusing figure of pathos—the nurturing savage. In order to facilitate the ultimate roles of extractors and extracted, the indigenous woman's familiarity had to be neutralized. Thus the pathos of raped mothers ultimately could be laid at Europe's door, where it signified disdain for the Spanish and disregard for ultimately monstrous women.[31]

The monstrosity of the native mother had an important visual corollary. A mid-sixteenth-century Portuguese artist, for example, depicted the devil wearing a Brazilian headdress and rendered his demonic female companions with long, sagging breasts.[32] Toward the end of the century, a multivolume collection of travel accounts published in Latin and German augmented the evolving discourse of European civility with visual images of overseas encounters.[33] As Bernadette Bucher has shown, the early volumes of Theodor de Bry's *Grand Voyages* (1590) depicted the Algonkians of Virginia and the Timucuas of Florida as classical Europeans: Amerindian bodies mirrored ancient Greek and Roman statuary, modest virgins covered their breasts, and infants suckled at the high, small breasts of young attractive women (see Figures 1, 2, and 3). As Joyce Chaplin has illustrated, the English encounter with Native American bodies would ultimately "gesture towards racial identification of the body" as English settlers compared themselves favorably to Native Americans whom they saw as weak.[34] None-

Figure 1. Young virgin covering her breast. From Thomas Hariot, *A brief and True Report of the New Found Land of Virginia*, in Theodor de Bry, *Grand Voyages*, vol. 1 (Frankfurt am Main, 1590), plate 6. Courtesy of the John Work Garrett Library, Johns Hopkins University.

theless, even years before the English arrived in the colonies, visual and literary images were laying the groundwork for an ideology of European superiority. Thus the visual depictions of Native women were always in flux. In the third de Bry volume, *Voyages to Brazil*, published in 1592, the Indian was portrayed as aggressive and savage, and the representation of women's bodies changed. The new woman is a cannibal with breasts that fell below her waist. She licks the juices of grilled human flesh from her fingers and adorns the frontispiece of the map of Tierra del Fuego (see Figures 4 and 5). Bucher argues that the absence of a suckling child in these depictions is essential to the image's symbolic weight.[35] Their childlessness signified the women's cannibalism—they consumed rather than produced. Although women alone did not exemplify cannibalism, women with long breasts came to mark such savagery in Native Americans for English readers. As depictions of Native Americans traversed the gamut of savage to noble, the long-breasted woman became a clear signpost of savagery in con-

Figure 2. Woman suckling child. From *Eurom Quae in Florida . . .* , in Theodor de Bry, *Grand Voyages*, vol. 2 (Frankfurt am Main, 1591), plate 20. Courtesy of the John Work Garrett Library, Johns Hopkins University.

trast to her high-breasted counterpart. Other images of monstrous races, such as the headless Euaipanonoma, the one-footed Sciopods, and the Astomi who lived on the aroma of apples, slowly vanished from Europe's imagined America and Africa. Once Europeans reached Africa, however, the place of motherhood in the complex of savagery and race became central to the figure of the black woman. Unlike other monstrosities, the long-breasted woman—who, when depicted with her child, carried the full weight of productive savagery—maintained her place in the lexicon of conquest and exploration.

As he described one of the first slaving voyages made by Europeans

Figure 3. Native American woman with her child, two views. From Thomas Hariot, *A brief and True Report of the New Found Land of Virginia*, in Theodor de Bry, *Grand Voyages*, vol. 1 (Frankfurt am Main, 1590), plate 10. Courtesy of the John Work Garrett Library, Johns Hopkins University.

into West Africa, the Portuguese trader Gomes Azurara pinpoints the precise location of African women for European slave traders and settlers in the economy of production and control:

But rather they returned to their ship and on the next day landed a little way distant from there, where they espied some of the wives of those Guineas walking. And it seemeth that they were going nigh to a creek collecting shellfish, and they captured one of them, who would be as much as thirty years of age, with a son of hers who would be of about two, and also a young girl of fourteen years, who had well-formed limbs and also a favorable presence for a Guinea; but the strength of the woman was much to be marvelled at, for not one of the three men who came upon her but would have had a great labour in attempting to get her to the boat. And so one of our men, seeing the delay they were making, during which it might be that some of the dwellers of the land would come upon them, conceived it well to take her son from her and to carry him to the boat; and love of the child compelled the mother to follow after it, without great pressure on the part of the two who were bringing her.[36]

Figure 4. Woman (at left) holding leg. From *Memorabile Proviniciae Brasilae . . .* , in Theodor de Bry, *Grand Voyages*, vol. 3 (Frankfurt am Main, 1592), 179. Courtesy of the John Work Garrett Library, Johns Hopkins University.

Those who would capture African women to exploit their labors in the Americas would have to grapple with, and harness, those women's dual identity as workers and parents; once having done so they would inaugurate a language of race and racial hierarchy in which that dualism was reduced to denigration and mobilized as evidence of European distinction.

English travelers to West Africa drew on American narrative traditions as they too worked to establish a clearly demarcated line that would ultimately define them. Richard Hakluyt's collection of travel narratives, *Principal Navigations* (1589), brought Africa into the purview of English readers. *Principal Navigations* portrayed Africa and Africans in both positive and negative terms. The authors' shifting assessments of Africa and Africans "produc[ed] an Africa which is familiar and unfamiliar, civil and savage, full of promise and full of threat." Sixteenth-century ambivalence about

Figure 5. Women on map of Tierra del Fuego. From *Vera et Accurate Descriptio e orum omnius Quae Acdiderunt Quinque navibus, anno 1598*, in Theodor de Bry, *Grand Voyages*, vol. 9 (Frankfurt am Main, 1602), 56. Courtesy of the John Work Garrett Library, Johns Hopkins University.

England's role in overseas expansion required a forceful antidote. In response, Hakluyt presented texts that, through an often-conflicted depiction of African peoples, ultimately differentiated between Africa and England and erected a boundary that made English expansion in the face of confused and uncivilized peoples reasonable, profitable, and moral.[37]

The bodies of women on the West African coast, like those of their New World counterparts, symbolized the parameters of the colonizing venture. But because England's contact with West Africa took place in a historical moment marked by a determination to "plant" valuable American colonies with equally valuable workers, the imagined African woman's body in English writings was more rigidly deployed and thus far less likely to appear as an object of lust or even potential beauty. English writers regularly directed readers' attention to the topic of African women's physiognomy and reproductive experience. In doing so, they drew attention to the complex interstices of desire and repulsion that shaped European men's appraisal of Amerindian and African women. Sixteenth- and seventeenth-century writers conveyed a sexual grotesquerie that ultimately made African women indispensable, because it showed the gendered ways of putting African savagery to productive use. Although titillation was certainly a component of these accounts, to write of sex was also to define and expand the boundaries of profit through productive and reproductive labor.

The symbolic weight of indigenous women's sexual, childbearing, and childrearing practices moved from the Americas to Africa and continued to be brought to bear on England's literary imagination in ways that rallied familiar notions of gendered difference for English readers. John Lok's account of his 1554 voyage to Guinea, published forty years later in Hakluyt's collection, reinscribed Africans' place in the human hierarchy. Borrowing verbatim from Richard Eden's 1555 translation of Peter Martyr's description of the "New Worlde," Lok described all Africans as "people of beastly living." He located the proof of this in *women*'s behavior: among the Garamantes, women "are common: for they contract no matrimonie, neither have respect to chastitie."[38] This description of the Garamantes first appeared in Pliny, was reproduced again by Iulius Solinus's sixth century *Polyhistor* and can be found in travel accounts through the Middle Ages and into the sixteenth and seventeenth centuries.[39] As he struggled to situate his new expertise on Brazil, sixteenth-century writer André Thevet noted that he was not surprised by the easy dissolution of family ties among native Brazilians because this was also the case among the "ancient Egyptians . . . before they had any laws."[40] Traders to the New Worlds of Africa and the Americas did their homework before departure and grew adept at mobilizing symbols that resonated with their readers. Eden's Martyr has a long descriptive passage on African oddities; its reference to Garamante women's absence of "chastity" is followed by one to a tribe who "have no speeche, but rather a grynnynge and chatterynge. There are also people without heades cauled Blemines, havyinge their eyes and mouth in theyr breast."[41] Because he did not reproduce the entire paragraph, Lok suggested that, by the end of the sixteenth century, the oddities of Africa could be consolidated into the particular symbol of women's sexual availability.

William Towrson's narrative of his 1555 voyage to Guinea, also published by Hakluyt in 1589, further exhibits this kind of distillation. Towrson depicted women and men as largely indistinguishable. They "goe so alike, that one cannot know a man from a woman but by their breastes, which in the most part be very foule and long, hanging downe low like the udder of a goate."[42] This was, perhaps, the first time an Englishman in Africa explicitly used breasts as an identifying trait of beastliness and difference. He went on to maintain that "diverse of the women have such exceeding long breasts, that some of them will lay the same upon the ground and lie downe by them."[43] Lok and Towrson represented African women's bodies and sex-

ual behavior in order to distinguish Africa from Europe. Towrson in particular gave readers only two analogies through which to view and understand
African women—beasts and monsters.

Some thirty years after the original Hakluyt collections were published,
other writers continued to mobilize African women to do complex symbolic work. In 1622, Richard Jobson's *The Golden Trade* appeared in London, chronicling his 1620–1621 trading ventures up the Gambia River.[44]
Jobson described strong and noble people on the one hand and barbarous
and bestial people on the other, and African women personified his nation's
struggle with the familiar and unfamiliar African—a struggle that can also
be located along the axis of desire and repulsion. Jobson's association with
the "Fulbie" and "Maudingo" people furnishes evidence of this struggle.
He described Fulbie men as beastlike, "seemingly more senseless, than our
Country beasts," a state he attributed to their close association with the
livestock they raised.[45] Unlike many of his contemporaries, Jobson regarded
African women with admiration. In contrast to Fulbie men, the women
were "excellently well bodied, having very good features, with a long blacke
haire."[46] He maintained that the discovery of a "mote or haire" in milk
would cause these dairywomen to "blush, in defence of her cleanely meaning."[47] This experience of shame encapsulated a morality and civility to
which only women had access. Among the "Maudingos" of Cassan, newly
married women "observ[e] herein a shamefast modestie, not to be looked
for, *among such a kinde of blacke or barbarous people*."[48]

Despite his well-meaning description of African women, Jobson
recorded their civil behavior only when it deviated from what he and his
readers expected. His appreciation of "Fulbie" women and "Maudingo"
people was predicated on their ability to exceed his expectations. This kind
of appreciation of the exceptional is a rhetorical move that would recur
again and again in the language of slaveowners and legislators. Exceptional
African women were rewarded only insofar as they reinforced white female
behavioral norms. To Jobson, African women proved the precarious nature
of African civility. His narrative, even at its most laudatory, always rested
on the inferiority of African peoples. Although he described the history of
kingship and the great importance of ancestral honor among the Maudingos, Jobson still contended that "from the King to the slave, they are all
perpetuall beggers from us." His "wonder" at women's modesty alerted his
readers to the culture's abnormality and, implicitly, to its larger absence of
civility. Even as he depicted them positively, women became part of the

demonstration that, despite kings and history, these Africans were barbarous and ripe for exploitation.

Unlike many of his contemporaries, Jobson leveled his open-eyed gaze primarily at male African sexuality. In a unique twist on the consequences of the curse of Ham, Jobson maintained that African men carried the mark of the curse in the size of their sexual organs: they "are furnisht with such members as are after a sort burthensome unto them, whereby their women being once conceived with child . . . accompanies the man no longer, because he shall not destroy what is conceived." Jobson's interpretation of the penis corresponded to others' ideas about women's breasts. Both sexual organs were seen as pendulous and distended, somehow disembodied from their owner, and physically burdensome. Subsequently he returned to the subject of women only in terms of their subjugation to men, certain that "there is no other woman [that] can be under more servitude."[49]

Other English publications continued to locate evidence of savagery and legitimate exploitation in women. After Hakluyt died, Samuel Purchas took up the mantle of editor and published twenty additional volumes in Hakluyt's series beginning in 1624.[50] In his translation of a fourteenth-century narrative by Leo Africanus, Purchas presented a West Africa sharply delineated from the civilized. Discussion of "the Land of Negros," for example, is preceded by, and thus set apart from, a long section on North Africa. "Negros," unlike their northern neighbors, lived "a brutish and savage life, without any King, Governour, Common-wealth, or knowledge of Husbandry." To confirm this savagery, Leo Africanus asserted that they were "clad in skinnes of beasts, neither had they any peculiar wives . . . and when night came they resorted . . . both men and women into one Cottage together . . . and each man choosing his [woman] which hee had most fanciee unto."[51] This indictment opened the descriptive passages on "Ghinea," thereby making women's sexual availability the defining metaphor of colonial accessibility and black African savagery. The nudity of African and Native American women was not incidental to their savagery. Nakedness was an essential part of most descriptions of native peoples in this period and became the precursor to discussions of women's physical and reproductive anomalies.[52]

In the next volume, Purchas published Andrew Battell's *Strange Adventures*.[53] Battell spent seventeen years in Angola, from 1590 to 1607, some as captive, some as escapee, and some in service to King James. For sixteen months, Battell stayed near "Dongo" with the "Gaga" people, "the greatest Canibals and man-eaters that bee in the World."[54] Like sixteenth-century observers in Brazil, he highlighted women's unnatural reproductive behavior. This "tribe" of fighters and cannibals rejected motherhood. According to Battell, "the women are very fruitfull, but they enjoy none of their children: for as soon as the woman is delivered of her Childe, it is presently buried quicke [alive]; So that there is not one Childe brought up."[55] Battell positioned his discussion of this unnatural behavior in such a way as to close the debate on African savagery. Savagery began, in his account, with cannibalism and ended with mothers who consented to the killing of the children they bore.

Purchas also published a translation of Pieter de Marees's *A description and historicall declaration of the golden Kingedome of Guinea*. This narrative was first published in Dutch in 1602, was translated into German and Latin for the de Bry volumes (1603–1634), and appeared in French in 1605. Plagiarism by seventeenth- and eighteenth-century writers gave it still wider circulation.[56] Here, too, black women embody African savagery. De Marees began by describing the people at Sierra Leone as "very greedie eaters, and no lesse drinkers, and very lecherous, and theevish, and much addicted to uncleanenesse; one man hath as many wives as hee is able to keepe and maintaine. The women also are much addicted to leacherie, specially, with strange Countrey people . . . [and] are also great Lyers, and not to be credited."[57] As did most of his contemporaries, de Marees invoked women's sexuality to castigate the incivility of both men and women. Women's savagery does not stand apart. Rather, it indicts the whole: all Africans were savage. The passage displays African males' savagery alongside their access to multiple women. Similarly, de Marees located evidence of African women's savagery in their sexual desire. Given the association of unrestricted sexuality with native savagery, black female sexuality alone might have been enough to implicate the entire continent. But de Marees further castigated West African women: they delivered children surrounded by men, women, and youngsters "in most shamelesse manner . . . before them all."[58] This absence of shame (evoked explicitly, as here, or implicitly in the constant references to nakedness in other narratives) worked to establish distance. Readers, titillated by the topics discussed and thus tacitly shamed, found themselves further distanced from the shameless subject of the narrative. De Marees dwelled on the brute nature of shameless African women. He marveled that "when the child is borne [the mother] goes to the water to wash and make cleane her selfe, not once dreaming of a moneths lying-in . . . as women here with us use to doe; they use no Nurses to helpe them when they lie in child-bed, neither seeke to lie dainty and soft. . . . The next day after, they goe abroad in the streets, to doe their businesse."⁵⁹ This testimony to African women's physical strength and emotional indifference is even more emphatic in the original Dutch. In the most recent translation from the Dutch, the passage continues: "This shows that the women here are of a cruder nature and stronger posture than the Females in our Lands in Europe."⁶⁰

De Marees goes on to inscribe an image of women's reproductive identity whose influence persisted long after his original publication. "When [the child] is two or three monethes old, the mother ties the childe with a peece of cloth at her backe. . . . When the child crieth to sucke, the mother casteth one of her dugs backeward over her shoulder, and so the child suckes it as it hangs."⁶¹ Frontispieces for the de Marees narrative and the African narratives in de Bry approximate the over-the-shoulder breast-feeding de Marees described, thereby creating an image that could symbolize the continent (see Figures 6 and 7). In 1634, Thomas Herbert drew the image of a female Hottentot "as a sort of she-devil nursing a child over her shoulder."⁶² Herbert wrote a lengthy "description of the Savage Inhabitants" of the South African cape, in which he treated men and women as identical. They were together uniformly marked—by nature or by culture—as surprisingly different from Europeans. Their hair "rather like wooll than haire, tis blacke and knotty" and "their eares are long and made longer by pondrous bables."⁶³ The only descriptions that distinguished women from men referred to an alchemy of the bodies and behaviors of savagery that simultaneously marked the boundaries of English civility.

They are very ceremonious in thanksgivings, for wanting requitals, if you give a woman a piece of bread, she will immediately pull by her [loincloth] flap and discover her *pudenda.* A courtesie commended them, I suppose, by some *Dutch*-ill-bred Saylor, for taught it they are, they say, by Christians. And English men, I know, have greater modestie.

While this detail was produced in service of English gentility and the titillation of readers, the easy and willing display of genitalia in exchange for bread spoke both to Hottentot immodesty and a relative state of undress. A brief note about their cannibalism was shortly followed by the illustration and a short descriptive paragraph that noted that "the women give their Infants sucke as they hang at their backes, the uberous dugge stretched over her shoulder" (see Figure 8).⁶⁴ Herbert's image is remarkable for the monstrous posture of the suckling child who apparently hangs from its mother's

INDIÆ ORIENTALIS

PARS VI.

VERAM ET HISTO-
RICAM DESCRIPTIONEM

AVRIFERI REGNI GVINEÆ, AD AFRICAM
PERTINENTIS, QVOD ALIAS LITTVS DE MINA VO-
cant, continens, Qua fitus loci, ratio vrbium & domorum, portus
item & flumirfa varia, cum variis incolarum fuperftitionibus, e-
ducatione, forma, commerciis, linguis & moribus,
fuccincta breuitate explicantur & per-
cenfentur.

LATINITATE EX GERMANICO DONATA

Studio & opera
M. GOTARDI ARTHVS DANTISCANI.

Illuftrata vero viuis, & artificiofiffime in æs incifis iconibus,
inque lucem edita

à

Iohanne Theodoro & Iohanne Ifrael de Bry fratribus.

Francofurti ad Mœnum ex Officina Wolfgangi Richteri, fumpti-
bus Iohan, Theodori & Iohan. Ifrael de Bry fratribus.

Anno M. DCIV.

Figure 6. Woman breastfeeding over her shoulder. Title page from *Verum et Historicam Descriptionem Avriferi Regni Guineaa*, in Theodor de Bry, *Small Voyages*, vol. 6 (Frankfurt am Main, 1604). Note the contrast between this later depiction and the early representation of a Native American woman in Figure 7. Courtesy of the John Work Garrett Library, Johns Hopkins University.

Figure 7. Women in Africa. From *Verum et Historicam Descriptionem Avriferi Regni Guineaa*, in Theodor de Bry, *Small Voyages*, vol. 6 (Frankfurt am Main, 1604), 3. Courtesy of the John Work Garrett Library, Johns Hopkins University.

back with an almost insect-like tenancy while holding the "uberous dugge" between its teeth. Among the visual depictions of over-the-shoulder breast-feeding, this is undoubtedly the most violent.

The image, in more or less extreme form, remained a compelling one, offering in a single narrative-visual moment evidence that black women's difference was both cultural (in this strange *habit*) and physical (in this strange *ability*). The word "dug," which by the early seventeenth century meant both a woman's breasts and an animal's teats, connoted a brute animality that de Marees reinforced through his description of small children "lying downe in their house, like Dogges, [and] rooting in the ground like Hogges" and of "boyes and girles [that] goe starke naked as they were borne, with their privie members all open, without any shame or civilitie."[65] Herbert too elicited the animal connection by drawing the Hottentot woman clutching entrails in her hand while her child latched on with the intensity of a parasitic arthropod.

As Englishmen traversed the uncertain ground of nature and culture,

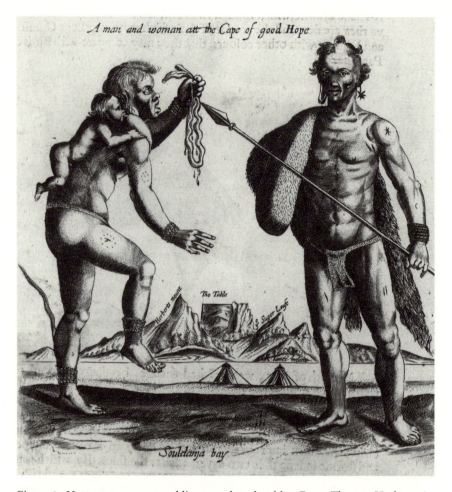

Figure 8. Hottentot woman suckling over her shoulder. From Thomas Herbert, *A Relation of Some Yeares Travaile Begunne Anno 1626* (London, 1634), 17. Courtesy of Harvard University.

African women became a touchstone for physical and behavioral curiosity both within Africa and in the Americas and Europe. Fynes Moryson wrote of Irish women in 1617 that they "have very great Dugges, some so big as they give their children suck over their Shoulders." But it is important that he connects this to being "not laced at all," or to the lack of corsetry.[66] While nudity—a state in which the absence of corsetry is certainly implicit—is constantly at play in descriptions of African women, the overwhelming physicality of the image is disaggregated from culture and instead becomes part of African female nature; something no amount of corsetry would set right. It is perhaps indicative of his national insularity in matters of the slave trade, that the Swiss physician Felix Spoeri commented on the length of enslaved women's breasts in seventeenth-century Barbados and explained it with an amalgam of nature and culture: "By nature slave women have very long breasts because they go about naked all the time."[67] In his 1670 publication on Africa, Nicolas Villaut suggested that the shape of African noses similarly resulted from the bad behavior of African mothers, "whose children sleeping many times whilst the mother is walking or at work, knock their noses against their shoulders and so in time they become flat; if they cry out for the teat, they throw their breasts over their shoulder and let them suck."[68] Drawing on Villaut, Robert Burton reproduced this speculation noting that

they give them the breast over their shoulders, and this may be the reason of the flatness of their Noses by their knocking them continually against the Back and Shoulders of the Mother . . . for it is observed that the children of their Gentry whose Mothers do not labour nor carry their Infants about them; have very comely Noses.[69]

Burton's addendum about class is quite important because it reflects the very real way in which the discursive landscape of appearance was disrupted by competing notions of class and sovereignty—the biological markers of racial difference that legitimate enslavement can here be interrupted by the behavior of the Gentry whose autonomy and freedom from enslavement might thus be assured. The confluence of mothers' abnormal bodies and their ability to inscribe racial characteristics on their children had long currency. Writing in the late eighteenth century, Johann Blumenbach also speculated that the pounding of a child's face on its mother's back shaped facial features. He claimed that the fact that such features could be seen on aborted fetuses was the result of a "natural degeneration" over time that meant that the artificial shaping of the nose had become natural.[70] And thus, again, the African woman embodied the behavioral and physical characteristics that degraded an entire race of people.

When John Ogilby compiled *America* in 1671, his more-than-600-page volume became the first comprehensive English introduction to the continent. His detailed and well-illustrated account of the Americas included the Columbus and Vespucci narratives (among many others) that I have dis-

ve. The reader learns of women in Hispañola who "destroy'd the
_heir Wombs, that they might not bear slaves for the Spaniards,"
and is again reminded of the ease with which women in the Caribbean give
birth, an ease reinforced by the inversion of men taking to their beds for
an extended celebratory "Lying-In" upon the birth of their first son. The
illustrations, while replete with nudity, cannibalism, and warfare, are
almost uniformly of well-proportioned women: the sagging breasts of the
fifteenth century have all but disappeared (see Figure 9). However, in the
last quarter of the text, the reader's visual sense of Indian women is altered.
Suddenly the women on the maps of Granada and Guiana tell a familiar
tale with their breasts; a tale explicated in his appendix on Chile, where
Ogilby explains that "some of them have such great breasts, that throwing
them over their shoulders they suckle their Children."[71] These scattered
images of sagging breasts in the late seventeenth century can only be read
as distinct from the sixteenth century evocations of Amerindian women's
bodies. For Ogilby, the breasts seem to signify a set of concerns with Granada, Guiana, and Chile, perhaps as a means of situating them as distinct
from other parts of the Americas. Just as African women's physiognomy
became shorthand for savagery, the shifting image of America also became
home to such physically inscribed differences (see Figures 10, 11, and 12).
But the enduring connection between African women's sexuality and difference at this point spoke specifically to the increasingly apparent needs of
the English market for slaves and the inevitability that African women and
men would satisfy that need.

African women's Africanness became contingent on the linkages
between sexuality and a savagery that fitted them for both productive and
reproductive labor. Women enslaved in the seventeenth and early eighteenth centuries did not give birth to many children, but descriptions of
African women in the Americas almost always highlighted their fecundity
along with their capacity for manual labor.[72] Erroneous observations about
African women's propensity for easy birth and breast-feeding reassured colonizers that these women could easily perform hard labor in the Americas;
at the same time, such observations erected a barrier of difference between
Africa and England. Seventeenth-century English medical writers, both
men and women, equated breast-feeding and tending to children with difficult work, and the practice of wealthy women forgoing breastfeeding in
favor of sending their children to wet nurses was widespread.[73] English
women and men anticipated pregnancy and childbirth with extreme uneas-
iness and fear of death, but they knew that the experience of pain in child-

Figure 9. Frontispiece. From John Ogilby, *America* (London, 1671). Courtesy of
New York Public Library.

Figure 10. Native American woman suckling over her shoulder on map of Granada. From John Ogilby, *America* (London, 1671), 316. Courtesy of New York Public Library.

Figure 11. Native American woman with sagging breasts on map of Guiana. From John Ogilby, *America* (London, 1671), 341. Courtesy of New York Public Library.

Figure 12. Native American woman suckling over her shoulder in Chile. From John Ogilby, *America* (London, 1671), 360. Courtesy of New York Public Library.

birth marked women as members of a Christian community.[74] As Saidiya Hartman argues, the absence of pain—either in childbirth or at the receiving end of the lash or branding iron—becomes "absolutely essential to the spectacle of contented subjugation" and to the notion that Africans are in fact improved by slavery.[75] Pain-free and disinterested delivery of children could only strike the contemporary English reader as a matter of astonishment and wonder. Upon further reflection, the connection between African women's reproductive lives and their suitability for hard manual labor would link their status with their bodies in a way distinct from but related to the biology of race. Roxann Wheeler has recently argued that "the performance of labor is a more reliable index of status than other activities or physical attributes."[76] But the double meaning of the terms labor and travail, as well as the need to articulate a social space for Africans in the context of emerging socioeconomic ideologies of difference, biology, and lifelong forced labor, collapsed the performance of work into the bodies of African women.

African women entered the developing discourse of national resources through an emphasis on what Europeans perceived to be their mechanical and meaningless childbearing. Initially, metaphors of domestic livestock and sexually located cannibalism touched on notions of reproduction for consumption. Neither Native American women and men, nor the children they produced—"fattened like capons"—added anything to English coffers. By about the turn of the seventeenth century, however, as England joined in the transatlantic slave trade, assertions of African savagery began to be predicated less on consumption and cannibalism and more on production and reproduction. African women came into the conversation in the context of England's need for productivity. Descriptions of these women that highlighted the apparent ease and indifference of their reproductive lives created a mechanistic image that ultimately became located within the national economy. Whereas English women's reproductive work took place solely in the domestic economy, African women's reproductive work embodied the developing discourses of extraction and forced labor at the heart of England's design for the Americas. By the eighteenth century, the contrasting connection between the "inscrutable and sexually polymorphous" African woman and the "chaste maternal" English woman together offered the continent up to English consumption.[77]

By the eighteenth century, English writers rarely used black women's breasts or behavior for anything but concrete evidence of barbarism in Africa. In *A Description of the Coasts of North and South-Guinea*, begun in the 1680s and completed and published almost forty years later, John Barbot "admired the quietness of the poor babes, so carr'd about at their mothers' backs . . . and how freely they suck the breasts, which are always full of milk, over their mothers' shoulders, and sleep soundly in that odd posture."[78] William Snelgrave introduced his *New Account of Some Parts of Guinea and the Slave-trade* with an anecdote designed to illustrate the benevolence of the trade. He described himself rescuing an infant from human sacrifice and reuniting the child with its mother, who "had much Milk in her Breasts." He accented the barbarism of those who had attempted to sacrifice the child and claimed that the reunion cemented his goodwill in the eyes of the enslaved, who, thus convinced of the "good notion of White Men," caused no problems during the voyage to Antigua.[79] Having used the figure of the breastfeeding woman to legitimize his slaving endeavor, Snelgrave went on to describe the roots of Whydah involvement in the slave trade and its defeat in war at the hands of the Kingdom of Dahomey (both coastal cities in present-day Ghana). "Custom of the Country allows Polygamy to an excessive degree . . . whereby the land was become so stocked with people" that the slave trade flourished. Moreover, the wealth generated by the trade made the beneficiaries so "proud, effeminate and luxurious" that they were easily conquered by the more disciplined (read masculine) nation of Dahomey.[80] Polygamy and the abundance of women "unclaimed for monogamy," always an important trope of difference in travel accounts to Africa, signaled an unambiguous distance between Europe and Africa. Thus women's fecundity undermined African society from without and within as it provided a constant stream of potential slaves and depleted the manhood of potentially dangerous adversaries.[81]

Eighteenth-century abolitionist John Atkins similarly adopted the icon of black female bodies in his writings on Guinea. "Childing, and their Breasts always pendulous, stretches them to so unseemly a length and Bigness that some . . . could suckle over their shoulder."[82] Atkins then considered the idea of African women copulating with apes. He noted that "at some places the Negroes have been suspected of Bestiality" and, while maintaining the ruse of scholarly distance, suggested that evidence "would tempt one to suspect the Fact." The evidence lay mostly in apes' resemblance to humans but was bolstered by "the Ignorance and Stupidity [of black women unable] to guide or controll lust."[83] Abolitionists and anti-abolitionists alike accepted the connections between race and black women's monstrous and fecund bodies. African women bridged other important differences between Atkins and Snelgrave. Snelgrave, although he was an avid slave trader, believed that Africans and Europeans shared a single origin, while Atkins the abolitionist was convinced that the two were separate species.[84] It is particularly noteworthy then, that both men mobilized women's corporeal traits to further their quite different intellectual and political agendas.

The visual shorthand of the sagging-breasted African savage held sway for decades. In Peter Kolb's 1731 narrative of the Cape of Good Hope, the "Hottentot" woman sits smoking marijuana while her nursing child peers over her shoulder. The image, quite distinct from Herbert's monstrous "Hottentot" a century earlier, at first glance embodies a lethargy that might disrupt the notion of African women as constant workers. But she sits as if only for a moment, staff in hand, strong legs ready to be once again on the move; a woman not part of any discernable family or social group whose pipe, physique, and childrearing are clearly outside the realm of European femininity (see Figure 13).[85] In the 1745 edition of Ansham and John Churchill's *Collection of Voyages* (originally published in 1732 and reprinted three times by 1752), an illustration titled "A Description of the Habits of Most Countries in the World" prefaces a discussion of clothing (see Figure 14). The bottom half of the taxonomic illustration groups various semi-nude savages alongside Spaniards and Scots highlanders, thus ensuring that readers understand the connection between savagery and civility. Outside of complexion, the single most significant index of racial difference is to be found in the pendulous breasts of Hottentot and Negro women. Mexican, Virginian, and Floridian women appear nude, but they have the high unused breasts that identify them as outside the category of perpetual laborer. Even the female Moor suffers from the dangers of proximity to Negro women (both in geography and on the page); for peering out from beneath her veil she appears to be burdened with breasts determined to slope downward.

The distortion of African women's bodies then, became a given for eighteenth century writers. Whether the connection forged by earlier travelers and philosophers was used to critique European woman, as a weak gesture of cultural relativism, or to cement the role of Africans as necessary slaves, it is a ubiquitous part of Europe's critique of and encounter with Africa. When William Smith embarked on a voyage to map the Gold Coast for the Royal Africa Company in 1727, he was initially disinterested in ethnography. His first description of people comes more than halfway through the narrative when he writes "but before I describe the Vegetables, I shall

Figure 13. Hottentot woman suckling over her shoulder while smoking marijuana. From Peter Kolb, *The Present State of the Cape of Good Hope*, vol. 1 (London, 1731), plate 4.

Figure 14. "A Description of the Habits of Most Countries in the World." From
Ansham and John Churchill, *Collection of Voyages* (London, 1732). Courtesy of the
Library Company of Philadelphia.

take Notice of the Animals of this Country; beginning with the Natives, who are generally speaking a lusty strong-bodied People, but are mostly of a lazy idle Disposition."[86] His short description, followed by a section on "Quadrepedes," is organized primarily around accusations of polygamy and promiscuity in which "hot constitution'd Ladies" are put to work by husbands who treat them like slaves. As the narrative continues, his ethnographic passages, while always brief, are also always organized around sexually available African women. In Whydah, for example, the reader encounters female Priests inclined to whoredom, and he tells of an anomalous Queen in Agonna who satisfies her sexual needs with male slaves, hands down her crown to the resulting female progeny and sells any male children into slavery.[87] Like de Marees a century earlier, Smith is not averse to using African women to critique European women's fashions:

In Europe when our Children can go alone, how many Cares and Anxieties continually perplex us, nor do we think that we can ever take enough Care of them: but here they have none of this Trouble. Childrearing in this part of the World, is attended with no Expence of long Lying-in, Gossipping, etc. A Negroe Woman, I have been told, has been deliver'd of a Child is less than a Quarter of an Hour, and in their Labour they use no Shrieks or Cries; nay the very same Day it is customery for the Lying-in women to go to the Sea-Side and bathe herself, without ever thinking of returning to her Bed. Here are no Provision of any Necessaries for the newborn infant, and yet all its Limbes grow vigorous and proportionate, and I must deliver it as my Opinion that the contrary Practice in Europe makes so many crooked People.[88]

Despite the fact that women and their sexual identities stand in for Smith throughout his text both as evidence of African difference and as a backhanded criticism of European women, it is not until the final pages of the text that he performs an astonishing sleight of hand during which an African woman "speaks" of Africa and Europe. As Smith prepares to leave the coast, bound for Barbados and then to England, he is heartened by the company of Charles Wheeler who, he tells the reader, had been a factor for the Royal Africa Company for the past ten years and whose professed tales of Guinea "render'd his Company diverting." He then reproduces a first person account that runs some twenty-one pages, much of which is taken up with conversations between Wheeler and "her Ladyship," an African concubine given to Wheeler during a visit to a king.[89] While initially loath to accept this woman as offered, Wheeler succumbs and finds himself entranced.

Her lovely Breasts, whose Softness to the Touch nothing can exceed, were quite bare, and so was her Body to her Waste . . . and though she was black, that was amply recompenc'd by the Softness of her Skin, the beautiful Proportion and exact Symmetry of each Part of her Body, and the natural, pleasant and inartificial Method of her Behaviour. She was not forward, nor yet coy, when I pressed her lovely Breasts, she gently stroak'd my Hand and smiling met my Salute with equal Ardour and Fervancy.[90]

Having located the legitimacy of his desire (he later says that "had she been White, I should have begg'd her of the King"), and offered a veiled pornography of their encounter, he goes on to level a relentless critique of Europe's sexual behaviors through the voice of the savage "Lady." In response to her queries about the ways of the English, Wheeler (Smith) vents about the irrationality of English marital customs, of conventions ostensibly about chastity that lead to the ruin of England's best men and women, and ultimately about the civility of the savage. He closes his narrative by stating that "I doubt not by an impartial Examination of the Premises, it would be found, that we Christians have as many idle ridiculous Notions and Customs as the Natives of Guinea have, if not more."[91]

What is important about this use of the savage is not that it would have been particularly unusual at this time, but rather that it occurs exclusively through the voice of a female informant and through the behavior of African women. Perhaps Smith—aware of the danger of his words and thus channeling them through not one but two secondary narrators—relied upon her ladyship's queries not simply because of the titillating factor of having a savage woman say that "she believ'd, according to the Account I had give, few Women in Europe presented their Husbands with their Maidenheads" but because, as the sine qua non of savagery herself, her civility was that much more evocative. The rhetorical maneuver performed by Jobson's dairymaids and Ligon's Cape Verdean Queen Anne is echoed here, and its effect is to cement the position of the African lady in opposition to her European counterpart. Whether English writers used the African woman to criticize their own culture or to demonstrate their racial superiority, the images such writers used were the linchpins of England's emerging notion of itself.

One of a very few English woman in late eighteenth-century West Africa, abolitionist Anna Falconbridge yearned for cultural relativism when she noted that women's breasts in Sierra Leone were "disgusting to Europeans, thought considered *beautiful* and ornamental here."[92] But such weak claims of sisterly sympathy could hardly interrupt 300 years of porno-tropical writing. By the 1770s, Edward Long's *History of Jamaica* presented readers with African women whose savagery was total, for whom enslavement was the only means of civilization. Long maintained that "an oran-outang husband would [not] be any dishonour to a Hottentot female; for what are these Hottentots?"[93] He asserted as fact that sexual liaisons occurred between African women and apes and made no reference to any sort of African female shame or beauty. Rather, Long used women's bodies and behavior to justify and promote the mass enslavement of Africans. By the time he wrote, the Jamaican economy was fully invested in slave labor and was contributing more than half of the profits obtained by England from the West Indies as a whole.[94] The association of black people with beasts— via African women—had been cemented: "Their women are delivered with little or no labour; they have therefore no more occasion for midwifes than the female oran-outang, or any other wild animall. . . . Thus they seem exempted from the course inflicted upon Eve *and her daughters*."[95] If African women gave birth without pain, they somehow sidestepped God's curse upon Eve. If they were not Eve's descendants, they were not related to Europeans and could therefore be forced to labor on England's overseas plantations with impunity. Elaine Scarry has persuasively argued that the experience of pain—and thus the materiality of the body—lends a sense of reality and certainty to a society at times of crisis.[96] Early modern European women were so defined by their experience of pain in childbirth that an inability to feel pain was considered evidence of witchcraft.[97] In the case of England's contact with Africa and the Americas, the crisis in European identity was mediated by the construction of an image of pain-free reproduction that diminished Africa's access to certainty and civilization, thus allowing for the mass appropriation that was the transatlantic slave trade.

After Richard Ligon saw the black woman at Cape Verde, he pursued her around a dance hall, anxious to hear her voice, though she ultimately put him off with only "the loveliest smile that I have ever seen." The following morning he came upon two "prettie young Negro Virgins." Their clothing was arranged such that Ligon could see "their breasts round, firm, and beautifully shaped." He demurred that he was unable "to expresse all the perfections of Nature, and Parts, these Virgins were owners of." Aware of the image of African womanhood already circulating in England, he assured his readers that these women should not be confused with the women of "high Africa . . . that dwell nere the River of Gambia, who are thick lipt short nos'd and commonly [have] low forheads."[98] As though their breasts did not adequately set these women apart, Ligon used these qualifiers to highlight the exception of their beauty. Along with many of his contempoes, Ligon was quite willing to find beauty and allure in women who were ceptional—not "of high Africa"—but whose physiognomy and "education" marked them as improved by contact with Europe. Ligon encountered them in a domestic space, one familiar to him, and he sidestepped the discourse of savagery and painted a picture of seductive beauties that was understandable in part because of the familiarity of the setting.[99] In response to Ligon's pursuit, these women, like the beautiful woman he met the evening before, remained silent. Ligon tried, unsuccessfully, to test the truth of their beauty through the sound of their speech. Language had marked monstrosity for centuries; Pliny identified five of his monstrous races as such simply because they lacked human speech.[100] It appears that decent language, like shame, denoted civility for Ligon in the face of this inexplicable specter of female African beauty. Finally, Ligon begged pardon for his dalliances and remarked that he "had little else to say" about the otherwise desolate island.[101] To speak of African beauty in this context, then, was justified.

When Ligon arrived in Barbados and settled on 500-acre sugar plantation with 100 slaves, his notion of African beauty—if it had ever really existed—dissolved in the face of racial slavery. He saw African men and women carrying bunches of plantains: "'Tis a lovely sight to see a hundred handsom Negroes, men and women, with every one a grasse-green bunch of these fruits on their heads . . . the black and green so well becoming one another." Here in the context of the sugar plantation, where he saw African women working as he had never seen English woman do, Ligon struggled to situate African women as workers. Their innate unfamiliarity as laborers caused him to cast about for a useful metaphor. He compares African people to vegetation; now they are only passively and abstractly beautiful as blocks of color. Ligon attested to their passivity with their servitude: They made "very good servants, if they be not spoyled by the English."[102] But if Ligon found interest in beauty, as Jobson did in shame, he ultimately equated black people with animals. He declared that planters bought slaves so that the "sexes may be equall . . . [because] they cannot live without Wives," although the enslaved choose their partners much "as Cows do . . . for, the most of them are as near beasts as may be."[103] Like his predecessors, Ligon offered further proof of Africans' capacity for physical labor—their aptitude for slavery—through ease of childbearing. "In a fortnight [after giving birth] this woman is at worke with her Pickaninny at her back, as merry a soule as any is there."[104] In the Americas, African women's purportedly pain-free childbearing thus continued to be central. When Ligon reinforced African women's animality with descriptions of breasts "hang[-ing] down below their Navels," he tethered his narrative to familiar images of black women that—for readers nourished on Hakluyt and de Bry—effectively naturalized the enslavement of Africans. His contemporary, Felix Spoeri, wrestled with the image of over-the-shoulder breast-feeding in 1661 when he noted that "when slave mothers go to work, they tie the young children onto their backs. While they work they frequently give their children the breast, across the armpits, and let them suckle." In less outlandish terms then, Spoeri worked to reconcile the tension between mothering and hard labor.[105]

By the time the English made their way to the West Indies, decades of ideas and information about brown and black women predated the actual encounter. In many ways, the encounter had already taken place in parlors and reading rooms on English soil, assuring that colonists would arrive with a battery of assumptions and predispositions about race, femininity, sexuality, and civilization.[106] Confronted with an Africa they needed to exploit, European writers turned to black women as evidence of a cultural inferiority that ultimately became encoded as racial difference. Monstrous bodies became enmeshed with savage behavior as the icon of women's breasts became evidence of tangible barbarism. African women's "unwomanly" behavior evoked an immutable distance between Europe and Africa on which the development of racial slavery depended. By the mid-seventeenth century, what had initially marked African women as unfamiliar—their sexually and reproductively bound savagery—had become familiar. To invoke it was to conjure a gendered and racialized figure that marked the boundaries of English civility even as she naturalized the subjugation of Africans and their descendants in the Americas.

"The Number of Women Doeth Much Disparayes the Whole Cargoe": The Trans-Atlantic Slave Trade and West African Gender Roles

The images that set African women so firmly apart from their European counterparts would resonate in myriad ways on the shores of Western and West Central Africa. European traders originally enticed by gold soon turned their attention to human cargo, and over the course of the sixteenth and seventeenth centuries slave ships would cross the Atlantic with growing frequency. Even as they constructed images designed to ease their own passage into the economy of slave trading, European traders and travelers left evidence of the social and cultural environments from which they wrenched African women. Slave traders who took African women from their homes engaged in more than a theft of bodies—they pilfered fragmented systems of knowledge around the economies of work, family, and beliefs that would inform the future of these women in America in ways that were radically distorted from their pasts. To fully reconstruct the gendered lives of African women and men before they were enslaved is, obviously, impossible. But one can appreciate the impact of women's transport on developing African American cultures. African women carried their pasts into the Americas just as surely as did enslaved men.

Notwithstanding the predominant images of captive African men, African women and children together made up the majority of those transported to the Americas during the entirety of the transatlantic slave trade. While women were never the majority of the transports, it was only among involuntary migrants from the African coasts that anything approaching the sex ratio of societies of origin was reproduced in the Americas. The notion of a male majority in the trans-Atlantic trade is fundamentally flawed and, in light of evidence to the contrary, the conclusions that have emerged from assumptions about male majorities among transported Africans need to be reconsidered.[1] If African women were a significant proportion of those forcibly transported to the Americas, they were an overwhelming share of all female migrants, both voluntary and involuntary.[2] As they assessed their surroundings in the Americas, European settlers would have been struck by the prevalence of African women; particularly in relation to women of European descent. Slave traders bought and sold significant numbers of African women and European settlers purchased them and put them to work on American fields: how did that shape emergent notions of racial slavery? How did those women, in turn, navigate their enslavement in ways both similar to and divergent from male captives? And how do we understand the ways in which women's reproductive identities intersected with the demands of forced labor, both for the men who enslaved them and for the women themselves? An appreciation of the demographic reality of the slave trade allows us to more fully understand the importance and impact of sex ratios and West African gender roles on emergent culture in the Americas.

Transport

On February 12, 1678, English slave traders loaded three recently purchased women and the same number of men on the *Arthur*, a slave ship anchored in the Callabar River, at the Bight of Biafra, West Africa. The ship's factor, George Hingston, paid the "kinge of New Callabarr" thirty copper bars for each woman; for each man he paid thirty-six.[3] The following day, canoes brought eighteen women and fourteen men to the ship. The next day, only three canoes approached the *Arthur* and Hingston purchased three men, one woman, and some yams with which to feed them. For the next six and a half weeks this piecemeal loading pattern continued: small numbers of women and men purchased each day from individual canoes. Assuming that the three women who boarded the ship on February 12 survived, they would watch from the cramped cargo bays with increasing despair as more and more women, men, and children joined them in the hold.[4] It would slowly dawn on these women and men that their capture was irrevocable and that their future was in the process of complete transformation. As they struggled to locate themselves in relation to the violation of their capture, their sense of community would be gendered in various ways. Between February 10 and March 28, Hingston daily purchased groups of women and men: three men and three women on the 13th; four men and four women on the 18th; six men and six women on the 20th; three men, four women, and two girls on the 27th. Acutely aware of the pattern of his purchases, Hingston wrote on May 5 that :

This day wee bought 5 men and 5 women wee forgett nott your hon^ers Interest if possible to gett most men if they are any way promisinge but as yett wee find ye women generally Better than they men.[5]

While the agony of uncertainty and depredation was uniform for those captured in the trade, the sense of probable future would be quite different for those on the *Arthur* than those on other ships. Because these women were not outnumbered, they would understand their capture as defined by their community identity. Should they consider it, they might also understand that their collective reproductive identities were innately part of the justification for their capture. The captain of the *Hannah* loaded a total of 266 men and 132 women between February 19 and March 10, 1689. Not only were the women outnumbered by almost exactly two to one, but as the ship lay anchored at Arda on the Gold Coast men and women were purchased and loaded separately. On the first two days of purchases, groups of men numbering between three and thirty-one arrived on board, leaving a single group of three women to face 122 men below decks.[6] The realities of capture, holding, and transport were likely to impress upon women a sometimes extreme sense of isolation. For these women, their gender identity only highlighted their isolation, layering conjectural meaning onto the fragments of explanation for their capture. Were they to be prostituted to these men? To their captors? Made servants to them? The search for meaning would be inextricable from their isolation. Only once before the ship left Arda did men and women arrive in the same parcel. In the particular configurations on board the *Arthur* and the *Hannah*, the slow realization of the women that they were being treated as property would have been inextricable from their experience of the ratio of men to women. Indeed, if anything sets those transported from the Bight of Biafra apart from those transported from the rest of the coast, it may be the clarity with which they came to understand the implicit link between their new productive and reproductive purpose in the Americas.[7]

As the loading continued, at times Hingston turned back canoemen bringing captives "by reason of their remissing in Bringn't us provision." Without food, he would make no purchases. Provisioning remained a constant problem throughout the six weeks during which Hingston loaded African women and men into the *Arthur*. For the three women and their companions, the "problem" was dire. Fed only yams as they languished in a ship from which they could see the land they would never again set foot on, they began to "grow Leane." Hingston found this perplexing, as he believed that "they want fore nothinge haveinge doely as much provision as they Cann make use of." Like many slavers, he was committed to the notion that mortality rates could be at least partially explained through recourse to the "willfulness" and "intractability" of captive Africans. His delusion that they wanted for nothing must have been matched by their horror as only two weeks after the sale of these three women the people around them began to die. Death came to men and women, boys and girls, in relatively equal numbers; as it did for most of those who experienced the Middle Passage.[8] Scarce food, dying men and women, and the three to thirty more people thrown into the hold each day punctuated the weeks until the *Arthur* finally left the river for the Atlantic Ocean.[9]

Once the *Arthur* pulled out to sea, the death rate increased. Not a day passed during the voyage without a dead African woman or man, boy or girl, being tossed overboard. On April 22, Hingston noticed that "the winds [were] nott blowinge so fresh" and brought the 274 women and men out into the open air to be mustered. At this point, the sex ratio among the living captives was 1.3 to 1, men to women. As they emerged from the hold of the ship, a common language would have assisted both men and women in the *Arthur* as they mourned their capture and worried about their future. They came in small groups from "Bandy," "Donus," and Callabar—all Ibo-speaking trading centers clustered at the basin of the Niger Delta.[10] Because of the likelihood that the women aboard the *Arthur* originated from areas close to the coast, it is even more likely that the women spoke a common language than that the men did.[11] It is difficult to imagine the looks and words of terror the women exchanged as they glanced around at the expanse of the Atlantic Ocean. They had already been on board ship for two and a half months. Now they would be returned to the hold for the remainder of the two-month voyage to Barbados.

Five more weeks passed before they again breathed fresh air. Hingston brought the ship to Bridgetown, Barbados during the height of the island's sugar boom, and sold the surviving 144 men, 110 women, 9 boys, and 9 girls in a mere three days. By the end of the voyage, 49 men and boys and 33 women and girls had died. The island's slaveowners wasted no time relieving Hingston of his cargo and initiating the women and men who had survived the journey aboard the *Arthur* into the demands of sugar cultivation.[12]

The purchasing method George Hingston used aboard the *Arthur* was one of two employed by European slave traders. The forts of Elmina, Cape Coast Castle, and Accra—whose legacy still exists in the intersections of history and memory—evoke the trans-Atlantic slave trade more powerfully than slowly loaded ships anchored beyond the breakers. Captive women and men waited in the "Holes" of European fortresses up and down the Upper Guinea and Gold coasts. There they languished in "damp Trunks" that caused "great Mortality" until traders loaded them aboard slaving vessels.[13] As ships made their way down the coast, slave traders capitalized on ethnic and linguistic differences in their effort to maintain control over cargo and those held at the forts. Men and women from Senegambia, for example, would be transported as far as the Gold Coast to guard those loaded onto ships or to be permanently enslaved by Europeans on the coast. The Royal African Company directed agents at distant forts to exchange men and women with one another when obtaining slaves to work in the forts—so-called castle slaves or *garomattos*—so as to remove individuals from familiar landscapes that beckoned runaways. Orders to ship captains often included directives regarding captives for the forts: "We have indeed order'd our Agents at Gambia. . . . to pick out. . . . ten or twenty of the choicest young healthy men and women slaves and to send them down to you . . . and to receive from you in return as many young healthy Gold Coast Negroes as they may have occasion for at Gambia."[14] Those from the Bight of Biafra—like those on the *Arthur*—experienced the Middle Passage with women and men who shared related languages and proximous geographies. In contrast, for some, the encounter between far-flung ethnic groups that characterized the experience of enslavement in the Americas began in the fortresses that dotted the shorelines of the Gold Coast. In the fort, women observed other women across lines of ethnicity or culture and caught glimpses of their future—and sometimes of the pervasive role that their reproductive identities would play.

In December 1727, Cayoba, a woman enslaved at the Royal African Company's fort on Bence Island at Sierra Leone, escaped from the castle. Cayoba ran with three men, who had already been renamed Peter, Dick, and Monday, but five months after their escape they were recaptured and returned to the company. Only weeks later the Royal African Company agent discovered another escape plot, this time among the men and women destined for transport to the Americas; perhaps they were emboldened by

Cayoba and her companions. The agent punished the conspirators publicly, but his already tenuous authority was demolished five months later when castle slaves and "sale slaves" joined together once again and successfully attacked the whites, drove them out, and burned the castle.[15]

As they did for those awaiting departure on board ships, slavers treated sexual difference as a natural way of organizing captives, and thus women at slave forts forged connections with one another even before they left the coast. In the month following Cayoba's return to the fortress, another female castle slave named Moota gave birth to her third child and thereby raised her husband Jemmy Bomboy's wages by "a Barr."[16] At slave forts along the Gold Coast, the separation between "castle slaves" and those awaiting transatlantic transport was similarly marked by childbirth. While an unnamed female captive managed an escape from the fort in 1714, Quaguerry and Amaba petitioned the factor at Commenda near Cape Coast Castle for an advance on their pay because they "have many children to maintain and but 1ᵃ per month." Orders came from Cape Coast Castle to advance Quaguerry's pay "in consideration of her children being Large, but the Agents think Amaba's . . . children too young to be allowed anything yet."[17] The Royal Africa Company practiced a kind of English domestic slavery on the African coast, and the balance between the cost of children and the benefits accrued from them ultimately favored the latter.

In 1744, Royal African Company officials carefully delineated the ideal sex ratios of Castle slaves to be "as near as you can half the number of men and half of women."[18] Through tiny windows or iron doors, women waiting for sale from forts or castles caught glimpses of other women who labored as slaves even as they mothered their children. Among the myriad images and expectations that African women brought to their New World enslavement, women such as Moota, Quaguerry, and Amaba—who answered to white men and whose children accompanied them as they carried out labors in an alien land—were painful portents of their future.

As the weeks and months unfolded before them, those who came aboard the same ships or endured the same fortress walls and who continued to see one another on adjoining plantations or in and around port cities must have truly regarded themselves as kin—connected by an unfathomable ordeal of transportation, deprivation, and loss.[19] If their paths crossed, they must have shared a rare and poignant moment of recognition, one full of a tangible past. Months or years later, after being led from the holes onto ships and into New World plantations, facing the frightening prospect of sustaining themselves and potentially their children, their memories of both

Moota and Cayoba—the enslaved mother and the resisting woman—might reverberate. Moota and the children she bore but did not "own" would retrospectively stand as signs of all that enslavement in the Americas could mean. For in addition to the labor she would perform, the disease she would battle, the punishments she would endure, and the loss of her hold upon her future, a woman enslaved in the New World would contend with the jeopardy carried by her reproductive capacity. Her vulnerability to sexual exploitation and the lack of clarity about how to formulate a relationship to a child under slavery would compound the violation of enslavement. African women most emphatically embodied the ideological definitions of what racial slavery ultimately meant. The inheritability of slavery depended upon the biological capacity of African mothers and fathers to pass their social identity as enslaveable—marked as it was on their skin—onto the bodies of their children. Racial slavery, then, functioned euphemistically as a social condition forged in African women's wombs. As they surveyed the survivors of the Middle Passage on American shores, European men could hardly help but see in the bodies of African women and girls the physical manifestation of their own dreams for the future. These women, however coerced, enabled the process of creolization—a transformation both threatening and reassuring to New World slaveowners and one that fully constructed the environment in which enslaved women endured and resisted the institution of American racial slavery.

Demography

The historiography of the slave trade is vast and allows us to speculate, with some particularity, about the cultural consequences of shifting sex ratios and points of embarkation for the men and women who experienced both the Middle Passage and American slavery.[20] Examining demography also raises the question of the role of slaveowners in shaping the sexual and ethnic composition of their labor force. Planters' ethnic preferences, while clearly and passionately articulated, determined neither the ethnicity of the enslaved population nor its sexual composition.[21]

Enslaved persons embarked from points throughout West and South East Africa.[22] Slave traders loaded approximately 11 million Africans on board ships bound for the Americas between 1519 and 1867, of which 9.6 million survived the journey and disembarked on American shores.[23] The breadth of geographical origins and the sheer number of persons involved have led to an emphasis on the relentless heterogeneity of the Middle Passage; and it is true that care must be taken not to overgeneralize about ethnic identity based on ports of embarkation. The loose monikers that slaveowners applied to those they enslaved—"Coromantee" or "Ibo"—often violated linguistic and cultural specificities that were of paramount importance to those so labeled. Nonetheless, despite the vast territory from which enslaved persons were drawn, patterns of enslavement and transportation do allow us a degree of specificity. Contemporary African historians concur that the notion of an impossibly wide array of geographic and cultural origins funneling down to the coast can be set aside in the seventeenth and early eighteenth centuries. Rather, hard data on the totality of the trans-Atlantic slave trade—particularly in the early decades of the trade—enable a confident discussion of regional and ethnic origins among the enslaved. In aggregate terms, within West Africa, regional origins can be simplified to three regions: the Gold Coast, from which 12 percent of all captives originated; the Bight of Benin, with 22 percent and the Bight of Biafra, with 15 percent. Ten percent came from Senegambia and approximately 40 percent from West Central Africa with the remaining originating in Madagascar or Mozambique.[24] These large and broad figures can be further clarified by national trading relationships. Thus, 60 percent of those transported from the Bight of Benin disembarked in Bahia, Brazil, while three out of five captives unloaded in the British Caribbean came from either the Bight of Biafra or the Gold Coast. Moreover, during the fifty-year period following 1658, two out of three enslaved persons arriving to Barbados or Jamaica embarked from an area on the Gold Coast less than 200 miles long.[25]

Ethnic and regional origin is further disaggregated by gender. Regional origins and sex ratios are closely connected, particularly during the earlier periods of the slave trade when local factors did much to influence the sex ratios for Africans who constituted the cargoes of slave ships. In the seventeenth century, ships leaving the Bight of Biafra carried 20 to 25 percent fewer men than those leaving the Upper Guinea Coast or West Central Africa. Although as time passed the disparity between the regions diminished somewhat, in the eighteenth century the Bight of Biafra and the Bight of Benin continued to supply the highest ratios of women to men, while the Gold Coast, West Central Africa, and the Upper Guinea coast supplied the lowest.[26] The value of women in the African slave trade—a trade that drew captive women into the African interior—also meant that the decision to make a woman available to the transatlantic trade would be mediated by price; the cost of transporting a woman to a more valuable market would have to be less that the additional profit available as a result of transport. This means that women sold to the Americas likely originated from areas near the ports of export and were thus more likely to share linguistic and cultural experiences; and the prosaics of prices might translate into linguistic and cultural familiarities among women.

The men and women on board the Arthur experienced capture and transport in numbers that would have been familiar to many ensnared by the trans-Atlantic trade in the second half of the seventeenth century. During the entire period of the slave trade, the Bight of Biafra was the port of origin for more enslaved women than any other region of the African coast, with "ratios of women higher and those of men lower than. . . . [any] other regions of Atlantic Africa."[27] It is important to understand that, while in other regions of export men constituted larger proportions of the captives, the ratios also shift significantly over time (see Table 1). By the nineteenth century there were more males, fewer women, and more children. Thus, while 66 percent of all captives from the Gold Coast between 1701 and 1809 were male, in the years between 1662 and 1700, women made up 41 percent and men 49 percent of total transports.[28] During the second half of the seventeenth century, female captives consistently outnumbered men at the Bight of Biafra. On board the *Arthur* women made up 43 percent of the captives and their sale in Barbados proceeded without complaint.

Royal African Company officials in London consistently sent slave-ship captains to the West African coast under orders to "view well the

TABLE 1. REGIONAL PERCENTAGES OF MALES AMONG ADULT CAPTIVES IN THE TRANS-ATLANTIC TRADE TO THE AMERICAS

Region	1601–1700	1701–1800
Bight of Benin	59	16
Bight of Biafra	49	58
Gold Coast	54	66
Senegambia	74	69
Sierra Leone	75	64
South East Africa	—	67
West Central Africa	60	67

Source: David Eltis, Stephen D. Behrendt, David Richardson, and Herbert S. Klein, eds., *The Trans-Atlantic Slave Trade: A Database on CD-ROM* (Cambridge: Cambridge University Press, 1999).

Negroes that they may be sound and merchantable between the ages of 15 & 40 and that the major part be male."[29] The injunctions of the Royal African Company have been understood as simply formulaic orders that were carried out with little difficulty; the conclusion has been that European slavers purchased twice as many men as women for labor in the Americas.[30] The orders of the company, however, occasionally reveal a tone of entreaty rather than authority. "If you are carefull you may have two men for one female," or "endeavour all you can to have your Number of Males exceed the females," or "the number of women Exceeding [men] doeth much disparayes the whole Cargoe."[31] Its instructions, then, reflected the company's inability to dictate the terms of trade. They also illustrate the disjuncture between slaveowners' experience with working black women and Royal African Company officials' ideologies of male/female value. Despite English buyers' preference for male laborers, over the course of the entire period of the Atlantic slave trade adult men, although they were the largest group of persons transported, constituted less than half of the total number of adults and children brought to the Americas. Women, boys, and girls combined outnumbered them in the trade. In the last four decades of the seventeenth century women constituted almost 40 percent of those who crossed the Atlantic, men 50 percent, and children (those thought by slave traders to be under the age of fifteen) the remainder. During the eighteenth century, the proportion of children rose to 20 percent, women fell to 30 percent, and men maintained their previous proportion. Not until the nineteenth century would the proportion of women fall to around 15 percent, while men and children equally constituted the remainder.[32]

The relationship between sex ratios and ethnicity was never static. Internal factors in the Bight of Benin and all down the coast altered sex ratios from year to year. In response to high demand, for example, slavers sold equal numbers of women and men to European slave ships from the Gold Coast in 1688.[33] In the last years of the 1720s, the aftermath of Dahomean expansion into Allada at the Gold Coast caused increased numbers of dependent women and men from the immediate area to be offered into the trade.[34] Thus, in the late 1720s and 1730s, more females were exported from Whydah than at other periods. As with women captured by the European slave trade in 1688 from the Gold Coast, women from this area in the 1720s must have found their capture particularly shocking; it was a fate that more often fell to men. Farther north, on the coast of Senegambia, traders and rulers made it a practice to procure enslaved women for sale to Europeans as early as the mid-fifteenth century, but only in small and symbolic numbers. In 1455 two women and one man found themselves offered to Diago Gomes as a token of peace.[35] Some 150 years later, the African merchant Buckor Sano argued that all Europeans "earnestly desired" the enslaved Mandinka women he offered to an English trader.[36] The fate of these women as sexual offerings, while arguably quite different from that suffered by those transported from Senegambia to the Carolina rice fields, would still become part of the apparatus of comprehension, or misapprehension, for both women and men sold across the Atlantic as they struggled to understand their futures.

The causes of shifting sex ratios are still being explored, but African economic and sociopolitical relations rather than European demands explain the shifting proportions of women in the transatlantic trade. For example, patrilineal societies appear to have exported more women than societies ordered along matrilineal lines.[37] The value of women in regional African slave trades (to northern Africa or Asia) affected the willingness of local slavers to make women available to the Atlantic trade, where slave traders paid lower prices for women then men.[38] Arguments have been made that African women's value as agricultural producers kept them out of the trans-Atlantic trade, but women performed agricultural work throughout West Africa regardless of the ratio at which they were made available to the Atlantic slave trade.[39] For the most part, regions affected by consistent warfare or military upheaval exported fewer women. But the cultural parameters of warfare would also shape the gendered contours of the trade. The inevitability of decapitating male prisoners of war in the Bight of Biafra, for example, certainly resulted in low numbers of male enemies sold to slave traders from that region.[40] On the other hand, German trader David Van Nyendael wrote at the turn of the seventeenth century that in the city of Benin it is not "allow'd to export any Male slaves that are sold in this Country for they must stay there; But females may be dealt with at anyone's pleasure." Van Nyendael referred here to a state policy in place since 1560; enforcement of the policy began to dissipate only after the second decade of the eighteenth century.[41] This prohibition against trading in men may well be a key to both the reluctance of European traders to stop there and the resultant small numbers of men or women transported to the Americas from the Benin kingdom. Ultimately, neither European interest in male laborers nor African interest in female ones satisfactorily explains the patterns of sex ratios in the transatlantic slave trade. Rather, an ability for African elites involved in the trade to dictate its terms determined both the scope of the trade in African women and the direction in which they were sent. And of course, while English traders might have firmly believed that the women on board slave ships disparaged the whole cargo, it was those very women whose labor made possible some of the most valuable export economies in the Americas.

Ethnicity and Experience

If the experience of capture and transport dominated the lives of first gener-ation Africans enslaved in the Americas to the degree that we imagine, it is important to sort through the information that captives may have brought to their initial encounter with Europeans and with the terms of the captiv-ity. By the time they were purchased by Hingston, the women on the *Arthur* could not have been ignorant of the possibility of enslavement at the hands of Europeans. Europe's slaving vessels had been visiting the Bights since before the seventeenth century.[42] Economic upheavals and the desire for trade goods both cast a wide web of capture and sale for African women, men, and children. As wars and slave raiders disrupted the rhythms of daily life, people would have heard word of their vulnerability to the white man's ships. Women and men on the Upper Guinea Coast also were well aware of the dangers of capture and sale. As early as the sixteenth century the invading Mane pressed toward the coast, creating a cycle of capture and sale to European traders that endured for centuries.[43] As prisoners of war, men—who were exported at a rate three times that of women at the Upper Guinea Coast—were particularly vulnerable to European slavers. But as we know from the examples of Cayoba and Moota, women were neither pas-sive nor protected. The small numbers of women sold to the transatlantic trade from Senegambia were overwhelmingly Wolof and lived nearest the coast, in contrast to the male captives, who came from further inland.[44] Because they came from a highly stratified society marked by caste and social and political hierarchy, Wolof women would have had ready access to the idea of enslavement: Divisions between *jambur* and *jaam* (slave and free) and *Buur* and *Baadoolo* (citizen and subject) were firm, superseding women's importance as transmitters of biological heredity.[45] As ships took them away from their homelands, in hindsight, the consistent regional con-flicts would render their capture conceivable, and their shared geographical and ethnic identities would facilitate connections with other enslaved cap-tives, albeit along sex-segregated lines. Others, of course, would be caught entirely by surprise by the particulars of local trading rhythms.

The women who found their futures so starkly changed could only add the surprise of their capture to the larger fear and uncertainty that grew as ships languished on the Callabar River or in the "holes" that filled up at Elmina. As they contemplated their uncertain future, their thoughts must have turned to those left behind. Perhaps they thought of crops untended, which meant children unfed. As night fell, their thoughts might have wandered to the daily evening markets that were predominately run by women, where they had exchanged wares, gossip, food, or friendship. If they had been members of polygamous households, perhaps the dawning recognition that they would never again see their relatives would be tempered by the knowledge that another woman would step in to care for their children—a bittersweet solace indeed. They would soon realize that the Middle Passage and what followed would fundamentally transform the ways in which they had imagined their futures.

By all accounts, captured women on slave ships came from communities in which they shouldered important responsibilities. Slave traders who watched the way women worked in West and West Central Africa called these women "slaves" to African men—no doubt an accusation they leveled to exonerate their own role in the slave trade. While European observers denigrated women's agricultural work, all members of society depended upon this essential sphere of women's work and compensated for it at the markets. Women produced agricultural exports essential to regional economies both prior to and during the period of European contact. At the western Gold Coast, women sold food and textiles at large biweekly markets attended by more than 3,500 people.[46] Wilhelm Muller, a German minister who lived at the Gold Coast between 1662 and 1669, noted that "apart from the peasants who bring palm-wine and sugar-cane to market every day, there are no men who stand in public markets to trade, but only women. It is remarkable to see how the market is filled every day with. . . . women selling [food]."[47] Samuel Brun commented on the division of labor concerning cultivated crops at the beginning of the seventeenth century. He noted that at Cape Palmas (Liberia/Sierra Leone), men traded Malaguetta pepper for money, but they traded beads for rice "because the rice is the ware of women, while Malaguetta is that of the men."[48]

The marketplace was a public place where women exchanged more than goods. Muller wrote, "they strengthen their memories by zealously repeating the old stories. . . . young people and children listen to such discourse with avid ears and absorb it in their hearts."[49] One wonders how long after their transport to the Americas women were able to gather to "strengthen their memories" by evoking their memories of the market-place, their homes, and the physical landscapes of their former lives. Women at the Gold Coast formerly lived in houses in which each woman and her children maintained a separate apartment that opened onto a shared central area. Women decorated their "clean and tidy [homes] . . . with white or red earth which they consider . . . particularly beautiful."[50] One wonders what beauty they managed to unearth from soil in the Americas.

The shape of the physical landscape had far-reaching implications for the ways men and women lived their lives. For example, more than anything else, water shaped the daily life of Mandinka women and men on the Upper Guinea Coast. Surrounded by myriad rivers and dense mangrove swamps, the peoples who lived in this part of West Africa used the waterways for transport and for food. In 1455, the Venetian trader Alvise Cadamosto wrote of his ship being approached by huge canoes and noted that "they are constantly journeying . . . in their canoes, carrying women and men."[51] His attention to the women no doubt was precipitated by his own single-sex experience of maritime trades. They navigated canoes with as few as one or as many as sixty people aboard and devised systems of dikes, sometimes miles long, to flood and drain rice fields. The nature of agricultural work in this region required large-scale collective effort, effectively pulling all members of the society into the agricultural sphere. The huge dikes built to accommodate the draining and flooding of fields required the cooperation of hundreds of people. During the construction and planting, both men and women moved from their homes to the fields to tend the crop and manage the waters. Enormous markets took place every eight days, bringing thousands to buy and sell, some coming from as far as sixty miles away. In the process, they created enduring social networks and used canoes and riverways as transport to "frequent reunions for social, religious and political purposes."[52] Perhaps this level of social mobility/integration in part addresses the relative inability of European traders to extract significant numbers of captives from this area. (Fewer than 5 percent of all persons entering the slave trade in the late seventeenth and early eighteenth century embarked from Senegambia/Upper Guinea Coast.) Despite the fact that the Upper Guinea Coast was extremely well placed in terms of the length of time it took to get to North America (almost a third fewer days journey) and a desirable sex ratio among those sold (men outnumbered women three to one) European ships were attacked or otherwise foiled from trading at this part of the coast more often than at any other.[53]

This constant movement of peoples from place to place influenced patterns of cultural and economic acquisitions. Senegambian women covered themselves with elaborate scarification, an adornment that was wholly perplexing to European observers but was certainly an essential component to a girl's coming of age, both physically and spiritually.[54] Gri-gris prayer amulets were worn all along the coast. Women and men carried their belief systems on their persons, offering food and thanks and requesting blessings from a pantheon of gods before eating, stepping into a boat, or going to sleep. As Islam moved from North Central Africa toward the West African coast, evocations of Muslim prophets accompanied the "fetiches," bags and amulets worn around the neck, that were responsible for preserving the safety of those who traveled so widely by boat.[55] As women moved through the work that defined their day, the protective divine would accompany them.

Much has been made of the "matriarchal" origins of West African families. Perhaps more significant for women transported from the Slave Coast would be the experience of having lived, or served, in households headed by male-female pairs who ruled in tandem over their lineage. Such was the case for the Fon. Known as the Taninon, the female head's responsibilities came from her role as intermediary between the living and the ancestors of each Fon lineage.[56] Even a woman held in bondage by a Slave Coast family could have no doubt as to the potential authority and responsibility of women in Fon society. Linkages between powerful women and men were inherent to Fon cosmology. In the mid-seventeenth century, Allada was the focus of Christian missionary efforts. African catechisms prepared by the Capuchin friars allowed the name "Lisa" to refer to Jesus Christ. In Allada cosmology Lisa, a white man, and Mawa, a black woman, form a paired deity.[57] Among the Igbo, the creator was Chineke— representing both male (Chi) and female (Eke)—whose unity and complementarity formed the crux of Igbo cosmology.[58] As agricultural producers, conduits to the ancestors, complements to Jesus Christ, even armed guards at the king's palace at Dahomey,[59] women's multiple and pivotal role at all levels of society would travel with both men and women across the Atlantic.

Matters of the spirit would be balanced by the quotidian rhythms of lives left behind. Thinking back, a woman from the Gold Coast might remember being called upon to witness a marriage as a child of seven or eight. Apparently a small girl was compelled to "sleep in between [the bride and groom] and watch out that they do not touch each other for seven days" as part of a wedding ritual.[60] There is no telling what insights a young girl might carry with her, or how her sense of her own importance might be shaped, as a result of her role at the inception of a marriage. Women would carry many such childhood memories. Both mothers and daughters would feel the absence of the moment of puberty at which a girl came under her mother's care, to learn weaving, baking, and marketing.[61] For many, circumcision would have marked their girlhood. Among other things, the rite of circumcision initiated female children into a sisterhood, creating a bond of shared secrets and pain. In modern accounts, the rite is deeply laden with imagery that constructs a long-standing connection between girls and their mothers, grandmothers, and ancestors.[62] Once these women found themselves in American slave societies, slaveowners wrenched this most essential site of commonality between mothers and daughters from them. Enslaved mothers would be forced to devise new ritual spaces as substitutes.

Steps to assure women's fertility followed soon after decisions to marry. After a marriage announcement, the bride's friends ritually prepared her for conception.[63] Once pregnant, she would be "brought to the seashore in order to be washed" after being ritually dirtied by "a great number of boys and girls" on her way to the water.[64] It should be noted here that, as they had since their first trips to West Africa, Europeans continued to insist that childbirth came easily to African women—and thus articulated an argument for reliance on enslaved African women despite their simultaneous insistence that men were the most desirable laborers. "In the second or third day [after childbirth] they already go among people and do their housework and business," exclaimed one travel writer. His awe at the speed of women's recovery on the Gold Coast is perhaps contextualized by the length of time elite European women spent recuperating from childbirth; Adam Jones points out that the German word for childbed in fact meant "six-week bed."[65]

Mother and father prepared a feast after the child survived its first seven days. Some years later, while still children, both boys and girls underwent circumcision.[66] Faced with permanent exile, the women and men transported from the African coast would leave behind much of what defined them as members of specific sociocultural entities. At the same time, the memories and belief systems that dictated female circumcision or polygamous households or sexual abstinence as birth control would live on in the Americas even as enslaved women would mourn the inability to actualize some aspects of their past. Cultural traditions were renegotiated as women and men made sexual connections and gave birth to children

...ɪ—should they survive—they guided into an adulthood categorically at odds with their own pasts. Moreover, while the presence of people from other parts of the West African coast would alter the ascendancy of any traditions tied to particular ethnicities or cultures, the violence of the slavery system in the Americas would alter them even more.[67]

During pregnancy at the Bight of Benin, women and men initiated a sexual distance that extended at least a year and a half after a birth. "Not allowed even the Matrimonial caresses of her husband" from the moment of a discovered pregnancy, men and women cooperated to protect unborn children and to space childbirth.[68] Abstinence reflected an understanding of the relationship between intercourse and pregnancy as well as a mutual desire to protect women's energy and health from too-frequent pregnancies. Men as well as women, then, acknowledged and understood the physical demands of childbirth and nursing in ways that were lost on European observers. As they often did, European observers misconstrued birth spacing in their haste to denounce all African women as either enslaved by their men or "inclined to Wantonness." They associated what they saw as sexual freedom with "an absolute sterility [or] . . . a seldom pregnancy." Thus they believed that the woman who mothered only "two or three [children] in their whole lives" did so as a consequence of sexual promiscuity and its attendant diseases and disorders, not because of conscious efforts to space births.[69]

Some European observers believed the post-delivery period of abstinence lasted three months, and others commented upon a two- to three-year period of breast-feeding. Contemporary studies note the evidence that prolonged breast-feeding in tandem with postpartum sexual abstinence was an essential factor in African women and men's ability to regulate fertility. Present-day anthropological studies focused on the area of West Africa from Sierra Leone to the Bight of Biafra calculate the average duration of postpartum taboo to have been a year or longer. By abstaining from sexual contact or practicing coitus interuptus during breast-feeding, parents were able to assure manageable birth spacing and thereby increase the probability that their children would survive infancy.[70] On the opposite side of the Atlantic, prolonged breast-feeding accompanied by sexual abstinence was one of the few cultural practices transportable from West Africa to the Americas.[71]

Women from Senegambia, as were women all along the coast, were accompanied by the infants they carried upon their backs for "as long as they are breast-feeding them."[72] At the Sierra Leone estuary and the Sess

River at Cape Palmas, women carried infants "as long as they have them at the breast . . . in a kind of leather box, in which the little one is sat. They also tie it to their body to prevent accident."[73] At the Gold Coast, parents protected newly born children by anointing them with palm wine, adorning them with safeguarding fetishes, and strapping them to a mother's back until they could walk.[74]

As their sons neared adulthood, Mandinka mothers along the Gambia river prepared them for circumcision. When Samgully's mother saw her son leaving for a month long trading voyage aboard Richard Jobson's ship in 1623, Jobson wrote that she "overtook us . . . [and] on the shore made grievous moane to have him sent back . . . because she said he would be absent againe in the time of circumcision . . . and if we would not put him on shore, she would throw herselfe from the bane into the river." Ignoring her pleas, they left, but they returned in time for the next month's ceremony which she—or her female emissaries—watched over with care.[75] Further south along the coast, circumcision was not widely practiced and therefore women at the Gold Coast did not need to prepare their sons or daughters for circumcision. The inability to properly prepare one's child for circumcision rites in the Americas then would not be experienced as a loss for women and men from some regions and different expectations about ushering children into adulthood would be felt as important differences between enslaved mothers and fathers. Once in America, however, they too would contend with the broader inability to carry through essential practices associated with birth and child-rearing. The failure to protect a child "with all kinds of exquisite beads and with elegantly fashioned gold . . . through whose strength the tender child is to be protected against summan, the Devil, and against illness, injury and accident" must have cut deep into the hearts of men and women who became parents in the Americas.[76] Finally, even as they may have looked forward to death, it would come stripped clean of the ritual space it formerly occupied. Women who at the Gold Coast had attended to their dead with female-only mourning rites, "burying every body in the Town they were born," would know with dreadful certainty that their own death would occur in a ritual vacuum.[77] The loss of these and other rites of protection and initiation must have been felt as an almost unbearable violence.

While the transformation of human beings into chattel property began on the West African coast, the transaction at the point of sale simply initiated a long and drawn-out process of alienation and commodification. The violent dislocation of the Middle Passage made the proto-capitalist terms of trade visible to even the smallest child, while simultaneously rendering the experience all but indescribable from a distance. The violation at the heart of the Middle Passage is of course, the removal from home, and while one's ability to imagine the lost home is increasingly compromised by the passage of time, the degree to which lives continued to be lived in the Americas was immeasurably shaped by what had been lost. The memories that survivors of the Middle Passage carried with them became crucial as they faced the demands and definitions of slaveowners in the Americas. The alchemy of subjugation and resistance would be affected by myriad factors, but the clash between self-perception and racist violation is the key. The imaginary African woman—with her "indifferent" childbearing and "monstrous" body—would encounter the corporeal woman on board slave ships with disastrous and dislocating results. The following two chapters explore that encounter (from both the perspective of slaveowner and enslaved) as it reverberated in women's real and potential reproductive lives.

While African women continued to perform agricultural labor and to bring children into the world, they did so in entirely different circumstances that would radically alter their vision of the cultural meanings of their pasts and their futures. Women in the Americas would struggle as slaveowners drastically and violently altered the terms and conditions under which they performed agricultural work and tried to maintain traditions of familial work. As overwhelming as the physical toll of fieldwork was to women and men enslaved in the Americas, the place of reproduction in their lives almost immediately took on an entirely new and violent significance in their lives. Predicated as it was on the inheritability of race as a sign of debasement, enslavement destroyed any illusions that childbirth and the reproductive potential of women's bodies were somehow private, contained, or inconsequential to the larger process of the cultivation of staple crops and the extraction of wealth from New World colonies. In largely private acts of writing—the composition of wills and inventories— slaveowning settlers both crafted and evidenced their reliance upon the idea of reproduction even in the face of sky-high mortality and dismal fertility rates among the women and men whose bodies held such a promise of legacy.

Chapter 3

"The Breedings Shall Goe with Their Mothers": Gender and Evolving Practices of Slaveownership in the English American Colonies

Slaveowners in the early American colonies did more than simply appropriate the labor of others for their own gain. They hammered together an evolving set of social and cultural norms pertaining to Africans and their descendents that set in motion generations of violence wrought on both their bodies and their sense of self. Gender furnished one of the crucial axes around which the organization of enslavement and slave labor in the Americas took place. Having left an environment in which gendered notions of work firmly placed women's labor in household production, seventeenth-century English arrivals to the colonies confronted a situation in which African women constituted close to half of all available agricultural laborers.[1] Enslaved women performed work critical to the profitable and orderly functioning of slavery in the Americas, and as "women" became "workers," slaveowners developed language and practices to clarify that contradiction. I thus begin my discussion of black women's lives in the Americas by exploring the connection between the broad ideological currents around Africa and African women and the behaviors of early American slaveowners. Slaveowners and the enslaved came to the unfamiliar ground of racial slavery from decidedly different perspectives. The ways slaveowners constructed their lives as separate and distinct from the lives of those they enslaved profoundly shaped the terrain of violence, control, and negotiation African men and women navigated. Particularly as they wrote their wills, colonial slaveowners enacted a moral grammar through which they attained fluency in the practice of slaveownership.

For most early American slaveowning settlers, the act of writing was confined to matters of accounting or other immediate business. Inventories, bills of receipt, articles of sale, and logbooks or plantation records abound in far greater numbers than collections of personal letters, journals, or travel diaries. Large-scale ownership of land and persons was the purview of only a small proportion of land and slaveowners. Most slaveowning settlers were of the "middling sort," with that group's attendant economic insecurity and limited access to, among other things, education and the luxuries of a life of letters. Indeed, those who possessed the ability to write but lacked the urge to leave less prosaic evidence than their account books might have said that concerns with matters of life and death obviously took precedence over the contemplation of amorphous issues of race and identity. Nonetheless, as they articulated their desires about the dispersal of their estates—whether meager or considerable—through their wills, these slaveowners did in fact leave a record of sorts, a reflection of the shifting terrain of racial identity in the early English colonies.[2]

Certainly no act of writing was more permeated with the materiality of life and death in colonial America than that of writing a will. Frequently dated within months or even weeks of the testator's death, the wills are saturated with the widespread early mortality that characterized early American settlers' lives. At the same time, economic historians have commented widely on the relative reluctance of early American colonials to leave wills. Writing a will was costly, and the unpredictability of death in the colonies contributed to a large proportion of property owners dying intestate.[3] Moreover, demographic stresses altered both the materiality of inheritance and the intentionality of final testaments. In early Maryland, for example, the likelihood that a white couple would have more than two surviving children at the time of either of their deaths was extremely slim. It would be unlikely, then, for surviving children to struggle over complicated divisions of property, either real or chattel. The vagaries of mortality rates also meant that it was very likely that husbands would die before their wives, forcing them to contemplate the uneasy proposition of a wife's remarriage or return to England and the problem of protecting one's legacy from another spouse or the need to divest resources to make a journey back home. Finally, the evidence was pervasive that "newcomers" peopled the colonies and that one's place in the world was tenuous at best; there was no guarantee of one's own survival or that of one's heirs.[4] Nonetheless, despite the uncertainties of American life, birth rates among white settlers in the English colonies were significantly higher than birth rates in Europe as early as 1700, and by 1725 birth rates for enslaved Africans in North America had also surpassed those of Europeans at home.[5] The questions of legacy permeated the atmosphere even as both slaveowners and enslaved struggled to make meaning of the birth and death that surrounded them.

To write a will was also a necessary response to the shifting meanings of property and progeny in the Americas. Intestate estates in all southern colonies followed the English law of primogeniture (northern colonies followed multigeniture for intestate property), but in practice slaveowning settlers consistently disavowed primogeniture in their wills and deeds.[6] The law of entail was in fact omitted from South Carolina's 1712 legal code, with the result that many women inherited considerable estates in the colony.[7] Particularly when dispersing property in persons, early American slaveowners were not inclined simply to leave all to their eldest son. Land was customarily divided between sons, with the eldest receiving the land on which the family home stood. If the estate was large enough, both sons and daughters would receive slaves. Enslaved persons left to sons were often a bequest in entail, which meant that the terms of the will demanded that the inherited slaves had to be kept on the land. Daughters were far more likely to inherit enslaved persons in fee simple, unencumbered by entail.[8] Slaveowners understood the value of portable property for daughters and the fact that ownership of land meant nothing without workers to cultivate it. As a result, enslaved persons appear in probate records more often than they would have had simple primogeniture prevailed. Changes in customary English inheritance laws and practices reflected the new material realities of property and family among settlers, and as the terms of prosperity for white settlers in the southern and Caribbean colonies came to depend on racial slavery, so too did ideas about the relationships between wealth, property, and race.

Wills and other probate records thus trace the ways discourses of race, gender, and progeny were transforming and transformed by the quotidian realities of owning property in persons. The milieu within which early America's colonists functioned was deeply insecure. While there is no need to rehearse the myriad factors that compounded the vulnerability of settlers' physical, emotional, and economic safety in New World colonies, it is important to situate their probate records—evidence of the certainty of that vulnerability—in the light of the constant reminders that their footing in the Americas was rarely secure.[9]

Legislative efforts to regulate racial purity on the North American mainland similarly testify to the insecurity of early American life for white settlers. Slaveowning assemblies in Maryland and Virginia initiated drawn-out statutory processes of regulating contact between slave and free over the course of the seventeenth century, processes that would ultimately be borrowed by slave societies throughout the region. The rigidity of the final outcome obscures the process during which anxieties about connections between black, brown, and white bodies defined the central concern of those in positions of power. In 1664, Maryland passed a law that decreed that "whatsoever free-born woman shall intermarry with any slave . . . shall serve the Master of such slave during the life of her husband; and that all the issue of such free-born women, so married shall be slaves as their fathers were." Punishing white women for giving birth to black babies renders the apprehensions of the colony's slaveowners transparent, for even as racial categories came into focus for white settlers, interracial sexual and social contact belied the fixity of their own whiteness. At the same time, Virginia assemblymen enacted legislation to guide them through the emerging morass of racial identities. The essential difference between black and white women lay, according to the 1643 statute, in the relationship between them and the work that they did In this first act to legislate racial difference, black women's work was defined as permanent—tithable regardless of any change in their status from slave to free—while white women's could be free of tax.[10] The 1662 Virginia act that defined all children born of the bodies of black women as slaves, even if their fathers were free and white, simply cemented things further. The association between blackness and forced labor was now legally complete. Both pieces of legislation suggest that colonial slaveowners saw questions of racial constancy as critical and highlight the intensity of their quest to separate themselves from the women, and men, they enslaved. The concerns about sexual liaisons the Chesapeake legislators made explicit are the implicit foundations for laws regulating economic and social contact unsullied by sexuality between free whites and enslaved or free blacks throughout the English colonies.

The laws regulating interracial contact are a central index of how the very idea of race came into being for New World setters. However, there were other important changes in the worldviews of those settlers. Notions about the relationship between self and community among seventeenth- and eighteenth-century colonials evolved as ideological and emotional individuation gradually replaced the communality within which most Westerners found themselves enmeshed in the sixteenth and seventeenth centuries. Just as travel writing became part of the arsenal of those whose sense of national and ethic identity was beleaguered, so too did the language and parameters of slaveownership. Scholars have differed on the trajectory of the transition from a "we-self" to an individuated self. Some trace this course through literature or dream journals, others through the increased need of colonists to turn to the courts to resolve disputes that were previously untangled informally.[11] In my view, this process of individuation was enmeshed in the intersectionality of discourses about race and gender. As an individuated "American" self came into being, key notions of mastery over property were mobilized that defined both whiteness and masculinity. Robert Olwell has remarked that "it is a truism that those instances when slaves appear most prominently in the historical record were precisely those moments in their lives when they were most subject to their masters' scrutiny and power."[12] Probate records reflect one of those moments when the enslaved come under slaveowners' scrutiny, but they also reflect a moment in which unscrutinized suppositions about slaveownership, race, and gender infuse documents. The fact that these documents were also places where, through the whims or careful planning of an owner, an enslaved person could most certainly be made cognizant of her diminished power over her own self or children highlights the need to carefully sift through slaveowners' probate records before we turn, in Chapters 4, 5, and 6, to an exploration that centers on the lives of the enslaved.

With some important exceptions, colonial settlers rarely turned first to Africa to fulfill their needs for labor. Indentured English servants, alongside enslaved or indentured Native Americans, were the first wave of workers. Most of these workers were of course men. In that regard, patterns of labor in the New World followed a familiar Old World form. Ultimately, then, in the act of colonizing the Americas, English settlers—particularly those with the means and the will to appropriate the labor of others—transformed the very concept of laborer to adapt to New World realities. The lure of the New World—with wealth embedded in the landscape—inscribed masculinity firmly in the act of colonization. Over the course of the seventeenth century, women constituted no more than 25 percent of all English indentured servants sent to the Americas, but their new environment chafed against the historically defined boundaries of femininity. They found themselves neither exempted from the hard labors of New World settlements nor solely consigned to domestic labors.[13] Initially, white women performed fieldwork alongside white indentured and free men, but there was something unsettling to colonial assemblymen about white women in the field. Virginia lawmakers betrayed their assumptions about white women's work in Virginia tobacco fields through the tax laws that conveyed its temporary nature. The assumption that white women's work would eventually move from field to household was at the heart of lawmakers' willingness to overlook white women's labor as a source of official colonial revenue. Ambivalent lawmakers assumed that white women's work was circumscribable as they passed legislation that, logically, would have encouraged the use of tax free laborers to cultivate crops for export. Virginia legislators saw black women, on the other hand, as permanent laborers and thus a tithable source of revenue; when they enacted the tax law declaring this so in 1643 they provided evidence of the entanglement of race and gender ideologies from the onset.[14] No longer the adult white married male who lived separate from the master who employed him, the laborer in the Americas was distinguished by how he or she differed—physiologically, sexually, religiously, and linguistically—from his or her "employer."[15]

Like their counterparts in Virginia, Barbadian settlers looked to England and Ireland for servants in the first decades of the island's settlement, but they were quick to make the transition from servant to slave labor. In 1638, only a few years prior to the onset of the sugar revolution, approximately one-third of the white population on the island was indentured.[16] Slaveowners cast a wide net in their quest to obtain reliable laborers and initially were not unduly concerned about protecting those few white female servants who made the journey to the Americas from the rigors of the field, even as they explicitly located these women's value in their ability to offset white minorities through their procreative capacities. "Send me . . . any sort men women or boys . . . what I make not use off . . . I can exchange with others," wrote an early settler, and although the captain of an Irish ship carrying servants to Barbados in 1636 expressed concern that he had too many women on board, he received no complaints about the "lustye and strong Boddied" women he sold in only two days.[17] In the first half of the seventeenth century, indentured women cost exactly the same amount as indentured men; planters paid equally for servants from whom they logically must have expected to extract equal amounts of profit.[18] Eight years after the island of Barbados was settled by the English, the white population was close to 95 percent male, and while that stark imbalance shifted over time, it was not until the 1670s that white sex ratios fell as low as 3:1.[19] Unsatisfied with the numbers of white women on the island, planters in Barbados repeatedly called for "loose wenches" to augment the white population. In 1656, out of gratitude for Barbadian participation in Cromwell's expansion of England's naval power, Cromwell ordered 2,000 "young women in England" to be sent to the colony. At least 400 of these "gifts" arrived "in order that by their breeding they should replenish the white population."[20] In response to similar pleas from Martinique, the king of France sent almost 200 white "women of ill repute" from Paris to the French colony between 1680 and 1682. And in 1681, Governor Pouancay asked for 450 such women to bolster white settler populations in Saint-Domingue.[21] It is in the context of this other "labor" performed by women that the clear distinction between white and black women's work becomes somewhat muddled, for no rigid distinction between the procreative and the agricultural existed. Rather, as the 1643 Virginia statute illustrates, the issue was one of duration—all women must work, but some women work forever. Similarly, all women must procreate, but some women procreate for the social and economic good of their own community and others do so for the social and economic good of someone else's community.

All free white women were enmeshed in the project of settlement, domesticity, and the "peopling" of the new colonies. In an early promotional description of Carolina, women were tempted with the news that "if any Maid or single Woman have a desire to go over, they will think themselves in the Golden Age, when Men Paid a Dowry for their Wives; for if they be but Civil, and under 50 years of Age, some honest Man or other, will purchase them for their Wives."[22] And indeed they were wives and mothers, their procreative powers firmly fixed in social categories. Their domesticating bodies were important enough to become evidence of large-scale colonial successes. Samuel Wilson wrote of Carolina in 1682 that "the air gives a strong appetyte and quick digestion . . . men finding themselves more lightsome, more prone and more able to all youthful Exercises than in England; the Women are very fruitful and the Children have fresh Sanguine Complexions."[23] The remarkable curative powers of the colony restored youth to aging men, and fertility to their wives. In 1709, John Lawson wrote "it has been observ'd, that Women long marry'd, and without Children, in other Places, have remov'd to Carolina, and become Joyful Mothers. They have very easy Travail in their Child-bearing, in which they are so happy, as seldom to miscarry." So powerful a claim found itself reproduced verbatim in literature on the colony published almost twenty years later.[24] The combination of low white female population figures and the urge to domesticate the landscape of the Americas caused colonial pamphleteers to promote these colonies as especially conducive to motherhood to lure white women to American shores.

Yet not all white women would have the path to "joyful Mothering" so easily cleared. The difficulties faced by indentured women—women whose labors were contracted for a specific purpose—meant that some white women's fecundity would be punished, not celebrated. Laws throughout the English colonies penalized white servants who had the temerity to become pregnant during their service. As they wrestled with the relationship between race and status, colonial authorities understood the need for a certain elasticity in order to allow women of the 'lower sorts" to become mothers in the service of the crown's empire. Arguing that an indentured woman who married introduced "two competing masters" into a situation where mastery should reside with the holder of the indenture rather than the husband, and that pregnancy likewise interfered with the owners' demands on female servants, colonial legislators punished women who married or became pregnant while under indenture. The paramount importance of agricultural labor and patriarchal authority meant that "unauthorized" pregnancies that prevented a white female servant from completing her duties would be punished by further demands on her contractual time and, frequently, the forced indenture of the child.[25] Even as her pregnancy took place outside sanctioned social norms, it would become transformed into an economic gain. Such punishments, of course, allowed both the holders of the indenture and the larger colonial settlement to benefit from the reproductive labor of indentured servants, even when they did not sanction it.

Complicated attitudes toward the pregnancies of indentured white servants became a bridge to more explicit assumptions about black women's reproductive identities. Neither in Barbados nor elsewhere in the English colonies did English elites shrink at the notion of breeding the "lower sorts." White elites who conceived of indentured females as both laborers and breeders easily transferred those assumptions onto the more debased and despised bodies of enslaved Africans. Settlers steadily incorporated black women's sexual and reproductive identities into the economics of New World mercantile successes. Writing in 1620, a colonial agent for Bermuda asked for assistance in procuring "3 men able to worke, out of England, or lett me have 4 negroes: 3 men 1 woman."[26] The cost differential between slaves and servants does not explain why four enslaved workers would be considered the equivalent of three indentured servants, but the addition of the woman is perhaps more transparent. The agent imagined the "Negroe" woman capable of something a woman "out of England" could not render. Even those far removed from American slave societies understood and sought to capitalize on the duality of women's labors. In the 1650s, a document determining tax relief for settlers to the Americas outlined the number of slaves and the amount of land required to free the settler from taxation. The "negroes children from 8–12 years shall count two for one . . . under the eight years, three for one . . . [and] the breedings goeth with the mothers."[27] While the linguistic description of the infants as "breedings" catches one off guard, it is the seventeenth-century presumption that "Negroes" shall both work in American fields and produce taxable children that warrants our immediate attention.

This attention to the demographic problem posed by women and their small children was not limited to the fertility of enslaved Africans; Native American women too became part of the mathematics of "mastery." By the turn of the seventeenth century, North Carolina settlers understood slaveownership in terms of both black and brown bodies. Isaac Wilson, for example, enslaved "Negroe Phebe Indian Mall Negroe Patt and Negroe Maria," in 1706, his workforce exemplifying the connections between African and Native American women enslaved in this period.[28] In 1707, the South Carolina assembly established the Commissioners of the Indian Trade to regulate trade between English settlers and Native Carolinians, and shortly afterward John Archdale mentioned that the Yamasee brought "Spanish Indians" to Charlestown, "designing to sell them for slaves to Barbados or Jamaica as was usual."[29] Trade in Native American slaves followed quickly on the heels of settlers' arrival to the mainland colony in 1670, and by 1708 a third of the total enslaved population were Native Americans.[30] It is significant that Native American women were enslaved at a rate of three to five times that of Native American men. Men were more likely to be killed in the wars incited by settlers' demand for trade goods and slaves, while women and children became the logical extension of the trade in deerskins and baskets so essential to the colonial economy of the colony before the introduction of rice culture.[31] During a military expedition against the Tuscarora in 1713, for example, 558 persons were captured. One hundred and sixty six men were captured and the remaining 392 women and children were sold at the Charlestown slave market.[32] By the first decade of the eighteenth century, faced with a substantial number of enslaved Native American women, the Commissioners of the Indian Trade stipulated that "every slave be sold singly, unless a woman with her child."[33]

The Colonial Frontier

As planters struggled to delineate the new terms for defining and balancing white and Native American women's productive and reproductive labors, the shift from servitude to slavery meant that black bodies increasingly became the object of white planters' scrutiny. And indeed, one might expect large-scale slaveowners—surrounded as they were by the inescapable rhythms of sex and birth and death in the so-called Negro villages—to calculate the reproductive capacity of their plantations with care. But prior to the economic successes that made large plantations possible, slaveholdings were quite small, and economic gain was by no means assured. This "frontier" period of slavery, when slaveowner and enslaved person were mutually dependent upon one another for survival, has been characterized as a time of tenuous equalitarianism that "tempered white domination and curbed slavery's harshest features."³⁴ However, even these small-scale slaveowners managed to articulate an evolving sense of separateness from the enslaved as they imagined their own prospects and the future of their laborers.

On the island of Barbados, where tobacco cultivated by indentured servants in the 1640s gave way by the 1660s to sugar cultivated by enslaved Africans, one can see the distinctions between servants and the enslaved quite clearly. Barbados, founded as an English colony in 1627, went through a thirty-year period with only a nominal presence of enslaved Africans. Over the course of the 1640s, landowners brought greater numbers of enslaved laborers to the island as they diverted their holdings from tobacco fields to sugar works. Among the smattering of extant probate records for white Barbadian settlers in this period, few mention enslaved laborers. Of the seventy-eight wills written prior to 1660 that bequeath or mention laborers, forty-six (59 percent) concern only white servants and frequently include bequests made to them (see Table 2).³⁵ The extremity of the colonial frontier forged important bonds between masters and servants and, in some cases, caused masters to embrace a sense of responsibility for the future of those with whom they had worked so closely. Thus Christian Brockehaven wrote in August of 1651 that he "give[s] unto every Christian servant I have one hundred poundes of sugar a piece to bee payd unto them a month after they are free."³⁶ And John Turner wrote that he "give[s] to my servant Richard Payne one year of his time."³⁷ But as the realities of Barbados's new reliance upon African laborers sank in, along with the vexing problem of a dwindling ratio of whites to blacks, the island's land and slaveowners began to grapple with the shifting parameters of their own identity and future in the face of their ownership in perpetuity of black bodies.

As owners of other people, slaveowners were forced to confront the linkages between the future of their progeny and that of their property. In 1651, in one of the first surviving wills to bequeath an enslaved person in

TABLE 2. WOMEN AND CHILDREN IN SLAVEOWNERS' WILLS, BARBADOS, 1650–79

	1650–59	*1660–69*	*1670–79*
Total wills			
Wills containing slaves	48	138	235
Wills that name slaves	16	98	165
Wills that identify women	18	82	154
Wills that identify children	3	26	35*
Wills that use the term "increase"	4	13	32**
Wills that identify a parent	1	12	26
Willis that "couple" slave men and women	2	15	10
Wills that use the term "spouse"	0	2	4

*Two children are listed with no women; **two wills use "increase" without listing women.
Source: Recopied Will Books, Series RB/6, Barbados Department of Archives and History.

Barbados, a "negroe woman together with all moveables and nonmove-ables" and six acres of land is handed down to a wife until two children "come to age and then to bee equally divided betwixt her and the chil-dren."[38] This kind of division posed, I would argue, a very different prob-lem than that embedded in John Wilkinson's 1652 will in which a third of his property—his "plantation . . . containing forty-seven acres of land . . . alsoe with ye thirde of all household stuff as Brass, pewter, Linene bedding [and] all Christian servants, negroes, horses, cowes, assenegroes [and] stock of hogge"—went to his wife and the remaining two-thirds were to be divided among a son and three daughters.[39] Even though any probate court would have understood the first will to mean that each child receive assets equal in value, the impossibility of dividing one woman's body between two adult inheritors is a symbol in which reproductive futures were imbed-ded—only through her reproductive activity could "a negroe woman" be bequeathed to two adults. By collectivizing all "servants, negroes, and horses" on the other hand, the testator does not have to imagine the divi-sion of a single person between more than one heir. Thomas Kennett too, avoided the dilemma of such divisions when he bequeathed "nineteen acres or thereabouts, with one Irish servant with the time he hath to serve, [and] two women negroes together with all household stuff" to his three step-children, Peter, Robert, and Mary Fistam.[40] The three laborers would accrue to the three heirs with relative ease. Presumably, Mary would have to make do with a servant whose time would soon be up, while Peter and Robert would find themselves in possession of laborers whose future progeny would further enlarge their fortunes. But with an equal number of laborers and progeny, Kennett, like Wilkinson, did not have to struggle with slippery mathematics. The problem of dividing a single "negroe woman" among a white family was, at this early stage of slaveownership, solved through an implicit assumption about her fertility; that by the time the children came of age, the Negro woman might have children of her own to add to the equation. Such an unspoken referent would become increasingly explicit over time and would come to constitute a central component of slaveholders' individuation processes.

Robert Wilshire divided his property, after passing the expected third to his wife, among four children. The property they could anticipate coming into possession of included

Men negroes vizt. Peter, Tom, and Pendee; Woman negroe named Judith and two young negroes one aged three years ye other aged three months; A breeding mare, one foale about two months old; A breeding Cow, one heifer with calf, and one calfe about three months old.[41]

Judith's proximity to the breeding livestock is inscribed both in the text of the will and that of her life. For though she is not stamped with the descriptor "breeder," her childbearing successes and the similar way her "young negroes" and the foal and calves are described suggest that dividing her among four heirs presented only modest difficulties to Wilshire's executor. Wilshire himself could only have understood his investment in Judith as a wise one that would accrue long into the future and well past the point of his own demise. His estate was small, limited to a house, seventeen acres of land, the enslaved men, women, and children, and livestock. As he surveyed his properties shortly before his death, probably while ill, he would have been under no illusion about the scale of his achievements. Small acreage, probably given over to tobacco cultivation, four enslaved adults and two small children, offset perhaps by his stable and presumably healthy family—these were not the marks of certainty and success accumulated by the growing numbers of Barbadian landowners who transformed the island into a "global economic giant" and the single most valuable overseas asset to the English Crown by 1660.[42] By the same token, his ownership of Judith created a possibility far more vivid than that wrought by Peter, Tom, and Pendee or, alternatetively, than the profit that would accrue from the work of male or female indentured servants.

Wilshire's division of his property in persons aligned him with other slaveowners on the island and in the colonies, as they too contemplated their deaths and their (limited) property. Men who behaved differently, whose expressions connected them to enslaved persons rather than distanced them from them, were few and far between. John Copper fell ill in 1656 and died with neither a spouse nor children to leave his estate. Instead, after gifts of sugar to his brother and sisters, he freed his "negro woman Jugg" and "likewise I give unto my Negro man Will and my negro woman Battee there [*sic*] freedom." He provided a yearly allowance for them all and gave them ten acres of land and the houses that stood there "for them and their children." Copper was alone in his intersecting bequests of freedom, land, and support, and one suspects that his singularity reflected both his understanding of the materialities needed to support freedmen and women in mid-seventeenth-century Barbados and his unique desire to supply them. It should be noted that his connection to Jugg and Battee does not necessarily indicate an antislavery stance, as the other bequest he made was to his servant Robert Shepart, to whom he gave thirty acres and "a negro I also give him." But the fact that he left the future of Jugg and Battee's children in their own hands, and the care with which he stipulated the support he hoped would maintain those futures, suggests his awareness of the anomaly of his behavior. Cooper knew, in 1656, that Jugg and Battee and their children were supposed to have very different futures from the ones he imagined for them.[43]

Women such as Judith, who were subjected to speculation about the connection between their lives as mothers and their lives as slaves, served a related but very different purpose. Lorena Walsh and David Eltis have both argued that the experience of owning slaves allowed owners to moderate the cultural norms that would have constricted behavior toward English workers. "Africans could be made to function outside the conventions, especially those of gender, that the English had constructed for themselves" before traveling to the American colonies.[44] It is in their appropriation of African women's future children that slaveowners bear witness to their sense of slaveownership. Judith enabled Wilshire to understand the parameters of his role as an Englishman in the Americas; his ability to harness her future not only expanded his patriarchal largesse but also marked his masculinity and emerging whiteness. As a moderately successful planter in colonial Barbados, what differentiated him from his English or even New England counterpart was his ability to harness Judith's future. Aligning Judith with livestock while simultaneously subjecting her, her children, and Pendee, Peter, and Tom to symbolically impossible bodily division both illuminates and masks the material realities of Wilshire's final months on the island and the indeterminate years that led up to this unconsciously revelatory moment.

While they were typical in some regards, Wilshire and those he enslaved were quite unusual in others. Birth rates in Barbados among the enslaved were low in this period, and Judith's living children made her, and Wilshire's estate, unusual. Nonetheless, in the Barbados of the 1650s, well before enslaved children became a common part of slaveowners' inventoried property, slaveowners began to identify female slaves of childbearing years as "increasers."[45] Terminology such as "pickaninies" was rare—the more common terms such as "increase" and "produce" suggest that slaveowners understood quite early the value of the reproductive lives of laboring women in their evolving conception of themselves as owners of human property. And of course, on some level slaveowners understood fertility as residing primarily in enslaved women rather than men. Daniel McFarland, for example, bequeathed the one slave he owned thus: "My negro wench named Diannah and all her future increase."[46] Diannah's choice of, or access to, fathers for her "future increase" rested primarily with herself. Similarly, when Nicholas Bochet died, after leaving land and unnamed "negroes" to his sons, he left his daughter money and "one Negro Girl named Sarah together with Issue and Increase." Bochet too left the problem of paternity up to Sarah. Moreover, Bochet saw Sarah's sex, and thus her reproductive potential, as an essential aspect of the bequest. For "in case the said Negro Girl should happen to Dye . . . another of about the age of the said Negro Girl named Sarah" would be purchased by his executors.[47] They crafted their bequests in this way despite low rates of childbirth during the early years of settlement and transition to slavery and despite the intersections between their own struggles with infant mortality, imbalanced sex ratios, and desire for heterosexual companionship and those of the women and men they enslaved.

In 1654, ten years after the move to sugar production on the island but ten years before the economic boom that placed Barbados at the pinnacle of England's overseas empire, one visitor to the island claimed that

thes Negors they doue alow as many wifes as they will have, sume will have 3 or 4 according as they find thayer bodie abell: our english heare doth think a negor child the first day it is born to be worth 05 1., they cost them noething the bringing up, they goe all ways naked: Some planters will have 30 more or les about 4 or 5 years ould: they sete them from one to other as we doue shepe.[48]

While there is no evidence that plantations with thirty c
dren existed outside the writer's imagination, the hyperl
the planters this visitor observed anticipated wealth in th
children. The metaphor of "shepe" also suggests the overlap
of travelers and slaveowners to connect women's reproductiv
of livestock. Slaveowners linked the reproductive lives of men
to those of their agricultural commodities in gestures that reac
either to establish distance from or to distinguish between their own struggles with "increase." In 1654, for example, John James bequeathed two-
thirds of his property, which included eight acres of land and "nine negroes
young and ould, with one cow with certain stock of Hoggs [and] dunghill
Fowles," to his daughter. He reserved the remaining third of his property
for the use of his wife during her lifetime. After her mother's death, the
daughter would inherit the "said land negroes stock of hoggs fowles and
cowes [and] what they shall produce by their increase."[49] James imagined
that, along with chicks, foals, and calves, enslaved children might also arrive
to buttress the economic position of his wife and daughter. In acknowledg-
ing this possibility, he became the first of many Barbadian planters to apply
the term "increase" not only to animals but also to African women.[50]

When planters looked to "increase," they crafted real and imagined
legacies. In the absence of living slave children, their own children still
inherited the promise of future wealth. Slaveowners whose prospects might
have seemed somewhat bleak looked to black women's bodies in search of
a promising future for their own progeny. With such demographic expectations also came an articulation of the longevity of the slaveowners' enterprises and a greater certainty of a future in and for the colony. Though
clearly there was no guarantee, a planter could imagine that a handful of
fertile African women might turn his modest holdings into a substantial
legacy. Black women's bodies became the vessels in which slaveowners
manifested their hopes for the future; they were, in effect, conduits of stability and wealth to the white community. On David Davis's plantation,
for example, where eighty-six persons labored, sex ratios were assiduously
balanced. Davis knew that he made a profitable investment in these forty-
three black female workers (see Table 1 above).[51] Through careful patterns
of purchases, he constructed a gender-balanced group of men and women
while keeping an eye fixed firmly on the future. Davis behaved rationally
when he assumed that by carefully balancing the men and women he purchased to cultivate his land he would also expand his slaveholdings. That

dreams had not quite come to fruition at the time of the sale of his estate (only three of the twenty-nine adult women are listed with children) may speak to a variety of conditions. No evidence tells us how long the men and women on Davis's land lived together. Nor do we know whether Davis's treatment of them precluded either the development of intimacies or the physical well being to reproduce. Certainly both slaveowners and some enslaved women expected and worked to enact childbirth. But for enslaved women, to do so also meant to open themselves to the emotional dangers of reproduction in a slave society.[52]

As the 1660s unfolded in Barbados, planters worked assiduously to build their labor forces and in the process provide opportunities for sexual contact among the enslaved. Between 1662 and 1664, for example, some 206 slaveowners purchased enslaved Africans from the Company of Royal Adventurers.[53] The buying patterns of these planters reflect a pragmatism regarding female labor. Of these over 200 purchases, 125 purchased groups of slaves that included both women and men. Of these 125, the ratio of men to women was 2:1 or higher in only 22 groups. Sixteen purchased more women than men, thirty-four purchased equal numbers of women and men, and seventy purchased groups such as Richard Chapman did, in which there were eight men and six women. Seventy-nine purchased slaves of one sex. Of that group, forty-nine purchased only men while thirty purchased only women.[54]

These purchasing patterns suggest that, faced with a cargo of men and women, Barbadian slaveowners did not rush to purchase men, which would have left considerable numbers of women behind for the latecomers. Between 1651 and 1675, 46 percent of all enslaved persons arriving to the island were female, and by the 1660s Barbadian slaveowners saw women as valuable laborers whom they easily integrated into their work force.[55]

Indeed, they may also have begun to value them more systematically as potential reproducers. Fifteen slaveowners in the 1660s (18 percent of those who identified women in their bequests) explicitly paired individual men and women in their bequests. In doing so, they attempted to provide their legatees with the promise of the couple's labor and their future offspring. Bequests of a woman with many men or many women with few men do not indicate the same level of mindfulness about the possible future embodied by a male-female pair, but at the same time, a women's reproductive potential remained constant with or without the steadiness of an individual man called, by the slaveowner, her "spouse." Purchases in which sex ratios were less than perfectly balanced still held the promise of future increase.

Barbadian slaveowners were not alone in their early recognition of the multifaceted benefits that might accrue to them through the bodies of black women. English settlers on Nevis in 1678 enslaved a workforce in which women's presence was ubiquitous: 79 percent of all slaveowning households included adult women. It is more significant that, considering the lack of settler control over the sex ratios of the transatlantic slave trade, 70 percent of those households enslaved women in equal or greater numbers than men. Also, 76 percent of slaveowners who owned women also owned children under the age of fourteen.[56] It would be impossible and indeed illogical for the island's slaveowners to fail to comprehend the particular value that accrued to them through the ownership of African women. Moreover, the fact that so few slaveowners designated the enslaved as paired couples in their wills should not suggest that without such written recognition no such relationships were experienced by the enslaved or imagined by the slave-owner. There is a degree to which the intimate lives of the enslaved simply will not emerge from the colonial archive, but these moments in slaveowners' probate records are suggestive, and should be understood as such.

Probate records are occasional windows into the material and emotional disruption to enslaved women's bodily and familial integrity caused by the deathbed plans of ailing slaveowners. In some cases, a white woman's fertility caused the dispersal of a black woman's family. Judith Mossier, unsure, one supposes, about the fertility of the unnamed enslaved women and men she already owned, set aside money to purchase a "negro woman" who with her "increase" was to be kept for the use of Mossier's baby grand-child.[57] The enslaved women Katherine and Hannah each lost a daughter, Nanny and little Betty respectively, in Roger Peele's will. If Mrs. Peele gave birth to a daughter, Little Betty would return to her mother (who was owned by Roger Peele, II), but if Peele's wife bore a son, that unborn child would retain possession of Hannah's daughter.[58]

By the end of the 1660s, Barbadian planters acknowledged and antici-pated conjugal relations among the enslaved even as they acted in ways that violated them. The close proximity of small-scale ownership did not miti-gate slaveowners' appropriation of women's reproductive lives. John Red-way bequeathed his two adult slaves, both women, to his children at the beginning of the decade. He gave Besse to his daughter, while he gave his son the fertile and therefore more valuable Sibb, along with her two chil-dren. Though Sibb had already borne two children, Redway still reaped her

)ductive potential. He stipulated that "all [other] such children as she hereafter bring into this world" should also go to John Redway, II.[59] Nicholas Cowell wrote, "I bequeath to my said son two negro slaves by name Mingo and Beauty to have and enjoy the same with their produce and increase to him forever."[60] In 1668, Robert Shepheard also counted on slave children to pad his children's inheritance. He endowed his son with six enslaved women and men and "all such pickininy or Pickininyes as shall come of the said negroes." He left his daughter with "two negroes called by name Hagar and Doll as also to have all such children as shall come of the said two negroes."[61]

Few slaveowners recognized that the enslaved made choices of their own. Thomas Barnes of Christchurch, unlike most of his contemporaries, saw differentiations among the enslaved on his plantation. He described "Joe and Nassy his wife [and] Jude their daughter" as a family unit who stand out from "Peter, Violet, Hagar, and Adam." The former were connected while the latter were simply a gender-balanced group. Even if we take the words of the slaveowner literally, assuming then that the designation of Nassy as "wife" implied a familial connection that Joe and Nassy felt and not one that was simply imposed by Barnes, we are reminded that the penchant of planters for male-female pairings did not always reflect the emotional or sexual desires of the enslaved.[62] For slaveowners, regardless of the emotional realities of the enslaved, such pairings ultimately reflected their own desire to provide consistence support for their spouse, children, and relatives.

In search of stability, some early slaveowners actively engaged in proto-social engineering. Upon his death in 1658, William Baldwin, Sr. of Barbados bequeathed this potential to his godson William Sealy. He stipulated that "one able negro man and one able negro woman . . . be bought and delivered unto [Sealy] within six months" after his death. Baldwin thus provided his godson the "seed" of future slaveholdings (irrespective of the affinity or lack thereof between the two enslaved adults).[63] While there is no evidence here or elsewhere that these two were forced to have sexual relations, Baldwin explicitly treated the pairing of a male and female slave as a proper gift for a young would-be planter. In 1719 a Virginia slaveowner purchased two fifteen-year-old girls and wrote "Nothing is more to the Advantage of my son th[a]n young breeding negroes."[64] Phillip Morgan and Michael Nicholls, in a study concerned with the ways in which large numbers of women and children were enslaved in the Virginia Piedmont, argued that Piedmont slaveowners "almost always" stipulated the purchase of women rather than men when providing for their own heirs in wills.[65] Slaveowners understood that the colony's future and their own legacies lay in the working bodies of black men and women. The close proximity in which these slaveowners lived with the small numbers of women and men whom they so enumerated in their wills did not militate against their ability and willingness to appropriate infants as property and to treat African women and men as the chattel that slaveowners hoped them to be. For every slaveowner who preserved ties of affection or parentage among those he professed to own, there was a William Browne. In an act that aligned the consumable bodies of cattle with the producing bodies of black women and men, William Browne carefully listed the names of his cattle along with the *Cattle* list of men and women: "Bessie" under "Women" and "Bessy" under "Cows."[66]

Fading Frontiers

By 1675 Governor Atkins estimated a population in which the enslaved outnumbered whites by more than ten thousand, and in which black women outnumbered all other members of the population, both black and white.[67] While slaveowners appeared consistently anxious about the growing African population, they never considered stemming the tide. In the midst of complaints about control, and the bifurcation of a formerly united white identity, planters railed bitterly against the Royal African Company for not supplying adequate numbers of Africans at reasonable prices.[68] Reliance on African labor, both in the fields and throughout the colonial infrastructure, touched all aspects of life on the island. Land consolidation removed the incentive for whites to indenture themselves to Barbadian planters, and planters could "keep three Blacks who work better and cheaper than they can keep one white man."[69]

While Barbados's demography was unique in the American colonies— there were equal numbers of enslaved men and women from the start of the island's colonial history—the attitude of the island's slaveowners toward slave "increase" was quite typical. Slaveowners from Jamaica to Johns Island invested their hopes in the reproductive capacities of their human property. In 1678, Willoughby Yeamans helped secure the future for his cousin in the new province of Carolina. He ordered his attorney, Christopher Barrow, to "give my Cozen Mr. John Yeamans a Negro man and a Negro woman." Barrow immediately procured Jack and Aram in Carolina with "their profitts and increase" for John Yeamans. Barrow did not take Aram's fertility for granted; he purchased Aram and Jack along with their two children, Jack and Namy, ages three and one year, providing John Yeamans with a woman whose reproductive capacity was thus proven. Furthermore, Aram and Jack's established ability as parents meant that Barrow also purchased a couple whose desire to maintain and protect the integrity of their family unit made them a stable source of wealth.[70]

John Yeamans and his descendents would ultimately create a society in which Carolina rice planters, in the words of Richard Dunn, "ha[d] more in common with Barbados sugar planters of the seventeenth century than [just] large gangs of slaves."[71] In 1685 when Governor Joseph West temporarily left Carolina for New England some fifteen years after his arrival in the colony, he enslaved twelve persons, the majority of whom were female: four men, one boy, two women one "younge negroe girl," two "children Negroes" (one a girl, one whose sex is indeterminate), and two "Indian girles."[72] From the very beginning of Carolina's settlement, enslaved women and men from Barbados enriched the mainland colony and created the mainland's only slave society that did not pass through an intermediary stage of reliance on indenture or free labor. Elite society in Carolina would echo that of Barbados in many ways. Indeed, for some observers no separation existed between South Carolina and island colonies. In 1682 Thomas Ashe wrote that "the Discourses of many Ingenious Travellers (who have lately seen *this part of the West Indies*) . . . justly render[s] Carolina Famous."[73] In the face of frequent death, enslaved women from Barbados embodied the hopes of Carolina planters' for wealth. Newly arrived slaveowners in Carolina groped about for agricultural successes, experimenting with cattle, corn, olives, silkworms, and, finally, rice. But throughout they assumed that African women and men would provide labor. More specifically, as planters had in their wills in Barbados, elite planters in South Carolina continued to rely on enslaved couples as "seeds" for future enterprises, understanding that the value of enslaved women resided in their roles both as producers and as potential reproducers.[74]

Whites journeying north from the islands brought enslaved men and women and the assumptions derived from the fact of a reproducing labor force with them, secure in the knowledge that the labor of the enslaved would help build the new settlement. Like slaveowners in Barbados, those in Carolina relied on women and their children, as well as men, to produce commodities and to serve the economic needs of the planter-settler; they recognized the dual value embodied by enslaved women.[75] Their wills, inventories, and purchase records indicate an early reliance on female laborers and an early recognition of the value of women's "increase." The initial presence of enslaved women in Carolina linked Carolina slaveowners to the Caribbean. Planters' assumptions about the future of their own families and the place of slavery in the new colony continued to be shaped by the women they enslaved. As in Barbados, from the very beginning, planters anticipated and parceled out the actual and potential "increase" of enslaved women. By the 1720s, as Carolina became a full-fledged slave society, Barbados's slave labor force gradually reached a point of self-sufficiency, and both colonies' slaveowners moved toward new stages in their reliance upon, and relationship to, enslaved labor. Four decades later, as mortality rates declined in response to a slowdown in the growth of sugar production on the island, the slave trade to Barbados also declined in the context of the ability, and desire, of enslaved women and men to increase the black population naturally.[76] Faced with the experience of Barbadian slaveowners, with whom Carolina continued to share familial and commercial ties, mainland slaveowners were not indifferent to the value of enslaved woman's reproductive potential.

In the earliest Carolina inventories, the prices assigned enslaved men and women reflect the clash between received notions of masculine value and the pragmatic realities of a reproductive labor force. In relation to adult men, women's value was often calculated at a lower rate. And thus Fibro and Fullis were assessed at £19 each while Jney and Spindile could be had after their owner Richard Fowell's death in 1679 for £21 each. If one looks at Fowell's entire estate, however, another pattern appears. Along with Fibro and Fullis, Fowell enslaved Barbery and her two small boys, Julia and Ginny. The total value of women on his estate was £95, plus £9 for the two children. The remainder of his estate was comprised of only £60 worth of enslaved men.[77] Similarly, John Smith enslaved two adult women and three men. The men were valued at £52 while the two women, along with Maria's four "pickaninies," similarly were assessed at £52—each man at £17, the women at £16, but the children as a group at £20.[78] Enslaved women embodied the growing value of plantation holdings. In a lease of the Thorowgoods plantation at the turn of the eighteenth century, William Hawlett promised John and Elizabeth Lancaster half of all the plantation's profits accrued in a seven-year period. That included "halfe the Rice halfe the pease halfe the Corne halfe the Butter halfe the Cheese ye Calves halfe the Hoggs halfe the Lams and the halfe parte of all the Negro Children that shall be borne."[79] Women were ubiquitous among the human property of

new planters in Carolina, as was the assumption that these women's reproductive lives could or would enrich the slaveowner's progeny. In the first
decade of the eighteenth century twenty-one documents identify enslaved
persons; only six are all-male transactions (see Table 3). The remaining fifteen, or 71 percent, recorded the presence of both men and women. Hannah
Stanyard, for example, purchased Betty and Mingo and "the negro girl
called Jenny."[80] Diana and "all and every her Increase" left the household
of a cooper for that of a small landowner, necessitating a change not only
of "owners" but also of labor regimes—urban to rural.[81] In a family sale
that perhaps did not bring with it so much upheaval for those who were
moved, Robert Daniel transferred all the men and women he enslaved to
his son in 1709.[82] From Daniel's perspective, the six women and eight men
he owned all provided valuable labor on his Berkeley County land. Their
relationships with one another may have led him to assume that the women
would soon provide him, or his son, with additional valuable laborers. If
Daniel's characterization of them as spouses carried with it requisite ties of

TABLE 3. MEN, WOMEN, AND CHILDREN IN SLAVEOWNERS' WILLS AND
INVENTORIES, SOUTH CAROLINA, 1702–10

Date of probate item	1702	1703	1703	1704	1705	1705	1708	1708	1709	1709	1709
Men	9	1	1	0	0	0	1*	1*	0	0	1
Women	7	1	1	0	1	1	0	0	3	1	0
Parents	1	0	0	0	0	1	0	0	1	0	0
Children	3	1	1	0**	0	1	0	0	1	0	0

Date of probate item	1709	1709	1710	1710	1710	1710	1710	1710	1710	1710
Men	3	8	1	30	0	0	5	1	4	0
Women	2	6	0	29	1	1	5	0	2	2
Parents	0	0	0	3	0	1	0	0	1	0
Children	0	0	0	3	1	1	0	0	0	0

There are 21 surviving inventories from 1699 to the end of the proprietary period. *These
documents are sales of one boy. **This document is a sale in which men and women are not
individually identified but their "increase" is deemed part of the sale.
Source: Secretary of the Province Records, Miscellaneous Series, South Carolina Department
of Archives and History.

affection, "Paw Paw Tom and his wife Nancy [and] Tom Godfrey and his wife Hagar" no doubt felt pleased that they would not be separated from one another in the foreseeable future. The potential that other men and women on Daniel's plantation had for meaningful partnerships among themselves must have equally shaped the ways in which they conceived of their futures.

Essentially, as they surveyed their property and imagined their deaths, slaveowners supplemented the present value of enslaved persons with the speculative value of a woman's reproductive potential, doing so with relatively little regard to the behavior, or the sentiment, of the women they enslaved. On the Boowatt plantation, George Dearsley enslaved sixteen persons, including seven women. He bequeathed all of them in male-female pairings to his heirs. In doing so, he signaled hope more than certainty. While he left "one Negro man name James one Negro woman name Sarah one negro girle name Quasheba one boy name Harry," he did not link Quasheba and Harry to Sarah as family but rather as well-ordered sets. Only one of the seven women, Nancy, had given birth to a surviving child, Charles; her reproductive successes became part of Dearsley's most valuable—sex-balanced—bequest. The other couples remained childless.[83] Though their owner carefully provided the opportunity for his slaves to reproduce, these men and women either had fallen victim to the high rates of infertility, miscarriage, and infant death endemic among the enslaved or had availed themselves of emmenagogues or abortifacients to interrupt pregnancies.

When Richard Harris died in Carolina in 1711, he provided each of his children with coupled enslaved men and women. His eldest son received land and the house with Pompey, Catharina, and "her increase." His younger daughters each received a man and a woman with some livestock: "To my daughter Anne one slave boy named Jack and a slave girle named Flora and her increase and ten cows and calves and their increase."[84] Richard Harris's bequests are quite telling. Even though he was a small-scale slaveowner in the first decade of the eighteenth century, Harris's fortune—he enslaved eight people and owned more than thirty head of cattle—was considerable. He would have likely counted himself as part of a community of small-scale slaveowners in the process of slowly accruing wealth by borrowing against their holdings to acquire more land and more slaves.[85] At his death, Harris had not attained the vast fortune of his dreams, but black women's bodies lay at the center of his earthly achievements. As he looked forward to his family's future, he probably felt a certain sense of accomplishment that he had provided so well for his children by linking their futures to the future unborn children of his human property.

In the early life of the colony, however, the immediate realities of long-term survival on the sometimes-brutal colonial frontier would often override the need for stability that acquiring enslaved children might satisfy. Slaveowners with a precarious foothold in colonial settlements lived in close proximity to those they enslaved, but continued to hope that their coffers would be enriched by the birth of enslaved children. They were not the lords of vast plantation workforces isolated from laborers by their wealth and imposing plantation houses. Rather, they worked beside those they enslaved, sharing food and shelter out of necessity. But the "tenuous equalitarianism" of the pre-staple crop economy did not stop them from engaging in a most hierarchical display of immoral arithmetic. They paid close attention to the growth opportunities—rather than ties of affection—that sprang from the wombs of enslaved women. Only through a black woman's body could a struggling slaveowner construct munificent bequests to family and friends. By using the term and concept of "increase," he created a larger bequest than he actually possessed. Only the black mother embodied both productive and reproductive potential.[86] And recognition of her potential was not limited to those slaveowners struggling to become successful large-scale planters. Almost a hundred years after the moment at which Flora's future became linked to her reproductive behavior, Thomas Jefferson wrote that he "consider[ed] a woman who brings a child every two years as more profitable than the best man of the farm, what she produces is an addition to the capital, while his labors disappear in mere consumption."[87]

Pacifying Rebellious Negroes

Early slaveowning settlers' reliance on both the reproductive and manual labor of enslaved women was no anomaly. The rhythms of the slave trade and the policies of the colonial enterprise supported their assumptions about the literal and symbolic value of women workers. In 1665, the Proprietors of the colony of South Carolina wrote that land would be granted in parcels of up to 150 acres per settler, his dependents, and his servants. A group of men investing in Carolina known as the Barbadian Adventurers demanded that the law that required "one man armed" per fifty acres of land be changed to require "one person white or black" per 100 acres. The gender-neutral wording reflected the fact that female-only slaveholdings were not uncommon. Barbadian planters also knew that their interest lay in a land grant system that rewarded the introduction of slaves and servants equally. The Proprietors also understood this. In a 1670 letter, they clarified their language by claiming that "man-servant" always "means negroes as well as Christians." Moreover, by 1682, once settlement had begun and the amount of land grants had diminished to fifty acres per servant or slave, the Proprietors altered assumptions about both male and female laborers and quantities of land. The first white settlers received 150 acres for men servants or slaves, and 100 acres for women. After a decade of settlement, the gendered labor distinctions vanished as the authorities provided equal landgrants for the transport of male and females alike.[88]

Transplanted Barbadian slaveowners, known as "Goose Creek Men" for the community in which they settled, dominated local politics in the mainland colony's first generation. These legislators passed the first Carolina slave law in 1690. In crafting the "Act for the Better Ordering of Slaves," they borrowed extensively from the 1688 Barbados slave code.[89] As in Barbados and other West Indian slave societies, lawmakers in Carolina defined slaves as all those who had been "to all Intents and Purposes" slaves.[90] By using the ambiguous language of custom, they skirted the systematic realities of racial slavery that surrounded them. Slaveowners' legislation located the defining condition of enslavement in circular logic: one is a slave because one has been a slave. Carolina slaveowners' legislative language highlights their assumptions about the particular roles of enslaved women. Customary slavery is rooted in the bodies of women. If one is a slave because one has been a slave, *becoming* a slave takes place in the act of birth. For those who were transported to the colony as slaves, capture and transport had fixed their status. The need to further define those who were enslaved occurred only when Africans in the Americas began to have children. The language of customary slavery became important only with the birth of children whose status needed to be codified and articulated, and thus only through the bodies of women. As Kathleen Brown has argued, women "became a means for naturalizing slave status with a concept of race."[91] In Virginia, the statute stating that the child of a slave should be a slave was explicated in 1662: "children got by an Englishman upon a Negro woman shall be bond or free according to the condition of the mother."[92] In a contrast more apparent than real, no explicit law in Carolina stated that the child of a slave should be a slave. From the perspective of an enslaved childbearing woman, however, the reality was tangible. For her, no ambiguity surrounded the certainty of her child's future as a slave; despite the vagueness of the statute, it left no real hope that her offspring would be free. Legislators developed the definition of slavery within her very body. Their linguistic pretense of "customary" slavery in the seventeenth century carried little meaning for the enslaved black woman who knew precisely how systematic racial "custom" could be.

While slaveowners understood the growing African population in terms of both economic gain and societal menace, they perceived the women they enslaved as a preventative against social unrest. In the 1650s, Richard Ligon advised all those interested in establishing a plantation on Barbados to enslave equal numbers of black men and women. By doing so, he suggested, the planter would avoid becoming besieged by African men who claimed to be unable to "live without Wives."[93] In fact, planters exhibited considerable inclination to construct slave communities ordered upon conjugal units of men and women.

Slaveowners in both Virginia and Carolina similarly believed that black women's sexual lives worked in their favor. In 1715, at the beginning of the Yamasee War, Carolina legislators arranged for a bargain. Threatened by a Native American offensive, South Carolina looked to Virginia for assistance. The Virginia legislators demanded that Carolina pay 30 shillings per month and "a Negro Woman to be sent to Virginia in lieu of Each Man Sent to Carolina to Work till their Returne." Virginia's slaveowning legislators apparently saw laboring black women as proper recompense for fighting white men. After brief consideration, the anxious South Carolina legislators responded that they deemed it "impracticable to Send Negro women . . . by reason of the Discontent such Usage would have given their husbands to have their Wives taken from them wch might have occasioned a Revolt also of the Slaves."[94] Virginia's request for women did not seem to surprise Carolina's legislators. The Carolinians understood that their military vulnerability necessitated a valuable exchange. After deliberation, however, they rejected Virginia's terms. For each of the 130 "poor ragged fellows . . . just handed from England and Ireland," Carolina legislators sent four pounds Carolina money, and no women, and then proceeded to turn to enslaved men to augment the ranks of the colonial militia. Negotiations around the military vulnerability of the colonies required a careful assessment of the derivation of multiple dangers; for Carolina's slaveowners, the dangers posed by the absence of black women, unruly black men, and presumably the loss of reproductive property, precluded allegiance to other Englishmen.

By 1715, then, enslaved women already constituted a critical site or negotiation with regard to both their sexuality and their labor. The exchange so angered Virginia legislators that they sent word to Carolina that in the future Carolina "shall perish before they shall have any assistance from [us]."[95] Virginia legislators couched their request in the language of labor, but they too may have sought the stabilizing effects of black women's sexual services, as did legislators in Carolina, who explicitly linked issues of sex, labor, and social control in their response to Virginia. Black women's value lay not only in the work of their hands but also in their potent ability to render volatile black men passive and restrained. By referring to the enslaved as "Husbands" and "Wives," Carolina legislators made it clear that they perceived virtually all adult slave women in the colony as coupled to men and acknowledged a certain dependency on the social networks of the enslaved. In the process, they revealed their precarious control of the young colony, conceding that they could not remove scores of these women without risking rebellion in the slave quarters. Evidence of such equations should no longer surprise readers well versed in the slippery linguistics of colonization and white supremacy. It can, however, point to the confluence at which the slaveowner met enslaved black men through literal and metaphorical enslaved black women. When slaveowners defined black women as pacifiers of black men's rebelliousness, they constructed a symbolic counterweight to the volatile environment of the early eighteenth-century mainland.

Carolina legislators didn't question the legitimacy of Virginia's request for women but countered with a lament about the inadequacy of their own numbers of black women. As they softened their refusal through a multivalent gesture, one that both paternalistically acknowledged the "human" needs of enslaved men and contributed to an emerging stereotype of black males who showed strong sexual needs and threatened unspeakable violence when their appetites were denied, they avoided expressing a more selfish motive. Carolina planters themselves, like their Virginia brethren, valued the presence of these women, who promised to combine plantation labor with sexual gratification, reproductive gain, and an inexplicit level of social control over an enslaved population that was rapidly outnumbering colonial slaveowners.

Plantation Regimes

By 1708, South Carolina was home to the only black majority on the mainland and by 1725, rice culture had taken over, bringing with it an explosion in slave imports and in the size and domination of plantation culture in the lowcountry. Similarly, in Barbados, by the end of the 1660s, the sugar revolution was in full swing, the white population of Barbados had leveled off at approximately 20,000 (from a high of 35,000 in the 1640s), and black Barbadians outnumbered whites by at least two to one. Sugar plantations totally dominated the geographical, economic, and social landscapes.[96] As slaveholdings became larger, the interplay between intimacy and dependency that characterized race relations in the frontier periods gave way to the drudgery and danger of monoculture cultivation regimes and the autonomy of black majorities and large plantations.

In 1683, there were 358 sugar plantations large enough to support their own sugar works on the island. (Some seventy-five more had been established by 1710.) These "slave villages" covered Barbados and were interspersed with more than 2,500 small farms with fewer than thirty acres; 72 percent of those small landowners were also slaveowners.[97] The size and terrain of the island, which was densely populated and relatively easily traversed, made it probable that families separated by probate could maintain some contact. The burgeoning population of enslaved creoles itself indicates the growing ability of men and women to navigate the social terrain of the island. Artisans and other creoles (mostly men) took advantage of slaveowners' faith in their "loyalty" to obtain incrementally more generous access to independent mobility. Indeed, as early as the late seventeenth century, some members of the enslaved community communicated with one another through written English.[98] Others relied on the ties of friendship and family that resulted from slavery's expansion across the island, which transformed disparate small slaveholdings into larger communities of family and friends.

The symbolic importance of black women's role in controlling growing populations of unruly black men did not contradict the eagerness with which slaveowners turned toward the male and female progeny of these women as unencumbered capitol. Planters sacrificed the relationship between mother and child to the economics of legacies. In the context of a slave society increasingly defined by the anonymity of absentee owners and large-scale property in persons, the intimacies embedded in the close quarters of speculative reproductive futures could be fully exposed in the terms of a slaveowner's will.

As property owners in Barbados felt increasingly committed to the permanence of the colonial venture, more and more of them went to the trouble and expense of writing wills that confined the wealth they accumulated to members of their family. When slaveowners considered their own mortality, the attention they paid to their human property did not, of course, extend to the realities of rising mortality and declining fertility rates among those women and men they enslaved. Enslaved women consistently constituted a central element of slaveowners' wealth, but proportionately fewer wills itemized children in the 1670s than did so in the previous decade (see Table 2 above). The sugar revolution was taking its toll on the small bodies of the island's most vulnerable inhabitants. Only 22 percent (thirty-five) of wills that mentioned women also mentioned children. Certainly the increased regimentation and concomitant violence of the plantation economy by the 1670s resulted in declining birth rates. That regimentation may have caused planters to neglect identifying "children," thereby distancing themselves from the evidence of the roles of enslaved women and men as parents and family members. At the same time, perhaps in an effort to shield themselves from the emotional and familial realities of life in the slave quarters, the number of planters who evoked enslaved women's fertility through the distancing notion of "increase" rose from 13 to 20 percent.

The act of bequeathing couples or women "with their produce" allowed the slaveowner surrounded by the increasingly inhumane rhythms of monoculture export to momentarily replace the image of female workers stooped over rows of ground with that of black mothers enriching the genteel lives of his children. In 1674 Robert Gretton of St. Michaels owned thirty-three enslaved women and men "both small and great" on his fifty-acre plantation. He wished to pass his success as a planter along to his children, and, in accordance with the social conventions of his day, he transferred the lion's share of his plantation to his son Robert. He similarly designed his daughter's gift to cushion her entry into the world—"two young negroes vizt. one youth a boy of about 14 or 16 years of age and one negro girl of the said age to be bought of a ship and delivered my said daughter at ye day of marriage."[99] Miles Brathwaite was also a representative provider. After his death in 1674, his daughters acquired "three negroe girles namely to each of them one." The remainder of his large estate—including enslaved male and female workers—went to his sons Nathaniell and John.[100] Some years later, the extraordinarily successful Robert "King" Carter made a similar gesture when he proposed that three enslaved girls should be purchased for his three male grandchildren—not his primary heirs, but boys he wanted to school in the mechanics of managing valuable property.[101] The boys appear to be the same age as the female recipients of such bequests in Carolina. Even small-scale owners such as Phillip Lovell followed similar conventions in parceling out enslaved women to daughters. He respectively bequeathed the enslaved girls Mary and Doll "together with all [their] increase" to his daughters Mary and Elizabeth. His son Edward received the land, one enslaved woman, and three enslaved men. Perhaps Lovell did this with the assumption that the produce of the plantation itself would ultimately generate the resources for Edward to acquire the new slaves who would naturally fall to Elizabeth and Mary—both of whom were in need of dower—from Mary and Doll.[102]

Ellis Rycroft owned Jugg and Tony, Nanny and Thom, and Peter and Peg—all "Negro boys and girls" who worked on his Christchurch plantation. He willed the six youngsters in pairs to his three younger children along with "their produce." His eldest son received three adults, Sambo, Rose, and Maria, "with their produce." As the eldest child and the one who bore his father's name, he should not have to wait quite so long for his property to begin to accrue.[103] In Barbados in 1676, William Death offered manumission only to his "negroe wench," after she had "fower children all liveing at one tyme." The children are pointedly not included in the promise of manumission under the assumption that this "negroe wench" would be so grateful for her freedom that she would easily walk away from the four children she offered in exchange. He also instructed that a "lusty able negroe either a man or a woman" be purchased for his heir George Harlow. He exhorted his executors to provide "a wife or a husband" for the "lusty negroe." This pair would presumably then provide the "seed" for Harlow's future riches.[104]

William Death's contemporaries shared his assumption that wealth in the form of children accrued from the ownership of slave women. That assumption was not misguided. Early in 1662 for example, William and Ann Duces sold their plantation and sixteen enslaved adults, eleven of them women. Of those eleven women, only two, Joane and Burch, were childless. Lily had four children, Mary and Susana each had three, Abigal, Judith, Nancy and Jane had two children each, and Bess had one.[105] High infant and childhood mortality rates certainly meant that many born on the Duces plantation would not survive their childhood. Nonetheless, enslaved women bore children, some of who survived to adulthood, lived among parents and kin, and in fact became parents themselves.

These children became part of the slaveowners' economy, and as such they also became part of the future of the slaveowners' family. When John Mullivax stipulated in 1675 that the "first negro child that shall happen to be born of the bodys of either . . . Bess or Maria shall be delivered unto" his grandson—he did so with an eye toward *his* future, not theirs.[106] At the

time of his death, the men and women enslaved by Mullivax had no children, but he hoped for the arrival of an enslaved child to expand both his
largesse—he enslaved only five people at the time he wrote his will—and
the fondness of his grandchild's memory of him. Jenny and her children
Nann and Cuffee were all that existed of Thomas Lee's estate. Her children,
who were likely emblematic of her exposure and vulnerability as the only
adult owned by Lee, were already part of his equation. Lee divided Jenny's
children among his own offspring and in the deposition given by his com-
mander hoped that "if it should happen that ever the negroe girle should
have a child . . . it should be for his daughter Margarett."[107] Margaret Ellacott's desire to provide money for her own daughter not only overrode recognition that enslaved mothers had similar maternal feelings but equated
any such feeling with that of cattle: "One negro girle by name Doll and her
encrease one cow by name Lilly and her encrease to be kept on my plantation . . . untill each of them shall be a year old and then sold (that is to say
the encrease) and [the money] delivered to my said daughter Lucretia."[108]
Edmond Dyne, well aware of the ties linking Hagar, her adult son Jacker,
and her grandson, bequeathed Hagar and Jacker to two of his own sons,
leaving Jacker's namesake Jack and Jack's mother to his own two daughters.[109] As their predecessors had since the 1650s, slaveowners acted to protect and ensure the future for their own progeny without regard to enslaved
women's ability to reproduce, their relationship to enslaved men, or their
relationship to their children.

This suggestion that slaveowners purposely attempted to create couples for the reproductive benefit of a planter's progeny was both common
and significant in colonial Barbados. William Trattle saw his familial duty
in terms similar to those of Robert Gratton. In 1674, Trattle left £100 to each
of his two nephews. He ordered the money to be "layd out in young negro
women, the said negro women with their offspring (if any) to be at [the
nephews] disposall when [they] shall attaine the age of twenty one
yeares."[110] He too was involved in a speculative gesture that embraced a
notion of livestock breeding even as he cannot be said to be engaged in
forcibly demanding that sexual intercourse take place between the "young
Negro women" and unnamed, random, enslaved (or free) men. Despite his
parenthetical disclaimer, Trattle saw black *female* bodies as the most valuable and ongoing reward for his beloved nephews. His assumption reflected
both the experiences and expectations of other planters. William Lesley, for
example, enslaved a woman named Dot who had had the dubious fortune
of bearing five living children before his death in 1674.[111]

As in Barbados, when intensive rice cultivation took hold of the colony of South Carolina, slaveowners faced with the tremendous growth of their slaveholdings looked to black women to both bolster their property and mitigate against quotidian violations. Although during the initial years of the rice boom the colony had entered a period during which birth rates fell, planters responded to an environment in which enslaved women's reproductive role in slavery had already been (and continued to be) evident. In 1737, an observer in North Carolina suggested that planters were quite mindful of enslaved women's reproductive value, writing that "a fruitful woman amongst them [is] very much valued by the planters, and a numberous Issue esteemed the greatest Riches in this country." He went on to suggest that slaveowners interfered in the lives of enslaved couples by obliging a woman to take a "second, third, fourth, fifth and more Husbands or Bedfellows" if children did not appear after a "year or two."[112] It is important to note that the manipulation of fertility here, as elsewhere, was perceived to be located in the body of the fruitful or fruitless woman, whose multiple husbands bore no reproductive responsibility. Thus, it was enslaved women who bore the burden and pain of slaveowners' clumsy manipulations and scrutiny. The particularized language of some slaveowners' wills elucidates slaveholding patterns. During the 1730s in South Carolina 13 percent of slaveowners who identified individual slaves in their wills brought specific men and women together in their bequests (see Table 4).

TABLE 4. WOMEN AND CHILDREN IN SLAVEOWNERS' WILLS, SOUTH CAROLINA, 1730–49

	1730–39	*1740–49*
Total number of wills	418	440
Wills containing slaves	132	149
Wills that name slaves	110	135
Wills that identify women	98	120
Wills that identify children	25	36
Wills that use term "increase"	27*	42*
Wills that identify a parent	22	35
Wills that "couple" slave men and women	15	23
Wills that use term "spouse"	2	4
Wills that identify siblings	1	3

*In both decades, two slaveowners use the term "increase" without specifying any women.
Source: Will Books, Records of the Secretary of State, South Carolina Department of Archives and History.

John Mortimer, for example, bequeathed two men, Simon and Sambo, and two women, Aedgi and Dido, to his wife. He split all other (unspecified in number) men and women among his children.[113] Isaac Child, a wealthy man who passed down land, slaves, and personal property to his sons, knew his sons would accumulate more with what he left them. To his grandson John, however, Isaac left "two negro children named Nanny and Sam," a gift that promised growth during John's minority and might even help to inculcate him into the mechanisms of slaveownership and the desire for capital accumulation at an early age.[114] Thus, the benevolence of an aging grandfather became the seed for a white child's future wealth. As for Nanny and Sam, there is no telling whether their relationship to one another produced the desired results.

Slaveowning men not only inscribed gendered value on the bodies of black women as they parceled out their holdings, they also used black women to confer attention on white women. Enslaved women were made visible through gender conventions that pertained to slaveowners' wives and daughters. The "mulatto girl called Jenny" became a talisman of Arthur Hall's love for, or sense of obligation to, his wife. Upon his death in 1732, among all those he enslaved, he named only Jenny. He bequeathed to his wife both property in Charlestown and Jenny "to her own separate use and behoof forever." His plantation and the other enslaved men and women went to his son, although until the son came of age, the "sixteen negroes to be kept with their Issue and Increase on the said Plantation and there to be employed and Ecercised under the Government of my said wife . . . for the purpose of maintaining and educating my young children."[115] Thus, while Arthur Hall must have owned other women, his desire to provide his wife with the particular gift of a "serving girl" unearths Jenny from archival obscurity. Jenny, and other women singled out from among the unnamed "negroes" divided among wives, sons, and daughters, suggest the particular primacy of place enslaved women held in the conscience and daily lives of South Carolina's slaveowners.

Black women found themselves used to signify largesse and particular attention or disapproval. When Robert Hume died in possession of more than eighty black men and women, he bequeathed only "a Negro Carpenter named Hampton" to his son, while giving to his daughter the slave Castor and his wife Diana, plus Antony, Clarinda, and her sons Will and Prince. The profits from his land also fell to his son and daughter, but Hume's brothers inherited the bulk of the enslaved men and women.[116] Hampton, Castor, Diana, Anthony, and Clarinda and her sons, became, in effect, the signs of a husband or father's particular and personal *gift* that was distinguishable from the inheritance share a wife or descendent of a slaveowner expected. In most cases, that gift took the form of a female body; women as a personalized message from the deceased.

One wonders about the extent to which Nanny, Sam, and other "gifts" like themselves were aware of slaveowners' cynical matchmaking.[117] Probate records suggest that most owners of large plantations passed the bulk of the enslaved as a unit to the eldest son. Younger children received single enslaved couples or individuals. Often, gendered ideology pertaining to white sons and daughters shaped the terms of those bequests. White daughters frequently inherited single enslaved women or girls—presumably with a nod to sociosexual conventions pertaining to gender and the "mastering" of African men.[118] When James Goodbe died, he shaped the terms of his bequests along conventional lines of gender hierarchy in a slave society. Goodbe gave each of his four sons land and slaves. To each of his daughters, however, whose futures as brides demanded a mobility that might be hindered by the possession of land, he left only cattle and slaves. Bequests such as Goodbe's suggest that, while they were inclined to bequeath slave property to all children, Carolina slaveowners reinforced the primacy of particular legatees through paired giving. Ultimately, of course, enslaved women did not embody isolated value. The Goodbe men each received a valuable couple—Toney and Phebe, Billy and Lena, Quaco and Linda, and Hercules and Judith. Murrial, Lucy, Sarah, Kary, Jena, Abigaie, and Grace went to the three daughters. The only white woman to receive the more valuable male-female pairing was his wife, who inherited Phebe and Primus.[119]

As the black populations of South Carolina grew, creating bonds of affection and kin as slaveowners bought, sold, and hired black women and men across county lines, the interplay between black desire for emotional sustenance and white desire for economic sustenance remains largely unreadable. How could Toney and Phebe, for example, not have recognized the implication of their pairing? Could they have been unaware of the explicitly sexualized dimension of their assigned labors? How must they have felt to know that their conjugal happiness represented a bulwark to the system that enslaved them? To the enslaved men and women who worked amid a large group of laborers, slaveowners' attempts to maintain a particular sex balance among them may have remained relatively invisible. The effect that Goodbe's legacies had on Toney and Phebe's affections for one another, assuming that they did not previously see themselves as a couple, is unknowable. But for those owned by men who emulated Noah, shackling them two by two, the slaveowner's intention could hardly have been opaque. If she actually cared for Toney, Phebe's gratitude for Goodbe's recognition of that emotional bond must have been shaded by the tacit understanding that the private life she shared with Toney supported the public life of the man who owned her. Should she ever bear a child, the baby would reinforce the economics that underpinned her emotional life.

The importance of women as reproductive property might be signaled in other ways as well. Twenty years after receiving slave couples from his father, Robert Daniel died. Tom Godfrey and Hagar and Pawpaw Tom and Nancy (transformed into Old Tom and Old Nanny) were the only survivors of the original fifteen Daniel inherited from his father. Over the years Daniel carefully replaced each dead, sold, or escaped enslaved woman or man with another of the same sex. Bess herself replaced one of the dead or gone females with her daughter Mareah, the only person marked as an offspring of one of the six enslaved women. When he wrote his will in 1732, seven years before his death, Daniel still owned fifteen slaves—eight men and six women.[120] The carefully prescribed gender parity, which he maintained over twenty years of slaveholding and reinforced by his bequests, furnishes evidence of his faith in the reproductive potential of his human property. Any frustration he may have felt at the absence of surviving children on the estate despite decades of care did not cause his plans to flag. Daniel ordered the executors of his estate to purchase for his wife, in addition to the bequest of the aforementioned fifteen men and women, "a negro boy and girl," a horse, and a featherbed; the boy and girl a message of regard, or obligation, to his wife from beyond the grave and a reflection of his lifelong conviction that an essential aspect of the value of the men and women he enslaved rested in their reproductive potential.

Although fewer children find their way into Carolina slaveowners' records in the 1730s, those records show that 25 percent of slaveowners' named children alongside women (see Table 3 above). In 1733, for example, Cato, Will, Cretia, and Phillis, the children of Carinda, along with Cloe, the child of Celia, were passed to the wife of their deceased owner together with their mothers.[121] In 1737, an unnamed child with her mother Venus passed to Phillip Combe's wife Martha.[122] In the inventory of Robert Hume's plantation, twenty-eight children were listed, only three motherless. Cyrus, his brother Will, and his sisters Diana and Mary lived with their mother Moll. Mindoe and her brother March lived with their mother Belinda. Only Cuffee, Minos, and Cudjoe appear on the inventory unlinked to a parent's name, and because African children constituted between 10 and 17 percent of the total number of African persons imported between 1735 and 1737, it is quite possible that they had been imported from West Africa.[123] In any case, these children populated the terrain of colonial South Carolina and stood as living testaments to the humanity and commodity of enslaved Africans. For Carolina slaveowners, Cloe, Mindo, and March and their counterparts personified slaveownership's exponential wealth and its foundational desecration. Well before the latter part of the century, when slaveowners in the Chesapeake, Carolina, and Georgia began to fuel the expansion of the lower South with the children born on coastal plantations, the understanding that enslaved children constituted a tangible and separable source of plantation wealth had taken root among the earliest setters in the colonies.

Shortly after the middle of the eighteenth century, birthrates in South Carolina surpassed mortality rates and the black population began to grow as a result of births rather than imports. Philip Morgan has found that by the second half of the eighteenth century the majority of slave sales in the colony involved groups, more than three-fourths of which were designated as family members either explicitly or implicitly.[124] An examination of slaveowners' inventories shows that a high proportion of slaveowners who enslaved women in the 1730s and 1740s also enslaved children and that by the beginning second half of the 1740s, while there was a small decrease in the percentage of households enslaving children, nearly all documents that identify children attach them to specific parents (see Table 5). This suggests a stability for enslaved families in the lowcountry that nonetheless grows out of a long-standing willingness of slaveowners to appropriate family formation among the enslaved along far more disruptive lines. Despite the fact

TABLE 5. WOMEN AND CHILDREN IN SLAVEOWNERS' INVENTORIES, SOUTH CAROLINA, 1736–45

	1736–40	1741–45
Total number of inventories—514		
Inventories containing slaves	106	201
Inventories containing women	95	192
Inventories containing children	67 (70%)*	122 (63%)*
Inventories identifying parents	61	118

*Percentage of all inventories containing women.
Source: Charleston Inventories, WPA Transcripts 102, 104, 105, 113, 114, 115, 120, 121, South Carolina Department of Archives and History.

that Henry Laurens wrote of the immorality of "separating and tareing asunder" slave families, enslaved women gave birth to many children prior to the development of the rice economy, and slaveowners had long ago forsaken an association between birth and humanity.[125] The connection between family formation and behavior that might reflect a mutual recognition of shared humanity between a slaveowner and the woman he enslaved seems tenuous at best.

As we saw in Chapter 1, childbirth became part of a series of symbolic icons mobilized by slaveowners that ultimately attempted to sever a black woman's hold on her humanity. Some slaveowners transformed childbirth, which they reduced to an inconsequential and painless act in between tilling rows of soil, into evidence of black people's connection to animals. In much the same way that Walter Johnson found for the antebellum period, colonial slaveowners made "a direct connection between the bodily capacity of the woman [they enslaved] and [their] own happiness."[126] Slaveowners "coupled" men and women, named them husband and wife, and foresaw their own future in the bellies of enslaved workers. Childbirth, then, needs to stand alongside the more ubiquitously evoked scene of violence and brutality at the end of a slaveowner's lash or branding iron. The scars from whippings or brandings stood as a visible "advertisement" that slaveowners equated human beings with chattel.

But as Kirsten Fischer argues, the connection between slaves and livestock was always predicated not on the belief that Africans were animals but rather in the evocation of a degraded but fully present humanity.[127] In other words, an enslaved person was branded "like" an animal in order to humiliate, not because she was an animal and was insensate. Thus, just as both Bessie and Bessy populated inventories and slaveowners assessed women's fertility on their balance sheets, they did so fully apprised of their own connections to their human property. Those connections found their way into colonial legislation almost immediately and attest to the particularly chilling balance between sex and racial slavery. It seems, then, that the ultimate contradiction—if we can even call it that—in the system of slavery was the banal, even thoughtless, coexistence of humanity (in the recognition of marital bonds) and inhumanity (in the appropriation of children and the unborn). This juxtaposition shaped the ways in which enslaved women and men could hope to articulate their own sense of family, parenting, or culture formation—all the things that constituted their lexicon of humanity. Each time a slaveowner's will was made public, or an enslaved woman overheard reference to a white child's ultimate interest in her own swelling belly or suckling infant, she responded by repositioning her self in relation to her child, her lover, and her reproductive capacity. Enslaved women and men were clearly not just the objects of slaveowners' probate records; they were also forced to respond to planters' ideas about their intimate decisions in immediate and painful ways. The decisions that slaveowners made directly affected the lives enslaved women and men led. As slaveowners composed their wills and ordered their inventories, enslaved women and men positioned themselves in relation to those who owned them, to the work they were forced to undertake, to one another, and to the children who died and survived their infancies.

"Hannah and Hir Children": Reproduction and Creolization Among Enslaved Women

Slaveowners spent years working through convoluted notions about reproduction and the women they enslaved. In so doing they enacted various degrees of intrusion and violence upon the bodies of women who had already endured both the Middle Passage and the destruction of their futures. Slaveowners' behaviors reflect their immersion in occasionally articulated notions of gender, race and power. The processes through which slaveowners arrived at their understandings about the reach of their power were deeply implicated by their assumptions about women's bodies and women's work. In turn, exercising that power had wide-ranging ramifications for the women and men caught in the grip of New World slavery. As slaveowners struggled to police the physical and political boundaries of their property and attach economic and social meaning to African women's bodies, women and men engaged in their own efforts to inscribe meaning onto their new lives. They chose partners and lost them to sale and disease, made babies and lost many of them, too. In other words, they struggled to impose their own meaning on a process of family formation that colonial slaveowners defined only in terms of their own sense of familial and societal security.

Both slaveowners and the enslaved understood that a process was underway. While it would not be until the mid-eighteenth century (at the earliest) that African communities in the North American mainland would reach the demographic benchmark that transformed them into African Americans, the creation of syncretic cultural forms in the Americas—the process of creolization—began in the historical moment most associated with mortality and a lack of natural increase. The cultural transformation that began when ships like the *Arthur* left the African coast was by no means dependent upon birth. Enslaved populations in the Americas that were defined by high mortality, skewed sex ratios, and low birthrates did not remain timelessly African. Even in places with the most violent and damaging work regimes, where mortality rates meant that workers would survive less than a decade and newly enslaved laborers to replace the workforce were a constant necessity, a process was underway. Cultural changes were happening regardless of mortality or childbirth rates. Yet childbearing retains a particularly important meaning in the experience of creolization. In the context of New World slavery, of course, creolization was in fact rooted in loss; in the despair of infant death and the altered meanings of women's fertility under the weight of burgeoning plantation regimes. As Ludmilla Jordanova argues, "feelings about reproduction are part of the cultural currency of a time and help shape people's sense of themselves."[1] To explicitly experience the alienation of reproductive labor (and I use this phrase mindfully), as enslaved Africans did, could not have helped but shape an enslaved woman's sense of herself as commodified even as the task of raising children into a life of violence and hard labor highlighted the skills necessary for navigating the new terrain. New and syncretic cultural forms emerged as strangers developed linguistic, familial, educational, architectural, or performative practices while becoming members of communities. Children, as well as young adults entering the Americas through the slave trade, made explicit the process of literal and symbolic reeducation that is at the heart of creolization.

Historians look at the process of cultural change in early slave societies as a way of assigning meaning and order to the conceptual framework of slavery; the varying degrees of natural increase in different slave societies helps scholars understand corresponding variations in African cultural retentions. Societies such as those in mainland North America with early natural rates of increase retained fewer African culture-ways, while those of the Caribbean or Latin America, where mortality rates consistently outpaced fertility, remained sites of vibrant and tangible links to the African past. There is a simplicity in this contrasting view of life versus death that is compelling. But in Barbados we can see that the clarity of the contrast between the mainland and the Caribbean became muddied as the island ultimately became home to the largest creole population in the Caribbean, where 90 percent of the black population was "island born" by 1800.[2] Even in the absence of natural increase, creolization evokes the language of generations and thus the transformations that accompany the shift from one generation to another.Rather than rehash old arguments about the usefulness of "Africanity" or African retentions as measures of the experience of slavery, this chapter explores the foundation upon which the notion of creolization rests.

When her owner died in 1654 somewhere on the island of Barbados, Bessie's life changed. Bessie, her children, and the other men and women with whom she lived were at the mercy of her owner's beneficiaries. Bessie is the only woman on this plantation whose name survives in the historical record. The other women enslaved on this plantation are recorded only as anonymous wives:

Negro man named Sam and his wife and piqueninies, Peter and wife and three piqueninies, Bessie and her piqueninies, Dick and his wife and two piqueninies, Adam his wife and two piqueninies, one Negro by name Abala.[3]

Whatever the circumstances were that created her solitude in the probate records and perhaps in her life, the death of her owner would force Bessie and the other families she lived among to prepare for the possibilities of further isolation—separation from children and friends in the immediate future. The sale of the men and women on the plantation separated Bessie, her family, and her peers; whatever ties of affinity connected them would stretch across the island. Bessie would have no assurance that she could keep her children or that they would even survive. The only certainty lay in the reality of their birth—events that had already irrevocably changed the terms of Bessie's enslavement.

As Saidiya Hartman has argued, the violation and violence of slavery is best understood not in "exhibitions of 'extreme' suffering or in what we see but in what we don't see."[4] Bessie stood alone with her children, a fact that would, of course, come to exemplify slaveowners' attitudes toward reproduction under slavery—it was solely the province of women. The invisibility of the father of Bessie's children—whether he was enslaved on another plantation, had died, or was the slaveowner himself—and the inability to predict where she and her children might find themselves after her owner's will cleared probate constitute a core experience of early American racial violence. Although they were perhaps initially unaware of the unprecedented act of legislation that linked children's status to that of their mothers, women such as Bessie would come to understand the contradictory relationships between themselves and their children. Uninterrupted by even a tacit nod toward paternity, the mother-child dyad came into being at the behest of slaveowners intent on calculating their own patriarchal powers through the ownership of human property.

It is important to know that among middle- and upper-class whites, it was not until the eighteenth century that children began to be "naturally associated" with their mothers instead of their fathers.[5] "Bessie and her piqueninies" constitute a linguistic model of cultural ideas that in 1654 already clearly separated black and white women's experience of reproduction. The fact that Bessie's owner designated her and the other enslaved persons on his plantation as members of nuclear families is both evocative and cautionary; evocative because, as "wives" and mothers in the first years of the sugar revolution on Barbados, Bessie and the women with whom she was enslaved remind us that dual identities as family members and laborers made up both the language of English slaveownership and the experience of enslavement from its inception, but cautionary because the use of the term "wife" is almost nonexistent among slaveowners describing their human property—Bessie is the norm, the "wives" are anomaly (see Table 2 above). Despite being occasionally listed alongside adult men, enslaved women's familial identity, when acknowledged, was almost universally linked to their children. "Wives" existed, on rare occasions, to satisfy the passions of black men; but routinely to confer such a marital identity on women whose commodification depended on their fictive identity as unencumbered by emotional connections, would lay slaveowners bare to the moral contradictions at the heart of their economy.

For every Bessie in Barbados there were myriad women who were unable or unwilling to bear children. Although slaveowners responded early and eagerly to reproductive potential, Bessie lived in a society marked far more regularly by death than by birth. The disease environment of the New World was devastating for everyone. Native mortality rates in the aftermath of the Columbian encounter are exemplified by Hispaniola, where 18 percent of the population died each year between 1492 and 1517, decreasing the population from over a million to 10,000.[6] Europeans and West Africans also succumbed in record, though less dramatic numbers to the disease environment created by Europe's settlement of the Americas. Smallpox, malaria, dysentery, yellow fever, dengue fever, influenza, and hookworm combined to create an environment in which life expectancy plummeted for all who disembarked from ships onto American shores. Differentials in immunities (or evolutionary biology) played an essential role in the development of the slave trade; mortality for West Africans in southern and Caribbean colonies during summer months was substantially lower than for their European counterparts. Slaveowners looked at those death rates and assured themselves that Africans were naturally fit for hard labor despite the fact that in northern colonies the situation was reversed. Death rates, then, caused most of those who searched for economically rational investments in long-term laborers to bypass enslaved Africans in the north and indentured white servants in the south.[7] Economic rationality and the luck of tropical immunities notwithstanding, enslaved African men and women faced enormous physiological hardships in the Americas.

In addition to the many disease vectors that negatively affected fertility, environmental factors also shaped slave life. Maternal and paternal exposure to lead has been found to have negative effects on fetal health and to cause a decrease in fertility overall. Among the enslaved on the Newton plantation in Barbados—the site of the largest archeological excavation of slave remains in the Americas—more than one-third showed evidence of lead poisoning.[8] Malaria renders men temporarily infertile, and two exposures to malaria a year were not uncommon for the enslaved. Tetanus, whooping cough, pneumonia, and a range of debilitating conditions brought on by malnutrition all interrupted or destroyed enslaved women's fertility rates.[9]

All these factors contributed to a situation in which, according to Richard Steckel, even in North America enslaved women lost at least 54 percent of their pregnancies to stillbirth, infant mortality, and early childhood mortality.[10] Steckel's evidence comes from nineteenth-century plantation records; given the increased risk of infectious disease during the height of the slave trade, one can presume an even higher level of infertility, miscarriage, and infant death in the colonial period. Indeed, rates of natural decrease characterized the early years of colonial settlement only gradually, and not universally, giving way to natural increase in established colonies.[11] Despite the physiological obstacles on both sides, in North America black and white women's fertility rates gradually rose over the course of the colonial period, from 42 and 44 births per 1,000 population respectively between 1670 and 1699 to 56 and 58 per 1,000 between 1760 and 1789.[12] But even as children began to survive their childhoods, they did so under very unstable conditions. Mothers would have kept a careful and anxious watch over newborns who were "exceedingly small" and who suffered mortality rates twice as high as the infants of slaveowners and other whites.[13] Eager to maximize their workforce, slaveowners often interrupted breast-feeding as early as the third or fourth month, and malnourished infants and toddlers were quick and easy targets of infectious disease. The difficulties women enslaved in mainland colonies faced would be greatly magnified for women in parts of the West Indies, who suffered fertility rates nearly half that of women in North America.[14]

But Bessie and women across the seventeenth- and early eighteenth-century English Caribbean were present in numbers balanced enough to make the possibility of family formation pervasive, if not inevitable. In 1676, some 16,121 enslaved women in Barbados labored alongside 16,346 men.[15] In Nevis, the proportions were the same (see Table 6). The possibility that one could form a family would have been inseparable from the obstacles to that process. While slaveowners and the enslaved may have been unaware of the technical explanations for low fertility, miscarriage, and infant death, they would have clearly understood the reality that childbirth was problematic. Even as the planters' awareness of the benefits of reproduction among the enslaved crystallized, they acted in ways that undermined whatever family formation balanced sex ratios made possible. Perhaps those women who could give birth did so only under duress, after failed attempts to control fertility or to maintain sexual distance from men. Or, perhaps childbirth came to offer a virtual route home, a means to rearticulate what should have been in the face of the brutal unfamiliarity of American slavery. However a woman perceived it, reproduction would change the terms of enslavement not only for herself and the father of her children, but for childless black women and men who would watch the arrival of children with a mixture of tenderness and trepidation.

TABLE 6. WOMEN AND CHILDREN IN SLAVEOWNERS' HOUSEHOLDS, NEVIS, 1678

	N	Percent
Households	641	—
Slaveowners	275	—
Enslaved men	1422	—
Enslaved women	1321	—
Enslaved children	1106	—
Owners of women	218	79*
Owners of women in equal or greater numbers than men	154	70*
Owners of no women	40	14*
Owners of no men	39	14*
Owners of women and children	166	76**
Owners of children and no women	15	5*
Owners of women and no children	70	32**

*Percentages of slaveowning households. **Percentages of slaveowning households with women. Source: Oliver, *Caribbeana*, 3: 29–35, 70–81.

"The First Negroe Child that shall Happen to Be Borne"

"Motherhood" occupies mythic proportions in the African American historical narrative. The imaginary past is peopled with selfless women working endless hours to support their children—mamas with expansive hearts and bosoms and a ferocious protectiveness, warriors who shouldered weapons while nursing babies. Some scholars have proceeded from the assumption that fertility control was anathema to African cultures and therefore not an option for women enslaved in North America.[16] It has also been argued that low birth rates among enslaved women can be traced to their refusal to bear children whose future could only hold enslavement. Historians who question or oppose this argument usually do so at least in part out of a sense of disbelief that seventeenth- and eighteenth-century enslaved African women had the knowledge, as well as the desire, to affect the demography of their communities so radically.[17]

Understanding reproduction among a newly enslaved population must be grounded in understanding men and women's ability to control conception. Europe's classical literature reveals that before the Renaissance effectively suppressed the dissemination and discussion of contraceptive potions and suppositories, women and men had extensive experience with fertility control.[18] On the African side, ancient Egyptian and early Islamic writing demonstrate a similar familiarity with the mechanisms of conception.[19] In 1700, North Carolina traveler John Lawson described Native American women as in possession of "an Art to destroy the Conception" of a child.[20] Although neither the European nor the North African written record has much to say about the reproductive lives of West African women, the fact that women throughout Europe, North Africa, and the Islamic world used methods of pregnancy control, which they gleaned from the local pharmacopoeia, strongly suggests that West African women would have done so as well. The few references to contraceptives or abortifacients in Afro-American and Caribbean sources support the notion that women and men transferred knowledge of fertility control from Africa to the Americas. Maria Merian, an entomologist in seventeenth-century Surinam, wrote extensively about enslaved and Native women's use of plants to induce abortion:

The seeds of this plant are used by women who have labor pains, and who must continue to work, despite their pain. The Indians, who are not treated well by the Dutch, use the seeds to abort their children, so their children will not become slaves like they are. The black slaves from Guinea and Angola have demanded to be treated well, threatening to refuse to have children.[21]

Among the African plants transported to the Caribbean were okra and aloe, both of which were used as abortifacients. Knowledge about using snake-root and cotton roots as emmenagogues survived the Middle Passage; plants from European and Native American pharmacopoeias joined these West African plants in the New World to help women control reproduction.[22] In the nineteenth-century American South, a physician reported enslaved women using vaginal suppositories and infusions of gum, camphor, and rue, all of which were relatively effective contraceptives that were noted in medieval records. Among eighteenth-century white settlers, the question then was not whether a fetus could be aborted but what guilt one could hide by doing so. When faced with what he presumed was an unwanted pregnancy in the first part of the nineteenth century, Harriet Jacobs's owner, Dr. Flint, intimated that he could have "helped" her to prevent or end the pregnancy.[23]

The possibility of successful fertility control must coexist with a recognition of all that would make a woman physically or psychologically unwilling or unable to bear a child. Nutritionally inadequate diets lowered fertility, and the labor regime rendered many women unable to conceive or to carry fetuses to term. But in addition to external suppressers of fertility, many women may have taken steps to avoid conception. At the very least, the extreme contrast in fertility rates among enslaved women in the Caribbean and those of the American South suggests that the question of fertility control must be taken seriously.[24] Women enslaved on plantations where planters' regimes negatively affected their fertility may have seen the absence of pregnancy as proof of an emmenagogues' effectiveness or evidence that the deities too were reluctant to bring another life into such a place. Moreover, when an attempt to control fertility failed, an unwanted but unstoppable pregnancy might have illustrated one's powerlessness as much as one's agency. I would like to avoid romanticizing these women who, like Bessie, come into focus at least in part because of their children. Presuming that Bessie loved and nurtured these children is dangerous, for ambivalence toward and distance from her "pickininies" would have been as logical an emotion as any for Bessie and the other mothers with whom she was enslaved. It becomes difficult, if not impossible, given the realities of disease, overwork, and fertility control, to accurately situate enslaved women's experience of childbirth and parenting. Mechanisms for interrupting the violation of enslavement could certainly have included a with-drawal from voluntary intimate contact, from the extension of self in community. In that context, the birth of a child would have done nothing to alleviate sorrow; indeed, it would only have made the load heavier.

Enslavement could not have been fully transformed by family forma-tion, even as we look to fictive and natural kin ties to assess the emotional wholeness of black life in its aftermath. Emotional attachments exposed one to further abuse. Enslaved women viscerally experienced their embodied contradiction. As the mother of a three-year-old child and a three-month-old infant in 1654, Judith had already added motherhood to the fixed equa-tion of her enslavement. Her reproductive capacity became part of her owner's mathematics, when he died, it became part of her experience as an enslaved woman. Both her potential and actual "increase" doubtless caused her great anxiety, if not anguish. The division of the estate—Judith and her children and Peter, Tom, and Pendee—would inevitably separate Judith from the father of her children, if not from the children themselves.[25] Such instability was as intrinsic to motherhood under slavery as Judith's children were to her life as an enslaved woman. Judith experienced an enslavement marked by an enormous degree of uncertainty that was manifested in the bodies of children whose future was out of her control.

Although Barbados was on the path to becoming a society fully satu-rated by slavery in the 1650s, Judith, and the men and women with whom she shared the condition of enslavement would not have yet fully encoun-tered the regime that was soon to come. Rather, they would be part of smaller slaveholdings that put them into daily contact with slaveowners. Over the course of the 1650s, the black population rose from 28 percent to 51 percent of the island's total inhabitants, but even well into the following decades, slaveowners with 1–19 enslaved persons would outnumber those who owned 20–59 and those who owned 60 or more by five to one.[26] In other words, while the black population would ultimately outstrip the white population, women such as Judith and Bess did not experience their repro-ductive or familial identities in isolation from slaveowners and the anxiety that proximity would have caused. At the same time, as women enslaved throughout the Caribbean did in the late seventeenth century, Judith would find herself in a community in which the numbers of men and women were evenly balanced and where, at least in Barbados, childbirth was not an anomaly.[27] Judith's identity as a parent with surviving children isolated her from the majority of women enslaved in Barbados in this period, but as the years unfolded other women would share Judith's situation and perhaps struggle with her to define themselves with and against the children they brought into slavery.

While an increasingly outnumbered white population struggled with a changing island, many enslaved women had to balance the demands of labor with those of childrearing. By the turn of the 1660s, there was a rise in the number of children inventoried in the estates of deceased slaveowners. Of the wills itemizing women in this period 31 percent (26) also mention children, though only 14 percent of slaveowners explicitly name a woman as a parent. Slaveowners' desire to add children to their balance sheet did not carry a corollary of recognition, and women would reap little reward from bearing these children. Having children did not change a woman's economic situation or decrease her work load in the sugar fields. The children simply became part of the plantation inventory. In the 1650s, ten out of thirty-three plantations with adult men and women contained children, by the 1660s twenty-two out of forty-eight did so (see Table 2 above). Throughout the decade slaveowners enumerated "Children," "small ones," "Pickaninies," or women "with one child" or "with two children." Moreover, as in the decade before, sex balance was the norm among inventoried slaveholdings (see Figures 15 and 16).

By the 1660s, then, even as slaveowners imported massive numbers of people from the West African coast, many women enslaved in Barbados were involved in a process of reproduction and acculturation that had widespread consequences. Planters who bequeathed the unborn children of enslaved women knew this, as did enslaved men and women themselves. On the 350-acre Fisher Pond plantation in St. Michael, for example, the slave population was inventoried twice over two years. In September 1667 there were sixteen children on the plantation; a year later, there were nineteen.[28] It is reasonable to assume that the additional children belonged to one or more of the forty-six adult females on the plantation because at this stage children rarely entered the trans-Atlantic slave trade.[29] Regardless of their provenance, however, the children's education and protection became the responsibility of the women and men with whom they lived and, ultimately, worked. While for slaveowners, the plantation became the dominant unit of production, for the enslaved, the presence of children (even for those who did not give birth) functioned as an equally important unit of cultural reproduction. These children symbolized more than anguish and upheaval for their mothers. After the Middle Passage and during the interminable reality of forced labor, reproduction could afford women and men

Number of persons
enslaved on each
inventoried plantation

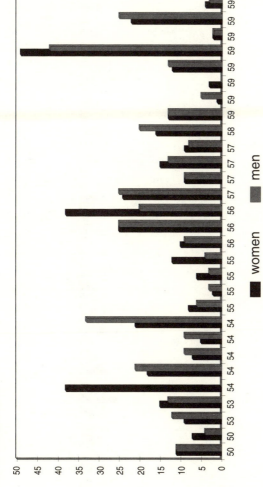

Year in which estate is inventoried

Figure 15. Men and women on inventoried plantations, Barbados, 1650–59. Each entry represents a single plantation inventoried the year of the owner's death; no entry is duplicated. Source: Deed Books, Series RB1, Barbados Archives, Cave Hill, St. Michaels.

Number of persons
enslaved on each
inventoried plantation

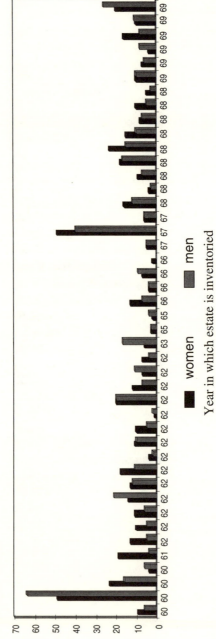

Figure 16. Men and women on inventoried plantations, Barbados, 1660–69. Source: Deed Books, Series RB1, Barbados Archives, Cave Hill, St. Michaels.

an opportunity to ground themselves, to manifest strength and persistence through children. Time and again, those historians have deemed the least fertile and the least likely to reproduce became parents in an environment where the basic assumptions about parenting could not be guaranteed.[30] It is not without irony that parenthood was simultaneously the area in which slaveowners could most severely undermine the lives of the enslaved.

There is an obvious if contradictory connection between the brutal growth of slaveownership and the development of creole communities, and enslaved women would find themselves reminded of that fact as they and their children, sometimes together and sometimes separately, found themselves marked as a source of bourgeoning wealth; even as, in the same breath, their identities as parents were simultaneously acknowledged and dismissed. In 1682, Mareah and "one pickannie by name Quashe" and Bess and "her child that she hath" were bequeathed respectively to their owner's two daughters.[31] The next year William Brooks bequeathed Busha "and her pickanney named Betty . . . and Busha's [future] increase" to his daughter.[32] In 1682, Thomas Spiar acknowledged three of his six adult slaves as parents on his plantation in St. James. "Cumba and hir two children, Nell Cow and hir child, Buck and hir five children."[33] On the St. Michaels's plantation of John Leddra, only one of the four women named was childless. Cate had Bess and James, Maria had Gibbs, and Alice had Harry. Only Lewcretia had no children.[34] Slaveowners used terms like "her child" to suggest women's autonomy over their offspring even as their actions spoke otherwise. The tension in the slaveowners' minds between the acknowledgment of parent-child bonds and the destruction of those bonds through the mechanics of slaveownership and inheritance echoed the attitudes of seventeenth-century travelers and traders to Africa and the Caribbean who claimed that Africans were animals yet could not completely jettison their humanity. For "Cumba and hir two children," the relationship between their humanity and their exploitation was marked by a different tension. Women such as Cumba, Cate, and Mareah brought to childbirth complex sets of fears and desires. To "own" even while being "owned" required women in the process of acclimating themselves and their children to the slavery system to incorporate that sense of "ownership" in contradictory and unexpected ways.

Cumba and Mareah's condition as enslaved fieldworkers was perfectly clear both to them and to those around them; their condition as parents was less so. Their sense of connection to their children cannot be assumed. Likely born on another continent themselves, they must have struggled mightily with the conditions into which their children were born. Perhaps their lives were inflected by a desire to improve the present through the presence of children, who so profoundly direct a community's vision toward the future. Perhaps the birth of their children was part of a conscious creolization. Indeed, from the moment of their birth, enslaved children symbolized the intersections of the past and the present; their names bore witness to the process underway. In 1661, Bombo and Equa's children were named Jack, John and Kate. In 1667, men and women named their children Quaqua, Cumba, Arubo, Coggo, Cosse.[35] As African-born men and women chose, or were made to choose, English or African names, they mobilized complicated connections between the past and the present. The birth of children signaled creolization at its most elemental level as enslaved women and men forged familial relationships across ethnic and national boundaries. Myriad African and Afro-European pasts came together in the Barbadian present. Bette Madigascoe and Dutch Moll, for example, lived alongside mulatto Toney, a boy named Mannuel, and a woman called Aimbo.[36] Lilly named one of her sons Callebar, perhaps in honor or remembrance of her own homeland.[37]

When the planter Henry Drax departed Barbados temporarily for London, he left detailed instructions for the overseer of his plantation. By the 1670s Drax enslaved three generations on his plantation, exemplified by Moncky Nocco—"who has beene an Excellent slave . . . his mother, wifes, and family."[38] By identifying Moncky Nocco as head of the family, Drax effectively appropriated Nocco into Drax's own notion of gender and authority and ignored the probability that, inside the family and the black community on the plantation, as an elder woman, a parent, and a grandparent, Nocco's mother undoubtedly occupied an honored and influential position. Nocco's family's African past is made visible as Drax identifies more than one wife and is reinforced by Drax's preference for "Cormantee" to be purchased in his absence, possibly a reflection on Nocco. Newly arrived West Africans would mean a constant renewal of the family's ties to their ancestral home and to the vaunted position of an elder woman. While Drax's respect for Moncky Nocco's family ties was unusual (Drax instructed the overseer to distribute extra rations to Nocco, who portioned them out to his family, in reward for his good service), his misunderstanding of the Nocco family configurations was probably typical. Typical too would be the need of Moncky Nocco's mother to function carefully in two forms of the same families—one of which she headed, the other of which was headed by her son. The Nocco family's generational ties and cultural bilingualism became increasingly representative of the lives of enslaved

Africans in Barbados. Throughout the island cultural transformation occurred as women born in West Africa gave birth to West Indian children.

In 1668, on the 97-acre plantation of John Weale and Romas Clarke in St. James, fifteen men and twenty-three women labored in the cane fields and boiling house. The names of a handful of these men and women—Corminty Maria, Cormanty Nanny, Cormanty Gunny, New Bayers, and New Mingoe—reflect either their origin or their status as recent arrivals to the island. Whether in an attempt to manufacture some sense of stability or maintain hold on their humanity, more than half these enslaved women had set in motion the inevitable process of transforming the African past by becoming mothers—six had one child, three had two, one had three, and two had four each.[39] Epho Jenne's son was simply named Jack.[40] Whether chosen by his mother or by his owner, the name "Jack" signified major change—both for Jack and for his mother. Both the man who owned them and the woman whose name suggests her African ethnicity must have understood the difference between "Jack" and "Epho Jenne." For Epho Jenne, the birth of Jack in Barbados was transformative. It marked the realities of creolization and the violation visited on men and women whose single names reflect at the very least the encroachment of English cultural referents and at the worst disrespect and disregard. Obliterated and mispronounced African names did violence to a crucial part of African culture and symbolized the willingness of Europeans to engage in many other kinds of violence toward the Africans they enslaved.

If women enslaved in Barbados who survived a Middle Passage that sapped them of strength, hope, and the tangibility of their future, looked toward childbirth with the notion of reclaiming at least one familiar cultural process, they must have been shaken by the new terms and consequences of reproduction. Jack would speak English as well as Epho Jenne's native tongue. He would remain uncircumcised. He would come of age in a society in which his ethnic identity merged with that of people his mother saw as strangers—Mende, Akan, Bakongo, Madagascar—his own Ibo heritage gradually melding into something new. But, of course, the very fact of Jack's birth would have been part of the process by which those strangers became known. Whether it was as attendants at his birth or as those who taught him to communicate across linguistic lines, schooled him in safe behavior when out of Epho Jenne's sight, or cared from him after her death—or for her after his—those "strangers" became connected to Jack at his birth and through him engaged in both his and their creolization. Faced with the shifting meanings and consequences of childbirth, enslaved women staked an enormous claim by bringing children into the world. A planter might presume tht he owned her, but a woman's children could become woven into the fabric of her assertion of autonomy, even in the face of constant challenge.

The relationship between production and reproduction was fraught with violence and the threat of familial disruption. Enslaved women would have been keenly aware of the oppositional stance of a slaveowner who, in the words of a woman enslaved in the nineteenth century, "had little to will his heirs, except such property as he was unable to grasp."[41] Staking the claim of parental authority meant inviting vulnerability. On William Brey's plantation in St. Michaels, there were more than twice as many women as men. In the years preceding the 1662 sale of Brey's property, three of the thirteen women he enslaved became mothers as they worked the 56-acre sugar plantation. Maria had two children and Peg and Nambo each had one. Brey's deed of sale to James Cowes and George Neeham anticipated the possibility of future sales. All property—"negroes, horses, or cowes"— could be sold in the future except for "Nambo a negroe woman with her child Grace and the rest of the Negroe children."[42] Nambo may have felt secure as a result of this provision, assuming she knew of it, but Maria and Peg clearly could not. Nor could the women on the St. Michaels planta- tion—should they be aware of the terms of their sale—look forward to childbirth, knowing before they even conceived them that they would be severed from their children. Brey's stipulation that Nambo and her child not be sold away from the land had multiple implications. Brey's relation- ship with Nambo led him to protect her from separation from her child and home. The relationship, however, had its limitations; it was not endur- ing enough to lead to her manumission. Nor did Brey extend this "compas- sion" regarding the separation of parents and children to other mothers. While the children could not be sold, he did not offer their mothers such protection. The children's value resided in their ongoing connection to the plantation. Their emotional needs would have to be met by Nambo if eco- nomic necessity required their own mothers to be sold away.

This kind of intricate attention to the details of legacy grew out of the particularities of small-scale slaveholdings. Faced with limited resources, middling planters divided their property with care. However, as we saw in Chapter 3, in the moment of "summoning the scribe" the intimacy of owner-slave interaction on small plantations or within households rarely worked to the benefit of emerging black families. Bell, Maria, and Minikin found themselves bequeathed, along with a man named Jack, to Elizabeth

Lolely's son John. In the process, they were separated from their children—a "small negro girl named Jane" and "a small negro called Betty"—who went to Lolely's two daughters.[43] The fate of Orage, a woman enslaved by Patrick Dun, was worse. Dun willed the child Peter, presumably Orage's son, to his son George. Another son, James, in turn acquired possession of Orage. Orage then had to witness the replication of her own fate on her daughter. Dun gave Annis, a female child, to his wife Catherine under the instruction that "the first negroe child boy or girl that shall be borne out of the body of . . . Annis" would be given to Robert Dun.[44]

John Redwood owned only nineteen acres of land, which he worked alongside Besse and Sanders. His death meant probable separation for the two, who may or may not have grown attached to one another. He bequeathed Sanders to his wife and Besse (who was more valuable because of her reproductive potential) to his only son.[45] Samuell Adams's death meant certain agony for Jugg. He bequeathed her to his son while her daughter, Great Dido, went to his daughter Margarett.[46] Similarly, Thomas Morris promised his children equal division of Besse's existing and future children, acting on the understanding of the plantation household as it had evolved by the 1660s.[47] Anxious to provide for their white families with small numbers of black bodies, slaveowners did so at the expense of ties of consanguinity and bonds of affection among the enslaved. Enslaved women who had shared living space and worked side by side with slaveowners would find that all pretense of intimacy or even recognition dissolved in the face of small-scale slaveowners' reflections on their own ties of family and affiliation.

"Coming" to Carolina: Complications of Creolization and Intra-Atlantic Slave Trading

While it was quite probable that families separated by the final wishes of slaveowners would stay on the same island, it also happened that slaveowners' movements could put much greater distances between members of families or plantation communities. There was no smooth linearity to this transformation from individuals to community. Well before the secondary slave trade that so devastated the lives of the enslaved in nineteenth-century America, early American settlers crisscrossed the Caribbean and the American Atlantic in search of fortunes. In the era of the slave trade, while those forced movements may have actually reconnected enslaved Africans with others from a common linguistic or geographic background as Coromantee from Barbados found Coromantee from South Carolina; for many, a second or third sea voyage would only mean more layers of uncertainty, illness, and fear.

Many black women and men made voyages from Barbados to Carolina. The women Jugg and Dilloe and their sons were part of a group of five men, eight women, and five children who made the journey from Barbados to the new settlement of Carolina before 1672. As testimony to their earlier lives together, three of the children bore the names of the men who accompanied them. The familiarity of the members of the group may have somewhat eased their fear and uncertainty as they left Barbados. Like all sea crossings, the journey to the new colony was marked by uncertainty. Few, except the wealthiest slaveowners, could shoulder the economic risk of transporting large groups of enslaved women and men during initial years of the settlement. Sent with George Thompson, a merchant and member of council in Barbados, the eighteen were lucky to travel together and find comfort in each other's company.[48]

Most of the first black arrivals, however, came in much smaller and less reassuring pairs.[49] These were couples brought by settlers unsure of their ability to survive in the new settlement and unwilling to risk large-scale transportation of enslaved property, but probably secure in their belief that in transporting a man and a woman they transported the possibility of future slaveholdings. Some settlers eschewed the transport of enslaved men and women altogether because it was too risky financially. Even as the source of labor rested primarily on the shoulders of the enslaved, some brought only indentured servants. Indeed, in the first years of settlement, servants outnumbered free whites four or five to one.[50]

But settlers continually brought enslaved women and men to the new colony in small numbers. Sara's experience was common. A twenty-one-year-old woman enslaved in Barbados by John Ladson, Sara accompanied Ladson alone to Carolina in 1678, leaving behind friends and family and fearing the consequences of what was possibly her second transatlantic sea voyage. One can only assume that the fact that Sara traveled alone with Ladson exponentially increased the probability that he would demand sexual contact with her, which would have magnified her predictable fear of sea travel, a frontier outpost, and the loss of any superficial or significant relationships on Barbados. Her upheaval and isolation continued shortly after their arrival, when Ladson sold her.[51] When Sara arrived in the new settlement, it had been only a few years since the first load of passengers from England and Barbados disembarked from the *Carolina* at Old Town, on the west bank of the Ashley River, in spring 1670.[52] Her initial sense of shock would have been profound, but despite the changes in place and servitude, she would soon have made connections with other Africans and their descendants. A mere decade after the earliest settlers arrived, one observer noted that "without [Negro slaves] a Planter can never do any great matter."[53] Sara's Barbadian past would serve as a point of connection to many other enslaved women and men. The new colonial venture on the mainland brought white and black men and women together from throughout British America, but as Peter Wood has shown, after only two years of relocations, "almost half of the whites and considerably more than half of the blacks in the colony had come from Barbados."[54] Once transported to the new colony, enslaved transports found familiarity with others who had been enslaved in Barbados and together they adjusted to the new regimes of forced labor and the new site in which it was to be performed.

In the context of involvement in a new settlement, those who had come to a full and nuanced understanding of life in one slave society found themselves thrown into an entirely new colonial settlement where, suddenly, fixed notions of race, labor, and identity became fluid again. For those individuals, the creolization process began anew. When John Yeamans left the island of Barbados for Carolina in 1671, he entrusted "Hannah and hir children" to his wife. She was not, therefore, among the eight enslaved men and women Yeamans took to Carolina on the initial voyage. The year she spent in Barbados with members of her community following his departure must have been filled with uncertainty. It was not until the following year that her future became clear, when Hannah and two of her children—Jupeter and Joane—came to Carolina. Yeamans forced her to leave her son Tony behind.[55] Three years after Hannah's arrival in the mainland colony, Yeamans died. She and her children were among the twenty-six slaves who survived him in the new colony. Some five years later, Hannah had managed to accumulate enough autonomy and capital to return to the island of Barbados, alone this time. Through her own work, or the benevolence of an owner, she was manumitted and baptized in the parish of St. Michaels on January 20, 1681. Records for the parish record her baptism and note that, she had "gone for Carolina."[56] Thus, over the course of a decade, Hannah journeyed, at the very least, three times between the two colonies.

Each time she disembarked she stepped into familiar worlds that she inhabited with her children and her peers, worlds in which material and symbolic cultures formed enduring links, connecting the lives lived in the mainland with those in the English Caribbean. Hannah would hear the strains of banjo music on both the mainland and the island colony, and would understand the power of Obeah to either heal or hurt.[57] But in Carolina, instead of an island transformed into a landscape dominated by "gardens," where trees and forests had given way to rows upon rows of sugar cane, Hannah and her children would find themselves acclimating to a wilderness. Hannah may have had a memory of an uncleared and forested Barbados, but her children certainly would not. Women in early Carolina would work dispersed across the lowcountry, at cattlepens or as part of groups of workers processing tar or clearing land on isolated tracts. The shock of Carolina would run deep, but, after an assessment of the situation, might turn into appreciation for the absence of supervision and the diffuse nature of authority in the early period of the colony. Nonetheless, as we have seen, such characteristics of the frontier economy could be misinterpreted as an egalitarianism that would leave one's autonomy intact when an owner died; should Hannah fall victim to that misapprehension, she would—as would her peers—have been disappointed by the illusory autonomy of the new colony.

As time passed, familial and other personal connections between black Barbadians and Carolinians faded and Africans and Afro-West Indians in Carolina and throughout the Southern mainland developed ties and identities distinct from their recently shared geographies. The connections between the islands and the mainland, which have primarily been understood by historians in terms of the political and socioeconomic factors that affected slaveowners, would be experienced quite differently for the enslaved. While she could not always dictate the circumstances, Hannah's children, alive or dead in at least two English colonies, influenced her travels. Her return to Barbados (in search of Tony?) and subsequent re-return to Carolina (having buried him?) positioned her in her community as a woman whose identity was forged in the crux of motherhood and mobility.

Hannah was not alone in experiencing mobility and motherhood as linked. Many of the women who moved from place to place did so as mothers. Abinibah, for example, was sold in 1705 with her son Cuffee to a merchant in Charlestown. Five years later, ill health forced the family that then owned her to move back to Barbados. In 1710, Abinibah also moved in the company of a woman named Cornelia and "one Negro boy named Morat," leaving Cuffee behind—dead or alive. Apparently without all her children—for Cuffee is lost to her and Morat could have been either her or

Cornelia's son—she moved from a merchant to a planter household, and left those she knew to endure a sea voyage to a place that may or may not have been familiar to her and her small child.[58] On Abinibah and Morat's journey to Barbados, a larger group of enslaved women and men from Carolina joined them. To clear his debt to a Barbadian planter, Stephen Gibbs of Charlestown sent eight enslaved men and women to an island planter. Old Abigail and her adult daughter Bess may or may not have been related to Old Jack Smith and Young Jack. Similarly, Jupiter and the boy Little Jupiter could have been connected to the women by ties of family or affinity. Lowrus and the girl Nancy are the only two of the eight not clearly related to one another by name or inference.[59] Together they endured what was for some a second sea crossing to meet the needs of a would-be planter.

Men and women enslaved on mainland colonies whose roots lay in the West Indies as well as West Africa occupied a difficult position. Over time, a Caribbean background became a mark of difference rather than a point of connection for new arrivals to Carolina. As slave traders imported growing numbers of enslaved men and women from the African coast, the Barbadian roots of the South Carolina slave community grew increasingly tenuous. Over the course of the eighteenth century, enslaved persons from Barbados—and the West Indies in general—fell from more than half the total enslaved population in Carolina to as little as 15 to 20 percent, and the influence and importance of the Barbadian past slowly receded from the collective Carolina experience.[60] Even before their proportion began to diminish, the very circumstances of their arrival separated them from men and women who had survived the Middle Passage. The passage from Barbados to Carolina did not produce the same experience as the lengthy journey from the West African coast with its diseases, crowded conditions, inadequate food and water, and high mortality rates.[61] Unlike the men and women arriving from West Africa, those coming from Barbados came in small cargoes. Between 1717 and 1719 the average ship from the African coast arrived in Charlestown with 72 men and women, while ships coming from the West Indies averaged only 14 passengers of African descent.[62] Those transported from Barbados did not experience the same degree of terror of the unknown. They came along with slaveowners, sharing with them an awareness of their mutual past, an anticipation of their future, and an understanding of the owner-slave relationship as it had already developed. That understanding would become increasingly important as they struggled to situate themselves among other Africans in the new colony. Their familiarity with the expectations and configurations of slavery in the Americas would move some into the role of mediator between newly arrived Africans and owners anxious to clarify their position in the colony.

Parenting and Loss in Carolina

Prior to the rice boom, black women enslaved in Carolina came primarily from American ports, and laid a foundation of sorts.[63] As the economy and the population of enslaved women and men grew, African imports increased, creating a population that was both increasingly African and consistently creole—enslaved persons who either had children or were themselves acculturated to the Americas.[64] Even as African import numbers outpaced Carolina-born slaves, both the value and the danger of women as reproducers were absolutely clear to slaveowners. In 1714, Carolina legislators noted "the number of negroes do extremely increase in this province, and through the afflicting providence of God, the white persons do not proportionally multiply."[65] Probate records indicate that, faced with a black population in which men continued to outnumber women, slaveowners seemed to balance their slaveholdings to assure a steady, if outnumbered female presence on many plantations. Slaveholdings balanced along gender lines meant that women enslaved in the new colony would find themselves, again or still, faced with the presumption or even expectation that they should create families. Between 1711 and 1729, 114 wills and bills of sale of Carolina slaveowners survive. While they are outnumbered, enslaved women are found in almost all extant slaveowning documents in the period. Of those, only fifteen documents in which slaveowners identified enslaved adults by name or sex contain no women (see Table 7). Like their counterparts in Barbados, Carolina slaveowners found that newly enslaved Africans were the primary means of immediately increasing their own wealth and the size of their slaveholdings. No one articulated a position on the logic of "breeding" the enslaved. Nonetheless, the inherent supposition that racial slavery enabled slaveowners to practice a slaveownership overladen with reproductive capacity prevailed, and women and men caught in its grasp would have fully understood the parameters of their most personal lives. In a rare explicit example of the potential for slaveowners to enact violence and manipulation through the potential children of an enslaved woman, the Indian woman Diana "with a young child at her breast" was to remain enslaved "until she hath borne another child," at which point her owner willed her manumission.[66]

TABLE 7. WOMEN AND CHILDREN IN SLAVEOWNERS' WILLS, SOUTH CAROLINA, 1711–29

	N	Percent
Number of wills	314	—
Wills containing slaves	114	—
Wills identifying slaves by name	97	85*
Wills identifying only men	15	28
Wills identifying women	82	72
Wills identifying children	50	43
Wills identifying parents	19	17
Wills using term "increase"	37	32

*Percentages of total documents containing slaves.
Sources: Secretary of the Province Records, 1711–1719, 1711–1717, 1714–1717, 1709–1725, 1714–1719, 1719–1721, 1721–1722, 1722–1726; and Will Book 1732–1737; South Carolina Department of Archives and History

Even as slaveowners clarified the connection between racial slavery and reproduction, the physiological and emotional realities of enslavement on the colonial frontier left many women without children. The realities of enslavement for women in Carolina and the definition of their "increase" as property provided ample reason for enslaved women to fear childbirth. Only a year after the death of their owner in 1710, for example, three of ten women and men on Dorothy Daniell's plantation had died. Surrounded by death on a struggling colonial frontier, Mary, Flora, Betty Comber, and Susanna not surprisingly remained childless. Alongside Panto, Joe, and Bransoe, the women would spend the next three years working for various landowners in order to pay off their owner's debt before being put to the "use and benefitt" of a minor grandson. In that context, it was unlikely that they would have children in the future.[67] Although the terms of the next three years of enslavement provided them with opportunities to forge connections with other enslaved women and men on plantations around the area, they could hardly have felt secure about their future.

Most women and men enslaved in Carolina in the first decades of the eighteenth century would have had a sense of uncertainty about their future in the colony. From the moment their predecessors set foot on the banks of the Ashley River—coupled but isolated on frontier outposts, their ability to feed and shelter themselves inextricably tied to labor performed alongside their owners—women would work in many ways. Their reproductive lives were tied to the life and work of the colony. Alongside planters' demands on their time and labor, enslaved women in Carolina also worked to construct families for the children they bore, and they did so in ways that were not always transparent to white observers. In 1706, the Society for the Propagation of the Gospel in Foreign Parts sent Francis LeJau to Carolina. In letters home, he critiqued Carolina society, both free and enslaved.[68] LeJau's letters home reflect his palpable distress about Carolina society, both black and white. Like many missionaries the Society sent to Carolina, LeJau focused on the ongoing difficulties he experienced in his efforts to reach the black population.

The evil I complain of is the constant and promiscuous cohabitating of slaves of different sexes and nations together. When a man or a woman's fancy dos alter about his party they throw up one another and take others which they also change when they please—this is a general sin for the exceptions are so few they are hardly worth mentioning.[69]

The "promiscuous disorder" of the enslaved would become an ongoing theme in LeJau's reports as, to his frustration, while refusing to "better order" their marriage choices, enslaved women and men protected their ability to impose internally derived order on their most intimate decisions.[70] LeJau's religious imperative made him unable to see anything but chaos in the personal lives of the enslaved, when in fact autonomous emotional choices represented hard-won freedom from interference and Christianity. The few enslaved men and women who incorporated Christian notions of nuptial morality into their marriage choices in Carolina, were "hardly worth mentioning."[71]

As they worried about the behavior of black couples, other Anglican clergymen from the Society for the Propagation of the Gospel turned a more hopeful eye toward black children, seeing them as targets for proselytizing throughout the first decade of the eighteenth century. In 1707, the Rev. William Dunn of Charlestown complained to the society of his "extreme difficult[y]" in persuading slaveowners to allow him to give religious instructions to the enslaved. "However I have persuaded some of them to let their slaves come at last to hear Sermon every Sunday, and likewise to cause the Children of their slaves to be taught to read."[72]

Dunn knew that enough children existed to make the likelihood of instructing them a significant inroad in the efforts to Christianize the black community.[73] In 1708, Governor Johnson estimated the colony's population for the lords proprietors. The population of enslaved men and women had grown since his last report; there were 300 more men and 200 more women than there had been in 1703. He reported that enslaved men outnumbered enslaved women (1,800 men to 1,100 women) but that since 1703 the number of "Negro children slaves" had doubled (from 600 to 1,200). This represented a higher rate of increase than the rate among white children (from 1,200 to 1,700), and a clear indication that childbirth and childrearing were integral to the experience of enslavement, even in such a new colony.[74] In the first decade of the eighteenth century, the enslaved population of South Carolina thus contained roughly equal numbers of men, women, and children. Prior to the 1720s, when a spike in African imports would lead to male majorities, Carolina slaveowners lived surrounded by the effect of relatively equitable sex ratios—the black children that populated the colony. As a result, they would, to the best of their ability, consistently work to maintain demographically balanced slave populations on their plantations, which in turn would speak volumes to the women and men they enslaved.

In his study of sex ratios and birth rates among blacks and whites in one South Carolina parish in 1726, Peter Wood contrasts birthrates among enslaved women with those of free white women to illustrate the toll work took on the bodies of women who might otherwise have been mothers.[75] I would argue, however, that the comparison of black to white women, while essential to our understanding of the ways slavery mutated black women's reproductive rates in contrast to those of women wh were not enslaved, draws attention away from the essential fact that, despite the worsening conditions of enslavement, black women continued to bring children into the world. The knowledge that in St. George's Parish in 1726 the average white woman had more than two children (2.24) while the average black woman had just over one child (1.17) highlights the trauma that accompanied the intense labor regime and dislocation of enslavement in the colony. But for their mothers and fathers, those 1.17 children became a significant part of their experience of and response to enslavement, even if the meaning embedded in their bodies is far less visible then the children themselves.

In 1713, Arrabell would illustrate clearly and heartbreakingly the tension that was at stake for enslaved women throughout the diaspora. Arrabell lived with seven women and nine men in Berkeley County. Three of the women were mothers and a fourth two-year-old child was cared for on the plantation in the absence of a named parent. The population of enslaved Africans would shortly eclipse that of white settlers, and Arrabell and the women around her may have begun to feel portents of the changes that were about to engulf the colony. They must have watched the aftermath of many slaveowners' deaths and searched for a way to shield themselves and their children from separation and distribution among their heirs. Through the birth of their children, enslaved women may have seen a means to reappropriate what should have been theirs all along. Arrabell's child's name appears to indicate poignantly the struggle inherent in reproduction in this most unstable moment in the development of a slave society. Arrabell called her child "Mines"—as she could little else in the burgeoning slave society of South Carolina.[76] And, of course, even as she staked this claim, she and her child were sold. The next sale may have been the one that irrevocably reminded her that Mines could not actually be hers.

Those women who could and did keep their children close were involved in a series of negotiated relationships with slaveowners. In 1706, Parthenia was assigned to tend to a two-year-old white child, Sarah Sindrey, who had been orphaned her mother died. While raising her own children, Primus, Lucy, and Hagar, Parthenia cared for the child under the supervision of her guardians. The degree to which Parthenia was able to focus on her own growing family—she had two more children by 1711—while also watching Sarah Sindrey is not clear. Neither are Parthenia's feelings as Sarah's older brother Gilson Clapp left to trade for slaves in the Gambia once he came of age. When he returned in 1718, her need to protect herself and her family would certainly have caused her to refrain from expressing any criticism of this venture to his young sister. Meanwhile, Parthenia would watch her own daughter come of age as Hagar made Parthenia a grandmother only fifteen days after Parthenia herself gave birth to twins. The next year, Hagar had her second child and was shortly thereafter "delivered to her mistress"—Sarah, who, at the age of seventeen, had married early that year. Thus, the child she had cared for became the owner of Parthenia's own child and grandchildren. Lines of authority were complicated things. Hagar named her second child Nanny, presumably in homage to an

Old negroe woman called Nanny good for nothing which [Gilson Clapp] took away . . . and kept on his plantation and would not cause her to return tho he was often requested soe to doe.

Sarah's guardian's pique at Clapp's obstinate refusal to relinquish Nanny is suggestive. Perhaps Nanny was someone to whom Clapp felt connected; perhaps, given Hagar's regard for her, she was a woman senior to Parthenia, a grandparent on the baby's father's side. In any case, Hagar then had two older women in her life with whom she was connected by either blood or affection. Thus Parthenia's daughter and grandchildren were indeed hers, at least for a time. But Sarah's marriage did not assure her future in the colony or her husband's financial success, which meant that Parthenia and Hagar and Nanny's extraordinary lives together remained always interruptible.[77]

Parthenia and her large family lived in close proximity to the Sindreys. It is easy to imagine the stress that proximity caused. Shared space occurred on both small and large holdings and undoubtedly both fostered and destroyed ties of affection between enslaved women and men. In accordance with the terms of his wife's will in 1711, for example, William Beard sold "one negro man named James one Negroe woman his wife named Sarah and one negroe girl the daughter of James and Sarah . . . named Jenny."[78] The family had been enslaved in Charlestown by a cooper, and necessarily shared small spaces both with one another and with the couple who owned them. Indeed, the close quarters of life in Charlestown may have been instrumental as James and Sarah met, connected, and brought a child into the world.

It is difficult to correlate the relationship between plantation size, ownership patterns, and reproduction. Probate records offer only snapshots of communities that were in motion. For Mary, Diana, Elray, Sausee, and Sabyna, a 400-acre plantation owned by Peter Robert on the south bank of the Santee River shaped a far different experience of enslavement than the Charlestown house in which Parthenia labored.[79] Like Mrs. Beard, Peter Robert constructed his slaveholdings with an eye toward gender parity. These five women worked the plantation alongside seven men, negotiating connections under the eye of a slaveowner who certainly hoped for reproductive fruit in addition to the provisions and staple crops they produced. While the greater diversity of the community of twelve men and women might appear more conducive to intimate ties, other factors such as work regimes, disease, lack of familiarity, and ethnic diversity could have impaired them. Seven men and five women also labored on Robert Fry's land, but not one of these women remained childless. Jenny and Sue respectively had six and four children. Appraisers listed Peter and Frank with their mother Moll, while Betty and Nanny each had a single child.[80] On the other hand, of thirty-seven women enslaved by Thomas Lynch, only two had children, this despite the fact that appraisers named eight of the women as "wife" or partner to a particular man.[81] On the small plantation belonging to Henry Livingston, both women enslaved there, Phillice and Satyra, had children. These women lived and worked alongside seven men. In an environment of such limited female community, the extraordinary disparity in their numbers would profoundly affect many aspects of their lives on the Livingston plantation, including, presumably, the ways they parented their children.[82] No matter what the proportion of women or the numbers of women with living children, those enslaved in Carolina would be keenly aware of the presumptions about their potential for reproduction.

As the rice boom took its toll and natural increase gave way to an increasingly African-born population, children born in the 1730s must have appeared increasingly precious to the black men and women around them. At the same time, many enslaved adults may have seen the presence of children as yet another window of vulnerability through which slaveowners had access to their lives and might have given thanks that fewer children existed to attract the attention of speculating slaveowners. Only one slaveowner's will in the 1730s explicitly separated parents and children, but it is impossible to ascertain how many other parents and children lost one another in the bequests of dying slaveowners.[83] William Swinton enslaved more than fifty adults on his plantations, seventeen of them women. Unlike most of his peers, Swinton singled out none of these women or men in his will. Rather, he divided them straightforwardly between his wife and children.[84] His divisions cut through the heart of the enslaved community. Twelve of the women had no children, although their monetary value in the inventory—on par with the value of the men—reflects the centrality of their work in the field. Judith, Beck, Rose, Sobina, and Mall, the mothers on the plantation, shared something with each other that may have separated them from the majority of the women on the plantation.[85] The experience of childbirth separated one slaveholding from another just as it separated some women from others.

As the community of men and women enslaved in Carolina grew, it became less homogeneous. Enslaved Africans from as far north as the Upper Guinea Coast and as far south as Angola would find themselves sharing living quarters. Similarly, men and women born in the West Indies would be grouped alongside those born in Carolina or in the Bight of Benin. Added to the mix of ethnic identity would be the factor of parenthood. As women such as the five mothers on Swinton's plantation labored alongside the twelve childless women, their children may have bridged differences in origin and language. Yet their pregnancies may also have erected a barrier between them and the other twelve women, who could have seen their pregnancies as evidence of an indistinct separation between the slaveowners' desires and the safety of enslaved women. As they labored for

Swinton, these seventeen women would struggle to overcome many differences—their identities as parents among them.[86]

Women who appear in the historical record alone could have been mothers of children who had died or could have been owned by men who ignored their motherhood or took their children from them. Despite the fact that some increase occurred during the 1720s, for example, mothers appear explicitly in only nineteen (23 percent) of the 82 wills and sales in which women are named (see Table 7 above)—constituting a total of only twenty-four women such as "Hagar and her children named Combo and London."[87] But children, described in the wills as either "boys or girls" or "children," appear in 50 of those 82 records, or more than half the records containing women. This is an important contrast with the available evidence for the previous decade. In the first decade of the eighteenth century (see Table 3 above), 53 percent of the documents that identified women also identified children and 40 percent of inventories itemizing women also identify women as mothers. Although more children are listed in slaveowners' records between 1711 and 1729, fewer are listed alongside parents. While this could be evidence that separating children and parents was commonplace, it may also reflect a slaveowner's reluctance, even as he or she took careful stock of the varied fertility of the women they enslaved, to assign the emotionally loaded category of "mother" to an enslaved woman.

The absence of explicit designations of enslaved women as parents, despite the appearance of children in 60 percent (50 of 82 records) of these records which span the boom years of Carolina's rice economy, suggests that as slaveowners focused their energies on devising successful export crops and bolstering the slave population with rising imports, in the face of the economic possibilities of parent-child relationships among black men and women slaveowners grew increasingly unwilling to even tacitly acknowledge the emotional qualities of such relationships. According to wills and inventories in South Carolina from 1711–29, 58 percent of slaveowners owned populations in which the number of women equaled or exceeded the number of men (see Table 8). Sixty-five percent of all enslaved persons mentioned in these transactions shared the experience of enslavement with members of the opposite sex. The experience of the enslaved in South Carolina was not exceptional. Enslaved men and women on the island of Montserrat experienced their enslavement in similar terms. Seventy-eight percent of all slaveowners enslaved women, and of those who used women workers, 67 percent enslaved them in numbers equal to or greater than men. A remarkably similar pattern existed in St. Christopher

TABLE 8. MALE:FEMALE SEX RATIOS IN SLAVEOWNERS' WILLS AND INVENTORIES, SOUTH CAROLINA, 1711–29

	Number of slaveholdings
Male majorities—34	
6:0	1
4:0	2
2:0	3
1:0	12
4:1	1
3:1	2
2:1	3
3:2	3
5:3	1
8:5	1
7:5	1
7:6	1
Female majorities—31	
1:2	5
2:3	3
3:4	2
5:7	1
5:8	2
4:7	1
1:3	3
1:4	3
1:5	1
0:1	6
0:2	3
0:3	3
0:4	1
Equal ratios	
1:1	17

Sources: Secretary of the Province Records, 1711–1719, 1711–1717, 1714–1717, 1709–1725, 1714–1719, 1719–1721, 1721–1722, 1722–1726; and Will Book 1732–1737; South Carolina Department of Archives and History.

and Montserrat; in St. Christopher 83 percent of all slaveowning households enslaved women and 78 percent of those enslaved women in numbers equal to or greater than men (see Tables 9 and 10).

Sex-balanced slaveholdings reflect slaveowners' pragmatic deployment of labor categories along newly inscribed gender lines, but they do not say much about the toll of rice cultivation and sugar fields on body and spirit.

TABLE 9. WOMEN, MEN, AND CHILDREN IN SLAVEOWNERS' HOUSEHOLDS, ST. CHRISTOPHER, 1707/1708

	N	Percent
Households	227	—
Slaveowners	188	100
Owners of women	188	83*
Owners of women in equal or greater numbers than men	147	78*
Owners of men only	27	12*
Owners of women only	36	16*
Owners of women and children	138	73**
Owners of women and no children	1	—
Owners of children and no women	1	—

*Percentages of slaveowning households. **Percentages of slaveowning households with women.
Source: Oliver, *Caribbeana*, 3: 132–39.

TABLE 10. WOMEN, MEN, AND CHILDREN IN SLAVEOWNERS' HOUSEHOLDS, MONTSERRAT CENSUS, 1729

	N	Percent
Households	245	—
Slaveowners	213	100
Owners of women	166	78*
Owners of women in equal or greater numbers than men	112	67*
Owners of men only	9	4*
Owners of women only	22	19*
Owners of women and children	176	82**
Owners of women and no children	20	—
Owners of children and no women	—	—

*Percentages of slaveowning households. **Percentages of slaveowning households with women.
Source: Oliver, *Caribbeana*, 4: 302–11.

Women owned on larger plantations might very well have experienced creolization in the complete absence of childbirth. From George Logan's perspective, his property was plagued by childlessness. Logan, a wealthy owner of land and slaves, mentioned sixty-three enslaved persons, including twenty-five women, in his 1720 will.[88] Despite the gender imbalance on his plantation, Logan recognized the importance of a female presence among those he enslaved. In the terms of his bequests he spread men and women into even groups of twelve to twenty, each of which he connected to a parcel of land. Logan bequeathed the women "with their increase" but did not indicate whether the division of the men and women he enslaved preserved or severed their emotional ties. The terms of his will ultimately forced the eight women and twelve men bequeathed to his eldest son to reconfigure or abandon their ties to the five women and seven men bequeathed to his daughter. And while the men and women Logan parceled out to his children found themselves enslaved on a relatively large plantation, Logan designated not one woman as "mother," nor did he name a single person "child." For these women and men, Logan's appreciating for balanced sex ratios did not translate into visible family formation, although it is important not to presume that the invisibility of these women and men's emotional lives was more profound than that of women and men who did have children.

Elsewhere, on the larger plantations of Richard Beresford, where the sex ratio among the enslaved mirrored Logan's, four of six women were listed with "suckling children" at one plantation and two of seven had "suckling children" at the other.[89] When Edward Hext died in 1742, only one of seven women on his plantation had no children; all the others had two or more, culminating in "Judey and her 5 Children, Jack, Will, Phebee, Lucy, and Satira."[90] Outnumbered by men three to one, these women and their children brought themselves, the men they embraced, and the children they bore into a community in the process of creolization, but their experience of creolization was in no way less violent than that of their childless counterparts.

For slaveowners, arranging their property so as to encourage reproduction could have only positive outcomes. And, indeed, a third of those slaveowners who transferred enslaved women in their wills or sales explicitly referred to the potential for enslaved women to have children by utilizing the term "increase" (see Table 7 above). As long as planters maintained relatively balanced sex ratios among the enslaved, large plantations meant regular interaction with a variety of persons of the opposite sex. With such interaction came opportunities for collective and emotional sustenance in the face of an increasingly demanding labor system, but it also carried with it the increased exposure to slaveowners' interference. For example, Doll, enslaved in Charlestown by Tayier Hall, had two daughters at the time he sold her. Sarah, on the other hand, remained childless. Hall anticipated more children from both women when he sold them "with their and every of their increase," and it remains unclear as to which woman had more successfully navigated the terrain of her enslavement.[91]

For enslaved women and men, these connections brought increased vulnerability. The threat of the community's dissolution loomed every time a slaveowner became ill, and upon an owner's death, that threat could be realized in a way that the enslaved experienced viscerally. In 1739, Andrew Broughton, for example, enslaved more than twenty-six men and women. In his lists of adult men and women Broughton identified Lawrence as Jack's father, Phillis as the mother of Duck, Duck as the mother of Bristoll, Grace as the mother of another Bristol, and Lucy as the mother of Nanny. While he carefully recorded these familial ties, he did so only to avoid confusion over names, for he allowed none of these parents and children, with the exception of Duck and Bristoll, to stay together. The children went separately to his wife and daughters, and the parents became part of his son's inheritance. When Broughton bequeathed enslaved women and men with "their issue and increase," he did so having already witnessed generations form among the men and women he enslaved and thus with the full knowledge that he was destroying families.[92]

When Jeremiah Miles died, he left land and slaves to both his wife and his two daughters. He named, alongside "their [present] and future increase," six enslaved women as part of his wife's inheritance.[93] These six women would leave the eleven other women and sixteen men with whom they had labored. The bonds forged through shared living had deepened through the presence of children. At the time of the planter's death, nine of the fifteen women were mothers, each with a single child. Neither his will nor the inventory of his property suggest to which men these women were connected, but it seems fair to assume that these men and women and children understood themselves to be members of a community in the process of reproducing itself. This last fact must have been noted by Miles, among those he purchased were "boys and girls" carefully matched—six of each at the time of his death.[94] The bequest of these women and men to Miles's daughter certainly wrought havoc on ties of community. They became dower, and upon the marriage of a Miles woman, they would be absorbed into the plantation holdings of her husband. The consequences of such marriages for the enslaved would have to be dealt with when they transpired. But for women on Miles's plantation such as Flora—the mother of an infant child, Hagar, at the time of Miles's death—the birth of their children and their connection to the men who fathered them set in motion a ess of community formation and acculturation that was hardly unusual in the Carolina low country.

By the end of the 1730s, white Carolinians imported more than two thousand enslaved Africans a year through Charlestown. The black population would grow to 36,700 by 1740, more than twice as large as the white.[95] Gilson Clapps (Sarah Sindrey's brother who spent time trading for slaves in the Gambia before settling in Carolina), like Miles, enslaved equal numbers of men, women, boys, and girls on his plantation. Unlike the women on Miles' plantation, however, only one of those eighteen women had a child. Clapps's childhood memory of Parthenia's fecundity must have taunted him as an adult; while he looked forward to "future Issue and Increase" from these women, at the time of his death that optimism had not been borne out.[96] It is not possible to ascertain the origins of the women on the Clapps plantations, but they may well have been predominantly African, a fact that would have affected both their fertility and their proclivity to reproduce. The demands slaveowners directed against black women and men increased alongside their understanding that access to the slave trade meant expendable and easily replaced laborers. For those enslaved men and women who were Carolina-born or acclimated to the colony, creolization exposed them to a particularly insidious injustice. Slaveowners responded to the sympathies developed between black men and women by attempting to manipulate those emotions to "make them more tractable."[97]

The desire for "tractability" among the enslaved would increase after September 9, 1739. In the aftermath of the Stono Rebellion (discussed below in Chapter 6), the legislature instituted prohibitive import duties on enslaved Africans, effectively calling a decade-long halt to slave imports, which caused the proportion of Africans in the enslaved population to drop over the course of the 1740s.[98] In the face of the transformations brought to the colony by the Stono Rebellion, beliefs about women as producers and reproducers remained constant. Despite the conviction that the black population represented enormous potential dangers, growing numbers of slaveowners perceived enslaved women as potential mothers. In the 1730s, 28 percent of testators used the term "increase"; 35 percent did so in the following decade.

Enslaved women in this decade had children despite the fact that they lived in an environment marked by the dangers of a slaveowning class gripped by the specter of black revolt. In the years immediately following Stono, as the African population diminished proportionally, the proportion of inventoried slaveholdings in which mothers and infant children were present in slave communities remained as high as it had been prior to the drop in slave imports (see Table 5 above). Women bore children prior to the halt in the African slave trade and the imposition of increasingly punitive measures of social control, and they continued to do so afterward. In 1740 Dinah and Sitera each had three children; the two other mothers on the plantation where they were enslaved had two and one child respectively.[99] When Walter and Judith Dallas died in 1740, their combined estates contained eight women, five men, and eleven boys. Six of the eight women were mothers; Cate and Maria each had three children, Sabina had two and Nancy, Mariah, and Grate had one each.[100] Forty-two slaveowners' inventories survive from 1742; and on twenty-eight inventoried plantations (66 percent), children had been born. For these women, like those enslaved by Isaac Dubose, slavery and motherhood existed side by side, and both exposed them to violence equal to that unleashed by the rebels at Stono. Fifteen men and five women labored on Dubose's extensive landholdings along the Santee River in Craven County. The five women he enslaved all had children. Grace, Grace, and Hannah each had two children, and Sarah and Desire each had one.[101] According to Dubose's will, after his death the land and the twenty men and women were parceled out to his children. Only one apparent family group seemed to have been protected; Sarah, her child Amerett, and a man named Dublin became the property of Dubose's wife.[102] There could be no telling whether the risk they shouldered—in the form of the emotional vulnerability of a parent/child bond—would now come to haunt them. For the moment, Sarah and her child were "protected." Sarah's family (presuming Dublin was a part of it) would be maintained. As for the four other women, their fate is less clear. Dubose's death must have instigated panic for the two Graces, Hannah, Sarah, and Desire. Dubose ordered Hector, Port, and Patrick sold, and questions about their relationship to the mothers and children Dubose enslaved cannot be answered. As Dubose's will shifted these women and men around to his heirs, their ability to protect their ties to one another would no doubt be tested. For them and for all other enslaved parents, the children made that test all the more important, and difficult.

Whether or not a woman was a mother at the time of a slaveowner's death is not always clear. In 1742 on all but eight of the twenty-eight inventoried plantations in which mothers were identified (69 percent) women without children outnumbered women with children. Childless women outnumbered mothers anywhere from 9:1 to 2:1. On the majority of these plantations (or fifteen) the ratio stood at 3:1 or 2:1. For many women and men, then, children were not as explicitly a part of the ordeal of enslavement as they were for those on Dubose's or Hext's plantations. Susanna Cordes enslaved Rinah, Nanny, Molly, Phillis, and Nancy alongside nine men, five "little boys," and one "girl." In addition to these women and men, Cordes inherited her share of silverware, plantation tools, bedding, and furniture.[103] The executors of the estate identified none of these women as mothers, and perhaps none ever gave birth to a surviving child. However, the executors' wording—"little boy Matthias"—suggests that at the very least, Matthias still needed a mother. And perhaps Molly, who appears directly above him in the inventory, took on that role. In the aftermath of Susanna Cordes's death, the particular worry or fear of a birth parent may have escaped these women and men. On the other hand, someone cared for the children around them, and in the absence of the word "mother," parenting still had to take place.

The women and men who parented other women's children on the estates of Carolina planters must have looked upon these children with truly mixed emotions. African women and men who arrived in South Carolina found evidence of the permanence of their enslavement in the multigenerational families that greeted them. While childbirth became part of the tools of control wielded by slaveowners who "rewarded" the enslaved with permission to visit, or punished them with separation from, families, it also served as evidence to those newly enslaved of endurance, vulnerability, connection, and pain. It is difficult to imagine for whom those emotions were more distinct; those whose relationships with one another led to the birth of children, or those who, upon arrival, glimpsed the parameters of their future in the small, enslaved, children for whom they came to be responsible.

The African arrivals to the South Carolina low country did more than shift the colony's demographic balance. They shifted the cultural balance as an unfamiliar African present replaced an acculturated Carolinian past. Women and men born in Carolina or the West Indies had been on the path "toward a unified Afro-American culture," but planters driven toward increasing profits reintroduced a tangible ethnic African present.[104] In and of itself, childbirth cannot stand in for the complexities of layered and oscillating acculturation in the face of a circular relationship to an African past. Nonetheless, the arrival of a child almost inevitably causes those who witness it to reflect on the future and the past. Belinda, enslaved by Robert Hume, who perhaps was born in the colony and was given a name that evoked a creole or English framework for her life, named her own children

Mindoe and March (the latter reflecting the West African practice of "day" names).[105] Both names evoked an African past, either one she herself had experienced, or one she revisited through the changing composition of the men and women around her. Yet both children would speak English without even a West Indian accent and would experience their lives in South Carolina as rooted firmly there. For women such as Belinda, parenthood in the 1730s would be particularly complicated. Embodying, as they did, the process of creolization in a community quite suddenly in the grips of a rejuvenated yet unfamiliar African past, Mindoe and March may have been painful—if loved—evidence of the unimaginably altered confines of a formerly African life. While natural increase among the enslaved all but ceased during this period of growth for the plantation economy, childbirth—with its complex accompaniment of creolization—continued to touch the lives of the enslaved.

Chapter 5
"Women's Sweat":
Gender and Agricultural Labor in the Atlantic World

While enslaved women grappled with the new dimensions and implications of their reproductive lives, they undertook considerable and onerous agricultural work.[1] The preceding two chapters have emphasized the connectedness of reproduction and enslavement by exploring the ways in which reproduction functioned foundationally in the development of racialist thinking, the onset of modern slaveownership, and the experience of enslavement. These chapters preceded a discussion of manual labor because in order to fully appreciate the degrees to which sex and gender infused the development of racial slavery, one must momentarily isolate the ideological and material valences of reproductive potential, of childbirth and loss, and of the multiplicities of "women's work" for the daughters of Africa. Early American slavery was fully imbued with assumptions about and measures taken against African women's gendered bodies. Slaveowners came to understand racial slavery as well as plantation management through a series of images, calculations, and experiences in which the notions of sex and race were fully intertwined. Enslaved women, and men too, from the moment they set foot aboard slave ships or were born in American colonies, came to understand their identity under slavery as marked by sex and race. It is from this point then, that we move on to a discussion of agricultural work, for to fully understand the role of reproduction in the lives of enslaved women, one must grasp the role of grueling work regimes for women who also suffered under the onslaught of this most fundamental appropriation of their labor.

Hard labor, daily and relentless, underlaid all ideologies of race and reproduction and all experiences of birth, parenting, and loss under slavery. The obscene logic of racial slavery defined reproduction as work, and the work of the colonies—creating wealth out of the wilderness—relied on the appropriation of enslaved women's children by colonial slaveowners. But, at the risk of stating the obvious, reproductive work did not alone define daily life. The effort of reproducing the labor force occurred alongside that of cultivating crops. And even as enslaved women engaged in a process of community formation that was simultaneously resistant and acquiescent and ultimately the inevitable byproduct of their dispossession and oppression, they struggled to protect their bodies and their spirits from the ravages of unrelenting hard labor.

An overdetermined connection between women and the domestic has dominated the ways we think about women's work. The very phrase conjures the domestic—cleaning, childcare, food preparation—and inevitably leans in the direction of the family. Images of enslaved female house servants tend to populate the collective imaginary with as much tenacity as do gentle-hearted mammies. But as slaveowners perused the bodies of their newly purchased human property, they quickly made decisions about the kind of work each was capable of performing and in almost all cases put women to work cultivating land. To be exempted from the field in favor of the house was a fate open to very few enslaved women, particularly in the colonial period, when the luxury of large houses and the niceties of china, silver, and fine furniture were still part of the slaveowners' imaginary future rather than their tangible present. It was far more likely that women would end up in the fields. Indeed, the entire system of hereditary racial slavery depended on slaveowners' willingness to ignore cultural meanings of work that had been established in England and to make Africans work in ways the English could not conceive of working themselves.[2] Once slaveowners received almost equal numbers of African men and women from slave traders, they inverted the gender ideology that they applied to white women and work.[3] As more and more enslaved persons were brought to the Americas, African women and girls found themselves in the fields. Early American slaveowners felt no compunction about using women for this kind of hard labor. As Thomas Nairne calculated the cost to the crown of sponsoring settlers to Carolina in the first decade of the eighteenth century, he speculated on the wealth that would be produced by transported settlers. "I will suppose for the present, that white Women and Children are of no Advantage (tho' 'tis not altogether so) and only reckon Men fit to Labour, and the Slaves of both Sexes."[4] During the crucial frontier period of slavery in the mid-eigthteenth-century Georgia lowcountry, for example, a contemporary stated that "in the planting and cultivation of fields the daily tasks of a good Negro Woman" was exactly the same as that of a man.[5] Another planter, outfitting a Florida plantation in 1769 wrote, "very strong and able wenches will do as much work as any man."[6] And on the island of Barbados, eighteenth-century Codrington Plantation owners calculated the monetary value of enslaved male and female field hands equally at £56.[7] As the role of African women in all manner of cultivation, production, and marketing in African societies was reduced to a singular drudgery on a white man's lands, the narrowing of their lives and skills would compound the violation of this new manner of work. It is ironic that the reliance of slaveowners on African women as fieldworkers made their economic role as significant to the American economy as it had been in Africa; African women on both continents produced the agricultural goods that were the base of the respective economies.[8] As they cleared fields and cultivated and harvested crops, enslaved West African women found themselves performing familiar tasks whose cultural meaning had radically changed.

The invisibility of enslaved women in the iconography of early American slave labor is a modern omission. For the men who put black women to work in the fields and for the women who worked there, women's capacity for backbreaking labor was hardly incidental. Indeed, it was central to developing racialist ideology; the "natural" difference between "Negroes" and Englishmen often was evidenced by black women's supposed ability to labor ceaselessly. As Europeans registered their "wonder" at African difference, the image of the black woman who "slaved" for lazy African men was both recurrent and necessary. The intellectual and social milieu from which English slaveowners emerged supported an approach to the organization of labor that fully exploited enslaved women's real and imaginary capacity for grueling agricultural toil.

Field Work: Sugar Fields

The diverse labor needs of the early American settlement have been well documented. While often rhetorically reduced to their most important export, "sugar islands" and other staple crop-producing colonies were actually sites of a wide array of work—ranging from road building to navigating small craft to blacksmithing and tailoring to carpentry and butchering. While clearly it would be wrong to present the sole undertaking of the early American slave society as producing monoculture crops, it would not be far from the truth to suggest that enslaved women found themselves

confined to the monotony and drudgery of the field more regularly than
their male counterparts.

As we saw in Barbados, as planters moved from tobacco culture
toward sugar, for example, almost all planters enslaved nearly equal numbers of men and women, and it was not uncommon for slaveowners to own
more women than men (see Figure 7 above). At the time of his death in
1659, John May's estate included three men—Pattorne, Tome, Oge, and an
unnamed "able negroe." With them were five women—Hagar, Mareah,
Nell, Jugge, and another unnamed "able negroe."[9] Thomas Kennett had
only female slaves; two unnamed women who labored alongside a male
Irish servant.[10] John Waterland owned four women; Jude, Maria, Mall, and
Hagar; two men, Mingo and Sambo; and two children, James and Peter.
English incorporation of colonial settlements and racial slavery into the
parameters of acceptable labor management required some dramatic ideological maneuverings and a fundamental restructuring of the notion of
women's work; a similar transformation of thinking about men's labor did
not occur. Outnumbered by women two to one, then, the men on Waterland's plantation would have been diverted to craft and stock work because
the four women would amply cover his twenty acres of land. But once
Waterland faced his mortality, Jude, Maria, Mall and Hagar became more
than simply workers; they were workers with riches embedded in their intimate behaviors. Calculating their contribution to his wealth, along with
their enduring value, Waterland attached Mingo and Hagar to the land in
his bequest to his eldest son. The others would ultimately be dispersed
between his wife and children, but together Hagar, Mingo, and their progeny would, with luck, carry young Nicholas Waterland far into the future.[11]

John Wolverstone also owned twenty acres of land in Barbados, but he
had purchased only women to work it—Anne, Hagar, and Jone. A "picka-
niney negroe" named Hopsey lived with them, but on his St. George's plantation he, and his son Benjamine after him, oversaw a female-only
workforce.[12] Anne, Hagar, and Jone, possibly balancing sexual demands
with the daily toil on a small struggling plantation, would also have to parse
out parenting responsibilities for Hopsey as they faced the uninterrupted
demands of the field and presumably shouldered "domestic" work for each
other and the Wolverstone men as well.

By the 1660s, women frequently outnumbered men on the larger plantations. In 1661, John Lewis's plantation contained nineteen enslaved adult
women, four enslaved men, and eight children.[13] Judith Powery's 200-acre
Hope Plantation in St. Thomas contained eighteen enslaved women and

eleven men in 1662.[14] The same year Philip Banfield's property included ten enslaved women, five men, and eight "pickaninies."[15] The numbers of women in the fields would also strike slaveowners surveying the workforce on their lands elsewhere in the English Caribbean.[16] The connection between physical and reproductive labors was already clear to the island's planters and, as we saw in Chapter 3, at the very moment at which Barbados power as a sugar producer was being established, the work these women performed in the field did not obliterate a recognition of their ability to also produce wealth in the form of enslaved children.

Forced to accommodate a demography that was determined on the African coast, slaveowners throughout the colonies struggled to bring their assumptions about gender and labor into line with this new labor force. The work of constructing colonial settlements, of manufacturing the goods and products ancillary to staple crops for export, further complicated the relationship between labor and gender. Slavery regimes did not erase the connections between domesticity and women. Indeed, slaveowners made the connection between domestic servitude and black women early on. Writing in 1675 from Barbados, one recent arrival complained that his white female servant was a "slut," but "until a neger wench I have, be brought to knowledge, I cannot . . . be without a white maid."[17] But the numbers of "Negro wenches brought to knowledge" meant that such connections were secondary and, moreover, fell under the purview only of the very rich.

By the mid-eighteenth century, such practices were solidified on plantations like the Roaring River plantation in Jamaica, where, for example, 76 percent (seventy of ninety-two) of enslaved women were field workers compared with only 33 percent (twenty-eight of eighty-four) of enslaved men. These women, it should be noted, were also the parents of forty-three boys and thirty-six girls, most of whom were too young to work at the time of the plantation's inventory in 1756.[18] It was to this pattern of consistent reliance on women as laborers that Michael Craton spoke in 1978 when he wrote of eighteenth-century Jamaica that "it was indeed a curious society, as well as an inefficient agricultural economy in which women for the most part were the laborers and men the specialists."[19] But of course, the importance of staple crops produced in the Americas to the domestic and colonial economies of Europe is evidence enough that enslaved women can hardly be said to have been inefficient manufacturers of American wealth.

Because of what we know about depressed fertility and increased infant mortality, we can safely say that most enslaved women found field-work, rather than childbirth or parenting, to be that which they experienced in common. Cutting eighty acres of cane was not the same as cultivating subsistence crops, but important connections existed between the rhythm of working plantations both large and small on the sugar islands and the mainland colonies. On small estates, both women and men worked the land. On larger plantations, however, enslaved men worked in the boiling house, tended cattle, or made barrels and worked with wood, leaving fieldwork to women. The refusal to allow enslaved women to occupy skilled or artisanal positions meant that the mobility that accompanied such work was also denied them.

The work of the field was, in part, responsible for the low fertility of enslaved women. However, many women still shouldered the burden of fieldwork alongside the difficulties of parenting under slavery. Robert Rumball enslaved twelve children, eleven women, and only five men on his 89-acre plantation in Barbados. The women Rumball owned lived on the small sugar plantation that had a sugar works. Two white female indentured servants did the domestic work. The work of sugar processing and animal husbandry (the plantation also contained a curing house and forty-two assorted livestock) fell to the five male indentured servants and most of the five enslaved men. This left the backbreaking work of the field to the eleven enslaved women—Grete Jugg, Wasshaw, Backoe, Great Marrea, Dido, Violettoe, Lille, Hagar, Affee, Frowna, and Little Marea—many of whom were also mothers to the twelve children who appear in Rumball's inventory under the heading "Negroe Children." Childbirth simply meant that the demands of the field had to coexist with the emotional and physical pull of parenthood.[20]

In the late seventeenth and early eighteenth centuries, then, cane fields were places in which women constituted a high proportion of the total work force. Indeed, in some places, the field became a female space as balanced sex ratios across the English sugar islands led to female majorities in the fields. Even when women's proportional representation in the slave trade declined, in many places—notably Jamaica—sex ratios on the plantations remained quite balanced. Thus, even though they were outnumbered in the population as a whole, women constituted more than half the work force—half the visible source of sugar's cultivation. On the Mesopotamia plantation in Jamaica, which enslaved 322 men and 216 women, the majority of fieldworkers were women (182 of 359); close to half the enslaved men worked as drivers, craft and stock workers, stock keepers, or marginal workers.[21] Similarly, on the eighteenth-century Beaulieu plantation in Saint-Domingue, there were eighty-seven men and fifty-four women, but women outnumbered men on the field more than two to one.[22] Despite the fact that men were imported at a ratio of 163 to 100 women over the course of the slave trade to Jamaica (1655–1807), on the estates, work gangs were close to even with ratios of approximately 105 men to 100 women.[23] Even where the larger population was still demographically weighted toward men, slaveowners' understanding of gender and work among the enslaved explained the preponderance of women seen in work gangs. On both small and large plantations, women spent their working lives in the field. On the sugar islands as well as in Carolina's rice swamps and Virginia's tobacco fields, occupational diversity existed almost solely for enslaved men.[24]

In the colonial period, slaveowners throughout the Americas became quite willing to put African women permanently to work in the fields, but they balked at allowing them access to any skilled tasks. Skilled work that supported domestic economies such as dairy work or weaving primarily remained the purview of white women—planters' wives who oversaw the work of overseers' wives or female servants.[25] Black women found themselves on the bottom of the work pyramid on the sugar plantations, exposed to hard labor and drudgery with little chance of escape to more skilled or protected positions. Women of African descent were presumed to be fully capable of the heavy lifting and wielding of rudimentary tools that fieldwork required and were found throughout the French Caribbean cutting cane. On the sugar islands of the French Caribbean, women were regularly assigned the fieldwork dismissed by one ecclesiastic observer as "the easiest of all labor."[26] They prepared the fields for planting, cut cane and did the often dangerous work of feeding sugar cane into the mills, a job that could maim or kill if it was not done with perfect timing and that, despite the need for precision, was often relegated to the evening, after enslaved women had worked a full day on the fields. It is not surprising that accidents were "certainly frequent among female slaves . . . particularly at night, when, exhausted by hard labor during the daytime, they fall asleep while passing the cane."[27]

Slave labor was not, of course, limited to sugar cultivation. Women worked on coffee plantations and cultivated indigo as well. An early eighteenth-century observer in Saint-Domingue for example, wrote of a sexual division of labor on the island's indigo fields; men hoed while women stooped to plant seeds and cover them with earth.[28] In seventeenth-century French Guiana, slaveowners sent enslaved women—even in advanced states of pregnancy—to do the public works projects such as road and fortress construction known as corvée labor. Returning from her corvée labor early after becoming ill, an enslaved woman named Doué gave birth to a stillborn son in April 1690; his death marked the limited expectations that shaped a life controlled by the demands of work.[29]

The connection between femininity and domesticity elicits images of cooks and child minders, but the reality was that few women of African descent escaped the field. During a 1706 raid on the island of St. Christopher, French forces absconded with a large number of enslaved persons. When they enumerated those they had lost, the English provided the occupational category each laborer filled and thus left an occupational breakdown for the island's forced laborers at a juncture when St. Christopher had already been settled for more than seventy years and four decades had passed since the turn to sugar cultivation. Of the captives, 64 percent had been field hands, 10 percent had worked in sugar factories, 14 percent had been domestics, and 12 percent had been artisans, overseers, or other "skilled" laborers.[30] Forty years earlier, planters would have been even less willing to divert ablebodied workers from fieldwork to the care and production of domestic luxuries.

Periods of gender parity would wax and wane according to the internal logic of the slave trade, leaving those West African women who survived the Middle Passage in a gender minority.[31] While Barbados was distinct in maintaining female majorities/gender parity during the entire slavery period, women enslaved on the other English sugar islands would continue to find themselves outnumbered in the quarters even as they labored in the fields alongside mostly other women. They were vulnerable to both white and black men, and their time spent in the fields would have been the only time in which they might achieve anything even approximating the female space that defined daily life in most West African cultures. In the context of closely supervised gang labor, the connection between their centrality to agricultural production in West Africa and to fieldwork in the Americas would be at best a numbing reminder of the violent contraction of their unfolding futures. Moreover, women's connections with each other and their sense of collective identity must have grown as a result of the sex ratios of the cane fields. In this regard, a world only nominally defined by their identity as parents presaged the community of mutual support, healing, and resistance evidenced among enslaved women in the antebellum American south.[32] Still, it is difficult to fully imagine the ways in which shifting meanings of gender and backbreaking agonies of hard labor came together to assign meaning to women's work in the colonial cane fields.

Fieldwork: Cattlepens

The slaveowners who made their way from Barbados and elsewhere in the West Indies to the mainland colony of Carolina in the 1670s constructed a labor system that mirrored the sugar fields in many ways. The Barbadian planters who introduced slavery to South Carolina caused the mainland colony to become a slave society from the very moment of its settlement.[33] Although indentured servants accompanied the initial white settlers and landowners, there was never any question that Africans and their descendents would perform the bulk of the colony's hard labor. Englishmen and women in Carolina cemented the connection between hard labor and black bodies even before their arrival. When South Carolina was chartered, land grants were awarded on the basis of the numbers of servants and slaves that settlers brought with them to the colony. Those with the means transported large numbers of laborers to increase the size of their land grants without fear that in the new colony their status as slaveowners would be undermined. In correspondence concerning the particulars of the settlement plan, the lords proprietors had been quick to clarify that land would be allocated equally for "Negroes as well as Christians"; in other words, those who brought slaves would be rewarded uniformly, in terms of land, with those who brought servants.[34] White settlers coming from the West Indies, where black labor had long since displaced white servitude, were obvious beneficiaries of this landgrant system. The future of Carolina was inextricably linked to enslavement, assuring settlers that land entitlements would be based on generous headrights. The care taken to ensure privilege for slaveowners who settled in the new colony illustrates two implicit assumptions on the part of by the new settlers: black laborers would constitute wealth and black laborers would produce wealth on the mainland.

While landgrants were distributed equally regardless of the race of a white servant or a Negro slave, the lords proprietors did distinguish between male and female laborers. First settlers would be granted 100 acres for the importation of white or black women, and 150 acres for white or black men. Rewarded proportionately more for the import of men than women, newly arrived slaveowning settlers were not blind to the gender conventions that prevailed around them regarding notions of hard labor. During the first twenty-five years of settlement, enslaved men outnumbered enslaved women by two to one.[35] Most of the early settlers to the colony who received warrants for land between 1672 and 1695 for transporting slaves, or servants and slaves, brought only men or male majorities. (35 percent and 25 percent respectively.) However, more than 20 percent brought pairs of men and women, and others brought only women or a majority of women. (9 and 5 percent respectively). Put another way, enslaved women were considered an investment valuable enough to offset disparities in land acquisition by 65 percent of all the first settlers who went to the expense of transporting laborers to the new settlement alongside themselves and their families.[36] In this moment at which slaveowners themselves momentarily controlled the ratios of men and women imported into a colony, it is particularly telling that women were a logical and consistent choice for transport to the new colony. The proof that women would work in Carolina's fields would be confirmed, and not only by looking backward to Barbados's sugar plantations. In the early years of the colony a brisk trade in Native American slaves also confirmed women's place in the mainland colony. Enslaved Indian women outnumbered men by close to five to one in the first decades of the colony's history, mostly because slaves obtained as a result of intertribal wars were more likely to be women and children—men were killed rather than taken as prisoners. John Wright enslaved fifteen black men and seventeen women, only four of whom were of African descent. Perhaps wishing to offset the black majorities that defined the English Island colonies, some looked to a different kind of female labor. When writing a promotional pamphlet for the colony, John Norris wrote that a small-scale settler should bring money to purchase "Two Slaves; a good *Negro* man and a good *Indian* woman," while a wealthier settler should plan to purchase

Fifteen good *Negro* Men. . . . Fifteen *Indian* Women to work in the Field. . . . Three *Indian* Women as Cooks for the Slaves and other Household-Business and Three *Negro* Women to be employ'd either for the Dairy, to attend the Hogs, Washing, or any other employment they may be set about in the family.[37]

The correlation between sex and race was rarely this extreme, nor would the intended designation of black women as domestics become a reality for more than a fraction of enslaved African women in the colony, but of the 4,300 enslaved persons in the colony in 1708, 1,400 were Native American. The vast majority of those 1,400 were women who worked alongside African and Afro-Caribbean women in the new colony.[38]

As the seventeenth century ended, the headright was reduced to 50 acres per laborer, male or female. The desire to reward the first generation of settlers—those willing to risk an uncertain future in the colony—had led

to the generous landgrants in the 1670s and 1680s; but the removal of gendered distinctions of labor by 1685 reflected the shifting understanding of
gender, race, and labor on the part of the colonial setters. It was perhaps in
deference to that shift that Peter Hearne Sr., imported a "negro woman"
only three months after he brought a single "negro man" to the colony in
1683. Hearne's choice of a woman would necessarily have been conditioned
by the transparent relationship between race and reproduction for seventeenth-century slaveowners. For those women and men transported to the
new colony, the confusion of the frontier was possibly abated by clarity
about the role they would be performing. The assumption that their working bodies promised more than just their labor on the land must have been
as clear to Jone and Andrew, transported together in April of 1673, as it was
more than twenty years later to Sam, Tony, Bess, and Jany, who arrived in
the colony with their owner and his wife in 1695.[39]

Others would soon join these men and women from the West Indies
and from West Africa and together they would embody Carolina planters'
hopes for wealth. They uncritically understood that enslaved women's value
resided both in their roles as producers and as potential reproducers, and
as they linked the reproductive lives of those they enslaved to their own
acquisition and distribution of wealth, they acted on that understanding in
ways that ultimately threatened enslaved men and women's humanity in
the most profound ways. The enslaved women who arrived in the mainland
colony from the West Indies and, in increasing proportions, directly from
West Africa during the frontier period found themselves adjusting to labor
conditions significantly different from those in the sugar fields or on their
native soil. The isolation of a new settlement may have provided relief from
the rigors of sugar cultivation, but it brought with it new exhaustions, dangers, and vulnerabilities. Many of the colony's first settlers raised cattle during the time it took to deforest the land to make way for crops. Tending
livestock was, for many enslaved Africans, a familiar task. Carolina's first
slaveowners were cognizant of the skills that West African men brought to
the settlement and relied upon men from the Fula, Wolof, and Mandinka
areas of West Africa—especially Senegambia—to tend the cowpens in the
upcountry. For enslaved men re-exported from the Caribbean pastoral agriculture was not only familiar, but would calibrate a sexual division of labor
destroyed by sugar cultivation—offering another escape from the woman's
work of the fields.[40]

The confidence slaveowners had in African men's abilities to tend the
large and free-ranging herds was not isolated, as we shall soon see, but for

the women who had not learned the fine art of managing free-ranging cattle, the Carolina frontier offered no immediate recognition, or rather exploitation, of their skills. Still enslaved men were not alone out there, nor were they alone in crafting parameters of their lives in Carolina with echoes from Senegambia. The women who accompanied them came from areas in West Africa where rice cultivation, on a small household scale, worked in tandem with tending cattle.[41]

Often a man and a woman, perhaps accompanied by a child, found themselves together on the cowpens, where their experiences of the familiar and the foreign would have to mesh. Jack and Jugg, for example, tended seventeen head of cattle on Francis Jones's bleak settlement. Jones's entire estate, aside from cattle and Jack and Jugg, consisted of some old pots and "one old bedstead, three old chests, two old chaires, one fourme, two stools, and one table top."[42] Likewise, in 1696, Mingo and Mall and a boy named Cudgeon tended thirty head of cattle and fifty-five pigs somewhere in the outer reaches of Carolina. When their owner died toward the end of the century, he could not claim even a single piece of furniture.[43] It is quite likely that the rudimentary tools with which Mall and Jugg pounded and winnowed rice escaped the eye of the estate's executors. Mortar and pestle and homemade straw baskets would, in time, be permanent parts of the colonial landscape. Before the turn of the eighteenth century, however, as tools that were solely the province of black women's "unimportant" innovation they would not warrant inventory.

Mall and Jugg lived their lives among men and boys in poverty and rural isolation on the colony's frontier. Other women enslaved on cattle lands were less isolated. Dido and Phebe and the Indian woman Betty were enslaved alongside Jeffry and Timbo and an Indian man called Leander on a large settlement where they were responsible for more than one hundred head of cattle and twenty sheep in addition to a crop of corn. The strength of their combined numbers and the succor of one another's presence did not protect them from their owner's financial mismanagements or their sale as a group to clear his debts. The owner was careful to include "ye Increase of ye said sheep slaves maize and cattle" in the terms of the sale, and the careful symmetry of his property in persons suggests that he had hoped for reproductive expertise where cattle-tending insight was deficient.[44]

As they struggled to survive the frontier, the women at these cattlepens probably nurtured emotional connections to the men enslaved alongside them; though they did not bring children into this world of cows, pigs, and meager living, whether they loved or hated Mingo, Jack, and the others is not for us to know. What is clear is that there were no "house servants" on the frontier. Women were just as likely to be wielding the sawbuck as their brethren, though it was only to them that their owner looked for reproductive wealth. During this period when the uncertainty of the future for white settlers could not have been clearer, white slaveowners invested limited resources in both male and female laborers. But women were an important part of the frontier, and the conviction that black male volatility needed to be mitigated certainly would have informed purchasing patterns. So would presumptions that women's capacity for labor made them investments that, unlike the import of luxurious household niceties, did not have to be put off until financial success in the new colony was assured. In all likelihood, the prosaic image of a black man and a white man sharing work on the sawbuck needs to make way for a clear understanding that the white man was undoubtedly thinking that, without an outlet for his sexual needs, the black man's continual and contained labor could not be assured. Moreover, the proximity of white owners and enslaved women cleared the way for white men to more easily identify black women as potential sexual outlets for themselves. As the slaveowning settler made his tentative way on the colonial frontier, he would certainly rely on his convictions about African women's ability to work and potential to reproduce as he made difficult economic decisions about investing limited resources into a labor force he might or might not be able to control.

During the first twenty-five years of the eighteenth century, deerskin trading, cattle raising, and the production of naval stores gradually gave way to methods of acquiring wealth that were far more ecologically invasive and, for enslaved women and men, cost much more in human terms. By 1708, the Carolina colony had become the only mainland colony with a black majority as the settlers turned their resources and attention to rice cultivation and transported rapidly expanding numbers of enslaved persons from the West African coast. In 1700 half of the enslaved persons in Carolina were African born; by 1710 that proportion had grown to two thirds.[45] The colony's transition to rice production brought with it a complicated change in women's work; both to the rhythms and rigors of their labors and to the cultural milieu in which they performed them. African laborers cleared the forested lands that soon gave way to rice plantations. Women and children worked alongside men. Enslaved Africans brought more than simple hard labor to the process of transforming the land; in both large and small ways they brought expertise that was recognized and exploited by white settlers albeit in ways that would ultimately destroy them. An observer described black male workers laboring after dark (when the winds had died down) "lopping and fireing," while women and children cut down shrubs and bushes. In 1679, Jean Barbot observed cultivation techniques among the Wolofs on the Senegal Coast. "They set fire to what is found on the land left fallow in previous years, then afterwards. . . . they turn it over and mix up the earth and the burnt material."[46] In 1707, John Archdale remarked that "little Negro Children" performed valuable complementary labor on plantations; their work, essential but light, freed adults for larger, more physically strenuous, jobs.[47]

The colony was beginning its unstoppable journey toward rice culture; it is a great irony that that journey both depended upon African expertise and was devastating to black bodies. In the small cattle-raising outposts of the backcountry, black women had used large mortar and pestles to process the rain-fed rice they grew on dry land. Free-ranging cattle, tended by men, cleared the fields after harvesting in an indigenous complementarity learned on the West African coast. When slaveowners took note of the crop, the move from garden to plantation happened with alarming speed and devastating results. As rice culture developed and the colony expanded in the early eighteenth century, the numbers of enslaved persons brought to Carolina directly from the West African coast rose rapidly.[48] In 1706, only 24 Africans entered the colony by ship. Four years later, 107 persons were forcibly transported from West Africa. By 1725, that number approached 2000 per annum.[49] White Carolinians quickly grasped the significance and scope of the society's changing demography. In a letter to English officials in 1699, Edward Randolph accurately assessed the numbers of white inhabitants but put the black population at four times the white—a figure at least twice their actual number.[50]

Slave import levels fluctuated greatly over these years (from 25 to 600 per annum between 1706 and 1723) and women whose pasts likely included labor in Barbados or elsewhere in the Americas were joined in small numbers by those coming from the West African coast. Childbirth and parenting must have occasionally provided a bridge that connected women and men whose pasts were so divergent and whose futures were now necessarily conjoined. As they parented, or mourned the conditions that made parenting impossible, they would also be caught up in the overwhelming demands for their labor in the forests or on the fields. Faced with cargoes they could not control, slaveowners' connection to a Barbadian tradition of slaveholding helped to create the ideological room for women in the fields. The fact that women provided valuable labor, and more valuable children, meant that as the colonial economy developed, slaveowners in Carolina followed the example set by decades of slaveownership in the English Caribbean and did not shirk from using women as laborers on Carolina plantations. Through their presence, their work, and their children, enslaved African women unwillingly contributed to the developing definitions of slavery and control in colonial South Carolina. Randolph estimated that 5,000 enslaved men and women could produce staples for export, with hundreds of others located in and around Charlestown in occupations central to constructing the colonial infrastructure. While the black population didn't reach 4,000 until 1708, his exaggerated numbers are offset by the precision of his assessment that enslaved persons were at the heart of the new colony's economic future.[51]

The Africans whose numbers began to eclipse those born in the West Indies or in Carolina in the first decades of the eighteenth century constituted the only black majority in the mainland American colonies. During the 1710s and 1720s, the population of enslaved women and men grew rapidly, jumping from 3,000 in 1703 to 12,000 in 1729 and 29,000 by 1739. The growing population did not escape the concern of travelers and observers. In 1730 The *Boston News-Letter* published a letter from Charlestown that reported that "we have a bout 28 thousand Negros to 3 thousand Whites;" and in 1741, a visitor to the colony suggested that "it is estimated that there are fifteen heathen slaves for every white man," though in the low country the actual ratio was closer to two to one.[52] Moreover, both the value and the danger of a reproducing labor force were absolutely clear to slaveowners. In 1714, Carolina legislators noted that "the number of negroes do extremely increase in this province, and through the afflicting providence of God, the white persons do not proportionally multiply."[53]

Probate records indicate that faced with a black population in which men continued to outnumber women, slaveowners seemed to balance their slaveholdings to assure a relatively even, if outnumbered, female presence on many plantations. For women enslaved on small plantations, the rice boom that would ultimately envelop the colony had not yet touched their lives. Enslaved on a plantation outside Charlestown in Berkeley County in 1716, Marina labored on the land alongside two other women, three men, a "negro boy" and a negro "Girle." The man who purchased Marina and the rest, assiduously balancing a workforce from whom he expected much, held out some hope that, in addition to the work he required from her, Sarah, and Hagar on this 350-acre plantation, one or more of them would augment his wealth through childbirth. The terms of the sale included "the increase and offspring of ye said Women," though neither Marina, Hagar, nor Sarah had yet complied.[54]

For other women, the shift toward a staple-crop export economy meant the opening up of space in domestic labor. As with the Caribbean, the proportion of domestic servants was quite small; it grew from 1 percent of all enslaved laborers at the start of the eighteenth century to somewhere between 5 and 10 percent by the turn of the nineteenth century.[55] When the tanner William Chapman died in 1711, for example, Moll found herself answering to not one but two new "Mistresses." Chapman willed that she "equally be divided" between two white women in Charlestown. Moll had previously worked surrounded by men—William Chapman, the "negro men Cudjo and Dick," and two black boys named Jack and Sam.[56] Now Moll would work in an atmosphere shaped by the housebound duties required of urban dwellers Mary Reynolds and Elizabeth Adams. Whether the shift worked to Moll's advantage is unclear. As town women who socialized with an artisan, it is likely that Reynolds and Adams were involved in some kind of commercial endeavors. Shopkeepers, grocers, and milliners—these "female" professions would have kept Moll hard at work.[57]

The joint ownership of Moll, while unusual, simply facilitated the mobility that characterized urban enslavement for the few enslaved women who found themselves in Charlestown. Urban settings throughout the Americas provided limited access to unsupervised movement for enslaved women. Indeed, not only creole women but also those born in Africa might find anonymity and autonomy in Charlestown. An Angolan washerwoman and an Angolan seamstress were both suspected of having supported themselves (and, ultimately, their ability to run away) by hiring themselves out to "free Negroes and others" in Charlestown.[58] The ability to work in a setting sheltered from the environment and the disease of the rice field, to walk unsupervised down the street on the way to market, to meet friends or family, were perquisites of women's domestic work that may have balanced the violation of living in close quarters with those who enslaved them; the considerable physical burdens of laundering, cleaning, sewing, and child care; or even the emotionally draining imperative to escape notice.

The Charlestown market was, for most of the colonial period and beyond, a space within which enslaved women gathered, sold their wares, and exchanged information and friendship with one another. Concern over the economic and community-building activity of these women erupted frequently in the city's legislature and newspapers. In 1747, a petition was presented to the assembly complaining "of the great Liberty and Indulgence which is given to those Negroes. . . . to purchase quantities of flour butter apples, &ca, all which they retail out to the inhabitants of Charlestown," who were "entirely ruined and rendered miserable" as a result.[59] Women were the majority of market traders, and as such they attracted the ire and rancor of many Charlestown residents, who resented being made dependent on "notorious" and "impudent" women.[60]

In other colonial southern cities as well, the dominant role of enslaved persons, particularly women, in the marketplace was a cause for alarm. By the middle of the 1760s, enslaved women in and around Savannah, Georgia, were plying their wares in the city's market both with and without their owners' consent.[61] Whites complained of women's behavior in the market in terms that, as Robert Olwell has shown, suggested direct insubordination and rebellion.[62] Their dependence on these market women for food and goods only fueled their ineffectual attempts to regulate the market and the mobility among the enslaved that the market both depended upon and generated.

The mobility of Esther, a "Girl" enslaved by the merchant and slave trader Robert Pringle at the end of the 1730s would bring devastating results. Pringle praised her skills and integrity, saying

She is a Very Likely Young Wench & can doe any House Work, such as makeing Beds, Cleaning Rooms, Washing, attending at Table, &c. & talks good English being this Province Born, & is not given to any Vice, & have always found her honest.

Her only vice, it seems, was an inability to stay away from her parents, who were also enslaved by Pringle and who lived on his plantation outside of Charlestown. He complained of her "goeing frequently to her Father and Mother, who Live at a Plantation I am Concern'd in about Twenty Miles from Town from whence there was no Restraining her from Running away there, & Staying every now & then."[63] As a result, he shipped her to Portugal, where he had business contacts, to be sold. The relative proximity of her parents proved too much for Esther, as it did for Pringle, who concluded that banishment to a non-English-speaking nation over 2,000 miles away was just punishment for this honest, skilled, and hard-working young woman's enduring connection to her parents. Esther's story, and her inability to protect herself from her owners' malicious caprice, augment the evidence of enslaved women's dominance in Charlestown markets, and the never-ending legislative complaints and decrees directed toward such women in a failed effort to reduce white dependence upon black women for foodstuff and wares.[64]

Marina and Moll and Esther (before her exile) experienced their enslavement under conditions quite separate from the majority of black women. Certainly connections such as those between Esther and her parents could have bridged the experiential gap between the rice fields and the houses of Charlestown, but regardless of their families' connection to the plantations, these women faced quite different dangers. Working in Charlestown during the early years of the rice boom insulated them from some physical labors and exposed them to others. For these particular women, their enslavement, sex, and childlessness may have provided the only obvious connections between them.

Fieldwork: Rice Swamps

Throughout the slaveowning south and Caribbean, one of the consequences of white commitment to slave labor was an unwillingness to invest heavily in more efficient but delicate equipment that would make the agricultural work done by the enslaved less labor intensive. The significant differences in the lives of enslaved people that accrued from the staple crops they cultivated were mediated, especially for the women who found themselves in fields of tobacco, rice, sugar, and coffee, by the work of the hoe. In the antebellum period, Frances Kemble described enslaved women as "hoeing machines," and recently, historian Leslie Schwalm has suggested that the hoe itself might be considered the "universal implement of slavery," one with particular significance for women across the Americas.[65] With the advent of rice culture in South Carolina, another implement served to reinscribe the difference and particularities of cultivation and culture in the lives of African and African American women—the mortar and pestle.[66]

The particular role of African women in the harvesting and processing of rice cannot be underestimated. In order to make rice edible, the indigestible outer husk must be removed while keeping the inner kernel whole. This involves a delicate balance of strength and finesse that was undertaken completely by hand until the advent of mechanized threshing in the 1760s and 1770s. Until that time, the only way to mill rice was with the mortar and pestle that was used by African women in Senegambia and Sierra Leone, and in South Carolina. Many questions have been raised about how rice culture was brought to South Carolina. Rice was a crop with which Englishmen were unfamiliar, and for some time the introduction of the crop with its complex system of water management—the use of dikes and dams to periodically flood and drain the fields—was attributed to some combination of planter ingenuity and grain brought by the captain of a slave ship from Madagascar. But the connection between West African slaves (particularly those from the Senegambia region, who came with a long tradition of both dry and tidal rice-cultivation skills) and the introduction of rice to the colony is compelling. Recent scholarship has cemented the link between the knowledge Africans from the Senegambia region brought, however involuntarily, to South Carolina and the development of the wet growing techniques that transformed the physical and economic landscape of the lower South.[67]

The turn to rice culture in the colony had devastating effects on enslaved women and men. Rice is among the most onerous and labor intensive food crops, and the duration of the growing season and the dangerous and repellent nature of the work placed it at the extreme end of any continuum of forced agricultural labor in the early Atlantic world. Cultivating the crop over the duration of its 14-month growing season involved clearing the land of trees, bushes, and shrubs in January and February; planting acres of seeds by hand and foot; weeding constantly with hoe and hand: spending weeks in knee- and waist-deep water scaring birds away from the ripening crop; harvesting and stacking the rice over the course of three to four weeks; and finally threshing, winnowing, and pounding the rice to remove the kernel from the husk. Runaway numbers peaked during the hoeing and weeding seasons of June through early August as enslaved men and women stole away in search of respite from the "laborious and tedious" task of hand-picking grass from around the rice shoots that had taken root.[68] But the pounding of the harvested rice had to be the most arduous and dangerous work over the course of the season of rice. Not until the 1770s would technology begin to replace the exhausting work of pounding rice by hand.[69] Slaveowners were mindful of the toll that this work on the health and lives of those they enslaved:

The worst comes last for after the Rice is threshed, they beat it all in the hand in large wooden Mortars . . . which is a very hard and severe operation as each Slave is tasked at Seven Mortars for One Day, and each Mortar contains three pecks of Rice. Some task their Slaves at more, but often pay dear for their Barbarity, by the loss of many . . . valuable Negroes.[70]

The constant work of lifting a ten-pound pestle, arms over one's head, for hours a day was exhausting, so much so that the task was often divided into two separate sessions in the mornings and evenings. The act of pounding the rice required not only physical strength but acumen as well. Pounding too strenuously would leave one with less-valuable broken rice and bring castigation on the worker whose exhaustion level was costing the plantation owner his profits. The information necessary to cultivate and harvest rice drew heavily on female West African expertise, as women who had for generations begun their day with the pounding of a small amount of rice for daily use found their relationship with the crop utterly transformed— beginning with the need to teach men how to efficiently and carefully perform this task.

The skills needed to cultivate rice successfully were transferred from African to Englishman and from women to men to women again. Women, whose knowledge of rice cultivation in Senegambia had been passed from mother to daughter for generations, found themselves in the difficult position of transferring their knowledge to men, whose enslavement would now be exacerbated by the indignity of performing women's work and the penalty for not performing it well. As Pearson has written, in the process of meeting the demands of the crop, slaveowners "dissolved the gender division of labor" that had characterized the early years of the colony as well as the West African past.[71] The introduction and construction of the tidewater cultivation levees, sluices, and dikes that transformed swamps into rice fields demanded an astounding amount of labor from enslaved women and men. Over the course of fifty years, the enslaved workers on a single seventeenth century Carolina plantation moved over 6 million cubic feet of earth in the construction of the rice fields, creating "an earthwork approximately one-half the size of Monks Mound, the largest pre-historic Indian mound in North America."[72] In the aftermath of the War of Independence, white observers noted the connection between the design of rice irrigation systems and military engineers' fortifications a link that was often materialized as enslaved men worked alongside military engineers in the construction of canals, thus cementing the connection between constructing irrigation systems and male knowledge.[73] While men had historically performed much of this work in Western Africa, the conviction held by South Carolina slaveowners that men and women would have "the same day's work in the planting and cultivating of the fields" suggests that slaveowners did not exempt women from the heavy work of moving earth to create the rice fields.[74] In this, enslaved women would follow the lead of the men, whose familiarity with hydraulic design was so essential to South Carolinian planters.

Rice culture in South Carolina differs from staple crop cultivation elsewhere in the New World not only because of the grueling demands of the
crop but because of the relationship between indigenous African female
knowledge and rice cultivation. As Judith Carney has so eloquently illustrated, the aural rhythm of a woman at her mortar and pestle pounding rice
for the day's consumption announced the new day all over the West African
coast. Women's expertise was of paramount importance at every stage of
the crop's cultivation in the West African rice region—from seed selection
to the use of the long- and short-handled hoe to the use of the mortar and
pestle to the construction and design of the fanner baskets for winnowing
and, finally, to cooking. For the first generations of enslaved persons in the
colony, that sound would continue to punctuate the day. As relatively isolated laborers on the colonial frontier, enslaved women and their families
might even have relished the familiarity wrought by the steady rhythmic
cadences of the mortar and pestle at the start of the day. But as South Carolina slaveowners wrested the crop from household use and applied it to
plantation agriculture, the cadence of the mortar and pestle would resonate
in entirely different ways. As Carney writes:

A task performed daily by African women in less than an hour became transformed
with commodity production into extended hours of daily toil by male and female
slaves over an abbreviated period of the year. The pounding of rice, the preparation
of a food that signals daybreak and the re-creation of community life in West Africa,
underwent a radical transformation on eighteenth-century rice plantations. As
workers arose to the first of two pounding periods, the striking of the pestle represented a new conception of time and labor, calibrated by the dictates of planter and
market.[75]

The continuity between rice culture in the lowcountry and on the West
African coast and the essential role of women's knowledge in that transmission should not suggest that women had less difficult work in the rice fields.
Among the enslaved in North America, those who toiled in the South Carolina rice fields suffered the highest mortality. The work was grueling, the
tasks stretched the workday out until well into the night, and the toll that
the pounding of rice took on the bodies of the enslaved was so extensive
that slaveowners took careful notice of the destruction of their human
property. One late-eighteenth-century planter reasoned that the value of
the hulled rice did not outweigh that of his laborers and wrote to his overseer that "if the Rice made at Goose-Creek is not yet beat out, I wd. Wish
to have it sold in the rough, to save Labour of the Negroes."[76] Nonetheless,

the unique connection between the African past and the Carolinian present must be accounted for in the lives of enslaved women in Carolina. The connection between women's knowledge and the life of Carolina planters raises intriguing questions about the ability of these women to negotiate spaces of autonomy. The task system of labor conceded to the enslaved by South Carolina slaveowners allowed for the development of slave economies and created a clear distinction between time in the service of the slaveowner and time in the service of oneself. The task system itself had African antecedents and may have developed from the transfer of knowledge and skills between the enslaved and the slaveowner.[77] Indeed, the parameters of the task system, which was in place as early as 1712, may have given rise to the natural increase among the enslaved that was evident in the early years of Carolina's settlement. We know that the space that resulted from task labor generated gardens and markets: perhaps it generated a different relationship to the future that children embodied as well.

On the other hand, in the accounting of rice and women's lives, the balance should tip toward misery. Women in the Carolina lowcountry watched as one of the most essential cadences of their former lives was utterly transformed. The quotidian task that had given shape to their morning would in its transformation become a reminder of all that no longer existed. Not just the mortar and pestle but also the weaving and basketry that once served the household and the life of the community would be transfigured by the rapacious demands of the slaveholder.[78] Not unlike the birth of a child, the agricultural work that gave meaning to one's life now gave meaning to someone else's life. But opportunities to reconfigure the balance of power in slave societies were everywhere and constituted an ongoing narrative thread in the history of racial slavery. Childbirth and the identifiable skills brought to cultivation and processing crops were themselves possible spaces in which to maneuver, even as they simultaneously concentrated the misery and violation enslaved women and men endured.

Chapter 6
"Deluders and Seducers of Each Other":
Gender and the Changing Nature of
Resistance

Women's experience of racial slavery at the hands of English colonizers suggests that the language of resistance and accommodation is always already insufficient. The dichotomies that emerge are uncomfortable. Women who became mothers enriched their captors' estates while simultaneously creating the communities that would foster profoundly complicated opposition to and compliance with American racial domination. Women who did not become mothers mourned the loss of their birthright or celebrated this blow to slaveowners' domination. "Resistance" and "accommodation" are static poles at opposite sides of a spectrum whose intent is to capture the wide range of responses to repression but whose effect, I would argue, is quite the opposite. Resorting to a binary view, even if one does so in service of illustrating the range of responses that run along the line between two points, suggests an ability to clearly delineate the meaning of various behaviors and does so while suggesting that there is consensus about the terms in play. Is there agreement about the interpretation of behavior under an oppressive regime? While we know that social behaviors are transformed under slavery, to presume that an unwillingness to follow orders, for instance, can be clearly interpreted is to presume too much.

It is a truism that the enslaved resisted their enslavement; to imagine otherwise is to reduce men, women, and children to the machine-like laborer who existed solely in the racial imaginary of slaveowners and their descendents. Refusing to separate "resistance" from the larger social-historical study of the African American past avoids the creation of an artificial divide through otherwise integrated aspects of daily life.[1] It allows for a fluid understanding of oppositionality in which the political is not segregated from the social or cultural, the unwillingness to conform to slaveowners' demands for efficiency is connected to the debilitating effects of forced hard labor on the body and the spirit, and the insurgent value of a trickster tale is not isolated from the experiential pleasure of a story told as the body and mind recover after a day of toil. The pleasure taken in the tale is inextricable from and dependent on its mutinous quality.

Nonetheless, an assumption that all behaviors under slavery were resistant culminates in precisely the same imaginary automaton. For in the vacuum of perpetual resistance, there is no pain, no suffering, no wounds. Perhaps no better evidence of this conflict in interpretive frames exists than childbirth in a system that both relied upon and devalued it. It is to that end that centering or isolating enslaved women's acts of political and economic autonomy is appropriate in a study that has explored the multiplicities of enslaved women's reproductive lives, lives that refuse easy categories of compliance or resistance. A reductive view of reproduction does not move us beyond binaries. If we see childbirth as nothing more than an opportunity to illustrate the ability of enslaved women to release a wellspring of motherlove onto benighted children whom they would sacrifice everything to save, we do no more than reinscribe ideologies of maternal caregivers grounded in outdated notions of separate spheres, the feminized emotional, and the dichotomies of public/private.[2] An examination of the complicated rewriting of motherhood that occurs in the context of New World slavery offers instead a narrative of shifting meaning and reconceived foundations as the private, domestic, and noneconomic woman's womb becomes the site of venture capitalism. This chapter explores enslaved women's urge to contest enslavement both inside and outside their identities as mothers.

Efforts to Control

A cursory glance at colonial slave laws pinpoints the perception slaveowners had of the enslaved: they were a different, dangerously plentiful, and rebellious sort of property.[3] The contradiction at the heart of slavery—the claim on the part of slaveowners that the men and women they enslaved were not fully human—is explicated in the compulsory need to prevent the physical mobility and urge toward social intimacy is at the heart of human community. Colonial slave codes were universally concerned with regulating the movements of the enslaved, a concern rooted in both the pragmatics of social control and in the ideological nexus of human beings who were both real and chattel property.[4] In one of the earliest slave laws in Barbados, legislators determined in 1672 that the enslaved were real estate rather than chattel. This juridical identity meant little in the context of lived experience, but it does highlight the vexing problem of movement for slaveowners determined to tie the enslaved to the land ("to the intent that the Heir and Widow . . . may not have bare Land, without Negroes to manure the same") as inanimate objects whose value mimicked that of a house or barn.[5] In crafting legislation to "Better order and Govern" enslaved women and men, slaveowners consistently addressed the issue of mobility in the opening clauses of comprehensive slave codes. Virginia slaveowners highlighted the "pretense of feasts and burials" as the cause of the "frequent meetings" among the enslaved that needed to be curtailed.[6] Slaveowners in Barbados in 1688 found it "absolutely necessary to the safety of this place, that all due care be taken to restrain the wanderings and meetings of Negroes and other Slaves at all times, more especially on Saturday nights, Sundays and other Holidays." Antiguan slaveowners in 1697 adopted the Barbadian code largely unchanged and thus also focused primarily on controlling mobility. The second clause of the Carolina act, the one that immediately followed the definition of who exactly was enslaveable, said that no one "shall give their Negroes and other slaves leave, on Sundays hollidays or any other time to go out of their plantation."[7]

For decades, Englishmen in the Americas had struggled with the consequences of disparate population growth; settlers on Association Island abandoned the colony when "the great number of Negroes" outnumbered them two to one.[8] John Drax expressed alarm at the rising rate of white emigration from Barbados and warned that this weakened state rendered the island's white population increasingly vulnerable to the "first Attempt." He suggested the creation of a manufacturing base on the island to replace costly imports and to "find Imployment for many of your poor [who] would continue not [to] goe off because they know not how to subsist in Barbados." To protect against the encroachment of slave artisans, the proposed jobs must be exclusive—"in this trade nor in any other [may] there be any Negroes employed except Artificers belonging to the sugar work."[9] As Carolina legislators would half a century later, Barbadian legislators blamed skilled slave labor and land consolidation for displacing the aspirations of poor working whites whose mobility led to white elite vulnerability.

On the other hand, as enslaved African men moved through the ranks of gang laborers and filled the positions of artisans, they too acquired mobility. Growing numbers of African blacksmiths, dockworkers, coopers, and haberdashers moved about the island, in and out of Bridgetown, making money for their owners and making connections for themselves. Unsuccessful efforts to curb white reliance on African artisans did not mitigate the considerable economic gains for whites that owned them. In retaliation against owners who allowed this, the Assembly proposed taxes on "every Negro where there is no sugar works." In his letter, Drax allowed for African artisans at sugar works only so long as their owners did not contribute to the problem of slave mobility by hiring them out.[10]

The concern around mobility poses interesting questions about gender and movement. As we have seen, enslaved women had little access to artisan positions. Domestic services like laundering, cooking, and cleaning would be open only to a minority of women. Undeniably slaveowners primarily targeted enslaved men for their unregulated wanderings, but occasionally women too enjoyed the freedom to walk to a neighboring plantation or into Bridgetown to meet with friends and family—on Sundays perhaps, or on days like the first of June 1671, when all work, drinking, or entertaining ceased in order to commemorate the end of a period of "grievous sickness and pestintiall distempor."[11] But gender circumscribed mobility as it did work. Men were more likely to become mobile communicators outside the small plantation communities on which women provided the bulk of the field labor. However, women created the need for those lines of communication as, through their bodies, they created ties of consanguinity.

In the context of a community increasingly defined as creole—in other words, one in which connection and intimacy were made visible by the birth of children—the attempt to control and curtail movement was, in many ways, both futile and intuitive. Connections among the enslaved were evidenced by childbirth itself, by the shift from African to European languages, by runaways aided and sequestered by friends and family, and by the ability and desire to plan and carry out revolts. Colonial legislators vainly passed laws disallowing communication among the enslaved on its most fundamental level. In Barbados, they prohibited the enslaved from "using or keeping of Drums, Horns, or other loud Instruments which may call [them] together, or give sign or notice to one another of their wicked designs and purposes." Similar legislation on the mainland focused on the ability to gather independently: In Carolina, "great numbers of slaves which do not dwell in Charlestown, on Sundays and holidays resort thither, to drink, querrell, fight, curse and swear . . . in great companies together, which may give them an opportunity of executing any wicked designs and purposes."[12] In order to prevent such gatherings, legislators turned to slaveowners, threatening them with fines for allowing those they enslaved off their property without legitimate reason and proper permission; control could not be wrested from the Sunday gatherers, so slaveowners were the logical target of frustrated legislators. Still, whether gathering in Charles-town, calling one another to clandestine meetings in Barbados's secluded groves, or attending feasts and funerals in Virginia, enslaved women and men traveled well outside the confines of rural plantations. As they moved from place to place, they carried with them the assumption that movement was their right; freedom of movement did not crumble in the face of regulatory attempts to limit it. The gathering of African peoples in private and in public places formed an essential part of their lives in the colonies.

If slave laws illuminate the extent to which enslaved men and women were moving all around the colonies, they also reflect another kind of movement as well, that of a slaveowning class's sense of racial identity. Slaveowners' legislation reflected a racial consciousness that developed over time, borne out in the owners' efforts to isolate themselves from those that they enslaved. In Barbados, as the planter class purchased more slaves, the legislative records of the island's council and assembly reflect growing anxiety about ethnic and religious differences among white colonists. In July 1661, for example, worry over English outmigration to other colonies led the council to request "three thousand Christian servants at the half yearly, [for] if wee are so supply'd then Jamaica or the Neighboring Collonys may probably bee furnish'd with a suitable number of freemen from us."[13] This desire for English settlers, which often manifested itself in pleas to the metropole to send white women to the colonies, cannot be conflated at this stage with a straightforward desire for "whites" to offset "blacks." Long-standing ethno-religious differences and conflicts confounded the logic of racial slavery. Thus, at the same time, the council ordered lists, by parish, of "siditious troublesome or dangerous" Irish, and prohibited all Irishmen residing in Barbados from commanding "any shallop or boats belonging to or in this Island."[14] During the same session, the council compiled "Reasons against the being and sort of the Quakers within this Island"—a list of grievances arising from Quaker refusal to serve in the military as well as from their "dayly" proselytizing.[15] And, of course, endemic inter-European rivalries further complicated any simplistic notion of "whiteness" or common cause. Later that year, the council ordered guns and powder and an island-wide mobilization in anticipation of an attack from the Spanish.[16] During the 1666 war with the Dutch, which not incidentally coincided with a period of rising white emigration from the island, fear of external attack led to the arming of enslaved men. On this occasion, the need to defend against a foreign invasion was stronger than the fear that armed slaves would rebel.[17] Carolina legislators also felt themselves beleaguered by "outsiders" who encroached upon the safety and security of the colony. Their fears were justified. Hostilities with neighboring Native Americans alarmed and concerned Carolina's white settlers. Colonial policy exacerbated wars among Indians to guarantee favorable trading conditions for Carolina colonists dependent on the Native American trade.[18] Deerskin figured prominently alongside the foodstuffs and naval stores that served as Carolina's economic mainstays, and, in their efforts to ensure constant access to Native American trading goods, colonial officials pursued policies that led to open rebellion between English settlers and a Creek-Yamasee alliance in 1715, the Yamasee War, and placed white Carolinians squarely in the middle of a large regional Indian slave trade.[19]

For much of the first decades of settlement, then, white Carolinians, like slaveowners in Barbados, focused attention on external sources of aggression such as the dangers posed by the Spanish and Native Americans. But an inevitable polarization took place when, in the wake of staple monoculture exports, rapid black population growth transformed southern and Caribbean English colonies one by one into slave societies. Growing numbers of Africans intensified the sense of isolation experienced by slaveowning settlers up and down the Atlantic, who misinterpreted the extent of their marginality.[20]

While population growth at this stage occurred as a result of the slave trade, the transformation of Africans into Afro-Americans drew the attention of slaveowners in search of evidence of their own mastery. As William Willoughby searched for viable methods of social control, he felt that only "different tongues and Animosities in their own Countrey have . . . kept them from Insurrection," suggesting that the process of acculturation was a source of danger because it mitigated linguistic and cultural distances and thus gave voice to latent discontent. Willoughby believed he possessed the skills to discern the loyal from the mutinous and claimed credit for maintaining peace among "Creolian" slaves, who were now able to plot together on the basis of the trust he had in some island-born men, "as are best approved of for their Fidelities and Abilities," to advise him.[21] Elsewhere colonial Assemblies similarly looked to "worthy" black women and men to protect them. In 1706, for example, Carolina came under attack by combined French and Spanish forces. In his report of the event, Governor Johnson described the lurking presence of warships at Charlestown harbor and gratefully noted that "notice [was] brought by a Negro that ye Enemy had been on shoar." Fear, self-interest, or loyalty motivated the unnamed black man to raise the alarm. His ability to assess and report on the immanent danger of foreign ships speaks to the presence of acculturated women and men like himself who were versed in the boundaries of the colony and the rewards of "loyalty" to the colonial authorities.[22] Four years later, Thomas Nairne reported on the practice of arming enslaved men in the colony's militias; Carolina legislators acted on their confidence that they maintained control over the colony when they handed a gun to a man who expected "his Freedom, [if] in the Time of an Invasion [he] kills an Enemy."[23] As Willoughby had in Barbados, slaveowning legislators saw the cooperation of enslaved militiamen and loyal informants as evidence of their own ability to maintain order and evoke responsibility among black men.

Such individuals held an essential place in the slaveowners' arsenal as they searched for a way to neutralize the volatile population they lived among, if only symbolically. Writing to the Board of Trade in 1730, William Chapman argued against the imposition of taxes on "the Blacks[.] We represent to your Lordships that this is in Effect a Duty on the British manufacturers, the Blacks being the produce thereof."[24] This attempt to erase human and social origins spoke to the economic and symbolic necessity of a neutralized enslaved labor force. Faced with an increasingly African-born population, the writer located them as men and women who were remarkable for the color of their skin rather than their place of origin. Like all imports, once in the colony they would become part of the colony—in essence, creole—but until then the "Blacks" were nothing but British products.[25] The conflict between slaveowning legislators' desire to see the enslaved as passive, undifferentiated, controllable brutes and their experience with men and women whose agency demanded something different continued—particularly over the behavior of "acculturated" men and women. To balance their dependence on enslaved laborers with their awareness of the coercion inherent in the slave system must have been quite a task for colonial slaveowners.

Even before Willoughby turned to creole men for counsel, efforts to control and regulate were explicitly embedded in the reproducing bodies of enslaved women. Women's role in protecting the colonies was perhaps more complicated. Enslaved women's sexual identity cut two ways: it could pacify black men's aggression or give rise to creole laborers who were sometimes a source of peace and sometimes a source of danger. The relationship between ethnicity and rebellion warranted incessant analysis among Carib-

bean slaveowners. Elsewhere in the British West Indies, Antiguan sl..
ers would be violently reminded of the potential for creole rebellion in 1737.
At the same time, Willoughby's conviction that danger lay in acculturation
would be tested by the wave of rebellions and revolts led by ethnic Africans
that crisscrossed the eighteenth-century Caribbean. Primarily led by men,
these revolts were undergirded by women who hosted gatherings, carried
information, and ran away to join maroon communities—sometimes with
children in tow. Faced with a recurring influx of ethnic Africans and the
undeniable evidence of their unhappiness, many slaveowners turned a
hopeful eye toward the large numbers of island-born creoles.[26]

A century and a half before Barbadian slaveowners embraced the abolition of the slave trade on the grounds that Africans posed a dangerous and,
in their colony, unnecessary evil, they had already begun to articulate their
assumption that it was Africanity rather than enslavement that caused defiance. As often was the case, pragmatic slaveowners contradicted legislative
efforts to control. In 1663 the Barbados Assembly considered "An Act rec-
ommending the christening of Negroe children"; some fifty years later, slaveowners in Carolina would do the same.[27] But neither Barbadian nor
Carolinian planters embraced efforts to instruct the children of enslaved
women in Christian rituals. Planters' reluctance to provide religious instruction for the enslaved dated back to the mid-seventeenth century.[28] Evocations of Christianity had a minimal effect on the daily lives of the enslaved
population, but they carried weight for legislators, who continued to hol-
lowly exhort that "all Negroe slaves and servants remaining in the said colony shall be Instructed in the Principles of the . . . [Christian] Religion And
that such who shall arrive at a competent knowledge therein be admitted to
the Sacrament of Baptism."[29] Despite the refusal of slaveowners to allow the
few available clergy regular access to the enslaved, the laws reflect the relationship between control, reproduction, and creolization. Christianity intersected with creolization. By symbolically transforming island-born children
into God-fearing Christians, legislators must have presumed a formula for
creating "worthy" creoles. There was also an unspoken assumption about
enslaved women in these laws: enslaved women's reproductive power was
both available and in use for the purpose of removing the perceived dangers
of Africanity in the form of ethnically based rebellion.

Despite their willingness to draw on notions of black loyalty to the
English flag, slaveowners were increasingly forced to understand the riptide
of discontent under the surface. It was, perhaps, with this in mind that the
Barbados council proclaimed in 1667 that acts and other important infor-

mation must now be "published" in Bridgetown "by sound of Trumpett" in lieu of drums.[30] More than twenty years earlier, Richard Ligon commented on enslaved drummers' skills in invoking "pleasure to the most curious eares."[31] In 1661, Felix Spoeri chronicled nightlong religious ceremonies among the enslaved that "consist[ed] of particular dances, [and] drumming on a hollow tree trunk over which an animal skin is stretched."[32] Whether or not it was pleasurable to European ears, drumming evoked Africa. By replacing the agitation of drumming with the thoroughly European, not to mention military, tones of the trumpet, white Barbadians calmed their nerves and more easily monitored networks of communication among the enslaved.

Despite the clearly articulated interest of Carolina's first settlers in opening the colony to slavery from its inception, slaveowners understood the black population as a source of considerable danger and with petulance and violence sought to subjugate them. In 1691, the colonial legislators wrote of the need to "prevent the Mischeives which (as the Number of Slaves Shall Increase) Too much Liberty may occasion," thereby fusing the issue of mobility and population growth in one neat sentence. The code included provisions for fining slaveowners who did not employ sufficient numbers of whites on their plantations and at their cattlepens.[33] In August 1720, when Carolina's legislators calculated the colony's population at 9,000 whites and 12,000 blacks, they complained that the "Pitch and Tar Trade prodigiously Increasing ha[s] occasioned ye Inhabitants to buy Blacks to the great Indangering [of] the Province."[34] The Board of Trade responded with admonitions that "no body . . . may have more Negroes than ten to a white man."[35] Although Carolina planters ignored this proposed proportion of black to white, in the face of an always growing black population, they responded to slave resistance quickly and violently. When slaveowners discovered a plot on the part of a group of enslaved men that spring, the men involved ran south in an attempt to reach safety in Florida. Their attempts to entreat the assistance of Creek Indian guides failed, and upon their capture, legislators ordered their execution by hanging and fire.[36]

Informants and Litigants

As the realities of forced labor propelled both enslaved laborers and slaveowning legislators into implicit or explicit efforts to reposition power in the colonies, enslaved women could not have been unaware of the conversations about creole children's propensity for accommodation and violence. It is no wonder that slaveowners perceived enslaved women as vehicles for increasing the distance between themselves and the dangerous lurkings of an Africanity exemplified by the rhythmic resonance of drums and counterweighted by slave children reciting the Lord's Prayer. But by the middle of the 1670s, enslaved men on the island had developed communication links that sustained an island-wide response to enslavement. In 1675, Barbadian slaveowners uncovered a full-scale insurrectionary plot to overthrow the plantation regime and establish an Ashanti- or Akan-style government and society in its place.[37] The belief on the part of the rebels that ethnic identity could be sustained and reproduced outside Africa is an important corollary to the desire of slaveowners to categorize the children of Africans as morally and culturally distinct from their parents. As news of the revolt came to light after three years of planning, members of the assembly mitigated their ignorance of such proximate rage by rallying the image of black conjugality. According to the Commissioners investigating the conspiracy, the revolt plans were so clandestine that "even . . . [the conspirators'] own wives" remained unaware of them.

However, ultimately, a woman became aware of the plans and used information about the impending revolt for her own end. Days before its intended inception, Fortuna, enslaved on the Hall plantation in St. Peters, revealed the plot and brought the conspiracy to a halt. Once slaveowning legislators quashed the conspiracy, they freed Fortuna "in Recompense of her Eminent Service to the Good of this country in Discovering the Intended plotted Rebellion of the negroes."[38] Little else is known about Fortuna, least of all her motivation for providing information that sent over 100 men to jail and seventeen to the gallows. It may have been that Fortuna's act testifies to the divide between ethnic Africans and creoles. It is significant that the insurrectionists were "almost exclusively Coromantee," and Fortuna's willingness to separate her fate from theirs certainly reflected a deep perceptual chasm between herself and them.[39]

While for the most part enslaved men were those who used occupational mobility to their advantage, Fortuna took the opportunity to seize her own mobility upon the heels of men's plans for freedom. Her reasons for doing so may have been utterly selfish or they may have grown out of a desire to protect and provide for members of her own family. Fortuna's gender, her occupational location, and the presence or absence of her kin all shaped the priorities that propelled her into the assembly chambers and from there to her freedom. But the action that so clearly set her aside from Coromantee men did not necessarily connect her to creole women. On the same day the assembly freed Fortuna, they paid Marroa, another Negro woman, twenty shillings for her "Diligent attending the Assembly."[40] The small sum and the language suggest that she waited upon the assemblymen, perhaps cleaning the meeting hall. Her silence, in light of her artisan's mobility and proximity to powerful white men, stands in sharp contrast to Fortuna's revelation, suggesting the multiplicities of women's responses to the terms of their enslavement, race, gender, and location.

Enslaved women threw their weight against the confines of their enslavement in many different ways. The tactics with which enslaved women expressed their anger, grief, and desperation about enslavement were obviously not strictly embodied—in other words, it was not just about regulating their fertility or raising children. While occupational diversity was outside most women's experience, some were able to use their occupational category to expand the boundaries of their lives. In 1734, members of the Court of Common Pleas in Carolina heard a "plea of tresspass" brought by "Phillis a Free Negroe Woman." Phillis brought suit against Samuel Fox (probably a working white man, as he signed the register only with his mark) for his failure to pay her wages for her work "nurs[ing] and tend[ing his] Infant Child." She had cared for and lodged this child for a full year and brought Fox to court when he refused her payment of the promised 2.8 pounds sterling.[41] The court found in her favor, and Fox registered his promise to pay the money.

Phillis was one of the "Negroes in Trade" that local merchants had recently petitioned the assembly to control. Although she barely fits the definition of an artisan or skilled worker, as a black woman who utilized the legal mechanisms of the colony with aplomb, she did, of course, pose a threat. It was at about the same time that Phillis appeared in court that white artisans organized a petition asking the Assembly to ban the use of enslaved persons as skilled workers. The petitioning traders surely did not think of a woman such as Phillis as on a par with the carpenters, black-smiths, coopers, and sawyers who threatened their livelihoods. But black female litigants during the slavery period used the courts to reduce their own powerlessness and to oppose white gender stereotypes about them.[42] Perhaps the traders understood that. Their petition grew out of a moment in which the visibility of black men's access to the trades—and its destabilizing consequences for working whites—was highlighted by the anomaly of a black woman's successful use of the courts against one of their own.[43]

Phillis's presence in court could not have failed to command attention from the multitude of participants who lined the halls or milled about outside waiting for their turn before the judges. Did residents of Charlestown gossip about her audacity that February, or did the fact that Samuel Fox was not a man of means minimize attention to the case? In either instance, the behavior of black women in the city of Charlestown certainly warranted attention from legislators interested in social control. Through their work as marketers and sellers of goods, some women managed to move outside the plantation orbit just as enslaved men did through their work as artisans or craftsmen. While selling the produce from their provision grounds, these women moved from plantations into town, creating and cementing relationships as they went. Late in the eighteenth century a *South Carolina Gazette* columnist would accuse black market women of working in tandem with one another to "exclu[de] . . . every white person" from purchasing foodstuff at reasonable rates.[44] By that time, forms of autonomy in the hands of black women had become a daily reality for black and white residents of Charlestown. In hindsight, some Carolinians came to understand the original legislators' attempts to curtail the market-driven wanderings of African women and men, yet many others would have celebrated their failure to do so.[45] The presence of market women in Charlestown and throughout the English colonies was a constant reminder of the ineffectual nature of legislation in the face of pragmatic desires for consumer goods and the tenacious efforts of black women to protect this space of autonomy and mobility.

The particular place of enslaved women occupied a complicated position. In March 1743, legislators rewarded the enslaved woman Sabina for informing them of "the Design of several negroes to desert to St. Augustine."[46] Only she could assess whether the reward from the lieutenant governor sufficiently compensated for causing the capture and execution of one of the deserters. Her information should have shown the legislators that "the Designs" of the enslaved increased exponentially with their ability to navigate Carolina, an ability that accompanied acculturation. Indeed when a Spanish ship, flying a "Flag of Truce" lingered too long in Charlestown harbor, legislators feared that the Spaniards would be apprised of weaknesses in the colony's defense by "conversing with our slaves": men and women able to assess and inform upon the colony's weaknesses.[47]

The weaknesses of the colonies were, of course, myriad. They were made manifest not only in the ability of creole women and men to navigate the cultural terrain of the colony but also in the very process by which those men and women came into being. In January 1746, Kate drew the attention of the legislators. Committed to jail the previous June, Kate had languished there ever since. Without providing any other information, the legislators noted that Kate had murdered "a Negro Child" belonging to a man other than the one who owned her. Kate "had been reputed Mad for twelve months before she committed the said murder" and had confessed "with every Circumstance" to the crime.[48] Both the unknown causes of her madness and the circumstances that led her to murder a child whose relationship to her is unclear are buried beneath legislative debate over who should shoulder the cost of her imprisonment. One wonders about Kate and her family, whether her "madness" was in fact predicated by the sale of her own child to another plantation, and whether it was thus her own child she killed as a result. The legislators gave little further thought to her beyond her financial cost to them, perhaps knowing that to do so would bring them closer than they wished to the violence and, indeed, madness that lurked among the "increasing" women who constituted their labor force and their wealth. They maintained a distance from women and men whose actions, individual and collective, threatened to disrupt the orderly business of export production.

Runaways

While conflict with the Spanish and neighboring Native Americans displaced by English settlers demanded considerable attention from Carolina legislators, the problem of black resistance constantly caused alarm. In 1687, two women, one of whom carried a nursing infant girl, and eight men escaped Carolina by boat to St. Augustine, Florida, and thus formed the first group of escaped slaves from Carolina whose flight is recorded in the colonial records. The women were not named, but we know that the mother was wife to Mingo and that the three of them were enslaved together by Samuel De Bordieu. Their escape was a desperate one: Mingo had allegedly killed someone in the process. These men and women converted to Catholicism, married, and found work in Spanish Florida, the women as domestics in the home of the Spanish governor. When approached, Governor Quiroga refused to return the runaways to their English enslavers, although he offered to pay for them in the future and, in a gesture certain to have reeked of sarcastic taunting to English settlers who claimed to be ready to execute an enslaved person for repeated petty theft, said he would be willing to prosecute Mingo should the charges against him be substantiated.[49] In 1696, Don La Redno Del Torres St. Callas, governor of St. Augustine, had both "negroes and negroes women" in his custody and was loath to return them.[50] A decade after the 1706 attack, Carolina officials began listing annual accounts of "Negro and Indian Slaves taken . . . and carried to St. Augustine," and losses to individual planters near the southern boundary ranged from one to thirty enslaved workers "taken and carried" per year.[51] Hardly unwilling captives, black Carolinians continuously headed south. They understood that Spanish authorities would free them upon their arrival, and they needed little additional enticement to cross the border into Spanish Florida.[52]

Slaveowners anxiously looked for ways to mitigate the economic and moral threat of runaways to their enterprise. In the summer of 1721, legislators congratulated one another when Harry—for reasons unknown to us and to them—returned to Carolina from St. Augustine, having fled to escape enslavement at the hands of the widow Perry. Once he was back in Carolina, the governor recommended rewarding him for the information he provided and, of course, for his "faithfulness."[53] As the decade unfolded, the assembly was far more likely to involve itself in the inevitability of runaways than in the unlikely event of their return. Harry's return, apparently on his own initiative, stands as an anomaly in the complex narrative of enslaved workers "enticed," "captured," and "runaway" to St. Augustine.

Although formal negotiations between the two colonies' governments took place throughout the 1720s and 1730s about the question of escaped black women and men, rarely did those negotiations occasion return.[54] Slaveowners petitioned the assembly for monetary compensation for the loss of killed, absconded, or executed slaves. The assembly debated each request while railing against Spanish "theft" of enslaved men and women, sending a ship to St. Augustine late in 1722 to demand the return of seven runaway slaves.[55] Twenty years later, the problem had increased tenfold. In November 1738, at least seventy enslaved women and men found their way to St. Augustine, occasioning a series of unsuccessful international negotiations for their return to South Carolina.[56]

Less than a year after Harry's return, an enslaved woman similarly brought attention to herself from the colonial assembly. Flora found the terms of her enslavement so unbearable that she braved the wilderness that lay between her and St. Augustine to head there with her child, to the dismay of both her owner and the legislators.[57] Flora's flight—abetted through networks of communication between black people—appears less of an anomaly than Harry's. She chose to run in the context of a network of information, possibly propelled by the reality that her child's future would be entirely out of her hands if she did not. She escaped only a week after a Spanish expedition, which included a free black man, arrived in Charlestown. The unnamed man had the temerity to speak with the enslaved in Charlestown, a liberty that enraged the assemblymen. The legislators "believe[d] he can have no other view then to Entice them from their Masters," indeed, to "carry off" enslaved women and men from Charlestown.[58] The assembly's frustration with those who would not accept the confines that slaveowners wanted to impose upon them is palpable: "We think it very Improper that the Negroe that is come with [the Spanish] should . . . talk with the Town slaves[.]" It is significant that this posture of indignation was absent during discussions of the women who headed toward St. Augustine.

Slaveowners regularly used the language of seduction as they fumed against those responsible for the absence of their slaves. In the 1688 version of the Barbadian slave code, legislators disallowed slaveowners "of the Hebrew Nation residing in any Sea-Port Town" to enslave more than one male, "be he man or boy"—thereby suggesting both a diminished manliness on the part of Jewish settlers who were unable to control masculine Africans as well as a feminine passivity on the part of enslaved women who could be owned in any number without apparent danger.[59] But that language did not distinguish between the mutinous behavior of men and women. Where one might expect to find a degree of self-righteous and sexualized hubris around Spanish "enticement" or "use" of African women, the legislators discussed women's absences with a straightforwardness that suggests that they did not see women's resistance as either unexpected or differentiated from that of their brethren. Feminized enslaved men *and* women were "enticed" away to St. Augustine by masculine Spaniards or "decoyed" away by manly Indians.[60] Slaveowners negotiated the enterprise of control through language that relegated both black women and men to the mutable and weak—the feminine.

Enslaved women who were so defined upset the balance of the slaveowners' equation with decisions couched in the immediacy of their lives. Perhaps Flora listened carefully to what the English-speaking black man in Charlestown had to say. Could he have directed her way south, telling her of natural landmarks to assure that she maintained the proper course, convincing her that the hardship of the journey would be mitigated by the relative freedom that awaited her? Whether she decided to escape before or after his arrival in Charlestown, she would have found a kind of familiarity if she and her child arrived in Florida. There were other women from Charlestown already there. The very day her owner reported her absence, another Carolina slaveowner reported news of his own. Two enslaved negro women, Abigail and Dinah, and one enslaved Indian woman named Peggy who ran from him, had been located "in the hands of the Spaniards at St. Augustine."[61] For these mothers with small children, Spanish Florida figured as a powerful site of emotional and physical safety. Presumably, Abigail and Dinah welcomed Flora and her child with joy and relief. If Flora arrived safely, their common bonds of experience at the hands of Carolina slaveowners would facilitate a mighty connection.

Ties of affection between mothers, children, and other adults transformed other mothers into runaways as well. In the summer of 1732, Delia ran away from James Searles with the child she still nursed. Delia had not been enslaved in the colony long enough to perfect her English, but she had lived in Carolina long enough to make some strong and important connections to other enslaved persons. One of these was Clarinda, another woman from the Searles plantation. Clarinda spoke "very good English," already had been enslaved by at least one other owner, and cared enough for Delia to link her fate to a woman whose child hampered both their mobility. Delia or Clarinda either retained boat-handling skills from her past or had the gumption to assume that navigating a twenty-five-foot long, three-foot wide canoe as a vehicle of escape could not be that difficult.[62] In addition to their mutual willingness to brave the waters, they also appear mutually willing to share the burden of Delia's child. The dangers of escape multiplied with the presence of a dependent baby. Clarinda's travel with the child implied a connection to Delia and her baby as well. For these two women, mothering constituted not an individual but a collective responsibility. And, indeed, it may have been the child itself who provided the impetus for these African women, at different levels of acculturation and acclimatization, to join one another in the attempt to leave behind their enslavement.

Delia's and Clarinda's bid for freedom did not occur in isolation. Between 1732 and 1739, slaveowners placed 195 advertisements in the *South Carolina Gazette* for runaway slaves (see Table 11).[63] Male runaways outnumbered female runaways three to one—191 men to 61 women. These numbers, however, obscure the impact of female runaways, since flight did not always involve a single person. Men were far more likely than women to escape collectively. In one-fourth of all reported instances, men ran together. But women almost always fled alone. Delia's and Clarinda's

TABLE 11. RUNAWAYS IN SOUTH CAROLINA, 1732–50

	1732–39	*1740–50*
Advertisements	195	299
Male runaways	191	287
Male maroonage	139	231
Female runaways	61	91
Female maroonage	57	86
Women with children	7	21
African women	4	4
Mustee women	10	1
Women "well known" or "this country borne"	3	13

Source: Lathan A. Windley, ed., *Runaway Slave Advertisements: A Documentary History from the 1730s to 1790s* (Westport, Conn.: Greenwood Press, 1983).

choice to tie their fates to one another was unusual; they are the only pair of women reported fleeing together in this period. There are two other instances of women in groups, both of which involve both women and men. In 1732, Amoretta and Sarah, "being very clever Negroes," banded with Jack, Hercules, and Monday to escape from William Webb's plantation (shortly after being relocated from another plantation) by canoe. This group is one of two reported in which men and women ran together. Barbary, pregnant, and her husband Pompey in January 1739 were the other.[64] Ultimately, women constituted 57 of 196 instances of *petit maronage* (29 percent), and 61 of 252 individual runaways (24 percent).

The confines of slavery became so unbearable for some women that 11 percent of them, like Delia and Clarinda, willingly shouldered the risks of running with a child.[65] For these women, the intensity of their desire to protect themselves and their children is self-evident. Certainly Jeney exhibited extraordinary tenacity when she left her new owner, in the wake of her former owner's death (a common precondition for the decision to run) and "carried with her three children."[66] Were all the children hers? The language of the advertisements does not make that clear. Nonetheless, Jeney's emotional ties to the children, biologically or fictively hers, overrode her desire to expedite an individual escape.

Although most women ran alone, they likely ran toward friends or family. Only 6.5 percent (4 of 61) were described as having been born in Africa: these women might not as yet have forged familial or community bonds. Slaveowners called 16 percent (10 of 61) of the women "Mustee," indicating their ties to more than one ethnic community in the colony. Advertisers either listed the remainder as "Carolina born" or indicated, through other descriptive language, that they were fully integrated into the Carolina community. For example, "Sabina . . . speaks good English and is Daughter to a Negro woman named Tulah."[67] While few mothers took the extreme step of escape with dependent children, most women's escape was facilitated by their membership in families or communities from whom they could expect succor. For women who parented under slavery, children could both propel them to run and compel them to stay. Despite the hopes of slaveowners in the pacifying power of black women, family could act both as a pacifier and as an instigator of action. In the face of a labor force that always contained women, slaveowners had to struggle to maintain an image of black women as a source of calmness and a tool for the control of unrest.

Revolts

White Barbadians responded in ways to be expected in the immediate aftermath of the 1675 conspiracy. As planters discovered, tried, and executed those involved, they directed violence at the slave community that reverberated far beyond those directly involved in the attempted uprising. Legislators ordered at least thirty-five men executed after investigating the conspiracy. They caused eleven of the conspirators to be beheaded and dragged their decapitated corpses through the streets of Speightstown.[68] The legislative measures that were taken to more carefully control and rigorously punish those who planned to revolt resulted in whippings and executions of "rebellious Negroes" throughout the next decade. Legislators housed the accused in Speightstown during their interrogation and dutifully reimbursed the owners of the executed men.[69] They passed laws to "Restrayne the too frequent wanderings and meetings of Negroes and to Punish such Crimes, Insolencys and Outrages as shall be Committed By them."[70] Desperate to explain this conspiracy, the slaveowners looked to forces outside the island and to outsiders in their midst. The council and assembly forbade the importation of "Indian slaves" from the "Adjacent collonyes" into Barbados. These Native Americans were styled "a People of too Subtill Bloody and Dangerous nature and Inclination to be remained."[71] They soundly condemned Quakers for bringing the enslaved into their Meetings "under pretense of converting . . . them to the Christian beliefe" and passed laws to forbid or "restrayne" that activity.[72] A few years later, the Jewish community, always highly taxed by the council and assembly, came under censure for its dealings with the enslaved; in 1679, the island's legislators passed "An Act to Restrayne the Jews from keeping and trading with Negroes." In 1683, when rumor spread of another rebellion, legislators had the five enslaved persons whose "threatening language" prompted the scare whipped and one executed by fire.[73]

The 1675 conspiracy had been an attempt to reproduce an old "home"—to bring ethnic African political and cultural institutions to Barbados.[74] The failure of the conspiracy may well have been contingent on similar attempts to reproduce "home" in the bodies of lovers and children. For some years preceding the 1675 conspiracy, the tanner James Lydiatt enslaved Isabella and her husband Toney in Speightstown. Lydiatt owned only Isabella, Toney, and their children. Given Lydiatt's profession Toney was, no doubt, accustomed to an artisan's autonomy and responsibility. After the conspiracy of 1675 officials held the conspirators in a private home in Speightstown for "Examination."[75] Nearby, Isabella and Toney may have harbored mixed feelings as the aftermath of the attempted revolt unfolded. If they sympathized with the rebels, they knew that their own security and that of their three children, Betty, Laurence, and Sabara, dictated maintaining distance from the conspirators. Perhaps they even felt some sense of relief that their family had survived the wave of executions and repression that followed the conspiracy's betrayal. In September 1676, however, the death of James Lydiatt shattered Isabella's family as much as the executions of the previous year shattered the conspirators' families. In order to satisfy Lydiatt's debts, his executors "disposed of" all five. In so doing, they destroyed the stability of the "home" Tony and Isabella had previously found in one another, just as certainly as stopping the insurrection destroyed the hopes for "home" harbored by others enslaved on Barbados.[76]

Four years after the 1675 conspiracy, William Bullard gave voice to what must have been a common sentiment by stipulating in his will that "if any of my negroes after my decease should prove refractory unruly and incorrigible than I allow my [wife Grace] to make sale of such negroe or negroes."[77] The conspiracy and its aftermath made clear the reality that "Refractory" and "incorrigible" behavior could signal dangers beneath the surface of even faithful servants. The fear that any black person could end up involved in organized violence must have reminded Barbadian planters that the familial connections upon which the edifice of "loyal creole slave" was constructed presupposed connections of greater importance to enslaved men and women than "loyalties" to planters—and could not be so easily harnessed.

For those men and women who found themselves negotiating intimacies alongside the demands of enslavement, the outcome was not inevitable. The irregular rhythms of birth, slaveowners' plans for women's increase, and the proportion of women listed as mothers did not alter perceptibly during the course of the fifteen years before and after the conspiracy. However, in the two years immediately following 1675, the number of recorded births among enslaved women dropped. Shortly afterward, by 1682, children appeared in wills five times as often as they had in 1676 and 1677, and by the end of 1684, between 14 and 42 percent of slaveowners wills identified enslaved children (see Table 12). It seems plausible that women responded to the sudden and increasingly dangerous climate of retaliatory violence by not bearing children until after the immediate crisis had passed. It is equally possible that in the aftermath of the conspiracy, slaveowners neglected to record children. The vision of blacks as violent rebels may have temporarily obliterated the other image—blacks as mothers and fathers. Either scenario would not have boded well for those enslaved women and men—parents and partners—caught in the turmoil of slaveowners' escalating perception of the enslaved as potential rebels.

In 1692 the contradiction of parenting and childbirth under slavery erupted when Afro-Barbadian creoles planned a slave revolt.[78] These men and women (of the fifty-one executed rebels, four were women) were the children of mothers who had struggled to maintain familial integrity in the face of a society wholly invested in slave labor. As slaveowners grew increasingly confident about their ability to control (and discern loyalty among) the enslaved population, they relied on growing numbers of creole black men to serve in the island's militia, effectively believing in their own ability to discern the safe from the dangerous. In turn, the organizers of the 1692 revolt relied on black militiamen as informants, turning the notion of safety on its head.[79] The island's legislators quickly moved past their sense of betrayal at the hands of "trusted men" and used the rebels' island birth against them. Legislators reported to the crown that the 1692 rebels lacked the brutal follow-through of Africans, that as creoles they were ineffective rebels. Slaveowners diminished the fear generated by island-born rebels by labeling the conspirators both transparent and effete.[80] If we remember the connection between creole slaves and reproducing women, we see an appropriation of women's bodies as symbolic tools of social control in the

TABLE 12. WOMEN AND CHILDREN IN SLAVEOWNERS' WILLS, BARBADOS, 1670–84
(PERCENTAGES IN PARENTHESES)

	1670	*1671*	*1672*	*1673*	*1674*
Total wills	55	89	57	63	87
With slaves	28	16	28	28	28
With women	14 (50)*	10 (62)*	18 (64)*	14 (63)*	21 (75)*
With children	8 (57)**	3 (33)**	2 (11)**	5 (35)**	5 (24)**
With parents	3 (21)**	3 (33)**	2 (11)**	5 (35)**	4 (19)**
Using "increase"	3 (21)**	3 (33)**	3 (16)**	1 (7)**	3 (14)

	1675	*1676*	*1677*	*1678*	*1679*
Total wills	67	61	51	77	94
With slaves	15	21	20	29	32
With women	9 (60)*	15 (71)*	16 (80)*	18 (62)*	19 (59)*
With children	2 (22)**	1 (5)**	—	4 (22)**	5 (26)**
With parents	2 (22)**	1 (5)**	—	2 (11)**	4 (21)**
Using "increase"	2 (22)**	3 (15)**	3 (19)**	4 (22)**	7 (21)**

	1680	*1681*	*1682*	*1683*	*1684*
Total wills	94	102	73	62	84
With slaves	37	39	34	32	43
With women	21 (57)*	27 (69)*	24 (70)*	28 (87)*	29 (67)*
With children	3 (14)**	7 (19)**	10 (42)**	6 (21)**	8 (27)**
With parents	1 (5)**	—	9 (37)**	5 (18)**	8 (27)**
Using "increase"	4 (19)**	4 (15)**	3 (11)**	1 (3)**	6 (21)**

*Percentage of women in wills in which slaves appear. **Percentage in wills in which women appear.
Source: Recopied Will Books, Series RB6, Barbados Archives, Cave Hill, St. Michaels.

language of the 1692 legislative report. The women who bore these rebels became evidence of safety and thus served a purpose for slaveowners at odds with the future women imagined for their children. The rebels may well have embodied their mothers' longing to wrest a future from the hands of slaveowners through the birth of children destined to rise up and out of slavery. But slaveowners took a great risk as they attempted to reduce the symbolic, as well as the real, threat of the enslaved. By mobilizing black mothers into their rhetorical arsenal of control, slaveowners created a precarious mental barrier between themselves and an undifferentiated violent black populace.

In the end, the symbolic meaning of these imaginary "safe" black mothers and their even safer children had its own meaning among the enslaved. Aside from a plot discovered in 1701, the conspirators of 1692 orchestrated the last recorded Barbadian revolt attempt until 1816. Hilary Beckles argues that there were so few eighteenth-century slave revolts in Barbados because white society became more militarized; the prospect of revolt was more dangerous for the enslaved in eighteenth-century Barbados than it had been in the seventeenth century.[81] I would suggest, however, that one must also consider the growth of family ties to explain the gap between revolt attempts. Enslaved men and women in eighteenth-century Barbados lived in communities increasingly marked by the birth and death of children and by the development of familial ties. Perhaps the presence of their own families magnified the potential dangers of violent resistance to slavery.

The 1692 conspirators sought to take control of the society they created. Unlike their precursors in 1675, they did not intend to recreate African political or cultural institutions on New World soil. Rather, they intended the revolt to guarantee their freedom and prosperity as Afro-Barbadians. We can only assume that the impulse to do so was reinforced by the presence of their mothers and fathers, their own children, and the children of the men and women around them. These creole sons and daughters both embodied life's possible parameters in a slave society, and made smaller the range of reasonable risks. The presence of children offered proof of enslaved men and women's humanity regardless of the dehumanizing process of enslavement or radical attempts to break free of it. As family members, or as those who lived among families, potential rebels might refocus their attention on actions that did not endanger lives. Meetings in town, unauthorized movement, or clandestine relationships all would become part of daily attempts to navigate the confines of enslavement without putting parents, siblings, or children into mortal danger.[82]

On February 26, 1734, word reached the Carolina Assembly that "several Large Companies of Negroes [have been] Meeting very Lately at Different Places." According to the assemblymen, "frequent Robberys Insolencys and unrestrained Libertys of most Slaves at this Time" were fomented and cultivated at these meetings. Fearful of an insurrectionary plot, the assembly identified ten individuals who were enslaved by various planters in the countryside, and brought them to Charlestown for interrogation. Among them was "Mr Godin's Washer Wench." The freedom of movement she commanded (she frequently "was sent" into Charlestown) might have been mparable to that enjoyed by Phillis, the woman who sued for wages due in the Carolina Court of Common Pleas that year. Perhaps Phillis and the washerwoman knew one another. According to the assembly, the enslaved involved in the plot had "constant communication with one another" as they met and talked both in Charlestown and on outlying plantations.[83] Phillis, Flora and her child, the washerwoman, and others like them took their place alongside their male counterparts in ways that raised no *particular* alarm for the legislators. This silence on the matter of women's resistance suggests a ubiquity that historians have overlooked.

White elites in South Carolina, both in the government and on the plantations, understood their labor system as one that depended upon the growth of the slave population through both imports and childbirth. The wider concerns of balancing a growing enslaved population with mechanisms of control brought slaveowners to a heightened awareness of the interplay between acculturation, population growth, and social control. In the aftermath of the Stono Rebellion of 1739—the largest slave revolt in eighteenth-century mainland America—the Assembly enacted prohibitive duties on imported slaves, essentially stopping the importation of enslaved men and women from Africa and the Caribbean for the next decade.[84]

In enacting these taxes on African slaves, assemblymen did not fear a depletion of the enslaved population. While the halt to African imports indicated that slaveowners understood the African trade as a source of unrest in the colony, the 1740 Negro Act also reflects slaveowners' understanding of the dangers of acculturation among black men and women. As Leon Higginbotham has argued, the language of the 1740 act was not concerned with protecting white colonists from "wild and savage" Africans (as the 1712 act was) but rather with keeping black South Carolinians in "due subjection and obedience." This shift in language is significant both as Higginbotham notes—a move from protection to maintaining profit—and as a reflection of the consequences of reproduction and acculturation.[85] In the preamble to the 1740 Negro Act passed in the aftermath of the Stono Rebellion, childbirth continued to be intrinsic to the definition of enslavement:

All negroes . . . mulattoes and mustizoes who now are, or shall hereafter be, in this Province, and all their issue and offspring, born or to be born, shall be . . . absolute slaves.[86]

The 1740 Negro Act went on to explicitly wrench any and all personal liberties from black men and women.[87] The writers of the 1740 Negro Act prohibited a wide range of activity such as buying and selling merchandise, keeping canoes or raising livestock, gathering or traveling in groups on roadways, renting houses or living quarters, or being taught to write—all the potential activities of acculturated or creole men and women. In addition, the act provides evidence that the legislators understood that enslaved women and men, through reproduction and through family formation, already created and reinforced their acculturated identities.

Ten years after the Stono Rebellion of 1739, legislators reviewed and revised Carolina's 1740 Negro Acts. One Act stated that a slave who "delude[d] or entice[d]" others to run away should be put to death. However it also noted that

doubts have already, and may hereafter arise, where a number of Slaves are actually found proceeding out of the Province, either in Boats, Canoes or otherwise, and no Evidence appearing who amongst them was the Deluder or Seducer or Provider of the said Boats, Canoes, Ammunition, and so forth.[88]

To clarify the situation, legislators declared that all men or women found in the above situation "shall be presumed to be reciprocally Deluders and Seducers of each other," and all put to death. The language "deluders and seducers of each other" did not take into account the possibility that none of the enslaved were deluded and ignored the reality that all had seduced the legislators. It could hardly have been otherwise. The legislators were men long accustomed to the linguistic oxymorons the dialectics of "femininity" and female laborers, production and reproduction, the black majority and white supremacy necessitated. To preserve the many fictions about slavery they had created, slaveowning legislators had to see those who threw their collective weight against the boundaries of enslavement as victims of seduction.

Women were careful observers of the colonial landscape and responded to moments of unrest as did enslaved men. The proportion of women who appeared in runaway advertisements placed after the Stono Rebellion did not substantially change. Women constituted 24 percent of the total advertised runaway slaves between 1740 and 1749; in the decade prior to the Stono Rebellion they accounted for 31 percent (see Table 11 above). The substantial change occurs in the number of women who ran either while pregnant or with their children; in the later years, more women who escaped slavery did so with their children. In the 1740s, 23 percent of all female runaways ran with one or more children. Nancy ran "with her child" some time in late 1740. Though her owner William Stone hazarded no guess about her destination, her flight no doubt responded to individual circumstances that were made more unbearable by the presence of her vulnerable child.[89] Most women who ran with children did so alone, although presumably they ran toward someone. Pompey buttressed her desire to escape the bonds of enslavement with the support of a man who may have been the father of her children. She and her two children ran away with "an Angola Negro Man," and their flight illustrates the ties of kin and affinity forged both particularly between creole and ethnic Africans and generally, as both were "very well known in Town and Goose Creek."[90]

Unlike the women who ran away prior to the Stono Rebellion, many of Pompey's cohort ran with others and those who did ran with men.[91] Partnerships formed in slavery between men and women were evidenced not only in the lists of slaveowners' property but also in the decisions those men and women made about how to resist their enslavement. In September 1747, a slaveowner placed the following ad in the *South Carolina Gazette*:

Runaway . . . on the 11 of July last a Negro Fellow named Mingo, about 40 years old, and his wife Quane, a sensible wench about 20, with her child a Boy about 3 years old, all this Country born: Also Cudjoe a sensible Coromantee Negro Fellow about 45 years old, stutters, and his wife Dinah an Ebo wench that speaks very good English, with her two Children a Boy about 8 years old, and a Girl of about 18 months.[92]

Quane and Dinah may have had little in the way of a common past—one was born in slavery and the other was transported to it—but that was not an obstacle to their shared present. Certainly their mutual experience of motherhood played an essential role in their decisions to run away with their partners. Perhaps Dinah, as the older of the two, advised Quane on parenting, reminded her of a lost African past, or convinced her that eight years of attempting to parent under slavery provided reason enough for flight.

The ethnic modifiers; the ages of Mingo, Quane, Cudjo, Dinah, and the children; Cudjo's stutter; Dinah's proficiency in English; and the simple fact that ties existed between the four adults strong enough to bridge barriers of ethnicity and individualism in this collective bid for freedom are all glimpses of personhood that are for the most part impossible to obtain from slaveowners' probate records. Dinah's children reflect the fact that some women born in Africa were among those to whom slaveowners successfully looked for reproductive value. Dinah's experience also suggests that parenting became part of the arsenal of survival and resistance for some African women in slavery. On a more general level, Dinah and her children suggest a possible shift in the effect that childbearing had on women. Proportionally two times more mothers with children were advertised as running away after the Stono Rebellion than before. (As saw above in Table 5, the proportional number of enslaved children inventoried in the aftermath of the Stono Rebellion dropped slightly, although the willingness or ability of slaveowners to recognize parental ties between women and children rose.) Had the regime of the plantation become more unbearable? Had the prospect of raising a child in slavery become less tolerable? Or did the emotional toll of forced separation propel more women to run with their children rather than face the terms of a slaveowner's will?

The 1739 Rebellion in Carolina was evidence of the consolidating power of the institution of slavery vis-à-vis African ethnicity and ethnic identity. The embargo on African imports changed little in terms of the economic landscape of the colony—rice and indigo production remained the same—and slaveowners did not manifest concerns that the institution of slavery would be damaged by lack of African imports. Just as Angolan men carried out the largest mainland slave rebellion in colonial American history and forced Carolina legislators to fundamentally interrogate the dangers of "africanity," so women at various stages of the creolization process emerged from the records in startling ways.

In early 1749 Kate, Susannah, and Sue became embroiled in an intricate and tangled conspiracy. Conspiracies are vexing pieces of history because they equally reflect an always simmering rage of discontent on the part of the enslaved and an always present quicksand of hysteria on the part of the slaveowners. The conspiracy of 1749 is particularly confusing to sort out because it ultimately seems to come down to the desire of a slaveowner to keep an enslaved woman by his side through an elaborate scheme to reward her with freedom for informing about a plot that perhaps never existed. In 1748, Joe, an enslaved man owned by James Akins, was accused of having burned down a barn on Akins's property some three years earlier. Justice was swift and brutal. He was publicly hanged, and Kate, who was also owned by Akins and was implicated in Joe's crime, was ordered sold from the colony—her proximity to such irreverent violence apparently was reason enough to warrant her banishment. Shortly afterward, it was revealed that Joe and a large group of other enslaved women and men in the area had been involved in a conspiracy to revolt and flee the colony and that in the aftermath of his death his cohorts planned to avenge his execution by staging the revolt on the one-year anniversary of his hanging. Atkins had not followed the orders of the court, and Kate remained on his plantation when she and Susannah, who had been married to Joe, allegedly informed Akins about the plot, causing him to bring it to the attention of the authorities.[93]

The events that followed generated eighty pages of testimony in the South Carolina council journal as over 100 enslaved persons and sixteen free whites were accused of, provided testimony of, denied, and recanted evidence of a widespread plan to revolt that involved men and women enslaved on close to two dozen plantations in four parishes along the Cooper River. The conspiracy is remarkable for many reasons—its extent, the temporary imprisonment of whites on the basis of black testimony, and the lack of punishments in its aftermath—but what is most remarkable about it is the central role women played in its evolution and disclosure. While only nine of the 104 named conspirators were women, three of its four primary architects were Kate, Susannah, and Sue. Moreover, it is likely that Kate's relationship with James Akins and his unwillingness to banish a woman his neighbors claimed he cared for more than "his own Wife and Children" set the entire crisis in motion.[94]

On January 23, 1749, James Akins, having allegedly been informed of the plot by Kate and Susannah, brought Agrippa into town to make a confession before the magistrate to a plot forged in the Summer of 1748 by himself, three women, and six other men to escape the colony after "coming to Town [to] set the Town and Magazine afire."[95] While on their way to harvest oyster shells, Agrippa and the other men and women passed an evening in the home of Pompey, a driver on the Vanderdussen plantation, and his unnamed wife. While they ate and played music, the plan took shape. White boatmen and cobblers and others became implicated, accused of inciting and aiding the conspirators. Upon hearing Agrippa's story, Governor Glen immediately called for some fifteen enslaved men to be brought to Charlestown to be interrogated, and Akins similarly brought Susannah into Charlestown to confirm Agrippa's testimony. Within days, twenty-one enslaved and seven free white men were charged in the conspiracy, the militia was ordered on guard, and Governor Glen requested the assistance of the Royal Navy to keep watch because of fear that the revolt had not been contained.

The conspiracy, whether it was real or not, speaks volumes about the rhythm of slave life in colonial South Carolina. The men and women involved, who made their plans while undertaking legitimate business for their slaveowners, traveled among twenty-four plantations that stretched over hundreds of acres. Their testimony spoke of their day-to-day activities; they piloted boats and gathered in one another's homes for meals and barbeques and weddings. Their activities reveal a community in which boundaries between fieldworker and artisan or driver were quite fluid and in which talk of resistance—if not actual acts of revolt—was ubiquitous. Moreover, the pages of the testimony suggest that slaveowners responded to enslaved women's presence in Carolina in ways that reveal contours of gendered ideology. Atkins testified that Kate and Susannah were trustworthy; they had initially informed on Susannah's husband, Joe. Akins used Joe's alleged arson and execution to legitimize Kate and Sue's testimony; as he did so he charged that Joe had threatened both of them with physical violence for their loyalty to whites. Akins claimed that Kate and Sue came to him for protection after Joe threatened them with rape and violence.

Joe had some time before asked them if they would leave this Province and go off with him and with others that would go off and that Will and George soon after asked the same two Wenches if they liked what Joe had proposed to them some time before . . . to which they answered that they did not and that. . . . the said two wenches in formed [Akins] that the said Joe had greatly threatened them for telling what they did and said if they told any more of that matter . . . he *would do all the mischief he could and knock their Brains out* and then go off.[96]

Akins also understood that Susannah, as Joe's wife, commanded a kind of testimonial authority. Whether free or enslaved, Susannah had lost her husband to his criminal refusal to accept his position as a slave. Her willingness to inform upon his accomplices positioned her well; Akins would have seen her loyalty to him and to the slaveowning community as heightened by the personal pain she had suffered as a result of her husband's execution.

In addition to Kate and Sue and Susannah's involvement in the plot, there are many women, beginning with Pompey's wife, who, while unnamed and unindicted, existed at the center of the community of slaves who so provoked the colonial authorities that winter. Toney, for example, had learned of the plans for revolt on the occasion of his wedding when he "had invited George and Joe on his Toneys going to take a wife who had been Georges Wife before."[97] This woman who had married George and then Toney is not named, but her identity as a conduit of community and evidence of a kind of marital flexibility among this population cannot be overstated. Both she and Pompey's wife suggest that in this county, where men only slightly outnumbered women, perhaps their relative absence from the records of this and other revolt attempts has more to do with the eyes and ears of magistrates and less to do with an intentional withdrawal of enslaved women from the conversations about resistance and revolt that clearly permeated the landscape. These women were wives and mothers. Susannah, for example, drew on her role as a mother when she sent her young son out as a lookout—presumably a welcome if nerve-wracking break from his usual task of watching over his younger siblings—when Akins unexpectedly came to the woods around the plantation.[98] And indeed, when Susannah finally recanted her testimony, she referred to her identity as a wife, claiming that "she had been in a sort of Prison ever since Joes Death and chained for days together."[99] She said that Akins had followed her around for days, apparently relentlessly "talking to her about white Peoples being about the Plantation and Enticing the Negroes to runaway,"

she said she did not know what thing that Kate told her she had stood out as long as she could but her Master had made her say it that she is now convinced that if she continues to say as she formerly did these People that she had accused must suffer innocently . . . and that she believes Kate was the first beginner of it.[100]

Kate never retracted her story. Despite being "very solemnly pressed to consider what she was about," she maintained the veracity of the conspiracy on the part of both the enslaved and white men she had implicated. The governor declared the whole thing a "forgery" and both women, along with Robin and Sue, were ordered sent to the Workhouse immediately and to then be "sent off this Province." Akins "assured his Excellency [that] he would readily and chearfully" do so, and the whole affair came to an official close on February 7, 1749. Upon his death ten years later, James Akins's inventory included a woman named Kate, hinting that perhaps Akins had again avoided dispossessing himself of a woman whom his neighbors and family suspected had become far too intimate with her owner.[101] It appears that Robin, Susannah, and Sue suffered the intended banishment, as they do not reappear in the Carolina inventories. Susannah's "prison" had been transported, though if her sentiments were genuine, she was at least saved the anguish of implicating the innocents with whom she had made a home. Kate, on the other hand, must have constructed an entirely new prison— one in which she exchanged the ties of community for the isolation of her owners' affection.

The 1749 Carolina conspiracy explicitly reveals something that is implicit for the entire colonial period. Women lived and worked alongside enslaved men and in that capacity they resisted and accommodated to enslavement in ways that both were inflected by gendered conventions of mothering and femininity and resituated the meaning of motherhood, resistance, and political authority. Kate's proximity to Akins's emotional machinations is unusual, but her interpretive stance is perhaps less so. She watched the landscape for an opportunity to grab hold of some autonomy and did so in the context of a community defined by ties of work, friendship, marriage, sex, love, jealousy, and betrayal. The messiness of it all speaks volumes about what it meant to navigate the colonies as an enslaved woman.

Epilogue

The women whose lives inform this study deserve and demand our attention. They deserve it because women existed at the center, not the margins, of the colonial landscape—in all its economic, social, political, and moral realms. Women enslaved in the American colonies found themselves at the intersection of ideologies that would profoundly shape the colonial experience as a whole. As early American settlers puzzled through the problem of creating an economic return out of a hostile landscape, the ability and willingness to commandeer the labor of others on the basis of the alchemy of race was crucial. Women of African descent redefined familiar categories of work, race, inheritance, and parenting even as the categories remained, and still remain, in play. The very fact that we can talk about women who were enslaved in early America is a testament to the changes wrought by introducing new analytic categories of race, gender, and class to historical studies. This study has been my attempt to follow the interventions of revisionist history to their necessary conclusions.

When we invoke race and gender as critical analytic categories, we set in motion radical changes. The way we understand the configuration of power, the individual and collective meaning attached to events, the construction of communities, the rhythms of cultural encounter and transformation, the very terms of change are all transformed; for if one dismantles the assumptions about antecedents, then all that follows necessarily unfolds along fundamentally altered lines. If we "know" that Sally Hemmings stood by holding the candle that illuminated Jefferson's desk as he penned the Bill of Rights, we need to realign our notion of fundamental freedoms. His ability to consider his own freedom from bondage is not simply a freedom embodied in whiteness but one delineated by sex and gender. The concept of freedom, which Edmund Morgan linked more than thirty years ago to slavery, is problematized yet again. But "problematized" is not always the same as "transformed." In the end, Sally Hemmings is an anomaly by virtue of her notoriety. How many other names of African American women are so firmly etched on the historical record? Her sisters are reduced to their physicality, their anonymity belied by bodies that worked to both produce and reproduce the nation's most valuable resources. Origin myths are powerful. And we must continue to ask what, precisely, "transformation" might mean.

Despite the fact that the academic and intellectual community has changed since the creative upheavals of the 1970s, the academy continues to be fundamentally segregated. Although disciplinary boundaries are more porous, those boundaries still hold, and our intellectual interests are interpolated with our bodies such that attention to historical subjectivity is overwhelmingly assumed to be the province of historians whose own subjectivity is an object of scrutiny. We struggle to convert critiques of narrow visions of the past into constructive scholarship. We define the communities we study and find them bounded not so much by their own uniformity as by our own still-inadequate notion of boundaries. I don't pretend that *Laboring Women* is a model of complex inclusivity, but it is the product of an intellectual and political environment that rejects isolated categories of identity in an effort to inch toward a more unstable vision of the past and, potentially, of the present.

On the most reductive level, this study has illustrated simply that African women were there. They were crucial to all facets of racial slavery—to the generation of profits for those who owned and oversaw enslaved laborers and to bourgeoning notions of race as a tangible index of human distinction. I have argued that to write the history of racial ideology without gender is to omit the most fundamental reality of race as a trope—its heritability. Without understanding how the categories of race and gender inform each other, one is left with a one-dimensional sense of how these categories were mobilized and why they resonated with such clarity and violence in the lives of early modern Europeans.

The connection between Africa and brute agricultural labor was forged in the heady mix of economic greed, prurient voyeurism, and rigid categories of "us" and "them." The illustrated travel narratives centered African women as crucial objects of European interest, objects that stood (and still stand) in for the lived experience of women working on American plantations. Of course, the symbolic importance of African women in laying the groundwork for the trade in human beings does not stand in for women's actual experience of the Middle Passage, as Atlantic creoles, or, ultimately, as the labor force responsible for transforming empty fields into valuable export crops. To write these women back in to the narrative of the history

history of women, and the history of colonial America is to

...s soon as we do so, as soon as they become visible, we must ...pple with the interpretive and social consequences both of their lived experiences and of our own gesture of acknowledgement. And thus, what begins as perhaps an uncomplicated impulse becomes a much more complicated and difficult exercise in reconfiguring the past. One must ask whether centering women's use as objects is a logical or useful method for centering women as subjects. The gerund "laboring" that opens the title of this study explicitly suggests the multiplicities with which I am concerned. The work women did under slavery was simultaneously agricultural and reproductive, and the interplay between the two arenas is dependent also upon the symbolic work these women performed. While I am satisfied with the relationship between the various categories of work I evoke, I admit to a degree of unease about giving the symbolic primacy of place by opening this study with a chapter on images. Indeed, there is a tension through this study between the ideological work of enslaved women in travel narratives or probate records, their manual work in fields and in slaveowners' households, and the creative work of fashioning meaning in and through their identities as lovers, mothers, laborers, or even combatants. But ultimately I believe that tension is resolved precisely by the effort to construct meaning in a radically unfamiliar landscape. New World slave societies clearly prove the lie of the split between ideology and experience. And it is only by foregrounding the changes wrought by the institution of slavery upon all involved that one can locate the social categories such as work and family in the context of no-longer-familiar structures of meaning.

The archive yields very little without a struggle, and the effort to wrench meaning itself creates meaning all its own. I hope that my efforts to clarify the interpretive act are clear. I do so not to distance myself from the lives of the women and men about whom I write but rather to open up the possibilities of interpretation and to ask readers to do the same. The relationship between image and experience, always a vexed one in historical studies, is particularly vulnerable to rhetorical violence as historians work to create new maps of the notions of race and gender in early America. The archives do not allow women enslaved in early American colonies to speak. The absence of their literal voice in the documents does a violence that flows into current historical studies with almost unbearable ease. The process began from the initial moment of their subjugation at the hands of

European slave traders, and because of that link, the impossibility of recovery is inextricable from the moral imperative to attempt it.

Harriet Jacobs, Sojourner Truth, Elizabeth Keckley, and the women whose voices were captured through WPA interviews carefully crafted their stories. As Nell Painter has recently illustrated, even women whose narratives were wrenched from them exerted considerable control as they mustered efforts to retain their autonomy and direct their future. Still, it can be argued that there is a liability for the historian in their self-conscious narrations, for there is no question that women of African descent in the nineteenth century—particularly those whose literacy sanctioned their humanity—were fully aware of the context in which they spoke. Indeed, their texts are saturated with explicit references to the political and moral valence of their literacy. Harriet Jacobs provides the most salient example with her apologies to her readers around her unwillingness to touch upon her experience of sexual violation. Perhaps the inability of most African women in the seventeenth and eighteenth centuries to record their own texts becomes a way for the historian to avoid constructing a history of triumphant "sheroes" relentlessly articulating their resistant powers. Such one-dimensional women become part of the very tangle of racial violence that flesh-and-blood women mobilized their voices against and therefore serve little purpose in the process of reinscribing the humanity of those described again and again as less than human.

To write, then, of early American communities without attending to the process by which individuals constituted themselves as members of communities interwoven by violence as well as affinity is to reproduce the very act of erasure on which the entire colonial enterprise rests. It is not enough to say "There also were slaves there," when in fact those who were enslaved constituted an essential part of the colonial community. Historians must attend to the evidence of African women's presence in early America. For women of African descent, their demographic representation and the ideology that was mobilized to confine them, while not entirely equivalent, overlap in significant ways. David Eltis's evidence that four out of five women to cross the Atlantic before 1800 were African provides us with a startling entry point; the demography takes us aback. The historiography of the Atlantic colonies has systematically ignored women of African descent even while claiming to attend to all "significant" members of colonial communities. There is certainly a danger in deeming subjects worthy of inquiry solely on the basis of their numeracy, but in the context of their constructed invisibility, demography can be revealing. Readers familiar with the enduring richness of Peter Wood's *Black Majority* understand the radical potential of demography. In light of demographic realities and the stubborn unwillingness of our predecessors to acknowledge men and women who were not of European descent, social historians have been quick to mobilize the subversive potential of numbers as a corrective to histories driven by politically self-conscious evidence left by the property owners, elected officials, and spiritual leaders who people the past.

But just as demography can be inherently subversive, it can also function as a mediating device—as a way to preserve that which is or is desired to be unknowable. I have mobilized the figures of women and girls in the slave trade as the foundation for an argument that both depends on demography and transcends it. Over the course of the eighteenth century, the numbers of women in the trans-Atlantic trade steadily declined because of rising imports of children. The subsequent shift in women's proportionality on American and Caribbean plantations needs to be carefully examined, but both the presence and the absence of women in the rice, sugar, tobacco, and cotton fields carry gendered systems of meaning. My argument throughout this study has been that gender is always already in those fields, not that the exploitation of enslaved women's work in agriculture meant that gender distinctions disappear in the face of brutal work regimes. Therefore, while demography is critical, it cannot simply stand alone. Women's presence and absences in the Americas together constitute the context in which different meanings were attached to women's bodies and women's work.

Gender then—the range of interpretive possibilities around which socially inscribed identities are formed—is crucial to the work of early African-American history. The early modern Atlantic world came into being through innumerable acts of violence and violation perpetrated under the rubric of economic gain, nationalist conflict, and, ultimately, conviction in racially conferred notions of hierarchy. The challenge, for historians of the early Atlantic, at any rate, is to account for the equally innumerable acts of humanity, the ways in which men and women caught in the maelstrom of colonial upheavals reconfigured their subsequent sense of identity and possibility. Motherhood, for instance, cannot possibly remain unmodified when it is understood in the context of both the overwhelming commodification of the bodies of infants and their mothers, and the potential impulse women may have felt to interrupt such obscene calculations. I say "potential" because I am not interested in any account of behavior that rests on the flimsy grounds of the "natural." In such an account, a rejection of emotional connections, a refusal to protect, would be just as rational and likely a configuration of the mother-child relationship as was the bonds of motherhood that created Harriet Jacobs stunning seven-year ordeal—an story that has fast become an archetype of enslaved motherhood. I find the instability of the former possibilities far more compelling than the latter because it foregrounds my own contention that historically contingent factors shape human relationships in unpredictable, uncomfortable, and unsettling ways. While this is a position that begs for a scrutiny perhaps outside the purview of my own abilities, it is also one that requires an interruption of the kind of neatly inscribed notions of community we must now work to transcend.

Constrained by the vagaries of evidence and power, one must turn elsewhere—to travel accounts and probate records, to court cases and cargo lists—to evoke the range of possible experiences for women and men enslaved in the colonial period. An expansive methodology in and of itself is the obvious solution; it is not particularly innovative. But I am in search of an expansive methodology deployed in the service of, and open to the possibility of, contingency and the unknowability of the past.

Ultimately, I would like this study to have evoked a sense of the possible. Not just to refute any lingering suggestion that Africans in the Americas are a people without access to the furthest reaches of our historical experiences, but also to make clear that this, as are all projects engaged in the past, is a venture of profound, and profoundly creative, uncertainty.

Notes

Introduction

1. For connections around and across the Atlantic, see Julius S. Scott, "The Common Wind: Currents of Afro-American Communication in the Era of the Haitian Revolution," Ph.D. dissertation, Duke University, 1986, and Peter Linebaugh and Marcus Rediker, *The Many-Headed Hydra: Sailors, Slaves, Commoners, and the Hidden History of the Revolutionary Atlantic* (Boston: Beacon Press, 2002). For an overview of some of the larger themes of the Atlantic as a space of historical inquiry see David Armitage and Michael J. Braddick, eds., *The British Atlantic World, 1500–1800* (New York: Palgrave Macmillan, 2002).

2. Ira Berlin and Philip D. Morgan, "Introduction," in *Cultivation and Culture: Labor and the Shaping of Slave Life in the Americas*, ed. Ira Berlin and Philip D. Morgan (Charlottesville: University Press of Virginia, 1993).

3. Peter H. Wood, *Black Majority: Negroes in Colonial South Carolina from 1670 Through the Stono Rebellion* (New York: W.W. Norton, 1974); Kathleen M. Brown, *Good Wives, Nasty Wenches, and Anxious Patriarchs: Gender, Race, and Power in Colonial Virginia* (Chapel Hill: University of North Carolina Press, 1996); Philip D. Morgan, *Slave Counterpoint: Black Culture in the Eighteenth-Century Chesapeake & Lowcountry* (Chapel Hill: University of North Carolina Press, 1998); Ira Berlin, *Many Thousands Gone: The First Two Centuries of Slavery in North America* (Cambridge, Mass.: Harvard University Press, 1998); Kirsten Fischer, *Suspect Relations: Sex, Race, and Resistance in Colonial North Carolina* (Ithaca, N.Y.: Cornell University Press, 2002).

4. David Eltis, *The Rise of African Slavery in the Americas* (Cambridge: Cambridge University Press, 2000), 96.

5. I take as a starting point Sharon Harley and Rosalyn Terborg-Penn, eds., *The Afro-American Woman: Struggles and Images* (Port Washington, N.Y.: Kennikat, 1978), but one could look back to Toni Cade Bambara, *The Black Woman: An Anthology* (New York: New American Library, 1970); Joyce Ladner, *Tomorrow's Tomorrow: The Black Woman* (New York: Doubleday, 1971); Gerda Lerner, *Black Women in White America: A Documentary History* (New York: Pantheon Books, 1972); and Angela Y. Davis, "Reflections on the Black Woman's Role in the Community of Slaves," *Black Scholar* 3 (December 1971): 2–15.

6. Evelyn Brooks Higgenbotham, "Beyond the Sound of Silence: Afro-American Women in History," *Gender & History* 1 (1989): 50–67, 50.

7. For works on the linkages between race and gender, see bell hooks, *Ain't I a Woman: Black Women and Feminism* (Boston: South End Press, 1981); Angela Y.

Davis, *Women, Race, and Class* (New York: Random House, 1981); Evelyn Brooks Higginbotham, "African-American Women's History and the Metalanguage of Race," *Signs* 17 (Winter 1992): 251–74; Elsa Barkley Brown, "Polyrythms and Improvisations: Lessons for Women's History," *History Workshop Journal* 31 (Spring 1991): 85–90; and "'What Has Happened Here': The Politics of Difference in Women's History and Feminist Politics," *Feminist Studies* 18 (Summer 1992): 295–311. For studies of women in slavery, see Deborah Gray White, *Ar'n't I A Woman? Female Slaves in the Plantation South* (New York and London: W.W. Norton, 1985); Barbara Bush, *Slave Women in Caribbean Society, 1650–1838* (Bloomington: Indiana University Press, 1990), Hilary McD. Beckles, *Natural Rebels: A Social History of Enslaved Black Women in Barbados* (New Brunswick, N.J.: Rutgers University Press, 1989); Elizabeth Fox-Genovese, *Within the Plantation Household: Black and White Women of the Old South* (Chapel Hill: University of North Carolina Press, 1988); Marietta Morrissey, *Slave Women in the New World: Gender Stratification in the Caribbean* (Lawrence: University of Kansas Press, 1988); and Bernard Moitt, *Slave Women in the French Antilles, 1635–1848* (Bloomington: Indiana University Press, 2001). These six are the only book-length studies of women in slavery to date.

8. Brown, *Good Wives, Nasty Wenches*.

9. Fischer, *Suspect Relations*. For more of this kind of scholarship, see the works of Sharon Block, "Coerced Sex in British North America, 1700–1820," Ph.D. dissertation, Princeton University, 1995; Jennifer Spear, "'Whiteness and the Purity of Blood': Race, Sexuality, and Social Order in Colonial Louisiana," Ph.D. dissertation, University of Minnesota, 1999; and Juliana Barr, "The 'Seductions' of Texas: The Political Language of Gender in the Conquests of Texas, 1690–1803," Ph.D. dissertation, University of Wisconsin, 1999.

10. Hazel V. Carby, "White Woman Listen! Black Feminism and the Boundaries of Sisterhood," in *The Empire Strikes Back: Race and Racism in 70s Britain*, Center for Contemporary Cultural Studies (London: Hutchinson, 1982), reprinted in *Black British Cultural Studies: A Reader*, ed. Houston A. Baker, Jr., Manthia Diawara, and Ruth H. Lindeborg, 61–86 (Chicago: University of Chicago Press, 1996), 68.

11. White, *Ar'n't I a Woman*, 29–46. See also Bush, *Slave Women in Caribbean Society*, 11–12.

12. For the most recent work on gender and the slave trade, particularly one that focuses on the cultural factors that shaped the sale of women, see G. Ugo Nwokeji, "African Concepts of Gender and the Slave Traffic," *William and Mary Quarterly* 3rd ser. 58 (January 2001): 47–68.

13. For discussion of the colonial frontier, see Ira Berlin, "Time, Space, and the Evolution of Afro-American Society on Mainland British North America," *American Historical Review* 85 (1980): 55.

14. For a discussion of experience and historical evidence see Joan W. Scott, "The Evidence of Experience," *Critical Inquiry* 17 (Summer 1991), 773–97. For racism and the discourse of reproduction see Dorothy Roberts, *Killing the Black Body: Race, Reproduction, and the Meaning of Liberty* (New York: Vintage Books, 1997).

15. Nancy Schrom Dye and Daniel Blake Smith, "Mother Love and Infant Death, 1750–1920," *Journal of American History* 73 (1986): 329–53.

16. Orlando Patterson, *Slavery and Social Death: A Comparative Study* (Cambridge, Mass.: Harvard University Press, 1982), 133; and Bush, *Slave Women in Caribbean Society.*

Chapter 1. *"Some Could Suckle over Their Shoulder,": Male Travelers, Female Bodies, and the Gendering of Racial Ideology*

1. Sidney Mintz and Richard Price characterize the conflict between the imaginary savage and the human being with whom the slaveowner has daily encounters as the contradictory characteristic of slaveownership in the Americas. Sidney Mintz and Richard Price, *An Anthropological Approach to the Afro-American Past: A Caribbean Perspective* (Philadelphia: Institute for the Study of Human Issues, 1976).

2. For an overview of the concept, see Henry Louis Gates, Jr., "Introduction: Writing 'Race' and the Difference it Makes," in *"Race," Writing and Difference*, ed. Gates (Chicago: University of Chicago Press, 1986), 1–20.

3. Richard Ligon, *A True and Exact History of the Island of Barbados* (London, 1657), 12–13.

4. Peter Erickson, "Representations of Blacks and Blackness in the Renaissance," *Criticism* 35 (1993): 514–15; Lynda Boose, "'The Getting of a Lawful Race:' Racial Discourse in Early Modern England and the Unrepresentable Black Woman," in *Women, "Race," and Writing in the Early Modern Period*, ed. Margo Hendricks and Patricia Parker, (New York: Routledge, 1994), 35–55; Kim F. Hall, *Things of Darkness: Economies of Race and Gender in Early Modern England* (Ithaca, N.Y.: Cornell University Press, 1995), 4, 6–7.

5. Ligon, *True and Exact History of Barbados*, 51.

6. P. F. Campbell, "Richard Ligon," *Journal of the Barbados Museum and Historical Society* 37 (1985): 259. For more on Ligon, see Campbell, "Two Generations of Walronds," *Journal of the Barbados Museum and Historical Society* 38 (1989): 253–85.

7. Hall, *Things of Darkness*, 29–61. In her masterful exploration of the interdependencies of "whiteness" and "blackness," Toni Morrison asserts that "the fabrication of an Africanist persona is reflexive; an extraordinary meditation on the [white] self; a powerful exploration of the fears and desires that reside in the writerly conscious. It is an astonishing revelation of longing, of terror, of perplexity, of shame, of magnanimity. It requires hard work not to see this." *Playing in the Dark: Whiteness and the Literary Imagination* (Cambridge, Mass.: Harvard University Press, 1992), 17.

8. Peter Hulme, *Colonial Encounters: Europe and the Native Caribbean, 1492–1797* (London: Methuen, 1986), 11, 18.

9. Arguments about the primacy of race or gender in the original construction of difference constitute an enormous theoretical literature. See, for example, Henry Louis Gates, Jr., who asserts that "race has become a trope of ultimate, irreducible difference" in "Introduction: Writing, 'Race,' and the Difference It Makes," 5. Hortense J. Spillers similarly argues that racial slavery—the theft of the body—severed the captive from all that had been "gender-related [or] gender-specific" and thus

was an "ungendering" process, in her "Mama's Baby, Papa's Maybe: An American Grammar Book," *Diacritics* 17 (Summer 1987): 65–81. I would posit that, rather than creating a hierarchy of difference, simultaneous categories of analysis illuminate the complexity of racialist discourse in the early modern period. On the connections between categories of difference see Anne McClintock, *Imperial Leather: Race, Gender and Sexuality in the Colonial Contest* (New York: Routledge, 1995), 61. On simultaneous categories of analysis, see Elsa Barkley Brown, "Polyrhythms and Improvisations: Lessons for Women's History," *History Workshop Journal* 31 (Spring 1991): 85–90; and for cautions on the dangers of erecting hierarchies of difference see Ania Loomba, "The Color of Patriarchy: Critical Difference, Cultural Difference, and Renaissance Drama," in Hendricks and Parker, *Women, "Race," and Writing*, 17–34.

10. Anthony J. Barker, *The African Link: British Attitudes to the Negro in the Era of the Atlantic Slave Trade, 1550–1807* (London: Frank Cass, 1978), 22.

11. Pliny the Elder, *Natural History*, 10 vols., trans. H. Rackham (Cambridge, Mass., Harvard University Press, 1938–63), 2: 509–27; and Herodotus, *The History*, trans. David Grene (Chicago: University of Chicago Press, 1987), 4, 180, 191.

12. Elizabeth A. Clark, "Generation, Degeneration, Regeneration: Original Sin and the Conception of Jesus in the Polemic Between Augustine and Julian of Eclanum," in *Generation and Degeneration: Tropes of Reproduction in Literature and History from Antiquity to Early Modern Europe*, ed. Valeria Finucci and Kevin Brownlee (Durham, N.C.: Duke University Press, 2001), 30; and Valeria Finucci, "Maternal Imagination and Monstrous Birth: Tasso's *Gerusalemme liberata*," in *Generation and Degeneration*, ed. Finucci and Brownlee, 65.

13. Richard Bernheimer, *Wild Men in the Middle Ages: A Study in Art, Sentiment, and Demonology* (Cambridge, Mass.: Harvard University Press, 1952), 33–41, 34. See also Peter Mason, *Deconstructing America: Representations of the Other* (New York: Routledge, 1990), 47–56.

14. *The Travels of Sir John Mandeville: The Version of the Cotton Manuscript in Modern Spelling*, ed. A.W. Pollard (London: Macmillan, 1915), 109, 119.

15. Sharon W. Tiffany and Kathleen J. Adams, *The Wild Woman: An Inquiry into the Anthropology of an Idea* (Cambridge: Schenkman, 1985), 63. See McClintock, *Imperial Leather*, 22–23, for more on what she labels the "porno-tropic" tradition of European eroticized writing on Africa and the Americas.

16. *A Treatyse of the Newe India by Sebastian Münster* (1553), trans. Richard Eden (microprint) (Ann Arbor, Mich., 1966), 57. See also Mason, *Deconstructing America*, 55, who links Vespucci's surprise at Indian women's firm breasts with expectations grounded in medieval imagery of wild women with sagging breasts. The language of "fylth" and shame also evoked sodomy and treachery for English readers. See Alan Bray, "Homosexuality and the Signs of Male Friendship in Elizabethan England," in *Queering the Renaissance*, ed. Jonathan Goldberg (Durham, N.C.: Duke University Press, 1994), 48. The wording of Münster's passage materializes many ideas of difference.

17. It is significant that this association with sagging breasts, unusual childbearing, and monstrosity emerged so early. Not until the sixteenth century did elite European women begin to use corsets to impose an elevated shape to their bodies,

and only then did the elevated breasts of corseted women became a marker of refinement, courtliness, and status. For more on corsetry, see Georges Vigarello, "The Upwards Training of the Body from the Age of Chivalry to Courtly Civility," in *Fragments for a History of the Human Body, Part Two*, ed. Michael Feher, Ramona Naddaff, and Nadia Tazi (Cambridge, Mass.: MIT Press 1989), 154–55. Very soon thereafter, the "unused" breast, preserved among the elite by employing wetnurses for their children, embodied the "classic aesthetic ideal," according to Londa Schiebinger. "Why Mammals Are Called Mammals: Gender Politics in Eighteenth-Century Natural History," *American Historical Review* 98 (1993): 382–411, 401. For a broader discussion of breasts' symbolic valence, see Marilyn Yalom, *A History of the Breast* (New York: Knopf, 1997).

18. Two years after the publication of Münster's *Treatyse*, Eden translated and published Peter Martyr, *The Decades of the New Worlde of West India (1533)* (London, 1555), another description of the Columbus encounters.

19. Münster, *Treatyse*, trans. Eden, 4; Martyr, *Decades of the New Worlde*, 2.

20. As Stephen Greenblatt has illustrated, the female "go-between" was crucial in encounter narratives. Greenblatt discusses the "go-between" through his analysis of Bernal Diaz's conquest narrative. He argues that Doña Marina, a native woman who becomes connected to the Spaniards, is the "object of exchange, agent of communication, model of conversion, the only figure who appears to understand the two cultures, the only person in whom they meet. . . . The site of the strategic symbolic oscillation between self and Other is the body of this woman." *Marvelous Possessions: The Wonder of the New World* (Chicago: University of Chicago Press, 1991), 143.

21. Münster, *Treatyse*, trans. Eden, 5; Martyr, *Decades of the New Worlde*, 3.

22. Münster, *Treatyse*, trans. Eden, quoted in Louis Montrose, "The Work of Gender in the Discourse of Discovery," *Representations* 33 (1991): 1–41, 4.

23. Montrose, "Work of Gender," 5. For more on gender and cannibalism see Carla Freccero, "Cannibalism, Homophobia, Women: Montaigne's '*Des Canibales*' and '*De l'amitie*,'" in Hendricks and Parker, *Women, "Race," and Writing*, 73–83; for the etymological relationship between Caribs and cannibalism see Hulme, *Colonial Encounters*, 13–42.

24. Benzoni, *History of the New World*, trans. W. H. Smyth (1572; reprint, London, 1857), 3–4.

25. Greenblatt argues that "wonder is . . . the central figure in the initial European response to the New World, the decisive emotional and intellectual experience in the presence of radical difference," in *Marvelous Possessions*, 14.

26. Hall argues that "the painted woman often represents concerns over female unruliness, [and] the power of whiteness. . . . Male writers continually accuse women of hiding their 'blackness' under the fair disguise of cosmetics." *Things of Darkness*, 89–90. See also Paul-Gabriel Bouce for an early eighteenth-century reference to popular English beliefs correlating the size of a woman's mouth to that of her vagina. In "Some Sexual Beliefs and Myths in Eighteenth-Century Britain," in Bouce, *Sexuality in Eighteenth-Century Britain* (Manchester: Manchester University Press, 1982), 29–46, esp. 31–32.

27. Benzoni, *History of the New World*, 8; emphasis in the original. For an

example of the consequences of the "Black Legend" for English settlers in the Americas, see Karen Ordahl Kupperman, *Providence Island, 1630–1641: The Other Puritan Colony* (Cambridge: Cambridge University Press, 1993), 92–96.

28. Ralegh, "The Discoverie of the large rich and beautifull Empire of Guiana," in Richard Hakluyt, *The Principal Navigations Voyages Traffiques & Discoveries of the English Nation*, 12 vols. (1598–1600; reprint Glasgow, 1903–5), 10: 39; cited in Montrose, "Work of Gender," 20.

29. Karen Robertson, "Pocahantas at the Masque," *Signs* 21 (1996): 561, argues that "representation of an Indian woman does involve a dilemma for a male colonist, as expression of the erotic may signal his own lapse into savagery." See also Montrose, "Work of Gender," 21.

30. Benzoni, *History of the New World*, 11 (emphasis added).

31. In eighteenth-century England, writers intent on displaying the *natural* role of motherhood for English women idealized the "savage mother" and in doing so created tension as the dichotomy of civilized English and savage Other slipped. See Felicity A. Nussbaum, *Torrid Zones: Maternity, Sexuality, and Empire in Eighteenth-Century English Narratives* (Baltimore: Johns Hopkins University Press, 1995), 48–53.

32. Hugh Honour, *The New Golden Land: European Images of America from the Discoveries to the Present Time* (New York: Pantheon, 1975), 54–55.

33. Theodore de Bry, ed., *Grand Voyages*, 13 vols. (Frankfurt am Main, 1590–1627). De Bry also published the series *Small Voyages*, 12 vols. (Frankfurt am Main: 1598–1628), chronicling voyages to Africa and the East Indies. Language training among the elite, particularly in Latin, meant that those with access to de Bry's volumes would possess the capacity to understand them; see Lawrence Stone, *The Crisis of the Aristocracy, 1558–1641* (Oxford: Oxford University Press, 1965), 672–702. For a discussion of the availability of books on reproduction and physiognomy see Patricia Crawford, "Sexual Knowledge in England, 1500–1750," in *Sexual Knowledge, Sexual Science: The History of Attitudes to Sexuality*, ed. Roy Porter and Mikulas Teich, (Cambridge: Cambridge University Press, 1994), 86.

34. Bernadette Bucher, *Icon and Conquest: A Structural Analysis of the Illustrations of de Bry's Great Voyages*, trans. Basia Miller Gulati (Chicago: University of Chicago Press, 1981); Joyce E. Chaplin, "Natural Philosophy and an Early Racial Idiom in North America: Comparing English and Indian Bodies," *William and Mary Quarterly* 3rd ser. 54 (January 1997): 231.

35. Bucher, *Icon and Conquest:* 135, 145. Bucher's analysis introduces a complex discussion of the morphology of consumption and an explanation that locates the reversal of production with consumption at the heart of anthropophagi in the icon of the sagging breast. See Bucher, *Icon and Conquest,* 73–120. For the formulation of the long-breasted woman in the Americas, see also Mason, *Deconstructing America,* 47–60; and for late seventeenth- and eighteenth-century use of the icon of sagging breasts, see Londa Schiebinger, *Nature's Body: Gender in the Making of Modern Science* (Boston: Beacon Press, 1993), 160–63.

36. Gomes Eannes de Azurara, *The Chronicle of the Discovery and Conquest of Guinea*, in *Documents Illustrative of the History of the Slave Trade*, ed. Elizabeth

Donnan, 1: 40. I am grateful to Prof. Stephanie Smallwood for drawing my attention to this passage and to its resonance for this project.

37. Emily C. Bartels, "Imperialist Beginnings: Richard Hakluyt and the Construction of Africa," *Criticism* 34 (1992): 517–38, 519. See Winthrop D. Jordan, *White over Black: American Attitudes Toward the Negro, 1550–1812* (Chapel Hill: University of North Carolina Press, 1968), 3–43, for further discussion of the fluidity of images of Africa in the early modern European imaginary. See also David Armitage, "The New World and British Historical Thought: From Richard Hakluyt to William Robertson," in *America in European Consciousness, 1493–1750*, ed. Karen Ordahl Kupperman (Chapel Hill: University of North Carolina Press, 1995), 52–75. Ultimately, the Hakluyt collection served as "a mythico-historical amalgam intended to introduce . . . conquest and colonization to Europeans." Bucher, *Icon and Conquest*, 22.

38. "The second voyage [of Master John Lok] to Guinea . . . 1554," in Richard Hakluyt, *The Principal Navigations, Voiages, Traffiques, and Discoueries of the English Nation*, 12 vols. (London, 1598–1600), 6: 167, 168; see also Martyr, *Decades of the New Worlde*, 356. "Garamantes" originally occur in Pliny, who describes them as an Ethiopian race that did not practice marriage. See John Block Friedman, *The Monstrous Races in Medieval Art and Thought* (Cambridge, Mass.: Harvard University Press, 1981), 15.

39. Barker, *African Link*, 121.

40. André Thevet, *The New Founde Worlde, or Antarctike*, trans. Thomas Hacket (London, 1568), 65–66; cited in Laura Fishman, "French Views of Native American Women in the Early Modern Era: The Tupinamba of Brazil," in *Women and the Colonial Gaze*, ed. Tamara Hunt and Micheline R. Lessard (New York: New York University Press, 2002), 72.

41. Martyr, *Decades of the New Worlde*, 356. In this paragraph, Martyr clearly borrows from Herodotus and Pliny. Monsters served a variety of functions in early modern literature, "from prodigies to pathology," and were an important part of descriptions of Africa "since Antiquity," according to Katherine Park and Lorraine J. Daston, "Unnatural Conceptions: The Study of Monsters in Sixteenth and Seventeenth Century France and England," *Past and Present* 92 (1981): 21–54, 23, 37.

42. "The first voyage made by Master William Towrson Marchant of London, to the coast of Guinea . . . in the yeere 1555," in Hakluyt, *Principal Navigations*, 6: 184. Jordan notes that "many chroniclers [of Africa] made a point of discussing the Negro women's long breasts and ease of childbearing," though he apparently takes such observations as fact rather than symbol in *White over Black*, 39–40. Schiebinger places the equation of African women's breasts with the udders of goats in a continuum of European imagery of, and relationship to, the breast. She notes that nineteenth-century ethnologists compared and classified breast size and shape much as they did skulls. Not surprisingly, they used African breasts, like African heads, to prove the linkage between Africans and animals. See Schiebinger, "Why Mammals Are Called Mammals," 402–3, 394. Philip Morgan asserts that, beginning with Richard Ligon, "Barbadians were the first coherent group within the Anglo-American world to portray blacks as beasts or as beastlike," in "British Encounters with Africans and African-Americans, circa 1600–1780" in *Strangers Within the Realm: Cul-*

tural Margins of the First British Empire, ed. Bernard Bailyn and Philip D. Morgan (Chapel Hill: University of North Carolina Press, 1991), 174.

43. Towrson, "The first voyage made by Master William Towrson," 187. Once he categorized women, Towrson relegated them to a passive role in the background of his interactions with Africans, despite the fact that they "worke as well as the men" (185).

44. Richard Jobson, *The Golden Trade or a Discovery of the River Gambra . . . by Richard Jobson* (1628: reprint, Amsterdam: Theatrum Orbis Terrarum ; New York: Da Capo Press, 1968).

45. Jobson, *The Golden Trade*, 35.

46. Jobson, *The Golden Trade*, 33

47. Jobson, *The Golden Trade*, 36.

48. Jobson, *The Golden Trade*, 56 (emphasis added).

49. Jobson, *The Golden Trade*, 58, 52, 54; and Greenblatt, *Marvelous Possessions*, 14.

50. Samuel Purchas, *Hakluytus Posthumus, or Purchas His Pilgrimes: Contayning a History of the World in Sea Voyages and Land Travells by Englishmen and Others*, 20 vols. (1624; reprint Glasgow: J. MacLehose and Sons, 1905).

51. "Observations of Africa, taken out of John Leo his nine Bookes, translated by Master Pory . . . ," in *Purchase His Pilgrimes*, 5: 517.

52. Drawing from Todorov's discussion of nudity in encounter narratives, Roxann Wheeler notes that remarks about African nudity are always qualified as European observers concede that in fact they are witnessing only partial nudity and that high social rank is often signified by clothing. Roxann Wheeler, *The Complexion of Race: Categories of Difference in Eighteenth-Century British Culture* (Philadelphia: University of Pennsylvania Press, 2000), 117.

53. "The Strange Adventures of Andrew Battell"(1625), in *Purchas His Pilgrimes*, 6: 367–517.

54. "Strange Adventures of Andrew Battell," 377–78.

55. "Strange Adventures of Andrew Battell," 32.

56. Pieter de Marees, *Description and Historical Account of the Gold Kingdom of Guinea*, trans. and ed. Albert van Dantzig and Adam Jones (1602; reprint Oxford: Oxford University Press, 1987), xvii.

57. De Marees, "Description and historicall declaration of the golden Kingdome of Guinea," in *Purchas His Pilgrimes*, 6: 251. I cite the Purchas edition rather than the modern edition in order to draw on the narrative that early modern English readers encountered.

58. De Marees, "Description and historicall declaration of the Golden Kingdome," in *Purchase His Pilgrimes*, 6: 258–59.

59. De Marees, "Description and historicall declaration of the Golden Kingdome," in *Purchase His Pilgrimes*, 6: 259.

60. De Marees, *Description and Historicall Account of the Gold Kingdom of Guinea*, 23.

61. De Marees, "Description and Historicall declaration of the Golden Kingdome," 259.

62. Linda E. Merians, " 'Hottentot': The Emergence of an Early Modern Racist

Epithet," *Shakespeare Studies* 26 (1998): 123–45, paragraph 26. Available online at http://search.epnet.com/direct.asp?an = 1531148&db = aph.

63. Thomas Herbert, *A Relation of Some Yeares Travaile Begunne Anno 1626* (London, 1634), 14. Available online at http://wwwlib.umi.com/eebo.

64. Herbert, *Relation of Some Yeares Travaile*, 17.

65. De Marees, "Description and historicall declaration of the Golden King-dome," 261. Oxford English Dictionary, 2nd ed., 1989.

66. Fynes Moryson, *Shakespeare's Europe: A survey of the Condition of Europe at the end of the Sixteenth Century, Being unpublished chapters of Fynes Moryson's Itinerary*, 2nd ed. (1617; reprint New York: Benjamin Blom, 1967), 485.

67. Alexander Gunkel and Jerome S. Handler, trans. and eds., "A Swiss Medical Doctor's Description of Barbados in 1661: The Account of Felix Christian Spoeri," *Journal of the Barbados Museum and Historical Society* 33 (May 1969): 7.

68. Nicholas Villaut, *A Relation of the Coasts of Africk . . .* (London, 1670), 157. Available online at http://wwwlib.umi.com/eebo

69. RB [Richard Burton, alias Nathaniel Crouch], *A View of the English Acqui-sitions in Guinea and the East Indies* (London, 1686), 8. Available online at http://wwwlib.umi.com/eebo

70. Londa Schiebinger uses Blumenbach's theories to highlight the connec-tion between race and sex in the Enlightenment in "The Anatomy of Difference: Race and Sex in Eighteenth-Century Science," *Eighteenth Century Studies* 23 (Sum-mer 1990): 392–93.

71. John Ogilby, *America* (London, 1671), 316, 360, 641.

72. Jordan, *White over Black*, 39.

73. Marylynn Salmon, "The Cultural Significance of Breastfeeding and Infant Care in Early Modern England and America," *Journal of Social History* 28 (1994): 247–70. For more on seventeenth-century wet nursing in England, see Valerie Fildes, *Wet Nursing: A History from Antiquity to the Present* (Oxford: Basil Blackwell, 1988), 79–100.

74. Linda Pollock, "Embarking on a Rough Passage: The Experience of Preg-nancy in Early Modern Society," in *Women as Mothers in Pre-Industrial England*, ed. Valerie Fildes (New York: Routledge, 1990), 45.

75. Saidiya Hartman, *Scenes of Subjugation: Terror, Slavery, and Self-Making in Nineteenth-Century America* (New York: Oxford University Press, 1997), 51.

76. Wheeler, *The Complexion of Race*, 65.

77. Nussbaum, *Torrid Zones*, 73–74. Ruth Perry argues that the valuation of "motherhood" developed in England alongside empire so that not until the nine-teenth century did "the production of children for the nation and for the empire constitute childbearing women as a national resource." "Colonizing the Breast: Sex-uality and Maternity in Eighteenth-Century England," *Journal of the History of Sex-uality* 2 (1991): 204, 205. And, indeed, there is a growing literature that explores the relationship between nineteenth- and twentieth-century imperialism and the inter-sections between childbearing and the national resources of colonial powers. See, for example, Anna Davin, "Imperialism and Motherhood," in *Tensions of Empire: Colonial Cultures in a Bourgeois World*, ed. Frederick Cooper and Ann Laura Stoler (Berkeley: University of California Press, 1997), 87–151. My own work and that of

Sharon Block, Kathleen Brown, Kirsten Fischer, and others suggest that the connections between reproduction and colonial identity were in fact in place some 200 years earlier. See also Greenblatt, *Marvelous Possessions*, 7.

78. Barbot, *A Description of the Coasts of North and South-Guinea*, in *A Collection of Voyages*, ed. A. Churchill (London, 1732), 36. See also J. D. Fage, "'Good Red Herring': The Definitive Barbot," *Journal of African History* 34 (1993): 315–20.

79. William Snelgrave, "Introduction," *A New Account of Some Parts of Guinea and the Slave Trade* (1734; reprint London: Cass, 1971).

80. Snelgrave, *New Account of Some Parts of Guinea*, 3–4.

81. Nussbaum, *Torrid Zones*, 79.

82. John Atkins, *A Voyage to Guinea, Brazil, and the West-Indies* (1735; reprint London: Cass, 1970), 50.

83. Atkins, *Voyage to Guinea*, 108.

84. Wheeler, *Complexion of Race*, 102.

85. Peter Kolb, *Present State of the Cape of Good Hope* (London, 1731) reproduced in Schiebinger, *Nature's Body*, 162.

86. William Smith, *A New Voyage to Guinea* (London, 1744), 142–43.

87. Smith, *New Voyage to Guinea*, 195, 208.

88. Smith, *New Voyage to Guinea*, 210.

89. Because of its length, its first-person narration, and its lack of appropriate punctuation, this section of Smith's narrative has been misunderstood as coming from him rather than his informant. Nussbaum, *Torrid Zones*, 78–79, and Wheeler, *Complexion of Race*, 130.

90. Smith, *New Voyage to Guinea*, 253–54.

91. Smith, *New Voyage to Guinea*, 257, 266.

92. Falconbridge's observation immediately follows a description of childbearing: "A few years after a woman is delivered, she takes her child on her back to wherever her vocation leads her." And while Falconbridge ascribes endemic bowleggedness among adults to this maternal practice; she notably does not go on to suggest that women's long breasts allowed them to nurse the children on their backs. Anna Maria Falconbridge, *Two Voyages to Sierra Leone, During the Years 1791–2–3*, in *Maiden Voyages and Infant Colonies: Two Women's Travel Narratives of the 1790s*, ed. Deirdre Coleman (London: Leicester University Press, 1999), 45–168, 74, emphasis in the original.

93. Edward Long, "History of Jamaica, 2, with notes and corrections by the Author" (1774), Add. Ms., 12405, p364/f295, British Library, London. Long was not alone in his delight at suggesting interspecies copulation. Londa Schiebinger details seventeenth- and eighteenth-century naturalists' investigations of apes. She notes that naturalists "ascribed to [simian] females the modesty they were hoping to find in their own wives and daughters, and to males the wildest fantasies of violent interspecies rape," in *Nature's Body*, 75–114, 78.

94. Robin Blackburn, *The Making of New World Slavery: From the Baroque to the Modern, 1492–1800* (London: Verso, 1997), 527–45.

95. Long, "History of Jamaica," p380/f304 (emphasis added).

96. Elaine Scarry, *The Body in Pain: The Making and Unmaking of the World* (New York: Oxford University Press, 1985), 15, 185–91. Hortense Spillers argues that

pain inflicted under slavery ungendered "female flesh," but I argue something different. While assertions about pain-free childbirth are, in a sense, an effort on the part of the slaveowner to ungender female flesh in order to make it labor, the discourse around women's work remains deeply gendered. It is simply that Europeans' gendered notions of differences between black women and black men include confidence in women's ability to do and proclivity for hard labor. See Spillars, "Mama's Baby, Papa's Maybe," 67–68.

97. Lyndal Roper, *Oedipus and the Devil: Witchcraft, Sexuality and Religion in Early Modern Europe* (London: Routledge, 1994), 203–4. See also Mary Poovey, *Uneven Developments: The Ideological Work of Gender in Mid-Victorian England* (Chicago: University of Chicago Press, 1988), 24–50. Poovey shows that, during mid-nineteenth-century debates over anesthesia for women in childbirth, members of the medical and religious professions argued that to relieve women of pain would interfere with God and deprive women of the pain that ultimately civilized them. See also Diane Purkiss, "Women's Stories of Witchcraft in Early Modern England: The House, the Body, the Child," *Gender and History* 7 (1995): 408–32, for the connection between pain-free childbirth and accusations of witchcraft. On the connection between midwifery and accusations of witchcraft, Carol F. Karlson notes that "the procreative nurturing and nursing roles of women were *perverted* by the witches," in *The Devil in the Shape of a Woman: Witchcraft in Colonial New England* (New York: W.W. Norton, 1989), 144.

98. Ligon, *True and Exact History of Barbadoes*, 13, 15–16.

99. Another example can be found in John Gabriel Stedman's relationship to the mulatto woman Johanna in his *Narrative of a Five Years Expedition Against the Revolted Negroes of Surinam: Transcribed . . . from the Original 1790 Manuscript*, ed. Richard Price and Sally Price (Baltimore: Johns Hopkins University Press, 1988). His attempts to persuade this almost-English woman to return to Britain with him failed in part because she understood what he did not—that her status as "exceptional" was contingent on her location in Surinam. Had she gone to England, she would have become, in effect, a "high African" woman. See Homi K. Bhabha, "Of Mimicry and Man: The Ambivalence of Colonial Discourse," *October* 28 (Spring 1984): 108, for a discussion of the symbolic importance of those who occupy the borders of colonial spaces.

100. Friedman, *Monstrous Races*, 29.

101. Ligon, *True and Exact History of Barbadoes*, 17. Henry Louis Gates, Jr. argues that the primary theme in Afro-American literature is the quest for literacy, a response to white assertions that blacks lacked "reason." Just as Phyllis Wheatley's literacy had to be authenticated by thirteen white male signatories, so all Afro-American writing was an oppositional demonstration of authentic intellect that "was a political act." Ligon's need to hear the voices of the black women who excited his lust and curiosity suggests a precursor to the black literary link between reading and reason. "The *spoken* language of black people had become an object of parody at least since 1769," Gates writes. *Figures in Black: Words, Signs, and the "Radical" Self* (New York: Oxford University Press, 1987), 5–6 (emphasis added). Ligon wrote during a period that predated that tradition of parody and instead located reason and civility in spoken language.

102. Ligon, *True and Exact History of Barbadoes*, 44.
103. Ligon, *True and Exact History of Barbadoes*, 47.
104. Ligon, *True and Exact History of Barbadoes*, 51.
105. Gunkel and Handler, "A Swiss Doctor," 7.
106. Greenblatt, *Marvelous Possessions*, 55.

Chapter 2. *"The Number of Women Doeth Much Disparayes the Whole Cargoe": The Trans-Atlantic Slave Trade and West African Gender Roles*

1. David Eltis, *The Rise of African Slavery in the Americas* (Cambridge: Cambridge University Press, 2000), 96–97.

2. While Eltis has noted that African women account for four out of five of all female migrants to the Americas before 1800, those figures need to be revised downward for North America as a whole. Drawing on Bernard Bailyn's estimates in *Voyagers to the West: A Passage in the Peopling of America on the Eve of Revolution* (New York: Knopf, 1986), Kathleen Brown has illustrated that women from Britain outnumbered African women by approximately 1.6 to 1 in North America. Kathleen Brown, "The History of Women in the United States to 1865 from a Global Perspective," unpublished paper, October 2002.

3. Price differentials between men and women were such that women—who commanded much more money when sold in the interior than in the Atlantic trade—were only made available to the trans-Atlantic slave trade when they were captured so near the coast that transport to the interior did not make financial sense. On the other hand, men captured in the interior would be routinely transported to the coast where they would fetch higher prices in the trans-Atlantic trade. See Paul E. Lovejoy and David Richardson, "Competing Markets for Male and Female Slaves: Prices in the Interior of West Africa, 1780–1850," *International Journal of African Historical Studies* 28 (1995): 282. At most embarkation points, women cost less than men did. The exception was Senegambia, the "only known region where Europeans paid equal prices for males and females." David Geggus, "Sex Ratio, Age, and Ethnicity in the Atlantic Slave Trade: Data from French Shipping and Plantation Records," *Journal of African History* 30 (1989): 41.

4. [George Hingston], "Journal Abourd the Arthur," December 5, 1677–March 31, 1678; Series T70, volume 1213, Public Record Office, Kew, London (hereafter T70/1213, PRO).

5. Hingston Journal, March 5, 1678, T70/1213, PRO.

6. "Invoice & Accounts for the ship Hannah," 1689, T70/1217, PRO.

7. Over the course of the seventeenth century, females leaving the Bight of Biafra constituted between 50 and 51 percent of total captives. I derive these figures from the CD-ROM interface of *The Trans-Atlantic Slave Trade: A Database on CD-ROM*, ed. David Eltis, Stephen D. Behrendt, David Richardson, and Herbert S. Klein (Cambridge: Cambridge University Press, 1999). As in figures that follow, this means that total percentages do not always reflect percentages on every slave-trad-

ing vessel. Information on sex ratio is not given for every ship; therefore, percentages are derived from available data.

8. For the trade as a whole there are small differences in mortality rates by age and sex—children were slightly more vulnerable than adults and men slightly more than women. See Herbert S. Klein, Stanley L. Engerman, Robin Haines, and Ralph Shlomowitz, "Transoceanic Mortality: The Slave Trade in Comparative Perspective," *William and Mary Quarterly* 3rd ser. 58 (January 2001): esp. 102 and Tables VII and VIII.

9. Hingston Journal, March 2, 1678, T70/1213, PRO.

10. Hingston Journal, April 22, 1678, T70/1213, PRO. For an argument that the linguistic similarities within African regions, coupled with long-standing familiarity with European languages, minimized the "Babel" that allegedly separated enslaved men and women from one another, see John Thornton, *Africa and Africans in the Making of the Atlantic World, 1400–1680* (Cambridge: Cambridge University Press, 1992), 216. Drawing on evidence that there were far fewer ports of embarkation for Africans than for Europeans, David Eltis also directly counters Mintz and Price's supposition that linguistic barriers created disaggregate "crowds" aboard slave ships. Eltis, *Rise of African Slavery*, 248–50.

11. See note 3 above.

12. Sex ratios among enslaved people disembarking on the island of Barbados between 1650 and 1700 were close to even, with males constituting between 52 and 58 percent; *Trans-Atlantic Slave Trade Database*.

13. Royal African Company to John Braithwate, Robert Cruikshank, and Benjamin Peake, July 9, 1730, Letter Book to Cape Coast Castle, 1728–1740, T70/54: 18, PRO.

14. Royal African Company to John Braithwate et al., July 8, 1731, T70/54: 47, PRO.

15. May 4, 1728 & October 25, 1728, Factors' Diaries, Bence Island 1727–28, T70/1465, PRO.

16. June 1, 1728, T70/1465, PRO.

17. 16–19 April 1715, Diary of William Baillie, Commenda, 1714–1718, Royal Africa Company Records T70/1464, PRO.

18. October 11, 1744, Royal Africa Company to Charles Orfeus, Gambia, T70/56, PRO.

19. Sidney Mintz and Richard Price see the genesis of Afro-American culture in the relationships forged on the slave ship. Thus, these women, as shipmates, became sisters by the time they set foot on the shores of Barbados. Sidney Mintz and Richard Price, *An Anthropological Approach to the Afro-American Past: A Caribbean Perspective* (Philadelphia: Institute for the Study of Human Issues, 1976), 22.

20. For his caution about the wisdom of the "numbers game," see David Henige, "Measuring the Immeasurable: The Atlantic Slave Trade, West African Populations, and the Pyrrhonian Critic," *Journal of African History* 27 (1986): 296–313. For the past two decades, economic historians have scrutinized the parameters of the Atlantic slave trade. Broadly speaking, aggregate numbers, regional and historical fluctuations, and age and gender ratios have been the foci of recent historical inquiry into the Atlantic slave trade. For synthesis and reviews of recent scholarship

see Paul Lovejoy, "The Impact of the Atlantic Slave Trade on Africa: A Review of the Literature," *Journal of African History* (1989): 365–97. See also Janet Ewald, "Slavery in Africa and the Slave Trades from Africa," *American Historical Review* 97 (April 1992): 465–85; and D. R. Murray, "Slavery and the Slave Trade: New Comparative Approaches," *Latin American Research Review* 28 (1993): 150–61.

The Atlantic trade is itself merely one element of a three-part system—the Atlantic, Oriental, and African slave trades. Six to seven million persons were transported in other trades. Patrick Manning explores the comparative weight and impact of each of the trades on African societies, in *Slavery and African Life: Occidental, Oriental, and African Slave Trades* (Cambridge: Cambridge University Press, 1990).

21. On ethnicity, see Daniel Littlefield, *Rice and Slaves: Ethnicity and the Slave Trade in Colonial South Carolina* (Baton Rouge: Louisiana University Press, 1981), 8–21. Hilary Beckles's assertion that planters in Barbados actively imported higher numbers of female laborers has been effectively challenged by the work of David Eltis and Stanley Engerman. Hilary McD. Beckles, *Natural Rebels: A Social History of Enslaved Black Women in Barbados* (New Brunswick, N.J.: Rutgers University Press, 1989), 7–23; David Eltis and Stanley Engerman, "Fluctuations in Sex and Age Ratios in the Trans-Atlantic Slave Trade, 1663–1864," *Economic History Review* 46 (1993): 311–12.

22. As synthesized by Michael Gomez, "There are seven general regions from which slaves were imported. The first, Senegambia, encompasses that stretch of coast extending from the Senegal River to the Casamance, to which captives from as far away as the upper and middle Niger valleys were transported. The second, Sierra Leone, includes the territory from the Casamance to Assini, or what is now Guinea-Bissau, Guinea, Sierra Leone, Liberia, and the Ivory Coast. Adjoining Sierra Leone is the Gold Coast, occupying what is essentially contemporary Ghana. Further east lay the fourth region, the Bight of Benin, stretching from the Volta to the Benin River and corresponding to what is now Togo, contemporary Benin, and southwestern Nigeria. The Bight of Biafra, in turn, comprised contemporary southeastern Nigeria, Cameroon, and Gabon. West Central Africa includes Congo (formerly Zaire) and Angola, and the seventh region, Mozambique-Madagascar, refers to southeastern Africa, including what is now Mozambique, parts of Tanzania, and the island of Madagascar." *Exchanging Our Country Marks: The Transformation of African Identities in the Colonial and Antebellum South* (Chapel Hill: University of North Carolina Press, 1998), 27.

23. David Eltis, "The Volume and Structure of the Transatlantic Slave Trade: A Reassessment," *William and Mary Quarterly* 3rd ser. 58 (January 2001): 26, Tables 1 and 2.

24. David Eltis and David Richardson, "West Africa and the Transatlantic Slave Trade: New Evidence of Long-Run Trends," *Slavery & Abolition* 18 (1997): 17.

25. Eltis and Richardson, "West Africa and the Transatlantic Slave Trade," 21; Eltis, *Rise of African Slavery*, 245–48; and Philip D. Morgan, "The Cultural Implications of the Atlantic Slave Trade: African Regional Origins, American Destinations, and New World Developments," *Slavery and Abolition* 18 (1997): 127. According to the database, while some 30 percent of embarkation points in Africa are unspecified

for enslaved persons arriving to Barbados in the second half of the seventeenth century, the percentages (rounded to the nearest whole number) are as follows:

Region	1651–75	1676–1700
Unspecified	30	25
Bight of Biafra	31	8
Bight of Benin	18	32
Gold Coast	18	14
Senegambia	—	5
Sierra Leone	1	—
South East Africa	2	5
West Central Africa	—	9

26. Eltis and Engerman, "Fluctuations," table 1; see also Geggus, "Sex Ratio," table 5.

27. G. Ugo Nwokeji, "African Conceptions of Gender and the Slave Traffic," *William and Mary Quarterly* 3rd ser. 58 (January 2001): 49, 52.

28. Eltis and Richardson, "West Africa and the Trans-Atlantic Slave Trade," 30–31 and Table 3.

29. Royal African Company to Captain Robert Conley, June 12, 1678, Copies of Instructions From the Royal African Company of England to the Captains of Ships in their Services December 10, 1685–April 16, 1700, T70/61: 38, PRO.

30. Claire Robertson and Martin Klein, "Women's Importance in African Slave Systems," in *Women and Slavery in Africa*, ed. Claire Robertson and Martin Klein (Madison: University of Wisconsin Press, 1983), 4.

31. RAC to Sam Morley, September 27, 1692, Instructions, T70/61: 99, PRO; and RAC to William Reeves, September 18, 1694, Instructions, T70/61: 115, PRO; and RAC to Petley Wybourne, January 3, 1688, Copies of Letters Sent by the Royal African Company of England to the Coast of Africa, T70/50: 86, PRO.

32. David Eltis and Stanley Engerman, "Was the Slave Trade Dominated by Men?" *Journal of Interdisciplinary History* 23 (Autumn 1993): 256.

33. By 1688 Whydah and Allada exported 20,000 men and women annually, mostly to the English. Robin Law, *The Slave Coast of West Africa, 1550–1750: The Impact of the Atlantic Slave Trade on African Society* (Oxford: Clarendon Press, 1991), 167.

34. Previously, Yoruba-speaking peoples from further inland constituted the majority of captives exported from Whydah and Allada. Law, *The Slave Coast of West Africa*, 187.

35. "Diago Gomes" in Richard Jobson, *The Discovery of River Gambra*, edited and with additional material by David P. Gamble and P. E. H. Hair (London: Hakluyt Society, 1999), 277 [264] (bracketed numbers are page numbers in the original publication).

36. Jobson, *Discovery of River Gambra*, 90 [140].

37. Eltis and Engerman, "Fluctuations in Sex and Age Ratios," 313–15.

38. Martin Klein suggests that the large numbers of enslaved women and chil-

dren in late nineteenth-century Sudan indicates that "vast numbers of women and children were absorbed as slaves within the Sudan even during the period of the Atlantic slave trade." See Klein, "Women and Slavery in the Western Sudan," in Robertson and Klein, *Women and Slavery in Africa*, 74.

39. Geggus argues that women's agricultural work shaped African traders' willingness to make them available to European slave buyers, while Eltis and Engerman take an opposing view. Geggus, "Sex Ratio, Age and Ethnicity," 37; Eltis and Engerman, "Fluctuations in Sex and Age Ratios," 313.

40. Eltis and Engerman, "Fluctuations in Sex and Age Ratios," 313–15; and Nwokeji, "African Conceptions of Gender and the Slave Traffic," 62.

41. David Van Nyendael, "A Description of Rio Formosa or . . . Benin," in William Bosman, *A New and Accurate Description of the Coast of Guinea*, (1704; first English edition London, 1705; fourth English edition London: Frank Cass & Co., 1967), 423–68, 462, 570n.

42. Portuguese settlements at Allada on the westernmost edge of the Bight of Benin had by the middle of the seventeenth century so influenced local rulers that in 1658 the King of Allada sent requests to Europe for priests to come baptize him. John Thornton, "On the Trail of Voodoo: African Christianity in Africa and the Americas," *Americas* 44 (January 1988): 264.

43. Walter Rodney, *A History of the Upper Guinea Coast, 1545–1800* (London: Oxford University Press, 1970), 38–70.

44. Gomez, *Exchanging our Country Marks*, 43. For a larger discussion of sex ratio and proximity to the coast see Manning, *Slavery and African Life*, 98.

45. Boubacar Barry, *Senegambia and the Atlantic Slave Trade* (1988; Cambridge: Cambridge University Press, 1998), 28–9.

46. Law, The *Slave Coast of West Africa*, 34–56.

47. "Wilhelm Johann Muller's Description of the Fetu Country, 1662–9," in *German Sources for West African History, 1599–1669*, ed. Adam Jones (Weisbaden, Steiner, 1983), 132–359, 243. Sixty years, later John Atkins similarly identified marketing as the provenance of women on the Grain Coast. John Atkins, *A Voyage to Guinea, Brazil, and the West Indies* (London, 1735; reprint London: Frank Cass, 1970), 100.

48. "Samuel Brun," *German Sources for West African History*, 44–90, 78.

49. "Wilhelm Muller," *German Sources*, 154. Walter Ong discusses the constant repetition of knowledge in oral cultures in *Orality and Literacy* (New York: Metheun, 1982), 24–35.

50. "Wilhelm Muller," *German Sources*, 201.

51. *The Voyages of Cadamosto* (1455/56) in Jobson, *Discovery of the River Gambra*, 253.

52. Rodney, *Upper Guinea Coast*, 16, 22, 32.

53. Eltis, *Rise of African Slavery*, 170.

54. See Jobson, *Discovery*, 55 [118]; for a fifteenth-century description see Cadamosto, 254.

55. Nicolas Villaut, *A Relation of the Coasts of Africk Called Guinee* (London, 1670), 46.

56. Edna G. Bay, "Belief, Legitimacy and the Kpojito: An Institutional History

of the 'Queen Mother' in Precolonial Dahomey," *Journal of African History* 36 (1995): 9.

57. Thornton, "On the Trail of Voodoo," 267.

58. Gomez, *Exchanging Our Country Marks*, 129.

59. Bay, "Belief Legitimacy and the Kpojito," 16.

60. "Wilhelm Muller," *German Sources*, 214.

61. Villaut, *Guinee*, 161.

62. For a discussion of the socio-symbolic value of female circumcision in contemporary African societies see Janice Boddy, "Womb as Oasis: The Symbolic Context of Pharaonic Circumcision on Rural Northern Sudan," in *The Gender/Sexuality Reader: Culture, History, Political Economy*, ed. Roger N. Mancaster and Micaela di Leonardo (New York: Routledge, 1997), 309–24; Hanny Lightfoot-Klein, *Prisoners of Ritual: An Odyssey into Female Genital Circumcision in Africa* (New York: Herrington Park Press, 1989). Both studies are critical of the practice but both also evoke the considerable power of the collective rite among girls and women.

63. "Wilhelm Muller," 216. *German Sources.*

64. Bosman, *New and Accurate*, 208.

65. "Wilhelm Muller," *German Sources*, 217, 335n.

66. Van Nyendael, "Description," in Bosman, *A New and Accurate Description of the Coast of Guinea*, 444; and Ogilby, *Africa*, 482. Ulsheimer also notes circumcision rites, but he only describes male circumcision. Ulsheimer wrote "these people have themselves circumcised, like the Jews." Andreas Josua Ulsheimer, "Andreas Josua Ulsheimer's Voyage of 1603–4," *German Sources*, 40.

67. Mintz and Price discuss the indiscriminacy with which any particular African carryover was either maintained or abandoned. New cultural institutions formed at the point at which women and men "exchanged ritual information." That exchange occurred when an individual with particular cultural knowledge stepped in to provide information about the birth of twins, for example, or the manner in which a house should be constructed. *An Anthropological Approach*, 23–24.

68. Van Nyendael, "Description," in Bosman, *A New and Accurate Description of the Coast of Guinea*, 444; Ogilby, *Africa*, 482.

69. Ogilby, *Africa*, 466.

70. R. R. Schoenmaeckers, I. H. Shah, R. Lesthaeghe, and O. Tambashe, "The Child-Spacing Tradition and the Post-Partum Taboo in Tropical Africa," in *Child-Spacing in Tropical Africa: Traditions and Change*, ed. Hilary Page and Ron Lesthaeghe (London: Academic Press, 1981), Table 3.

71. Herbert Klein and Stanley Engerman have examined fertility differentials between the West Indies and the Americas and maintain that different lactation practices explain different rates of reproduction in slave societies. North American women breast-fed for one year, while Caribbean women did so for two. Their work is supported by evidence on weaning in Barbados presented by Jerome Handler and Robert Corruccinni that confirms that enslaved children in Barbados appear not to be weaned until their third or fourth year. See Klein and Engerman, "Fertility Differentials Between Slaves in the United States and the British West Indies: A Note on Lactation Practices and Their Possible Implications," *William and Mary*

Quarterly 3rd ser. 35 (1978): 357–74; and Jerome Handler and Robert Corruccinni, "Weaning Among West Indian Slaves: Historical and Bioanthropological Evidence from Barbados," *William and Mary Quarterly* 3rd ser. 43 (January 1986): 111–17.

72. John Barbot *A Description of the Coasts of North and South-Guinea*, in *A Collection of Voyages*, ed. A. Churchill (London, 1732), 88.

73. Barbot, *A Description of the Coasts of North and South-Guinea*, 272.

74. Muller described a decorative bustle worn around women's hips that also served as a ledge upon which infants could be perched. "Wilhelm Muller," *German Sources*, 205.

75. Jobson, *Discovery of River Gambra*, 110 [153], 109 [153], 114 [155].

76. "Wilhelm Muller," *German Sources*, 161.

77. Villault, *Guinee*, 200–202.

Chapter 3. "The Breedings Shall Goe with Their Mothers": Gender and Evolving Practices of Slaveownership in the English American Colonies

1. David Eltis, *The Rise of African Slavery in the Americas* (Cambridge: Cambridge University Press, 2000), 98.

2. Kirsten Fischer has used bastardy and slander cases in colonial North Carolina court records to construct a complex analysis of nonliterate settlers' ideas about race and identity. Her work provides a crucial corollary to the analysis I present here. *Suspect Relations: Sex, Race, and Resistance in Colonial North Carolina* (Ithaca, N.Y.: Cornell University Press, 2001).

3. Lee J. Alston and Morton Owen Schapiro, "Inheritance Laws Across Colonies: Causes and Consequences," *Journal of Economic History* 44 (June 1984): 279.

4. Lois Green Carr and Lorena S. Walsh, "The Planter's Wife: The Experience of White Women in Seventeenth-Century Maryland," *William and Mary Quarterly* 3rd ser. 34 (October 1977): 553.

5. Robert W. Fogel, *Without Consent or Contract: The Rise and Fall of American Slavery* (New York: W.W. Norton, 1989), 124.

6. Alston and Schapiro, "Inheritance Laws," 278; for multigeniture in New England, see Toby L. Ditz, "Ownership and Obligation: Inheritance and Patriarchal Households in Connecticut, 1750–1820," *William and Mary Quarterly* 3rd ser. 47 (April 1990): 235–65.

7. Walter Edgar, *South Carolina: A History* (Columbia: University of South Carolina Press, 1998), 168.

8. C. Ray Keim, "Primogeniture and Entail in Colonial Virginia," *William and Mary Quarterly* 3rd ser. 25 (October 1968): 557; and Jean Butenhoff Lee, "The Problem of Slave Community in the Eighteenth-Century Chesapeake," *William and Mary Quarterly* 3rd ser. 43 (July 1986): 355. See also Lorena Walsh, *From Calabar to Carter's Grove: The History of a Virginia Slave Community* (Charlottesville: University Press of Virginia, 1997), 44–45.

9. That insecurity was clearly multivalent and by no means confined to the first generation of settlers. The language of successful Philadelphia merchants

reflected their own sense of circumspection, their "dependence on the opinion of others" and the ways in which their identity as successful men was shaped by this uncertainty and vulnerability in the face of gossip and slander. Toby L. Ditz, "Shipwrecked; or, Masculinity Imperiled: Mercantile Representations of Failure and the Gendered Self in Eighteenth-Century Philadelphia," *Journal of American History* 81 (June 1994): 80.

10. See Kathleen Brown's discussion of this tax levy in *Good Wives, Nasty Wenches, Anxious Patriarchs: Gender, Race, and Power in Colonial Virginia* (Chapel Hill: University of North Carolina Press, 1996), 116–20. For further discussion of the Maryland statutes, see Peter Bardaglio "'Shamefull Matches': The Regulation of Interracial Sex and Marriage in the South Before 1900," in *Sex, Love, and Race: Crossing Boundaries in North American History*, ed. Martha Hodes (New York: New York University Press, 1999), 114–15.

11. For an overview of interiority, see Mechal Sobel, "The Revolution in Selves: Black and White Inner Aliens," in *Through a Glass Darkly: Reflections on Personal Identity in Early America*, ed. Ronald Hoffman, Mechal Sobel, and Fredrika J. Teute (Chapel Hill: University of North Carolina Press, 1997), 163–205. On the development of a legal profession, see Cornelia Hughes Dayton, "Turning Points and the Relevance of Colonial Legal History," *William and Mary Quarterly* 3rd ser. 50 (January 1993): 7–17.

12. Robert Olwell, *Masters, Slaves, and Subjects: The Culture of Power in the South Carolina Low Country, 1740–1790* (Ithaca, N.Y.: Cornell University Press, 1998), 8.

13. David Galenson, *White Servitude in Colonial America* (Cambridge: Cambridge University Press, 1981), 23–26.

14. This tax law was the first colonial law that differentiated labor according to race. As Kathleen Brown has shown, it locates the defining racial moment in colonial Virginia in the bodies of laboring women. Brown, *Good Wives, Nasty Wenches*, 108–20.

15. Mindie Lazarus-Black, *Legitimate Acts and Illegal Encounters: Law and society in Antigua and Barbuda* (Washington, D.C.: Smithsonian Institution Press, 1994), 13.

16. Gary A. Puckrein, *Little England: Plantation Society and Anglo-Barbadian Politics, 1627–1700* (New York: New York University Press, 1984), 31.

17. William Hay to Archibald Hay, Barbados, September 10, 1645; cited in David W. Galenson, *Traders, Planters, and Slaves: Market Behavior in Early English America* (Cambridge: Cambridge University Press, 1986), 9; Richard S. Dunn, *Sugar and Slaves: The Rise of the Planter Class in the English West Indies, 1624–1713* (Chapel Hill: University of North Carolina Press, 1972), 57.

18. Galenson, *White Servitude*, 100.

19. Alison Games, "Opportunity and Mobility in Early Barbados," in *The Lesser Antilles in the Age of European Expansion*, ed. Robert L. Paquette and Stanley L. Engerman (Gainsville: University Press of Florida, 1996), 174. On the difficulty of accurately assessing the growth of both the slave and free population of Barbados between 1640 and 1680, see Dunn, *Sugar and Slaves*, 74–76.

20. Leo F. Stock, ed., *Proceedings and Debates of the British Parliaments*

Respecting North America (Washington, D.C.: 1930), 1: 248, cited in Richard Sheridan, *Sugar and Slavery: An Economic History of the British West Indies, 1623–75* (Baltimore: Johns Hopkins University Press, 1974), 237; see also Beckles, *White Servitude and Black Slavery in Barbados*, 47 and Hilary McD. Beckles, "The Economic Origins of Black Slavery in the British West Indies 1640–1680: A Tentative Analysis of the Barbados Model," *Journal of Caribbean History* 16 (1982): 50.

21. Bernard Moitt, *Slave Women in the French Antilles, 1635–1848* (Bloomington: Indiana University Press, 2001), 10.

22. *A Brief Description of the Province of Carolina* (London, 1666) in *Historical Collections of South Carolina . . . From Its Discovery to Its Independence in the Year 1776*, ed. B. R. Carroll, 2 vols. (New York: Harper and Brothers, 1836), 2: 17.

23. Samuel Wilson, *An Account of the Province of Carolina* (London, 1682) in Carroll, ed., *Historical Collections*, 27.

24. John Lawson, *A New Voyage to Carolina*, ed. Hugh Talmage Lefler (1709; reprint Chapel Hill: University of North Carolina Press, 1984), 91. For the reiteration, see John Brickell, *The Natural History of North Carolina* (Dublin, 1737), cited in Julia Cherry Spruill, *Women's Life and Work in the Southern Colonies* (1938; reprint New York: W.W. Norton, 1972), 46. For similar language from Pennsylvania writers, see Susan Klepp "Revolutionary Bodies: Women and the Fertility Transition in the Mid-Atlantic Region, 1760–1820," *Journal of American History* 85 (December 1998): 917–18.

25. Fischer, *Suspect Relations*, 102.

26. Thomas Durham to Sir Nathanie Rich, October or November 1620, in *The Rich Papers: Letters from Bermuda, 1615–1646*, ed. Vernon A. Ives (Toronto: University of Toronto Press, 1984), 218; cited in Alison Games, *Migration and the Origins of the English Atlantic World* (Cambridge, Mass.: Harvard University Press, 1999), 75.

27. "Privilidges Granted to the People of the Hebrew Nation That are to goe to the Wilde," n.d. (circa 1650), Papers Relating to the English Colonies in America, 1627–1699, Egerton Manuscripts, 2395, p. 46, British Library, London.

28. Isaac Wilson, Records of Perquimans Precinct Court, *Colonial Records of North Carolina*, ed. William L. Sanders, 10 vols. (Raleigh: State of North Carolina, 1886–90), 1: 650, cited in Fischer, *Suspect Relations*, 27.

29. John Archdale, "A New Description of That Fertile and Pleasant Province of Carolina, By John Archdale, 1707," in *Narratives of Early Carolina, 1650–1708*, ed. Alexander Salley (New York: Charles Scribner's Sons, 1911), 300. Note: it was not until the city was incorporated in 1783 that Charlestown became Charleston.

30. Most enslaved Indians brought to Charlestown from the back country were sold to Virginia or the West Indies, where their cultural isolation would make escape or resistance more difficult. Indeed, one of the precipitating factors leading to the devastating Yamasee War of 1715 was the conviction on the part of the Yamasee and the Creeks that agents sent to undertake a census of their villages were secretly planning to enslave them all. On Native American slavery in early Carolina, see Theda Perdue, *Slavery and the Evolution of Cherokee Society, 1540–1806* (Knoxville: University of Tennessee Press, 1979), 19–35; and James H. Merrell, *The Indians'*

New World: Catawbas and Their Neighbors from European Contact Through the Era of Removal (NewYork: W.W. Norton, 1991), 66.

31. Theda Purdue, *Cherokee Women: Gender and Culture Change, 1700–1835* (Lincoln: University of Nebraska Press, 1998), 67–68.

32. Gary B. Nash, *Red, White, and Black: The Peoples of Early America*, 2nd ed. (Englewood Cliffs, N.J.: Prentice-Hall, 1982), 134.

33. William L. McDowell, ed., *Journal of the Commissioners of the Indian Trade September 20, 1710–August 29, 1718* (Columbia: University of South Carolina Press, 1955), 186; cited in Perdue, *Slavery and the Evolution of Cherokee Society*, 28.

34. Ira Berlin, "Time, Space, and the Evolution of Afro-American Society on Mainland British North America," *American Historical Review* 85 (1980): 55. Berlin borrows from Peter H. Wood's *Black Majority: Negroes in Colonial South Carolina from 1670 Through the Stono Rebellion* (New York: W.W. Norton, 1974) in naming this equalitarianism "sawbuck equality."

35. Figures derived from Will Books, Barbados Archives Cave Hill, Barbardos.

36. Will of Christian Brockehaven, August 14, 1651, Will Books, Series RB6, Item 13, page 142, Barbados Department of Archives, St. Michael's, Barbados (hereafter RB6/13: 142, BA).

37. Will of John Turner, December 23, 1650, RB6/11: 459, BA.

38. Will of unknown, August 19, 1651, RB6/11: 523, BA.

39. Will of John Wilkinson, May 13, 1652, RB6/11: 507, BA. Note: "assenegroes" is a reference to mules.

40. Will of Thomas Kennett, November 5, 1659, RB6/14: 438, BA.

41. Will of Robert Wilshire, August 1, 1654, RB6/14: 553, BA.

42. Eltis, *Rise of African Slavery*, 196.

43. His behavior was probably not the result of a shared racial connection because blacks and mulattoes who owned property appear to be always so designated in the records. Will of John Copper, July 19, 1656, RB6/12: 144, BA. Jerome Handler and John Pohlman raised the question of Barbadian planters' manumission of enslaved women in relation to that of enslaved men. They found that manumission rates of women to men reflected gender ratios in the population as a whole. In other words, women were not being disproportionally manumitted as a result of sexual connections with white men. This is not what occurred in North America, where manumitted women outnumbered men. Handler and Pohlman stress throughout their study that the number of manumitted slaves in seventeenth-century Barbados was, in any case, "minute." "Slave Manumissions and Freedmen in Seventeenth-Century Barbados," *William and Mary Quarterly* 3rd ser. 41 (July 1984): 398–400.

44. Eltis, *Rise of African Slavery*, 220, 92n.; Walsh, *Calabar to Carter's Grove*, 31.

45. "Reasons of ye Planters of Barbados about Nonpayment of Custom," Thomas Povey, Booke of Entrie of Forreigne Letters, 1655–1660, Additional Manuscripts 11411, British Library, London. Hilary Beckles has argued that it wasn't until the 1670s that slaveowners in Barbados became aware of the economic potential embodied by enslaved children, and that in the 1650s slaveowners were actually hostile to women's reproductive capacity. Hilary McD. Beckles, "The Economic Ori-

gins of Black Slavery in the British West Indies, 1640–1680: A Tentative Analysis of the Barbados model," *Journal of Caribbean History* 16 (1982): 50, 54. The evidence I present below suggests otherwise.

46. Will of Daniel McFarland, January 31, 1733, South Carolina Department of Archives and History, Columbia (hereafter WB 32–37: 85, SCDAH).

47. Will of Nicholas Bochet, April 11, 1733, WB32–37: 45, SCDAH.

48. "Extracts from Henry Whistler's Journal of the West India Expedition, 1654," in *The Narrative of General Venables*, ed. C. H. Firth (New York: Longmans, 1900), 146. The wills of planters in the 1650s do not bear out Henry Whistler's observations.

49. Will of John James, January 24, 1654, RB6/14:432, BA. English common law stipulated that widows be left at least a third of their husband's property.

50. Jean Butenhoff Lee notes that in Virginia "masters planned to dispose of children still in the womb [or] . . . deliberated what to do with a woman's future increase." Jean Butenhoff Lee, "The Problem of Slave Community in the Eighteenth-Century Chesapeake," *William and Mary Quarterly* 3rd ser. 43 (July 1986): 359.

51. Sale of David Davis, May 30, 1710, SP 1709–25: 136, SCDAH.

52. In all but six documents in which women were mentioned—65 percent of them—young children accompanied enslaved women. Of those six, two women were accompanied by "boys" or "girls." Such language evokes a pubescent or adolescent child who may well have come to the colony via the Middle Passage. Three of the remaining groups of women were accompanied by "increase."

53. The restoration of the Stuart monarchy in England in 1660 reinvigorated English trade with Africa. That same year, the crown granted a charter to the Royal Adventurers for trade of all sorts, including slaves. From August 1663 through March 1664, the company delivered at least 3,075 slaves to Barbados. The initial company dissolved in 1667 and was replaced in 1672 by the Royal African Company. See K. G. Davies, *The Royal African Company* (London: Longmans, 1957), 40–44. The record of Barbados purchases covers 2,020 enslaved Africans sold to 206 slaveowners between 1662 and 1664. Barbados Ledger, 1662–1664, Company of Royall Adventurers, T70/646, PRO.

54. Two purchases did not identify the gender of the enslaved. Barbados Ledger, T70/646: 29, PRO.

55. Richard Sheridan noted that among all slave imports to Barbados through the Company of Royal Adventures in the 1660s, women constituted just under one half. Sheridan, *Sugar and Slavery*, 243. Planters' wills in the 1660s similarly reflect a proclivity for a sex-balanced labor force. Between 1660 and 1669, 138 slaveowners mentioned enslaved persons in their wills. Wills that itemized women jumped from 37 percent (eighteen) the previous decade to 59 percent (eighty-two) in the 1660s; 71 percent of slaveowners called the enslaved by name, and 73 percent of these wills contained women. Generally, in contrast with the 1650s, slaveowners in the 1660s appear more focused upon, or intimate with, the men and women they enslaved. The purchasing patterns revealed in the Royal African Company records carry over into the wills that itemize the enslaved. Most wills suggest balanced slaveholdings;

indeed, in the 1660s more wills mention no adult men than no adult women (twenty-six and ten respectively).

56. "Nevis Island Census, 1677–78," in Vere Langford Oliver, ed., *Caribbeana: Being Miscellaneous Papers Relating to the History, Genealogy, Topography, and Antiquities of the British West Indies,* 6 vols. (London, 1912), 3: 29–35, 70–81.

57. Will of Judith Mossier, June 14, 1668, RB6/10: 130, BA.

58. In the 1660s, thirteen (16 percent) slaveowners who mentioned women in their wills used the term "increase" to pass down future children. Another fifteen (18 percent) coupled men and women together in an act explicitly based on reproductive potential. Will of Roger Peele, June 27, 1668, RB6/10: 58, BA.

59. Will of John Redway, January 11, 1660, RB6/14: 503, BA.

60. Will of Nicholas Cowell, October 23, 1667, RB6/9: 321, BA.

61. Will of Robert Shepheard, July 1, 1668, RB6/10: 91, BA.

62. Will of Thomas Barnes, September 12, 1669, RB6/8: 33, BA.

63. Will of William Baldwin Sr., October 22, 1658, RB6/13: 226.

64. Will of Nathaniel Pope, May 26, 1719, Westmoreland County Deeds and Will Books, as cited in Philip D. Morgan and Michael L. Nicholls, "Slaves in Piedmont, Virginia, 1720–1790," *William and Mary Quarterly* 3rd ser. 46 (April 1989): 235.

65. Morgan and Nicholls, "Slaves in Piedmont," 235.

66. Inventory of William Browne, March 17, 1662, RB3/3: 276, BA. Carol Barash, noting a similar proximity between the enslaved and cattle in Jamaica, maintains that in doing so both are "consumed if not literally eaten" by the slaveowner anxious to emphasize the commodification of both the bodies in his possession. Carol Barash, "The Character of Difference: The Creole Woman as Cultural Mediator in Narratives About Jamaica," *Eighteenth Century Studies* 23 (Summer 1990): 413.

67. Governor Atkins to Board of Plantations, 3 February 1675, Entry of Papers, CO29/2: 55.

White men able to bear arms	10,000	Negro men	10,525
White male children	3,030	Negro boys	5,827
White women and female children		Negro women and girls	16,121
	8,695		
Total	21,725	Total	32,473

68. Journal of Assembly, April 16, 1675, CO31/2: 178. PRO.

69. Governor Atkins to Committee on Plantations, August 15, 1676, entry of Papers, CO29/2:91, PRO.

70. Willoughby Yeamans to Christopher Barrow, April 7, 1678, Records of the Register of the Secretary of the Province, 1675–1695 and 1703–1709, Secretary of State Miscellaneous Volume II, folio 58, SCDAH, Columbia (hereafter Sec. of State Misc. 2: 58, SCDAH.) John Yeamans was the son of Sir John Yeamans, first governor of the colony who died in 1674.

71. Dunn, *Sugar and Slaves,* 116.

72. Joseph West to Johna Lynch 20 June 1685, Register of Province Records,

1682–90, Book A: 203–4, SCDAH. I am grateful to Dr. Charles Lesser of the South Carolina Department of Archives and History for pointing me to this record.

73. Thomas Ashe, *Carolina, or a Description of the Present State of That Country . . . 1682* (London: 1682), printed in *Narratives of Early Carolina,* ed. Alexander Salley (New York: Charles Scribner's Sons, 1911), 139 (emphasis mine). The legacy of Barbados would resonate for black and white Carolinians in infamous ways as well. Death rates among whites in Bridgetown and Charlestown, the capital towns of Barbados and South Carolina respectively, at comparable periods of each colony's development are striking in their similarity. In both towns, the ratio of burials to baptisms approached four to one. Peter Coclanis, *The Shadow of a Dream: Economic Life and Death in the South Carolina Low Country, 1670–1920* (New York: Oxford University Press, 1989), 43. For more on the connections between the colonies, see Jack P. Greene, "Colonial South Carolina and the Caribbean Connection," *South Carolina Historical Magazine* 88 (1987): 192–210; Richard S. Dunn, "The English Sugar Islands and the Founding of South Carolina," *South Carolina Historical Magazine* 72 (1971): 81–93.

74. Ultimately, the cultivation of rice would create mortality rates for enslaved Africans that would also connect them with the Caribbean: Sugar plantations and the Carolina lowcountry were home to similarly devastating death rates, much higher than those on coffee, tobacco or cotton plantations. See Fogel, *Without Consent or Contract,* 127.

75. During the proprietary period (before 1719), while the largest number of assemblymen and deputies always came from England, Barbadian settlers consistently and closely made up the second largest group. Planters maintained a professional ascendancy in the ranks of legislators throughout the period, 60 to 70 percent of assemblymen. For tabulations of the high proportion of both Barbadians and slaveowning planters among South Carolina legislators, see Richard Waterhouse, *A New World Gentry: The Making of a Merchant and Planter Class in South Carolina, 1670–1770* (New York: Garland, 1989), 37–42. Speaking solely in terms of social conventions, Eugene Sirmans notes that as late as 1750 "there were still traces of a Barbadian influence in South Carolina as the [white] people retained some West Indian customs." Eugene Sirmans, *Colonial South Carolina: A Political History, 1663–1763* (Chapel Hilll: University of North Carolina Press, 1966), 229.

76. Michael Craton, *Testing the Chains: Resistance to Slavery in the British West Indies* (Ithaca, N.Y.: Cornell University Press, 1982), 257; and Barry Higman, *Slave Populations of the British Caribbean, 1807–1834* (Baltimore: Johns Hopkins University Press, 1984), 314. In discussing the emergence of "protonatalism" among slaveowners, Higman mentions that Barbadian legislators urged slaveowners to pay 5 shillings to a slave woman at the birth of a child, but that the practice "was not universal" (349). Perhaps Barbadian slaveowners' disinclination to reward childbirth is rooted in the earlier "naturalization" of childbirth in the eyes of Barbadian slaveowners. Why reward what already occurs?

77. Inventory of Richard Fowell, February 2, 1679, in Agnes L. Baldwin, List of Items Found in Inventories of Estates and Merchants Lists Recorded in South Carolina, 1670–90, Unpublished Guide, South Carolina Historical Society (hereafter, SCHS).

78. John Smith, 13 February 1682, in Baldwin, "List of Items Found," SCHS.

79. Sale of William Hewlett, August 23, 1704, SP 1714–15: 125, SCDAH.

80. Sale of Abraham Wright, February 28, 1703, SP 1709–25: 71, SCDAH.

81. Sale of Daniell Goble, May 20, 1705, SP 1711–17: 6, SCDAH.

82. Sale of Robert Daniel, October 17, 1709, SP 1709–25: 43, SCDAH.

83. Will of George Dearsley, June 20, 1702, SP 1711–19: 33, SCDAH.

84. Will of Richard Harris, April 7, 1711, SP 1711–19: 17, SCDAH.

85. Russell R. Menard, "Financing the Lowcountry Export Boom: Capital and Growth in Early South Carolina," *William and Mary Quarterly* 3rd ser. 51 (October 1994): 661.

86. For more on the particular nature of slave property in planter bequests, see Jean Butenhoff Lee, "Land and Labor: Parental Bequest Practices in Charles County, Maryland 1732–83," in *Colonial Chesapeake Society*, ed. Lois Green Carr, Phillip D. Morgan, and Jean B. Russo, 306–41 (Chapel Hill: University of North Carolina Press, 1988).

87. Edward Morns Betts, ed., *Thomas Jefferson's Farm Book: With Commentary and Relevant Extracts from Other Writings*, 2 vols.(Princeton, N.J.: Princeton University Press, 1953), 2: 46; quoted in Lee, "Land and Labor," 334, 53n.

88. Edward McCrady, *TheHistory of South Carolina Under the Proprietary Government, 1670–1715* (New York: Macmillan, 1901), 118; Wood, *Black Majority*, 15–20; Robert M. Weir, *Colonial South Carolina: A History* (New York: kto Press, 1983), 51–54; and A. Leon Higginbotham, Jr., *In the Matter of Color: Race and the American Legal Process, the Colonial Period* (Oxford: Oxford University Press, 1978), 165.

89. David Barry Gaspar, "With a Rod of Iron: Barbados Slave Laws as a Model for Jamaica, South Carolina, and Antigua, 1661–1697," in *Crossing Boundaries: Comparative History of Black People in Diaspora*, ed. Darlene Clark Hine and Jacqueline McLeod 343–66; (Bloomington: Indiana University Press, 1999); Dunn, "English Sugar Islands," 81–82; and M. Eugene Sirmans, "The Legal Status of the Slave in South Carolina, 1670–1740," *Journal of Southern History* 28 (November 1962): 464.

90. "An Act For the Better Ordering and Governing of Negroes and Slaves," [1696], in *Statutes at Large of South Carolina*, 7 vols., ed. David J. McCord (Columbia, S.C.: A.S. Johnston, 1840), 7: 352–65.

91. Brown, *Good Wives, Nasty Wenches*, 135.

92. Act XII, 1662, in William W. Herring, *Statutes at Large of Virginia*, 2 vols., (Richmond: Franklin Press, 1819–1820), 2:170; cited in Higginbotham, *Matter of Color*, 43.

93. Richard Ligon, *A True and Exact History of the Island of Barbados* (London, 1657),47.

94. Joseph Boone and Richard Beresford, Agents for the Commons House of Assembly in South Carolina, to the Council of Trade and Plantations, December 5, 1716, *Calendar of State Papers*, Colonial Series, January 1716–July 1717 (London: His Majesty's Stationery Office, 1930), 29: 216. See also Wood, *Black Majority*, 128–29.

95. *Calendar of State Papers*, 29: 216; Nash *Red, Black, and White*, 134.

96. Vincent Harlow, *A History of Barbados, 1625–85* (Oxford: Clarendon Press, 1926; reprint New York: Negro Universities Press, 1969), 338–39; and Jerome S. Han-

dler and Frederick Lange, *Plantation Slavery in Barbados: An Archeological and Historical Investigation* (Cambridge, Mass.: Harvard University Press, 1978), 28–29.

97. Handler and Lange, *Plantation Slavery*, 38–40

98. Beckles, *Black Rebellion in Barbados: The Struggle Against Slavery, 1627–1838* (Bridgetown, Barbados: Caribbean Research and Publications, 1987), 40–41; Craton, *Testing the Chains*, 110–11.

99. Will of Robert Gretton, June 10, 1674, RB6/9: 195, BA.

100. Will of Miles Brathwaite, November 5, 1674, RB6/15: 32, BA.

101. Robert "King" Carter, May 21, 1728, Robert Carter Letterbook, 1727–1728, Virginia Historical Society; cited in Philip D. Morgan, *Slave Counterpoint: Black Culture in the Eighteenth-Century Chesapeake and Lowcountry* (Chapel Hill: University of North Carolina Press, 1998), 381 n6.

102. Will of Phillip Lovell, November 15, 1674, RB6/13: 404, BA.

103. Will of Ellis Rycroft, July 14, 1677, RB6/13: 401, BA.

104. Will of William Death, December 23, 16[7]6, Will Books, RB6/12:507, BA.

105. Will of William Duces, February 25, 1662, Deed Books, RB3/3:252, BA.

106. Will of John Mullivax, January 6, 1675, RB6/9: 240, BA.

107. Deposition of William Forster, July 31, 1679, RB6/10: 194, BA.

108. Will of Margarett Ellacott, September 11, 1680, RB6/10: 328, BA.

109. Will of Edmond Dyne, November 16, 1680, RB6/14: 261, BA.

110. Will of William Trattle, September 5, 1674, RB6/13: 476, BA.

111. Will of William Lesley, December 13, 1674, RB6/9: 210, BA.

112. Bricknell, *Natural History*, 274, cited in Fischer, *Suspect Relations*, 165.

113. Will of John Mortimer, April 10, 1733, WB32–37: 104.

114. Will of Isaac Childs, November 5, 1734, WB32–37: 151, SCDAH. Childs's second son Isaac did indeed accumulate further property. When he died in 1743 he owned eighteen enslaved men and seventeen women, five of them mothers with living children. Inventory of Isaac Childs, July 1743, Charleston inventories, 1739–43, part II, WPA Transcript volume 114, no page number (hereafter WPA 114, SCDAH).

115. Will of Arthur Hall, 1732, Willbook 1732–37, p. 17, (hereafter WB32–37: 17, SCDAH).

116. Will of Robert Hume, December 16, 1736, WB37–40: 89, SCDAH.

117. It should be noted that in only two wills between 1730 and 1739 did slaveowners refer to male-female couples as "husband" and "wife." In the decade following the Stono Rebellion of 1739, that number rose only to four (or 3 percent of all named wills).

118. According to Allan Kulikoff's examination of wills in Prince George and Charles Counties, Maryland planters were inclined either to bequeath land to sons and slaves and other moveable property to daughters or to divide bequests of slaves along gender lines—daughters receiving female and sons male slaves. Allan Kulikoff, *Tobacco and Slaves: The Development of Southern Cultures in the Chesapeake, 1680–1800* (Chapel Hill: University of North Carolina Press, 1986), 202.

119. Will of James Goodbe, February 8, 1735, WB32–37: 280, SCDAH. Goodbe failed to mention Cloe and her child, both of whom appear in the inventory taken shortly after his death the year after he wrote his will. In addition, since the writing of the will Grace had had a child, who apparently would go to his daughter Eliza-

beth. Inventory of James Goodbe, October 2, 1736, WPA 104: 93–97, SCDAH. In his study of inheritance patterns in South Carolina, John Crowley notes that the association of slaves with the "residue" of a propertyowner's estate led to the liberal spread of wealth, via slaves, to younger sons and daughters. Crowley, "Family Relations: Inheritance in Early South Carolina," *Social History* 33 (1984): 51–57.

120. Will of Robert Daniel, June 1, 1732, WB37–40: 314, SCDAH.

121. Will of William Holmes, July 20, 1733, WB 37–40: 250, SCDAH. In the inventory, Celia is listed as Giles's wife, but that bond was meaningless to Holmes as he marks Giles, alongside eight other men, to be sold following Holmes's death. Inventory of William Holmes, February 19, 1738, WPA 104: 326–28, SCDAH.

122. Will of Phillip Combe, February 22, 1735, WB 37–40: 24, SCDAH.

123. Will of Robert Hume, December 16, 1736, WB37–40: 89, SCDAH. Entries of Negroes, Board of Trade Correspondence 1738, CO5/367:61, 67, 80, 87, 95, PRO. See also Wood, *Black Majority*, 340–41, for his detailed examination of African imports to the colony organized by age and regional origin. For all African imports between 1735 and 1740, he estimates that 12 percent were under age ten.

124. Morgan, *Slave Counterpoint*, 518.

125. Henry Laurens to John Lewis Gervais, August 16, 1783, typescript, Henry Laurens Papers Project, Columbia, South Carolina; cited in Morgan, *Slave Counterpoint*, 517 n.30.

126. Walter Johnson, *Soul by Soul: Life Inside the Antebellum Slave Market* (Cambridge, Mass.: Harvard University Press, 1999), 82.

127. Fischer, *Suspect Relations*, 175–81, 177, 181.

Chapter 4. *"Hannah and Hir Children": Reproduction and Creolization Among Enslaved Women*

1. Ludmilla Jordanova, "Interrogating the Concept of Reproduction in the Eighteenth Century," in *Conceiving the New World Order: The Global Politics of Reproduction*, ed. Faye Ginsburg and Rayna Rapp, (Berkeley: University of California Press, 95), 370.

2. Jerome Handler and Frederick Lange, *Plantation Slavery in Barbados: An archaeological and Historical Investigation* (Cambridge, Mass.: Harvard University Press, 1978), 167–68.

3. Anon., 1654, Davis Manuscripts, Box 7, Envelope 15, Royal Commonwealth Society, London.

4. Saidiya Hartman, *Scenes of Subjugation: Terror, Slavery, and Self-making in Nineteenth-Century America* (New York: Oxford University Press, 1997), 42.

5. Jordanova notes that one would never now save "men and children first." "Interrogating the Concept of Reproduction," 373.

6. Philip R. P. Coelho and Robert McGuire, "African and European Bound Labor in the British New World: The Consequences of Economic Choices," *Journal of Economic History* 57 (March 1997): 90 n.33.

7. Coelho and McGuire, "African and European Bound Labor," 102–11.

8. Jerome S. Handler, Arthur C. Aufderheide, Robert S. Corriccini et al., "Lead Contact and Poisoning in Barbados Slaves: Historical, Chemical, and Biologi-

cal Evidence," in *The African Exchange: Towards a Biological History of Black People*, ed. Kenneth Kiple (Durham, N.C.: Duke University Press, 1998), 148–49.

9. See Kenneth Kiple and Virginia Himmelsteib King, *Another Dimension to the Black Diaspora: Diet, Disease, and Racism* (Cambridge: Cambridge University Press, 1981) for a detailed discussion of exposure to disease under slavery.

10. Richard Steckel, "A Dreadful Childhood: The Excess Mortality of American Slaves," in Kiple, ed., *African Exchange*, 220.

11. Robert W. Fogel, *Without Consent or Contract: The Rise and Fall of American Slavery* (New York: W.W. Norton, 1989) 123.

12. Compared to those in England, fertility rates among both black and white women in North America were consistently high with approximately 15 more births per 1,000 than in England. See Susan Klepp, "Revolutionary Bodies: Women and the Fertility Transition in the Mid-Atlantic Region, 1760–1820," *Journal of American History* 85 (December 1998): 918, table.

13. Richard H. Steckel, "Birth Weights and Infant Mortality among American Slaves," *Explorations in Economic History* 23 (1986): 172, 177.

14. Fogel, *Without Consent or Contract*, 125.

15. Entry of Papers Relating to Barbados and the Government Thereof, [1676], Colonial Office series 29, vol. 2, folio 55, PRO (hereafter CO 29/2: 55, PRO).

16. According to John Blassingame, "Africans so highly valued children [that] they could [not] conceive of the European concept of celibacy." *Slave Community: Plantation Life in the Antebellum South* (New York: Oxford University Press, 1979), 162; see also Denise Paulme, "Introduction," in *Women of Tropical Africa*, ed. Denise Paulme, trans. H. M. Wright (London: Routledge, 1960), 14. For an overview of this historiography, see Cassandra Costley, "The African Roots of Some Afro-American Birth Control Practices," M.A. thesis, Morgan State University, 1993. Unfortunately, any attempt to focus on the specific question of African and Afro-American women's access to contraceptive and abortifacient information in the early modern period must ultimately end in a pastiche of suggestion and inference drawn from sources in the history of medicine, African anthropology, and Afro-American history.

17. Drawing on the complaints and observations of Jamaican planters, Stella Dadzie maintains that "there is a weight of evidence to suggest that [Jamaican] women slaves may have been exercising a conscious choice to control the extent of their own fertility." "Searching for the Invisible Woman: Slavery and Resistance in Jamaica," *Race and Class* 32 (1990): 27. According to Orlando Patterson a "gynecological revolt" occurred in eighteenth-century Jamaica, where enslaved women refused to reproduce. Orlando Patterson, *Slavery and Social Death: A Comparative Study* (Cambridge, Mass.: Harvard University Press, 1982), 133; Barbara Bush levels a critique at historians of slavery who fail to look to enslaved women's fertility control to explain low birth rates among the enslaved in *Slave Women in Caribbean Society, 1650–1838* (Bloomington: Indiana University Press, 1990). Perhaps the first scholar to situate abortion as resistance was Herbert Aptheker, who in a footnote equates abortion with "self-mutilation" as a way the enslaved "shorten[ed] their own misery and hurt their oppressors." *American Negro Slave Revolts* (New York: Columbia University Press, 1943; 5th ed. New York: International Publishers, 1987),

142–43. Deborah Gray White maintains a cautious stance "on whether slave women were guilty of practicing birth control and abortion." She looks instead to overwork and malnutrition to explain low birth rates among enslaved women. *Ar'n't I A Woman: Female Slaves in the Plantation South* (New York: W.W. Norton, 1985), 84–86. Herbert Gutman devoted a lengthy footnote to the discussion of herbal abortifacients. He dismissed the question of efficacy, claiming "it was their use, not their value which reveals most." Gutman examined the ability of enslaved women and men to maintain autonomy in their reproductive lives and thus did not explore the particular question of how that autonomy may have translated into decisions not to reproduce. *The Black Family in Slavery and in Freedom, 1750–1925* (New York: Vintage, 1976), 80–82.

18. John Riddle discusses the evidence of early fertility control and, draws upon modern day chemical analysis to show that some of the methods discussed contained scientifically significant contraceptive compounds. *Contraception and Abortion from the Ancient World to the Renaissance* (Cambridge, Mass.: Harvard University Press, 1992); Angus McLaren notes that "historians who ask *when* fertility first came to be 'controlled' avoid contemplating that perhaps it was *always* controlled." *A History of Contraception from Antiquity to the Present Day* (Oxford: Basil Davidson, 1990), 2.

19. In his study of medieval Arabic fertility control, B. F. Mussallam notes that "birth control is not simply an aspect of modernity, nor is it necessarily alien to pre-modern societies. . . . The remarkable secular decline in Western birth rates in the nineteenth and twentieth centuries was first achieved through the use of traditional, that is to say 'medieval' contraceptive methods." Modern-day diaphragms and chemical spermicides are the direct descendants of the intravaginal suppositories of the medieval period. *Sex and Society in Islam: Birth Control Before the Nineteenth Century* (Cambridge: Cambridge University Press, 1983), 9, 61. On Egypt and nineteenth-century West Africa, see Charles Finch, "The African Background of Medical Science," in *Blacks in Science: Ancient and Modern*, ed. Ivan Van Sertima, *Journal of African Civilizations* special issue 5 (1983).

20. John Lawson, *A New Voyage to Carolina*, ed. Hugh Talmage Lefler (1709; reprint Chapel Hill: University of North Carolina Press, 1984), 194.

21. Maria Sibylla Merian, *Metamorphosis insectorum Surniamensium*, ed. Helmut Decker (Leipzig, 1705; Insel-Verlag A. Kippenberg, 1975); as cited in Londa Schiebinger, *Nature's Body: Gender in the Making of Modern Science* (Boston: Beacon Press, 1993), 181, n.124.

22. Susan E. Klepp, "Colds, Worms, and Hysteria: Menstrual Regulation in Eighteenth-Century America," in *Regulating Menstruation: Beliefs, Practices, and Interpretations*, ed. Edienne Van de Walle and Elisha P. Renne (Chicago: University of Chicago Press, 2001), 27.

23. Matia Graham Goodson, "Medical-Botanical Contributions of African Slave Women to American Medicine," *Western Journal of Black Studies* 11 (1987): 198–203; reprinted in *Black Women in American History: From Colonial Times Through the Nineteenth Century*, ed. Darlene Clark Hine (New York: Carlson Publishing, 1990), 473–84; Herbert Gutman, *The Black Family in Slavery and Freedom, 1750–1925* (New York: Vintage Press, 1976), 81; Michel Laguerre, *Afro-Caribbean Folk*

Medicine (South Hadley, Mass.: Bergin and Garvey, 1987), 91–92; Riddle, *Contraception and Abortion*, 101–4, 138, 154; Kirsten Fischer, *Suspect Relations: Sex, Race, and Resistance in Colonial North Carolina* (Ithaca, N.Y.: Cornell University Press, 2002), 104–5; Harriet A. Jacobs, *Incidents in the Life of a Slave Girl: Written by Herself*, ed. Jean Fagan Yellin (Cambridge, Mass.: Harvard University Press, 1987), 57.

24. Barbara Bush's *Slave Women in Caribbean Society*, has argued precisely this point. For another such effort, see Christopher Morris, "The Articulation of Two Worlds: The Master-Slave Relationship Reconsidered," *Journal of American History* 85 (1998): 989.

25. Will of Robert Wilshire, August 1, 1654, RB6/14:553, BA.

26. David Galenson, *Traders, Planters, and Slaves: Market Behavior in Early English America* (Cambridge: Cambridge University Press, 1986), 4; Richard S. Dunn, "The Barbados Census of 1680: Profile of the Richest Colony in English America," *William and Mary Quarterly* 3rd ser. 26 (January 1969): 12, Table 3.

27. David Eltis, *The Rise of African Slavery in the Americas* (Cambridge: Cambridge University Press, 2000), 98.

28. Inventories of Edward Thorburgh, September 21, 1668, RB3/6: 135 and September 17, 1667, RB3/3:164, BA.

29. In the latter half of the seventeenth century boys and girls comprised respectively 8 and 4 percent of those exported to the Americas. David Eltis and Stanley L. Engerman, "Was the Slave Trade Dominated by Men?" *Journal of Interdisciplinary History* 23 (1992): 241. See also Eltis, *Rise of African Slavery*, 98, 106–7.

30. For a discussion of African women's infertility, see Allan Kulikoff, "A 'Prolifick People': Black Population Growth in the Chesapeake Colonies, 1700–1790," *Southern Studies* (Winter 1977): 398–403; and Herbert S. Klein and Stanley L. Engerman, "Fertility Differentials Between Slaves in the United States and the British West Indies: A Note on Lactation Practices and Their Possible Implications," *William and Mary Quarterly* 3rd ser. 35 (1978): 357–74.

31. Will of William Corley, January 3, 1682, RB6/8: 563, BA.

32. Will of William Brooks, June 2, 1683, RB6/12: 322, BA.

33. Will of Thomas Spiar, November 28, 1682, RB6/12: 167, BA.

34. Will of John Leddra, March 13, 1683, RB6/12: 273, BA.

35. Inventory of Edward Thornburgh, September 17, 1667, RB3/3: 164, BA; and Inventory of John Lewis, November 26, 1661, RB3/3: 428, BA. The absence of an easily identifiable African name does not indicate mimetic naming. Rather, English names may have been given prior to enslavement or may be the names of parents or grandparents, real or fictive, given to children in observation of traditional naming patterns. See John Thornton, "Central African Names and African American Naming Patterns," *William and Mary Quarterly* 3rd ser. 50 (October 1993): 727–42; and Cheryll Ann Cody, "There Was No 'Absalom' on the Ball Plantations: Slave-Naming Practices in the South Carolina Low Country, 1720–1865," *American Historical Review* 92 (1987): 563–96.

36. Will of Jeremial Egguiton, November 22, 1673, RB6/9: 20, BA.

37. Will of Robert Burton, June 5, 1675, RB6/9:278, BA.

38. [Col. Henry Drax], "Instructions which I would have observed by Mr Richard Harwood in the Management of My Plantation," ca. 1670–79, Rawlinson

A. 348, Bodlian Library, Oxford University Manuscript Collection, Oxford. This document has been identified and verified by Jerome S. Handler in *Supplement to A Guide to Source Material for the Study of Barbados History, 1627–1834* (Providence, R.I.: John Carter Brown Library, 1991), 56.

39. Inventory of John Weale and Romas Clarke, August 19, 1668, RB3/6:1, BA.

40. Will of Charles Lyder, June 23, 1674, RB6/13: 482, BA. Her name probably derived from Ibo.

41. Jacobs, *Incidents in the Life of a Slave Girl*, 196.

42. Inventory of William Brey, 1662, RB3/5: 196.

43. Will of Elizabeth Lolely, February 8, 1662, RB6/15: 252, BA.

44. Will of Patrick Dun, March 13, 1662, RB6/15: 205, BA.

45. Will of John Redwood, June 20, 1660, RB6/10: 100, BA.

46. Will of Samuell Adams, October 20, 1663, RB6/8: 426, BA.

47. Will of Thomas Morris, August 7, 1666, RB6/8: 132. BA.

48. Sec. of State Misc. 2:63, SCDAH, and Alice Leland Baldwin, *First Settlers of South Carolina, 1670–1700* (Easley, S.C.: Southern Historical Press, 1985), 231.

49. See Peter H. Wood, *Black Majority: Negroes in Colonial South Carolina from 1670 Through the Stono Rebellion*, (New York: W.W. Norton, 1974), 21.

50. Aaron M. Shatzman, *Servants into Planters: The Origins of an American Image: Land Acquisition and Status Mobility in Seventeenth-Century South Carolina* (New York: Garland, 1989), 59.

51. Sec. of State Misc. 2:73, SCDAH.

52. Settlers did not move to Charlestown until 1680.

53. Samuel Wilson, *An Account of the Province of Carolina . . . 1682* (London: 1682) in *Narratives of Early Carolina, 1650–1708*, ed. Alexander Salley (New York: Charles Scribner's Sons, 1911), 174.

54. Wood, *Black Majority*, 24. Wood's chapter "The Colony of a Colony" provides a full discussion of the political and social origins behind white Barbadians' relocation to and influence in Carolina (13–34). See also Richard S. Dunn, "The English Sugar Islands and the Founding of South Carolina," *South Carolina Historical Magazine* 72 (Summer 1971): 81–93; Jack P. Greene, "Colonial South Carolina and the Caribbean Connection," *South Carolina Historical Magazine* 88 (Winter 1987): 192–210; and Eugene Sirmans, "The Legal Status of the Slave in South Carolina, 1670–1740," *Journal of Southern History* 28 (November 1962): 462–73.

55. See Wood, *Black Majority*, 23, n.30.

56. 17 February 1682, Manumission Paper, Sec. of State Misc., 1:123, SCDAH. Joanne McCree Sanders, ed., *Barbados Records: Baptisms, 1637–1800* (Baltimore: Genealogical Publishing Co., 1984), 21.

57. Jerome S. Handler and Kenneth M. Bilby, "On the Early Use and Origin of the Term 'Obeah' in Barbados and the Anglophone Caribbean," *Slavery and Abolition* 22 (August 2001): 87–100; and Philip D. Morgan and George D. Terry, "Slavery in Microcosm: A Conspiracy Scare in Colonial South Carolina," *Southern Studies* 21 (1982): 127–45, 130.

58. Sale of Timothy Corbrow, October 13, 1705, SP 1709–25: 69, SCDAH; and Transport Application of Michael Mahon, November 9, 1710, SP 1709–25: 98, SCDAH.

59. Sale of Stephen Gibbs, November 7, 1710, SP 1709–25; 96, SCDAH.

60. Daniel Littlefield, "The Slave Trade to Colonial South Carolina: A Profile," *South Carolina Historical Magazine* 9 (April 1990): 69.

61. For discussions of the precise rate and causes of death during the Middle Passage see, for example, Joseph C. Miller, "Mortality in the Atlantic Slave Trade: Statistical Evidence on Causality," *Journal of Interdisciplinary History* 11 (Autumn 1991): 317–29; Richard Steckel and Richard Jensen, "New Evidence on the Causes of Slave and Crew Mortality in the Atlantic Slave Trade," *Journal of Economic History* 46 (March 1986): 57–77; Charles Garland and Herbert Klein, "The Allotment of Space for Slaves Aboard Eighteenth-Century British Slave Ships," *William and Mary Quarterly* 3rd ser. 42 (April 1985): 238–48; and David Eltis, "Mortality and Voyage Length in the Middle Passage: New Evidence from the Nineteenth Century," *Journal of Economic History* 44 (June 1984): 301–8.

62. Littlefield, "Slave Trade to Colonial South Carolina," 74.

63. Wood, *Black Majority*, 45.

64. Annual imports of enslaved men and women grew from an average of 275 in the 1710s to 900 in the 1720s and 2,000 per annum in the 1730s. Russell R. Menard, "The Africanization of the Lowcountry Labor Force," in *Race and Family in the Colonial South*, ed. Winthrop Jordan and Sheilia Skemp (Jackson: University Press of Mississippi, 1987), 93, Table 107.

65. "An Additional Act to an Act Entitled 'An Act for the Better Ordering and Governing Negroes and All other Slaves, 1714,'" *Statutes at Large of South Carolina*, ed. David J. McCord (Columbia S.C., 1840), 7: 365–68.

66. [Anon.] Fragmentary Will, 1721, SP, 1721–22: 160, SCDAH.

67. Will of Dorothy Daniell, October 15, 1711, SP1714–17: 44, SCDAH.

68. See the introduction in *The Carolina Chronicle of Dr. Francis LeJau, 1706–1717*, ed. Frank J. Klingberg (Berkeley: University of California Press, 1956), 1–14.

69. LeJau to the Society for the Propagation of the Gospel, September 15, 1708, Society for the Propagation of the Gospel Papers, South Carolina, vol. 16 p. 224, Lambeth Palace, London (hereafter SPG, South Carolina, 16: 224, LP).

70. "One of the most scandalous and common crimes of our Slaves is their perpetual changeing of Wives and Husbands which occasions great disorders." LeJau to SPG, October 20, 1709, SPG, South Carolina, 16: 237, LP. See also "I have proposed . . . that none of [the Negroes] that are not yet Marry'd pressume to do it without his masters consent and likewise those that are now marry'd do not part without the like consent." LeJau to SPG, June 13, 1710, SPG, South Carolina, 16: 266, LP.

71. The next year he wrote to the SPG that he had "refused to baptise and marry several sober slaves (their masters being unwilling)." LeJau to SPG, October 17, 1709, SPG, South Carolina, 2: 65, LP.

72. William Dunn to the SPG, April 21, 1707, SPG, South Carolina, 16: 153, LP.

73. For discussions of the impact of SPG ministers among enslaved Africans in South Carolina, see Wood, *Black Majority*, 132–42; and Margaret Washington Creel, *"A Peculiar People": Slave Religion and Community Culture Among the Gullahs* (New York: New York University Press, 1988), 67–80. For an earlier discussion of the religious experiences enslaved Africans brought to the Americas see Michael

A. Gomez, *Exchanging Our Country Marks: The Transformation of African Identities in the Colonial and Antebellum South* (Chapel Hill: University of North Carolina Press, 1998).

74. While imports contributed to some of the population growth, Peter Wood has documented natural increase among the enslaved prior to 1720. Governor Johnson to the Lords Proprietors, 17 September, 1708, Transcripts of Records in the British Public Record Office Relating to South Carolina, 1701–1710, pp. 203–10, SCDAH; Wood, *Black Majority*, 143–45, especially Table I.

75. Wood, *Black Majority*, 162.

76. Sale of John and Elizabeth Gibbes, May 7, 1713, SP 1711–17: 47, SCDAH.

While the true etymology of the name is uncertain, it could of course be a reference to mining or to a place name. I believe that it indicates the possessive. In her discussion of the meanings of mothering under slavery, Deborah Gray White states: "It was, ironically, an act of defiance, a signal to the slaveowner that no matter how cruel and inhumane his actions, African-Americans would not be utterly subjugated or destroyed. Slave mothers gave African-Americans the right to say collectively what one slave woman once said of her offspring: 'My child him is mine.'" *Ar'n't I A Woman: Female Slaves in the Plantation South* (New York: W.W. Norton, 1985), 110.

77. Elizabeth Sindrey, Estate Account Book, 1705–1721, South Carolina Historical Society, Charleston, South Carolina. Note, the spelling of Clapp's name changes in later probate records to Clapps.

78. Sale of William Beard, October 3, 1711, Secretary of the Province Records 1714–17: 43, SCDAH.

79. Sale of Peter Robert, April 14, 1716, SP 1714–17: 300, SCDAH.

80. Inventory of Robert Fry, November 23, 1736, WPA 104: 137–38, SCDAH.

81. Inventory of Thomas Lynch, December 20, 1738, WPA 105: 282–93, SCDAH.

82. Inventory of Henry Livingston, April 7 1739, WPA 113: n.p., SCDAH.

83. John Gough bequeathed "Betty the daughter of old Bess" and "Jubah daughter of Silvia," respectively to his sons Francis and Edward. He relegated Old Bess and Silvia to the arbitrary division of all "the negroes" among his four sons. Will of John Gough, December 29, 1738 WB 37–40: 568, SCDAH.

84. Will of William Swinton, February 20, 1741, WB40–47: 158, SCDAH.

85. Inventory of William Swinton, September 27, 1742, WPA 121: no page numbers, SCDAH.

86. African points of origin for enslaved persons disembarking in Carolina in the eighteenth century are very difficult to infer for the first twenty-five years of the century. During that period, a full 79 percent of the 6,509 persons arriving in the colony come from an unspecified African port. Moreover, only two of thirty-four voyages provided data on male percentages—offering a mean of 82 percent a percentage entirely unsupported by other data. In the next 75-year period, more data are available (see list). While 38 percent still originate from unspecified ports, sex ratios imputed from the slave trade database for this period continue to be very problematic. The number of voyages sampled are tiny (two, seven, and four) and

suggest male majorities (91 percent, 62 percent, 62 percent) that in at least one period are far too high.

	1726–50	*1751–75*	*1776–1800*
Unspecified	39%*	9%	19%
Bight of Benin	—	3%	—
Bight of Biafra	11%	9%	4%
Gold Coast	2%	12%	31%
Senegambia	9%	25%	13%
Sierra Leone	—	14%	15%
West Central Africa	39%	16%	16%

87. Will of Richard Smith, January 20, 1725, Will Book 1732–1737: 155, (hereafter WB 32–37: 155, SCDAH).

88. Will of George Logan, March 18, 1720, Sec. of Prov. 1719–21: 47, SCDAH.

89. Inventory of Richard Beresford, May 11, 1722, Sec. of Prov. 1721–22: 250, SCDAH.

90. Inventory of Edward Hext, May 3, 1742, WPA 121: n.p., SCDAH.

91. Sale of Tayier Hall, January 8 1718, Sec. of Prov. 1714–19: 183, SCDAH.

92. Will of Andrew Broughton, July 30, 1739, WB40–47: 197, SCDAH.

93. Will of Jeremiah Miles, February 2, 1736, WB 37–40: 540, SCDAH.

94. Inventory of Jeremiah Miles, February 28, 1739, WPA 113: n.p., SCDAH.

95. Russell R. Menard, "The Africanization of the Lowcountry Labor Force," in *Race and Family in the Colonial South*, ed. Winthrop Jordan and Shelia Skemp (Jackson: University Press of Mississippi, 1987), 104, Table 1.

96. Inventory of Gilson Clapps, 19 July 1738, WPA 105: 270–73, SCDAH; Will of Gilson Clapps, 6 February 1737 WB 37–40: 152, SCDAH.

97. Joyce Chaplin, *An Anxious Pursuit: Agricultural Innovation and Modernity in the Lower South, 1730–1815* (Chapel Hill: University of North Carolina Press, 1993), 56.

98. Menard, "Africanization of the Lowcountry," 81. The combination of prohibitive import duties and the economic depression caused by King George's War meant the black population fell to sixty percent of the colony's total population in the 1750s.

99. Inventory of Peter Pagett, May 8, 1740, WPA 120: n.p., SCDAH.

100. Inventories of Walter Dallas and Judith Dallas, May 9, 1740, WPA 120: no page numbers, SCDAH.

101. Inventory of Isaac Dubose, February 1, 1743, WPA 114: n.p., SCDAH.

102. Will of Isaac Dubose, June 12, 1742, WB40–47: 189, SCDAH.

103. Inventory of Susannah Cordes, March 8, 1743, WPA 114: n.p., SCDAH.

104. Ira Berlin, "Time, Space, and the Evolution of Afro-American Society on British Mainland North America," *American Historical Review* 85 (1980): 58. For a discussion of the particular ethnic component of the slave trade during the rice boom see Daniel Littlefield's chapter, "Rice Cultivation and the Slave Trade," in

Rice and Slaves: Ethnicity and the Slave Trade in Colonial South Carolina (Baton Rouge: Louisiana University Press, 1981), 74–114.

105. Will of Robert Hume, December 16, 1736, WB37–40: 89, SCDAH.

Chapter 5. *"Women's Sweat": Gender and Agricultural Labor in the Atlantic World*

1. According to Judith Carney, "the Diola of Casamance, Senegal refer to rice cultivation as a 'woman's sweat.'" Judith Carney, *Black Rice: The African Origins of Rice Cultivation in the Americas* (Cambridge, Mass.: Harvard University Press, 2001), 31.

2. David Eltis, *The Rise of African Slavery in the Americas* (Cambridge: Cambridge University Press, 2000), 220.

3. Eltis, *Rise of African Slavery*, 85–113; and Hilary McD. Beckles, *Natural Rebels: A Social History of Enslaved Black Women in Barbados* (New Brunswick, N.J.: Rutgers University Press, 1989), 29.

4. Thomas Nairne, *A Letter from South Carolina* (London, 1710), in Jack P. Greene, ed., *Selling a New World: Two Colonial South Carolina Promotional Pamphlets* (Columbia: University of South Carolina Press, 1989), 68.

5. Johann Martin Bolzius, "Reliable Answer to Some Submitted Questions Concerning the Land Carolina," *William and Mary Quarterly* 3rd ser. 14 (April 1957): 223–61, 257. This source was first published in 1751.

6. Ira Berlin, *Many Thousands Gone: The First Two Centuries of Slavery in North America* (Cambridge, Mass.: Harvard University Press, 1998), 168.

7. Harry J. Bennett, *Bondsmen & Bishops: Slavery and Apprenticeship on the Codrington Plantations of Barbados, 1710–1838* (Berkeley: University of California Press, 1958), 16.

8. Eltis, *Rise of African Slavery*, 92.

9. Will of John May, July 24, 1659, RB6/14:445, BA.

10. Will of Thomas Kennett, November 5, 1659, RB6/14:438, BA.

11. Will of John Waterland, February 3, 1660, RB6/14: 532, BA.

12. Will of John Wolverstone, May 26, 1663, RB6/15:262, BA.

13. Inventory of John Lewis, November 26, 1661, RB3/3: 428, BA.

14. Inventory of Judith Powery, March 19, 1662, RB3/2: 554, BA.

15. Inventory of Philip Banfield, May 11, 1662, RB3/2: 564, BA.

16. See references in *Caribbeana: Miscellaneous Papers Relating to the History, Genealogy, Topography, and Antiquities in the British West Indies*, 6 vols., ed. Vere Langford Oliver, (London, 1909–11).

17. John Blake to his Brother, November 1675 in Oliver, ed., *Caribbeana*, 55–56.

18. Richard Sheridan, *Sugar and Slavery: An Economic History of the British West Indies* (Baltimore: Johns Hopkins University Press, 1973), 257.

19. Michael Craton, *Searching for the Invisible Man: Slavery and Plantation Life in Jamaica* (Cambridge, Mass.: Harvard University Press, 1978), 142.

20. Will of Robert Rumball, September 14, 1660, RB6/14: 493, BA.

21. Richard S. Dunn, "Sugar Production and Slave Women in Jamaica," in *Cultivation and Culture: Labor and the Shaping of Slave Life in the Americas*, ed. Ira Berlin and Philip D. Morgan (Charlottesville: University Pres of Virginia, 1993), 62.

22. Bernard Moitt, "Women, Work, and Resistance in the French Caribbean During Slavery, 1700–1848," in *Engendering History: Caribbean Women in Historical Perspective*, ed. Verene Shepard, Bridget Brereton, and Barbara Baily (New York: St. Martin's Press, 1995), 159. Moitt goes on to argue that by the nineteenth century, female-majority field gangs were ubiquitous throughout the French Caribbean, a demographic situation acknowledged by historians but still under-theorized (162).

23. Dunn, "Sugar Production and Slave Women," 50–51.

24. For women's participation in work gangs in eighteenth-century Barbados, see Barbara Bush, *Slave Women in Caribbean Society, 1650–1838* (Bloomington: Indiana University Press, 1990), 121–24. For a discussion of labor and culture, see Ira Berlin and Philip Morgan, "Labor and the Shaping of Slave Life in the Americas," in *Cultivation and Culture; Labor and the Shaping of Slave Life in the Americas*, ed. Ira Berlin and Philip Morgan (Charlottesville: University Press of Virginia, 1993), 1–48; and David Barry Gaspar, *Bondmen & Rebels: A Study of Master-Slave Relations in Antigua with Implications for Colonial British America* (Baltimore: Johns Hopkins University Press, 1985), 93–128.

25. Eltis, *Rise of African Slavery*, 102.

26. Jean Pierre Labat, *Nouveau voyage aux isles de l'Amérique* (Paris: Guillaume, 1722), 3: 432; cited in Bernard Moitt, "Slave Women and Resistance in the French Caribbean," in *More Than Chattel: Black Women and Slavery in the Americas*, ed. David Barry Gaspar and Darlene Clark Hine (Bloomington: Indiana University Press, 1996), 239.

27. Labat, *Nouveau voyage*, 4: 206; cited in Moitt, "Women, Work, and Resistance," 165.

28. Elie Monnereau, *Le Parfait indigotier ou description de l'indigo* (Marseilles, 1765), cited in David Geggus, "Indigo and Slavery in Saint-Domingue," *Plantation Society in the Americas* 5 (1998): 191–92.

29. Moitt, "Women, Work, and Resistance," 162.

30. Richard S. Dunn, *Sugar and Slaves: The Rise of the Planter Class in the English West Indies, 1624–1713* (Chapel Hill: University of North Carolina Press, 1972), 198.

31. For balanced sex ratios in late seventeenth- and early eighteenth-century English sugar islands, see Dunn, *Sugar and Slavery*, 315–17. It is interesting that at the beginning of the nineteenth century, men outnumbered women in only six of sixteen British Caribbean slave societies. In Demerara-Essequibo (where the ratio was 130:100), in Berbice (128:100) and in Trinidad (123:100), the demographics were particularly skewed. In the Bahamas (104:100), St. Vincent (102:100), and Jamaica (100.3:100), they were closer to "normal." See Barry Higman, *Slave Populations of the British Caribbean, 1807–1834* (Baltimore: Johns Hopkins University Press, 1984), 117.

32. See Deborah Gray White, *Ar'n't I a Woman? Female Slaves in the Plantation South* (New York: W.W. Norton, 1985), 119–41.

33. Richard S. Dunn, "The English Sugar Islands and the Founding of South Carolina," *South Carolina Historical Magazine* 72 (April 1971): 81–93.

34. Lord Ashley to Sir John Yeamans, May 1670, in Langdon Cheves, ed., *The Shaftesbury Papers and Other Records relating to Carolina* (Charleston: South Carolina Historical Society, 1897), 164.

35. Peter H. Wood, *Black Majority: Negroes in Colonial South Carolina from 1670 Through the Stono Rebellion* (New York: W.W. Norton, 1974), 25.

36. Alexander S. Salley, *Warrants for Land in South Carolina, 1672–1711* (Columbia: University of South Carolina Press, 1973).

37. John Norris, *Profitable Advice for Rich and Poor* (London, 1712), in Jack P. Greene, *Selling a New World: The Colonial South Carolina Promotional Pamphlets* (Columbia: University of South Carolina Press, 1989), 128, 132., emphasis in original.

38. Mortgage of John Wright to Samuel Wragg, 15 June 1714, Charleston County Wills, #45, SCDAH; cited in Philip D. Morgan, *Slave Counterpoint: Black Culture in the Eighteenth-Century Chesapeake and Lowcountry* (Chapel Hill: University of North Carolina Press, 1998), 482. On Indian slavery, see Wood, *Black Majority*, 38–43; and Theda Perdue, *Slavery and the Evolution of Cherokee Society, 1540–1866* (Knoxville: University of Tennessee Press, 1979), 28.

39. Warrant for land for Peter Hearne, Sr., April 1683; Warrant for land for Mrs. Dorcas Smith, April 1673; Warrant for land for Francis Blanchart, July 1695; all in Salley, *Warrants for Land*.

40. Edward A. Pearson, "'A Countryside Full of Flames': A Reconsideration of the Stono Rebellion and Slave Rebelliousness in the Early Eighteenth-Century South Carolina Lowcountry," *Slavery and Abolition* 17 (August 1996): 22–50. For the African origins of Carolina animal husbandry, see Wood, *Black Majority*, 28–32; Walter Rodney, *A History of the Upper Guinea Coast, 1545–1800* (London: Oxford University Press, 1970), 24–5; and Timothy Silver, *A New Face on the Countryside: Indians, Colonists, and Slaves in South Atlantic Forests, 1500–1800* (Cambridge: Cambridge University Press, 1990), 172–76. For a review of various theories about the origins of cattle grazing see John Otto and Nain Anderson, "The Origins of Southern Cattle-Grazing: A Problem in West Indian History," *Journal of Caribbean History* 21 (1988): 138–53.

41. Carney, *Black Rice*, 85.

42. Inventory of Francis Jones, September 20, 1693, SP1692–1700:89, SCDAH.

43. Inventory, Anonymous, March 2, 1696, SP 1692–1700:237.

44. Sale of Alexander Mackey, 12 November 1711, SP 1711–17:18, SCDAH.

45. Morgan, *Slave Counterpoint*, 61. Russell Menard has asserted that equating rice with the rise in the importation of enslaved Africans is an oversimplification. Rather, using the work of Clarence Ver Steeg, he argues that the combination of naval stores and rice production, or "the general expansion of Lowcountry exports," together created the demand and economic means for the growth in slave imports. Russell R. Menard, "The Africanization of the Lowcountry Labor Force," in *Race and Family in the Colonial South*, ed. Winthrop Jordan and Shelia Skemp (Jackson: University Press of Mississippi, 1987), 94.

46. John Gerar William de Brahms, *Report of the General Survey in the Southern District of North America*, ed. Louis de Vorsey, Jr. (Columbia: University of

South Carolina Press, 1971), 93–94, quoted in Silver, *New Face on the Countryside*, 106–7. *Barbot on Guinea: The Writings of Jean Barbot on West Africa, 1678–1712*, ed. P. E. H. Hair, Adam Jones, and Robin Law, 2 vols. (London: Hakluyt Society, 1992), 1: 91; and Daniel C. Littlefield, *Rice and Slaves: Ethnicity and the Slave Trade in Colonial South Carolina* (Urbana: University of Illinois Press, 1991), 103–4.

47. John Archdale, "A New Description of that Fertile and Pleasant Province of Carolina, by John Archdale, 1707," in Alexander-Salley, ed., *Narratives of Early Carolina, 1650–1708* (New York: Charles Scribner's Sons, 1911), 310. He particularly discussed enslaved children's suitability for feeding silkworms. Planters' experiments in silk production were abandoned in the face of the successful introduction of rice to the colony. Silver, *New Face*, 147.

48. On the stages of Carolina's socioeconomic development, see Peter Coclanis, *The Shadows of a Dream: Economic Life and Death in the South Carolina Lowcountry, 1670–1920* (New York: Oxford University Press, 1989), 48–110, especially 61–63; Wood, *Black Majority*; and Clarence Ver Steeg, *Origins of a Southern Mosaic: Studies of Early Carolina and Georgia* (Athens: University of Georgia Press, 1975), 114–130.

49. Peter H. Wood, " 'More like a Negro Country': Demographic Patterns in Colonial South Carolina, 1700–40," in *Race and Slavery in the Western Hemisphere: Quantitative Studies*, ed. Stanley Engerman and Eugene Genovese (Princeton, N.J.: Princeton University Press, 1975), 144.

50. "Letter of Edward Randolph to the Board of Trade, 1699," in Salley, ed., *Narratives of Early Carolina, 1650–1708*, 207, and note 2. (New York: Charles Scribner's Sons, 1911).

51. Randolph was not the only observer to have difficulty estimating the ratio of black to white. See William D. Smyth, "Travelers to South Carolina in the Early Eighteenth Century," *South Carolina Historical Magazine* 79 (1978): 122.

52. *Boston News-Letter*, 22 October 1730, 2, cited in David A. Copeland, " 'The Proceedings of the Rebellious Negroes': News of Slave Insurrections and Crimes in Colonial Newspapers," *American Journalism* 12 (Spring 1995): 9; and *The Journals of Henry Melchior Muhlenberg*, trans. Theodore G. Tappert and John W. Doberstein, 3 vols. (Philadelphia: Lutheran Historical Society, 1942) 1: 58; cited in Robert Olwell, *Masters, Slaves and Subjects: The Culture of Power in the South Carolina Low Country 1740–1790* (Ithaca, N.Y.: Cornell University Press, 1998), 48.

53. "An Additional Act to an Act Entitled 'An Act for the Better Ordering and Governing Negroes and All Other Slaves, 1714,' " *Statutes at Large of South Carolina*, ed. David J. McCord (Columbia S.C., 1840), 7: 365–68.

54. Sale of John Hodgson, March 22, 1716, SP 1714–17:541, SCDAH. It is possible that the boy and girl were the children of one of the women owned by Hodgson. Given that Hodgson did not identify them with a parent, it is also possible that he purchased them.

55. Morgan, *Slave Counterpoint*, 244.

56. Will of William Chapman, January 2, 1711, SP 1711–19:14, SCDAH.

57. For discussion of the work of female artisans in Charlestown, see Julia

Cherry Spruill, *Women's Life and Work in the Southern Colonies* (1938; reprint New York: W.W. Norton, 1972), 276–92. Cara Anzilotti has argued that female land- and slaveowners in colonial South Carolina exhibited a conservativism that aligned them with patriarchal social and economic conventions and did not leave room for women to exercise slaveowning practices that might distinguish them from their male counterparts. "Autonomy and the Female Planter in Colonial South Carolina," *Journal of Southern History* 63 (May 1997): 239–68.

58. Elizabeth Bourquin, "Runaway Ad," *South Carolina Gazette*, May 23, 1761; cited in Morgan, *Slave Counterpoint*, 494.

59. Petition of Sundry Inhabitants of Charles Town, February 5, 1747, *Journal of the Commons House of Assembly*, ed. J. H. Easterby (Columbia: South Carolina Archives Department, 1958), 155.

60. Journal of the Commons House of Assembly, May 21, 1741, 18; also cited in Olwell, *Masters, Slaves, and Subjects*, 175.

61. Betty Wood, *Women's Work, Men's Work: The Informal Slave Economies of Lowcountry Georgia* (Athens: University of Georgia Press, 1995), 81–83.

62. Olwell, *Masters, Slaves, and Subjects*, 174.

63. Robert Pringle to Edward & John Mayne & Co., Lisbon, September 19, 1740, in *The Letterbook of Robert Pringle*, ed. Walter Edgar (Columbia: University of South Carolina Press, 1972), 247.

64. Morgan, *Slave Counterpoint*, 250–53; and Robert Olwell, "'Loose, Idle and Disorderly': Slave Women in the Eighteenth-Century Charleston Marketplace," in Gaspar and Hine, eds., *More Than Chattel*, 97–110.

65. Leslie Schwalm, *"A Hard Fight for We": Women's Transition from Slavery to Freedom in South Carolina* (Urbana: University of Illinois Press, 1997), 21.

66. I borrow the phrase "cultivation and culture" from the volume of the same name: *Cultivation and Culture: Labor and the Shaping of Slave Life in the Americas*, ed Ira Berlin and Philip Morgan (Charlottesville: University Press of Virginia, 1993).

67. Judith Carney's examination of the transmission of rice culture from Africa to America provides the most complete and compelling argument. Carney, *Black Rice*, 78–98. In addition, see Wood, *Black Majority*, 35–62; Littlefield, *Rice and Slaves*, 74–114; Joyce Chaplin, *An Anxious Pursuit: Agricultural Innovation and Modernity in the Lower South, 1730–1815* (Chapel Hill: University of North Carolina Press, 1993), 266; Pearson, "'A Countryside Full of Flames,'" esp. 33–34; and Michael A. Gomez, *Exchanging Our Country Marks: The Transformation of African Identities in the Colonial and Antebellum South* (Chapel Hill: University of North Carolina Press, 1998), 93.

68. Mark Catesby, *Natural History* (London, 1731, 1747), in *The Colonial South Carolina Scene: Contemporary Views, 1697–1774*, ed. H. Roy Merrens (Columbia: University of South Carolina Press, 1977) 100.

69. In 1787 Jonathan Lucas patented a water-driven mill for removing the husk from rice kernels. Carney, *Black Rice*, 132. For a discussion of the impulse on the part of slaveowners to develop mechanized milling of rice, see Chaplin, *An Anxious Pursuit*, 251–62.

70. Alexander Garden to Royal Society, April 20, 1755, Guard Book I, Royal Society of Arts, London; cited in Philip Morgan, *Slave Counterpoint*, 153. See also 151.

71. Pearson, "'A Countryside in Flames,'" 34. The skill of the processor resulted in more or less broken rice in the final product. Carney, *Black Rice*, 127.

72. Leland Ferguson, *Uncommon Ground: Archaeology and Early African America, 1650–1800* (Washington: Smithsonian Institute Press, 1992), xxiv. See also Carney, *Black Rice*, 91–97.

73. Chaplin, *Anxious Pursuit*, 267.

74. Bolzius, "Reliable Answers," 257.

75. Carney, *Black Rice*, 135.

76. Peter Manigault to John Owen, February 20, 1794, Peter Manigault Letterbook, South Caroliniana Library, University of South Carolina; cited in Chaplin, *Anxious Pursuits*, 252.

77. Carney, *Black Rice*, 99–101.

78. Dale Rosengarten, *Row upon Row: Sea Grass Baskets of the South Carolina Lowcountry* (Columbia: University of South Carolina and McKissick Museum, 1986); and Gomez, *Exchanging Country Marks*, 93.

Chapter 6. *"Deluders and Seducers of Each Other": Gender and the Changing Nature of Resistance*

1. For example, Neither Ira Berlin nor Philip Morgan devotes specific attention to resistance, although Morgan notes the omission and writes "the major triumph [of the enslaved] was the creation of an coherent culture—the subject of this book and *the* most significant act of resistance in its own right." Philip D. Morgan, *Slave Counterpoint: Black Culture in the Eighteenth-Century Chesapeake and Lowcountry* (Chapel Hill: University of North Carolina Press, 1998), xxii; Ira Berlin, *Many Thousands Gone: The First Two Centuries of Slavery in North America* (Cambridge, Mass.: Harvard University Press, 1998).

2. Patricia Hill Collins, "Shifting the Center: Race, Class, and Feminist Theorizing About Motherhood," in *Representations of Motherhood*, ed. Donna Bassin et al. (New Haven, Conn.: Yale University Press, 1994), 58.

3. David Barry Gaspar, "With a Rod of Iron: Barbados Slave Laws as a Model for Jamaica, South Carolina, and Antigua, 1661–97," in *Crossing Boundaries: Comparative History of Black People in Diaspora*, ed. Darlene Clark Hine and Jacqueline McLeod (Bloomington: Indiana University Press, 1999), 347.

4. Sidney Mintz and Richard Price point to this central contradiction in racial slavery in *An Anthropological Approach to the Afro-American Past: A Caribbean Perspective* (Philadelphia: Institute for the Study of Human Issues, 1976). See also Winthrop Jordan, *White over Black: American Attitudes Toward the Negro, 1550–1812* (Chapel Hill: University of North Carolina Press, 1968), 106.

5. By 1672, a secondary act allowing slaves to be removed from the land for the payment of Debts concludes that "Negroes shall be taken and deemed Real

Estate, to all other intents and purposes whatsoever, except what before excepted." "An Act declaring the Negro-Slaves of this Island to be Real Estates," 1668, and "A declarative Act upon the Act making Negroes Real Estate," 1672, in *Acts Passed in the Island of Barbados, 1643–1762*, ed. Richard Hall (London, 1764), 64, 93. This vacillation about the legal identity of the enslaved is at the heart of English laws, which were primarily concerned with the fact that the enslaved were " a special kind of property," as opposed to the Spanish conviction that the enslaved were an "inferior kind of subject." See Elsa Goveia, "West Indian Slave Laws of the Eighteenth Century," in *Caribbean Slave Society and Economy*, ed. Hilary McD. Beckles and Verene Shepard (New York: New Press, 1991), 350.

6. Leon Higginbotham, *In the Matter of Color: Race and the American Legal Process, the Colonial Period* (New York: Oxford University Press, 1978), 39.

7. "An Act for the Governing of Negroes," 1688, in Hall, *Acts Passed*, 112; Gaspar "With a Rod of Iron," 358; and "An Act for the Better Ordering . . . of Negroes," 1696, in *Statutes at Large of South Carolina*, ed. David J. McCord (Columbia, S.C.: A.S. Johnston, 1840), 353. See also Kathleen Brown, *Good Wives, Nasty Wenches, and Anxious Patriarchs: Gender, Race, and Power in Colonial Virginia* (Chapel Hill: University of North Carolina Press, 1996), 154.

8. Alison Games, " 'The Sanctuarye of our Rebell Negroes': The Atlantic Context of Local Resistance on Providence Island, 1630–41," *Slavery and Abolition* 19 (December 1998): 12.

9. Col. John Drax to Barbados Assembly, December 14, 1670, CO31/2: 15, PRO.)

10. Journal of Assembly, April 20, 1671, CO31/2: 24, PRO.

11. Journal of Assembly, May 17, 1671, CO31/1: 190, PRO.

12. Clause 7 in "An Act for the Better Ordering . . . of Negroes," in McCord, ed., *Statutes*, 353; and clause 2 in "An Act for the Governing of Negroes" in Hall, ed., *Acts Passed*, 112.

13. Journal of the Proceedings of the Governor and Council of Barbados, [1661], CO31/1: 49, PRO. See also the discussion on attracting white female servants and settlers in Chapter 3 above.

14. Journal of Council, July 11, 1660, CO31/1:10–11, PRO.

15. Journal of Council, July 27, 1660, CO31/1:13, PRO.

16. Journal of Council, June 11, 1660, CO31/1:1–6, PRO.

17. See Jerome Handler, "Freedmen and Slaves in the Barbados Militia," *Journal of Caribbean History* 19 (May 1984): 6, 20.

18. For discussions of the development of trade between Indians and colonists, see Joel Martin, "Southeastern Indians and the English Trade in Skins and Slaves," in *The Forgotten Centuries: Indians and Europeans in the American South 1512–1704*, ed. Charles Hudson and Carmen Chaves Tesser (Athens: University of Georgia Press, 1994), especially 310–13; and James H. Merrell, " 'Our Bond of Peace': Patterns of Intercultural Exchange in the Carolina Piedmont, 1650–1750," in *Powhatan's Mantle: Indians in the Colonial Southeast*, ed. Peter H. Wood, Gregory Waselkov, and M. Thomas Hatley (Lincoln: University of Nebraska Press, 1989), esp. 202–27.

19. Joel Martin suggests that a link exists between renegotiated relationships

with Native Americans and the white colonists' impulse to direct their needs for slave labor primarily toward the West Indies and West Africa. Martin, "Southeastern Indians," 308, 323; see also M. Thomas Hatley, *The Dividing Paths: Cherokees and South Carolinians Through the Era of Revolution* (New York; Oxford University Press, 1993), 33–34.

20. By 1668, fostered by a heightened awareness of his minority status, Lord Willliam Willoughby believed the Barbados black population to be "upwards of fourty Thousand," although modern estimates are half that. Richard S. Dunn, *Sugar and Slaves: The Rise of the Planter Class in the English West Indies, 1624–1713* (Chapel Hill: University of North Carolina Press, 1972), 75–76. Dunn estimates a population of 20,000 whites and 20,000 blacks in 1660.

21. William Willoughby to Lords of His Majesties Council, 9 July 1668, CO29/1: 115, PRO.

22. An Account of the Invasion of South Carolina in the Month of August, 1706, Secretary of State Correspondence, 1699–1724, CO5/382: 20–22, PRO.

23. [Thomas Nairne], *A Letter from South Carolina* (London, 1710), in *Selling a New World: Two Colonial South Carolina Promotional Pamphlets*, ed. Jack Greene (Columbia: University of South Carolina Press, 1989), 52.

24. William Chapman to Board of Trade, March 25, 1730, CO5/361: 88.

25. Chapman's maneuver should be contrasted with the proclivity of South Carolina slaveowners to exploit the multiple ethnicities of newly arrived Africans as a way to differentiate, to order, and to maintain a sense of mastery over the always-growing black population. See Daniel Littlefield, *Rice and Slaves: Ethnicity and the Slave Trade in Colonial South Carolina* (Baton Rouge: Louisiana University Press, 1981), 3–32. Michael Mullin suggests that slaveowners evoked Africans' particular ethnicity only during times in which the white population felt threatened. In this regard, it is useful to point to Carolinians' enduring use of ethnic nomenclature as an indication of consistent unease among Carolina slaveholders. Michael Mullin, *Africa in America: Slave Acculturation and Resistance in the American South and the British Caribbean, 1736–1831* (Urbana: University of Illinois Press, 1994), 14.

26. Jerome Handler and Frederick Lange, *Plantation Slavery in Barbados: An Archaeological and Historical Investigation* (Cambridge, Mass.: Harvard University Press, 1978), 167–68. For the Antiguan conspiracy, see David Barry Gaspar, *Bondmen and Rebels: A Study of Master-Slave Relations in Antigua with Implications for Colonial British America* (Baltimore: Johns Hopkins University Press, 1985).

27. Journal of Council, November 23, 1663, CO31/1: 82, PRO.

28. Richard Ligon, *A True and Exact History of the Island of Barbados* (London, 1657), 49–50.

29. Entry Book, February 4, 1667, CO29/1: 65, PRO.

30. Journal of Council, [1667], CO31/1: 183, PRO; and Journal of Council, [1661], CO31/1: 43, PRO.

31. Ligon, *True and Exact History of the Island of Barbados*, 48.

32. Alexander Gunkel and Jerome Handler, "A Swiss Medical Doctor's Description of Barbados in 1661: The Account of Felix Christian Spoeri," *Journal of the Barbados Museum and Historical Society* 33 (1969): 7; see also John Thornton, *Africa and Africans in the Making of the Atlantic World, 1400–1680* (Cambridge: Cambridge University Press, 1992), 224–30 for his overview of African percussive music in American slave societies.

33. Clauses 1 and 22, "An Act for the Better Ordering . . . of Negroes," 1696, in McCord, ed., *Statutes*.

34. Josiah Boone to Board of Trade, August 23, 1720, Board of Trade Correspondence, 1720–21, CO5/358: 14, PRO.

35. Board of Trade to Carolina Assembly, October 27, 1720, CO5/358: 47, PRO.

36. Josiah Boone, June 24, 1720, CO5/358: 7, PRO.

37. Anon., *Great Newes from the Barbados or a True and Faithful ACCOUNT of the Grand Conspiracy of the Negroes against the English* (London, 1676), 9. For a discussion of the intended rebellion see Hilary McD. Beckles, *Black Rebellion in Barbados: The Struggle Against Slavery, 1627–1838* (Barbados: Caribbean Research and Publications Inc., 1987), 37–41.

38. Journal of Assembly, November 25, 1675, CO31/2: 201, PRO.

39. Beckles, *Black Rebellion in Barbados*, 37. "Coromantee" referred to men and women from the Gold Coast, a region that supplied almost 20 percent of enslaved men and women in the 1680s. Handler and Lange, *Plantation Slavery in Barbados*, 22.

40. Journal of Assembly, November 25, 1675, CO31/2: 201, PRO.

41. Phillis a Free Negro Woman v. Samuel Fox, February court, 1734, p. 3, Judgment Book 1733/3–34/5, Records of the Court of Common Pleas, SCDAH.

42. Mindie Lazarus-Black, *Legitimate Acts and Illegal Encounters: Law and Society in Antigua and Barbuda* (Washington, D.C.: Smithsonian Institute Press, 1994), 52. For more on free black women's use of the courts in the Carolinas, see Kirsten Fischer, *Suspect Relations: Sex, Race, and Resistance in Colonial North Carolina* (Ithaca, N.Y.: Cornell University Press, 2002), 122–30.

43. Only two months after Phillis's court appearance, the assembly responded to the traders' petition, a document they had received some time earlier. April 9, 1734. Journal of Assembly, 1734: 126–38, SCDAH.

44. "The Stranger," *South Carolina Gazette*, September 24, 1774, quoted in Philip D. Morgan, "Black Life in Eighteenth-Century Charleston," *Perspectives in American History* New Series 1 (Cambridge: Cambridge University Press, 1984), 203.

45. Later, in clause 28 of the Carolina slave code, the lawmakers attempted to curtail the practice of allowing "slaves to do what and go whither they will and work where they please, upon condition that [they pay] their aforesaid masters so much money as . . . is agreed upon." This too was doubtless unsuccessful. McCord, ed., *Statutes*, 363.

46. Commons Journal, 3 March 1743, in Easterby, *Colonial Records*, 3: 264.

47. Commons Journal, 26 January 1745, in Easterby, *Colonial Records*, 4: 317.

48. Commons Journal, 15 January 1746, in Easterby, *Colonial Records*, 5: 43.

49. Jane Landers, *Black Society in Spanish Florida* (Urbana: University of Illinois Press, 1999), 24–25, n. 95; John J. TePaske, "The Fugitive Slave: Intercolonial Rivalry and Spanish Slave Policy, 1687–1764," in *Eighteenth-Century Florida and Its Borderlands*, ed. Samuel Proctor (Gainesville: University Presses of Florida, 1975), 3. For a discussion of freedom under the Spanish, see Jane Landers, "Gracia Real de Santa Theresa de Mose: A Free Black Town in Spanish Colonial Florida," *The American Historical Review* 95 (1990): 9–30.

50. Don La Redno to John Archdale, 1696, St. Augustine, in John Archdale Papers, Duke University Manuscript Department, Perkins Library, Durham, N.C.

51. "A List of Negroes and Indian Slaves Taken in the Year 1715," CO5/382: 102, PRO.

52. Not until 1733 would Spanish policy be explicitly focused on enticing the enslaved from Carolina. That year Philip V issued a *cedula* granting freedom to all runaways. He "hoped that the new policy would stimulate the mass exodus of slaves from Carolina." TePaske, "Fugitive Slave," 6.

53. Governor Nicholson to Assembly, August 11, 1721, CO5/425: 45, PRO.

54. In 1721, for example, Don Antonio Rexidor demanded the return of "three Slaves that were properly my own" from Carolina. Governor Nicholson maintained their justifiable capture, stating "that two of them did belong to Mr. John Smiley . . . taken from him by the Yamasee Indians and retaken again by our Indians." Antonio Rexidor to Governor Nicholson, received March 19, 1721, CO5/358: 325, PRO; and Governor Nicholson to Governor Marquis, March 19, 1721, CO5/358: 344, PRO.

55. Journal of Assembly, December 12, 1722, CO5/425: 377, PRO.

56. Commons Journal, January 19, 1739, and May 31, 1739, in Easterby ed., *Colonial Records*, 1: 596, 708.

57. Journal of Assembly, March 3, 1722, CO5/425: 285.

58. Assembly to Governor Nicholson, February 28, 1721, CO5/425: 281, PRO.

59. Clause 17, "An Act for the Governing of Negroes."

60. See, for example, Proclamation, January 5, 1722, CO5/425: 244; and Memorial of Robert Johnson, November 21, 1722, CO5/425: 368.

61. Petition of Robert Wilkinson, March 3, 1721, CO5/425: 285, PRO.

62. Clarinda and Delia's cooperative effort are evidence of a community among women of the sort that Deborah Gray White identifies in the antebellum period in *A'rn't I a Woman? Female Slaves in the Plantation South* (New York: W.W. Norton, 1985). Given the evidence of prolonged lactation, it is possible that Delia's child was as old as two years. "Delia and Clarinda," *South Carolina Gazette*, June 10–17, 1732, in *Runaway Slave Advertisements: A Documentary History from the 1730s to 1790s*, ed. Lathan A. Windley (Westport, Conn.: Greenwood Press, 1983), 3. Their comfort with the task of navigating the canoe may hint at their ethnic identity. Men and women from the Upper Guinea Coast were well accustomed to traveling by canoe.

63. The *Gazette* began its print run in 1732. Lathan Windley collects these ads, as cited above. For discussions of runaways that use the *Gazette* ads, see Peter H. Wood, *Black Majority: Negroes in Colonial South Carolina, from 1670 Through the Stono Rebellion* (New York: W.W. Norton, 1974), 239–68; Philip D. Morgan, "Colonial South Carolina Runaways: Their Significance for Slave Culture," *Slavery and Abolition* 6 (December 1985): 57–78; Daniel E. Meaders, "South Carolina Fugitives as Viewed Through Local Colonial Newspapers with Emphasis on Runaway Notices 1732–1801," *Journal of Negro History* 40 (1975): 288–319. For a study of a later period in South Carolina history, see Michael P. Johnson, "Runaway Slaves and the Slave Communities in South Carolina, 1799–1880," *William and Mary Quarterly* 3rd ser. 38 (July 1981): 418–41.

64. See Windley, ed., *Runaway Slave Advertisements*, 2, 36.

65. Philip Morgan cites the preponderance of women who ran away with children as evidence of "strong kin ties" and notes that while slaveowners suggested that one-third of male runaways left to "visit" family, they believed that over four-fifths of all female runaways ran to members of their families. Morgan, "Colonial South Carolina Runaways," 67, and n.38. Morgan finds that during the fifty-year period 1732–82, 11 percent of all female runaways ran with children. Morgan, *Slave Counterpoint*, 542, n.72.

66. "Jeney," *South Carolina Gazette*, 5 July 1735, in Windley ed., *Runaway Slave Advertisements*, 16.

67. "Sabina," *South Carolina Gazette*, 26 June 1736, in Windley ed., *Runaway Slave Advertisements*, 22.

68. Anon., *Great Newes from the Barbados*, 12.

69. Journal of Assembly, March 21, 1676, CO31/2: 207, April 20, 1676 CO31/2: 220, PRO.

70. Journal of Assembly, July 7, 1675, CO31/2: 185, PRO.

71. Journal of Assembly, June 13, 1676, CO31/2: 223, PRO. Even before the insurrection conspiracy, Governor Atkins speculated on the danger of Indians in the mainland. He suggested that those whites who left Barbados for other colonies regretted doing so when faced with "great prejudice from the Indians whose defection and numbers dayly increase . . . so most of the plantations on the continent . . . have received much damage by them." For Atkins, the fault lay with settlers who believed that prayers could redeem the Native American. Governor Atkins to Board of Plantations, February 3, 1675, Entry of Papers, CO29/2: 55–56, PRO.

72. Journal of Assembly, March 21, 1676 and April 18, 1676, CO31/2: 207, 216, PRO.

73. Vincent Harlow, *A History of Barbados, 1625–1685* (Oxford: Clarendon Press, 1926; reprint New York: Negro Universities Press, 1969), 326–27; and Hilary McD. Beckles, *Black Rebellion in Barbados: The Struggle Against Slavery, 1627–1838* (Barbados: Caribbean Research and Publications Inc., 1987), 40–41. Journal of Assembly, November 27, 1679, CO31/2: 370, PRO.

74. See Eugene Genovese, *From Rebellion to Revolution: Afro-American Slave Revolts in the Making of the New World* (New York: Vintage Press, 1981), for a discussion of the different forms slave revolts took. Genovese argues that not until the Haitian Revolution were slave revolts "modern" in outlook. The 1675 attempt in Barbados, because of the desire to reestablish old African ways of life in Barbados, was part of a "restorative" tradition. I would suggest that a more nuanced understanding of what it means to attempt to transplant old forms onto new soil is called for. See, for example, Gaspar, *Bondmen and Rebels*, Chapters 8 and 11.

75. Journal of Assembly, April 20, 1675, CO31/2: 220, PRO.

76. Will of James Lydiatt, September 16, 1676, RB6/13: 365, BA.

77. Will of William Bullard, January 11, 1679, RB6/13: 555, BA.

78. Beckles, *Black Rebellion in Barbados*, 43, table 8; and Edward Littleton to The Committee of Plantations, September 7, 1692, Board of Trade Correspondence, CO28/1: 174, PRO.

79. See Dunn, *Sugar and Slaves*, 256–58; Beckles, *Black Rebellion in Barbados*,

43–48; Gary A. Puckrein, *Little England: Plantation Society and Anglo-Barbadian Politics, 1627–1700* (New York: New York University Press, 1984), 164–65; and Michael Craton, *Testing the Chains: Resistance and Slavery in the British West Indies* (Ithaca, N.Y.: Cornell University Press, 1982), 111–14.

80. Craton, *Testing the Chains,* 110–11.

81. See Beckles, *Black Rebellion in Barbados,* 43–48.

82. Thomas Holt's 1995 presidential address to the American Historical Association is a reminder of the power of the everyday as the girder of racial and racist systems. While not directly concerned with the institution of slavery, Holt's essay evokes a more nuanced approach to the power of the mundane to shape one's identity in, and response to, slavery. I would argue that the birth of children, itself a marker of persistence and duration, contributed to the importance of everyday resistance over revolt or large-scale conspiracy. Thomas Holt, "Marking: Race, Race-Making, and the Writing of History," *American Historical Review* 100 (February 1995): 1–20. The classic work on day to day resistance remains Raymond A. Bauer and Alice H. Bauer, "Day to Day Resistance to Slavery," *Journal of Negro History* 27 (October 1942): 388–419. For more contemporary discussions of women and resistance to slavery, see Barbara Bush, " 'The Family Tree Is Not Cut': Women and Cultural Resistance in Slave Family Life in the British Caribbean," and Elizabeth Fox-Genovese, "Strategies and Forms of Resistance: Focus on Slave Women in the United States," both in *In Resistance: Studies in African, Caribbean, and Afro-American History,* ed. Gary Y. Okihiro (Amherst: University of Massachusetts Press, 1986), 117–32 and 143–65 respectively. For a position that centers women's resistance in family, see Mary Ellison, "Resistance to Oppression: Black Women's Response to Slavery in the United States," *Slavery and Abolition* 4 (May 1983): 56–63.

83. February 26, 1734, Journal of Assembly, 1734: 32, SCDAH. In the face of insurrection, slaveowners once again looked to external enemies of the state on which to place the blame. "Amidst our other perilous circumstances, we are subject to Many intestine Dangers from the great number of Negroes that are now amongst us," they complained. They lived surrounded by real and imagined slave insurrections that, in 1734, were apparently fomented by the French, who might "instigate them by artfully giving them an Expectation of freedom." Assembly to King George II, April 9, 1734, Board of Trade Correspondence 1733–38, CO5/363: 101, PRO. The report contains detailed concern about the encroachment of the French to the west of the colony, and their interference with the Indian trade.

84. For analysis of the rebellion and its aftermath, see Wood, *Black Majority,* chap. 12, "The Stono Rebellion and its Consequences," 308–26; see also John K. Thornton, "African Dimensions of the Stono Rebellion," *American Historical Review* 96 (October 1991): 1101–13.

85. Higginbotham, *In the Matter of Color,* 168.

86. "An Act for the Better Ordering and Governing Negroes and Other Slaves in This Province," 1740, *Statutes at Large of South Carolina,* ed. David J. McCord (Columbia: A.S. Johnston, 1840).

87. Wood writes "now the noose was being tightened"; *Black Majority,* 324.

88. Commons Journal, 17 May 1749, in Easterby, *Colonial Records,* 9: 120.

89. "Nancy," *South Carolina Gazette*, December 4, 1740, in Windley, *Runaway Slave Advertisements*, 43.

90. "Pompey," *South Carolina Gazette*, February 9, 1740, in Windley, *Runaway Slave Advertisements*, 40.

91. "Nanny and Clarinda, *South Carolina Gazette*, August 12, 1745, in Windley, *Runaway Slave Advertisements*, 65.

92. "Mingo and Quane," *South Carolina Gazette*, September 14, 1747, in Windley, *Runaway Slave Advertisements*, 79.

93. Philip D. Morgan and George D. Terry, "Slavery in Microcosm: A Conspiracy Scare in Colonial South Carolina," *Southern Studies* 21 (1982): 121–45. My discussion of the conspiracy draws from this article and transcripts of the council journal prepared by Robert Olwell. Morgan and Terry's article is the only in-depth discussion of the conspiracy, and while they initially discuss women's role in the testimony, their primary focus is elsewhere. I am deeply grateful to Robert Olwell for his generous and collegial gesture of making his transcripts available to myself and other scholars of early South Carolina during a seminar sponsored by the Program in the Carolina Lowcountry and the Atlantic World, Department of History, College of Charleston, February, 1999.

94. Morgan and Terry, "Slavery in Microcosm," 123, 126–27. Dr. William Bruce, a planter in St. Thomas and St. Dennis parish, made the allegation about James Akins's relationship with Kate.

95. Robert Olwell, " 'To Speak the Real Truth': Investigating a Slave Conspiracy in Colonial South Carolina," a document prepared from "A Journal of the Proceedings of His Majestys Honorable Council of South Carolina, From the 20th day of December 1748 To the 16th Day of December 1749," by James Bullock C[lerk of the] C[ouncil], 47 and 50; from a microfilm at the Library of Congress, originals held at SCDAH and PRO.

96. Journal of Council, 176, emphasis mine. I believe that the use of the term mischief suggests sexual violence of which neither Akins nor the women wanted to speak.

97. "To Speak the Real Truth," 78.

98. "To Speak the Real Truth," 129–30.

99. "To Speak the Real Truth," 162.

100. "To Speak the Real Truth," 163.

101. Morgan and Terry, "Slavery in Microcosm," 125, n.12.

Bibliography

Archival Sources

Cave Hill, Barbados. The Barbados Archives.
>Record Series RB6. Recopied Will Books, 1649–80.
>Record Series RB3. Recopied Deed Books, 1640–75.
>Record Series RL1. St. Michael: Baptisms, Marriages, Burials. 1647–1702.
Columbia, South Carolina. South Carolina Department of Archives and History.
>Records of the Secretary of State.
>Miscellaneous Records, Proprietary Series, 1671–1725. Secretary of the Province and Register of the Province volumes.
>Inventories of Estates, 1736–50.
>Wills, 1732–1750.
Charleston, South Carolina. South Carolina Historical Society.
>"List of Items Found in Inventories of Estates and Merchants Lists Recorded in South Carolina 1670–1690," by Agnes L. Baldwin, 1969.
>Gaillard Collection. In Theodore Gaillard Estate Book 1781.
>Letter Book of John Guerard, Charleston Merchant.
>Hume Family Papers.
>Benjamin Huger Rutledge Family Papers, 1675–1867.
>Broughton Papers. South Carolina Historical Society.
>Elizabeth Sindrey, Estate Account book, 1705–1721.
>Wragg Papers.
Kingston, Jamaica. Institute of Jamaica/National Library Manuscript Department.
>Manuscript 105, volumes 1–3. John Taylor, *Multum in Parvo or Taylor's Historie of his Life and Travells in America and other parts with An Account with the most remarkable Transactions which Annuall happened in his dais,* 1686–88.
London. British Library, Department of Manuscripts.
>Additional Manuscripts 11411. Thomas Povey Letterbook, 1655–60.
>Additional Manuscripts 12402–40. Edward Long Collection.
>Egerton Record Series 2395. State Papers Relating to Barbados and the West Indies, 1653–1679.
>Sloane Manuscripts 49. Journal of John Cox. . . . to Barbados and Antegoes, 1680–1.
>Sloane Manuscripts 2441. An Account of Barbados, 1684.

London. Lambeth Palace Library.
> Papers of the Society for the Propagation of the Gospel. South Carolina, 1702–44.
> Fulham Papers. South Carolina 1703–33.

London. Public Record Office, Kew.
> Colonial Office Records, Series 5 (South Carolina).
> Board of Trade Correspondence, 1720–1751.
> Entry Books of Letters. . . . re. the Proprietary and Colony of Carolina, 1663–1723.
> Land Grants, 1674–1765.
> Secretary of State Correspondence, 1699–1734.
> Sessional Papers, Council, Council in Assembly, and Assembly, 1721–51.
> Shipping Returns, 1716–1765.
> Colonial Office Records, Series 28 (Barbados).
> Board of Trade Correspondence, 1689–1751.
> Secretary of State Correspondence, 1689–1752.
> Colonial Office Records, Series 31 (Barbados).
> Sessional Papers, Council, Council in Assembly, and Assembly.
> Colonial Office Papers, Series 33 (Barbados). Shipping Returns.
> Public Record Office Papers, Series 30. Shaftesbury Collection.
> Treasury Office Papers, Series 70. Records of the Royal African Company.

London. Royal Commonwealth Society.
> Davis Manuscripts.

Oxford. Bodlian Library, Oxford University Manuscript Collection.
> Record Series Rawlinson A. 348. [Col. Henry Drax], "Instructions which I would have observed by Mr. Richard Harwood in the Management of My Plantation . . ." ca. 1670–79.

Published Sources

Ajigbo, A. E. "Prolegomena to the Study of the Cultural History of the Igbo-Speaking Peoples of Nigeria." In *West African Cultural Dynamics: Archaeological and Historical Perspectives*, edited by B. K. Swartz and Raymond Dummett, 305–25. The Hague: Mouton, 1980.

Alston, Lee J. and Morton Owen Schapiro. "Inheritance Laws Across Colonies: Causes and Consequences." *Journal of Economic History* 44 (June 1984): 277–87.

Anonymous. *Great Newes from the Barbados or a True and Faithful ACCOUNT of the Grand Conspiracy of the Negroes against the English . . .* London, 1676.

Appleby, John C. "English Settlement in the Lesser Antilles During War and Peace, 1603–1660." In *The Lesser Antilles in the Age of European Expansion*, edited by Robert L. Paquette and Stanley L. Engerman, 86–104. Gainesville: University Press of Florida, 1996.

Archdale, John. "A New Description of that Fertile and Pleasant Province of Carolina, by John Archdale, 1707." In *Narratives of Early Carolina, 1650–1708*, edited by Alexander Salley, 282–311. New York: Scribner's, 1911.

Armitage, David and Michael J. Braddick, eds. *The British Atlantic World, 1500–1800*. New York: Palgrave Macmillan, 2002.

Ashe, Thomas. *Carolina, or a Description of the Present State of That Country* (London, 1682). In *Narratives of Early Carolina, 1650–1708*, edited by Alexander Salley, 138–50. New York: Scribner's, 1911.

Atkins, John. *A Voyage to Guinea, Brazil, and the West Indies*. London, 1735. Reprint London: Frank Cass, 1970.

Baldwin, Agnes Leland. *First Settlers of South Carolina, 1670–1680*. Columbia: University of South Carolina Press, 1969.

———. *First Settlers of South Carolina, 1670–1700*. Easley, S.C.: Southern Historical Press, 1985.

Bambara, Toni Cade. *The Black Woman: An Anthology*. New York: New American Library, 1970.

Barash, Carol. "The Character of Difference: The Creole Woman as Cultural Mediator in Narratives About Jamaica." *Eighteenth-Century Studies* 23 (Summer 1990): 406–24.

Barbot, John. *A Description of the Coasts of North and South-Guinea*. Vol. 5 of *A Collection of Voyages*, comp. A. Churchill. London, 1732.

Bardaglio, Peter. "'Shamefull Matches': The Regulation of Interracial Sex and Marriage in the South Before 1900." In *Sex, Love, and Race: Crossing Boundaries in North American History*, ed. Martha Hodes, 112–40. New York: New York University Press, 1999.

Barr, Juliana. The 'Seductions' of Texas: The Political Language of Gender in the Conquests of Texas. Ph.D dissertation, University of Wisconsin, 1999.

Barry, Boubacar. *Senegambia and the Atlantic Slave Trade*. Translated by Ayi Kwei Armah. Cambridge: Cambridge University Press, 1998.

Bartels, Emily C. "Imperialist Beginnings: Richard Hakluyt and the Construction of Africa." *Criticism* 34 (Fall 1992): 517–38.

Bauer, Raymond A. and Alice H. Bauer. "Day to Day Resistance to Slavery." *Journal of Negro History* 27 (October 1942): 388–419.

Bay, Edna G. "Belief, Legitimacy and the Kpojito: An Institutional History of the 'Queen Mother' in Precolonial Dahomey." *Journal of African History* 36 (1995): 1–27.

Beck, Monica L. "'A Fer Ways Off from the Big House': The Changing Nature of Slavery in the South Carolina Backcountry." In *The Southern Colonial Backcountry: Interdisciplinary Perspectives on Frontier Communities*, edited by David Colin Crass, Steven D. Smith, Martha A. Zierden, and Richard D. Brooks, 108–36. Knoxville: University of Tennessee Press. 1998.

Beckles, Hilary McD. *Black Rebellion in Barbados: The Struggle Against Slavery 1627–1838*. Caribbean Research and Publications Inc., 1987.

———. "To Buy or to Breed: The Changing Nature of Labour Supply Policy in Barbados During the Eighteenth Century." Unpublished seminar paper, Department of History, Cave Hill Campus, University of the West Indies, Barbados, 1987/88.

————. "The Economic Origins of Black Slavery in the British West Indies 1640–1680: A Tentative Analysis of the Barbados Model." *Journal of Caribbean History* 16 (1982).

————. "From Land to Sea: Runaway Barbados Slaves and Servants, 1630–1700." *Slavery and Abolition* 6 (1985): 79–94.

————. "Historicizing Slavery in West Indian Feminisms." *Feminist Review* 59 (Summer 1998): 34–56.

————. *Natural Rebels: A Social History of Enslaved Black Women in Barbados.* New Brunswick, N.J.: Rutgers University Press, 1989.

————. "Rebels and Reactionaries: The Political Responses of White Laborers to Planter-Class Hegemony in Seventeenth-Century Barbados." *Journal of Caribbean History* 15 (1981): 1–19.

————. "Rebels Without Heroes: Slave Politics in Seventeenth Century Barbados." *Journal of Caribbean History* 18 (1983): 1–19.

————. *White Servitude and Black Slavery in Barbados, 1627–1715.* Knoxville: University of Tennessee Press, 1989.

Beckles, Hilary McD. and Karl Watson. "Social Protest and Labour Bargaining: The Changing Nature of Slaves' Responses to Plantation Life in Eighteenth-Century Barbados." *Slavery and Abolition* 8 (1987): 272–93.

Bennett, Harry J. *Bondsmen and Bishops: Slavery and Apprenticeship on the Codrington Plantation of Barbados, 1710–1838.* Berkeley: University of California Press, 1958.

Berlin, Ira. *Many Thousands Gone: The First Two Centuries of Slavery in North America.* Cambridge, Mass.: Harvard University Press, 1998.

————. "Time, Space, and the Evolution of Afro-American Society on British Mainland North America." *American Historical Review* 85 (1980): 44–78.

Berlin, Ira and Philip D. Morgan. "Labor and the Shaping of Slave Life in the Americas." In *Cultivation and Culture: Labor and the Shaping of Slave Life in the Americas*, edited by Ira Berlin and Philip D. Morgan, 1–48. Charlottesville: University Press of Virginia, 1993.

Bernheimer, Richard. *Wild Men in the Middle Ages: A Study in Art, Sentiment and Demonology.* Cambridge, Mass.: Harvard University Press, 1952.

Bhabha, Homi K. "Of Mimicry and Man: The Ambivalence of Colonial Discourse." *October* 28 (Spring 1984).

Block, Sharon. "Coerced Sex in British North America, 1700–1820." Ph.D. dissertation, Princeton University, 1995.

Bolzius, Johann Martin. "Reliable Answer to Some Submitted Questions Concerning the Land Carolina." *William and Mary Quarterly* 3rd ser. 14 (1987): 223–61.

Boose, Lynda. "'The Getting of a Lawful Race': Racial Discourse in Early Modern England and the Unrepresentable Black Woman." In *Women, "Race," and Writing in the Early Modern Period*, edited by Margo Hendricks and Patricia Parker, 35–55. New York: Routledge, 1994.

Brown, Elsa Barkley. "Polyrythms and Improvisations: Lessons for Women's History." *History Workshop Journal* 31 (Spring 1991): 85–90.

Brown, Elsa Barkley. "'What Has Happened Here': The Politics of Difference in Women's History and Feminist Politics." *Feminist Studies* 18 (Summer 1992): 295–311.

Brown, Kathleen M. *Good Wives, Nasty Wenches, and Anxious Patriarchs: Gender, Race, and Power in Colonial Virginia.* Chapel Hill: University of North Carolina Press, 1996.

Brun, Samuel. "Samuel Brun's Voyage of 1611–20." In *German Sources for West African History, 1599–1669*, edited by Adam Jones, 44–90. Wiesbaden: Franz Steiner, 1983.

de Bry, Theodore. *Grand Voyages.* 10 vols., London, 1590; Frankfurt am Main, 1594.

———. *Small Voyages.* 13 vols., Frankfurt am Main, 1597–1628.

Bucher, Bernadette. *Icon and Conquest: A Structural Analysis of the Illustrations of de Bry's Great Voyages.* Translated by Basia Miller Gulati. Chicago: University of Chicago Press, 1981.

Bull, Kinloch. "Barbadian Settlers in Early Carolina: Historiographical Notes." *South Carolina Historical Magazine* 96 (1995): 329–39.

Burnard, Trevor. "Theater of Terror: Domestic Violence in Thomas Thistlewood's Jamaica, 1750–1786." In *Over the Threshold: Intimate Violence in Early America*, edited by Christine Daniels and Michael V. Kennedy, 237–53. New York: Routledge, 1999.

Burton, Richard D. E. *Afro-Creole: Power, Opposition, and Play in the Caribbean.* Ithaca, N.Y.: Cornell University Press, 1997.

Bush, Barbara. "'The Family Tree Is Not Cut': Women and Cultural Resistance in Slave Family Life in the British Caribbean." In *In Resistance: Studies in African, Caribbean, and Afro-American History*, edited by Gary Y. Okihiro, 117–32. Amherst: University of Massachusetts Press, 1986.

———. *Slave Women in Caribbean Society, 1650–1838.* Bloomington: Indiana University Press, 1990.

———. "White 'Ladies,' Coloured 'Favourites,' and Black 'Wenches': Some Considerations on Sex, Race, and Class Factors in Social Relations in White Creole Society in the British Caribbean." *Slavery and Abolition* 2 (1981): 245–62.

Bynum, Caroline Walker. "Wonder." *American Historical Review* 102 (February 1997): 1–26.

Campbell, P. F. "Aspects of Barbados Land Tenure, 1627–1663." *Journal of the Barbados Museum and Historical Society* 37 (1984): 112–58.

———. "The Barbados Vestries 1627–1700, Part 1." *Journal of the Barbados Museum and Historical Society* 37 (1983): 35–56.

———. "The Barbados Vestries 1627–1700, Part 2." *Journal of the Barbados Museum and Historical Society* 37 (1984): 174–96.

———. "Two Generations of Walronds." *Journal of the Barbados Museum and Historical Society* 38 (1989): 253–85.

Canning, Kathleen. "Feminist History After the Linguistic Turn: Historicizing Discourse and Experience." *Signs* 19 (Winter 1994): 368–404.

Carby, Hazel V. "White Woman Listen! Black Feminisim and the Boudaries of Sisterhood." In *The Empire Strikes Back: Race and Racism in Seventies Britain*. Center for Contemporary Cultural Studies. London: Hutchinson, 1982. Reprinted in *Black British Cultural Studies: A Reader*, edited by Houston A. Baker, Manthia Diawara, and Ruth H. Lindeburg, 61–86. Chicago: University of Chicago Press, 1991.

Carney, Judith A. *Black Rice: The African Origins of Rice Cultivation in the Americas.* Cambridge: Harvard University Press, 2001.

————. "From Hands to Tutors: African Expertise in the South Carolina Rice Economy." *Agricultural History* 67 (Summer 1993): 1–30.

Chaplin, Joyce. *An Anxious Pursuit: Agricultural Innovation and Modernity in the Lower South, 1730–1815.* Chapel Hill: University of North Carolina Press, 1993.

Cheves, Langdon, ed. *The Shaftesbury Papers and other Records Relating to Carolina and the First Settlement on Ashley River Prior to the Year 1676.* Charleston: South Carolina Historical Society, 1897.

Childs, St. Julien Ravenel. "Kitchen Physick: Medical and Surgical Care of Slaves on an Eighteenth Century Rice Plantation." *Mississippi Valley Historical Review* 20 (1934): 549–54.

Clark, Elizabeth A. "Generation, Degeneration, Regeneration: Original Sin and the Conception of Jesus in the Polemic Between Augustine and Julian of Eclanum." In *Generation and Degeneration: Tropes of Reproduction in Literature and History from Antiquity to Early Modern Europe,* edited by Valeria Finucci and Kevin Brownlee, 17–40. Durham, N.C.: Duke University Press, 2001.

Clowse, Converse. *Economic Beginnings in Colonial South Carolina, 1670–1730.* Columbia: University of South Carolina Press, 1971.

Coclanis, Peter. *The Shadow of a Dream: Economic Life and Death in the South Carolina Low Country, 1670–1920.* New York: Oxford University Press, 1989.

Collins, Patricia Hill. "Shifting the Center: Race, Class, and Feminist Theorizing About Motherhood." In *Representations of Motherhood,* edited by Margaret Honey, Donna Bassin, and Meryle Mahrer Kaplan, 56–74. New Haven, Conn.: Yale University Press, 1994.

Copeland, David A. "'The Proceedings of the Rebellious Negroes:' News of Slave Insurrections and Crimes in Colonial Newspapers," *American Journalism* 12 (Spring 1995): 83–106.

Costley, Cassandra. "The African Roots of Some African-American Birth Control Practices." M.A. thesis, Morgan State University, 1993.

Craton, Michael. "Changing Patterns of Slave Families in the British West Indies." *Journal of Interdisciplinary History* 10 (1979): 1–35.

————. *Empire, Enslavement, and Freedom n the Caribbean.* Princeton, N.J.: Markus Wiener, 1997.

————. *Searching for the Invisible Man: Slaves and Plantation Life in Jamaica.* Cambridge: Harvard University Press, 1978.

————. *Testing the Chains: Resistance to Slavery in the British West Indies.* Ithaca, N.Y.: Cornell University Press, 1982.

Creel, Margaret Washington. *"A Peculiar People": Slave Religion and Community Culture Among the Gullahs.* New York: New York University Press, 1983.

Cressy, David "National Memory in Early Modern England." In *Commemorations: The Politics of National Identity,* edited by John R. Gillis, 61–73. Princeton, N.J.: Princeton University Press, 1994.

Crowley, John E. "Family Relations and Inheritance in Early South Carolina." *Histoire Sociale—Social History* 17 (May 1984): 35–57.

Curruccini, Robert S., Elizabeth M. Brandon, and Jerome S. Handler. "Inferring

Fertility from Relative Mortality in Historically Controlled Cemetery Remains From Barbados." *American Antiquity* 54 (1989): 609–14.

Curtin, Philip. *The Atlantic Slave Trade: A Census*. Madison: University of Wisconsin Press, 1969.

Davies, K. G. *The Royal African Company*. London: Longmans, 1957.

Davis, Angela Y. "Reflections on the Black Woman's Role in the Community of Slaves." *Black Scholar* 3 (December 1971): 2–15.

———. *Women, Race, and Class*. New York: Random House, 1981.

Dayton, Cornelia Hughes. "Turning Points and the Relevance of Colonial Legal History." *William and Mary Quarterly* 3rd ser. 50 (January 1993): 7–17.

Degler, Carl. "Slavery in Brazil and the United States: An Essay in Comparative History." *American Historical Review* 75 (1970): 1004–28.

Ditz, Toby L. "Ownership and Obligation: Inheritance and Patriarchal Households in Connecticut, 1750–1820." *William and Mary Quarterly* 3rd ser. 47 (April 1990): 235–65.

———. "Shipwrecked; or, Masculinity Imperiled: Mercantile Representations of Failure and the Gendered Self in Eighteenth-Century Philadelphia." *Journal of American History* 81 (June 1994): 51–80.

Donnan, Elizabeth. *Documents Illustrative of the History of the Slave Trade to America*, 4 vols. Washington, D.C.: Carnegie Institution, 1930.

Duke, William. "A List of the Names of the Inhabitants of Barbados in the Year 1638, who then poffefs'd more than ten Acres of Land." In *Some Memoirs of the First Settlement of the Island of Barbados*, 70–84. London, 1741.

Dunn, Richard S. "The English Sugar Islands and the Founding of South Carolina." *South Carolina Historical Magazine* 72 (1971): 81–93.

———. *Sugar and Slaves: The Rise of the Planter Class in the English West Indies, 1624–1713*. Chapel Hill: University of North Carolina Press, 1972.

———. "Sugar Production and Slave Women in Jamaica." in *Cultivation and Culture: Labor and the Shaping of Slave Life in the Americas*, edited by Ira Berlin and Philip D. Morgan, 49–72. Charlottesville: University Press of Virginia, 1993.

———. "A Tale of Two Plantations: Slave Life at Mesopotamia in Jamaica and Mount Airy in Virginia, 1799–1828." *William and Mary Quarterly* 3rd ser. 34 (1977): 32–65.

Dye, Nancy Schrom and Daniel Blake Smith. "Mother Love and Infant Death, 1750–1920." *Journal of American History* 73 (1986): 329–353.

Easterby, J. H., ed. *The Colonial Records of South Carolina*. Series 1, *The Journal of the Commons House of Assembly, November 10, 1736–March 19, 1750*. 9 vols.. Columbia: Historical Commission of South Carolina, 1951.

Edgar, Walter. *South Carolina: A History*. Columbia: University of South Carolina Press, 1998.

———, ed. *The Letter Book of Robert Pringle*. Columbia: The University of South Carolina Press, 1972.

Ellison, Mary. "Resistance to Oppression: Black Women's Response to Slavery in the United States." *Slavery and Abolition* 4 (May 1983): 56–63.

Eltis, David. "Mortality and Voyage Length in the Middle Passage: New Evidence from the Nineteenth Century." *Journal of Economic History* 44 (June 1984): 301–8.

———. "New Estimates of Exports from Barbados and Jamaica, 1665–1701." *William and Mary Quarterly* 3rd ser. 52 (October 1995): 631–48.

———. *The Rise of African Slavery in the Americas.* Cambridge: Cambridge University Press, 2000

———. "The Volume and Structure of the Transatlantic Slave Trade: A Reassessment." *William and Mary Quarterly* 3rd ser. 58 (2001): 17–46.

Eltis, David and Stanley Engerman. "Fluctuations in Sex and Age Ratios in the Trans-Atlantic Slave Trade, 1663–1864." *Economic History Review* 46 (1993): 308–23.

———. "Was the Slave Trade Dominated by Men?" *Journal of Interdisciplinary History* 23 (1992): 237–57.

Eltis, David and David Richardson. "West Africa and the Transatlantic Slave Trade: New Evidence of Long-Run Trends." *Slavery and Abolition* 18 (1997): 16–33.

Engerman, Stanley L. "Europe, the Lesser Antilles, and Economic Expansion." In *The Lesser Antilles in the Age of European Expansion,* edited by Robert L. Paquette and Stanley L. Engerman, 147–65. Gainesville: University Press of Florida, 1996.

Erickson, Peter. "Representations of Blacks and Blackness in the Renaissance." *Criticism* 35 (1993): 499–527.

Fage, J. D. "African Societies and the Atlantic Slave Trade." *Past and Present* 125 (November 1989): 97–115.

Fagg, David Webster. "St. Giles Seigniory: The Earle of Shaftesbury's Carolina Plantation." *South Carolina Historical Magazine* 71 (1970): 117–23.

Falconbridge, Anna Maria. *Two Voyages to Sierra Leone, During the Years 1791–2–3.* In *Maiden Voyages and Infant Colonies: Two Women's Travel Narratives of the 1790s,* edited by Deirdre Coleman, 45–168. London: Leicester University Press, 1999.

Fenhagen, Mary Pringle. "Letters and Will of Robert Pringle (1702–1776)." *South Carolina Historical and Genealogical Magazine* 50 (1949).

Finucci, Valeria. "Maternal Imagination and Monstrous Birth: Tasso's *Gerusalemme liberata.*" In *Generation and Degeneration: Tropes of Reproduction in Literature and History from Antiquity to Early Modern Europe,* edited by Valeria Finucci and Kevin Brownlee, 41–77. Durham, N.C.: Duke University Press, 2001.

Fischer, Kirsten. *Suspect Relations: Sex, Race, and Resistance in Colonial North Carolina.* Ithaca, N.Y.: Cornell University Press, 2002.

Fogel, Robert W. *Without Consent or Contract: The Rise and Fall of American Slavery.* New York: W.W. Norton, 1989.

Fox, George. *To the Ministers, Teachers and Priests (So Called and So Stileing your Selves) in Barbados.* London, 1672.

Fox-Genovese, Elizabeth. "Strategies and Forms of Resistance: Focus on Slave Women in the United States." In *In Resistance: Studies in African, Caribbean, and Afro-American History,* edited by Gary Y. Okihiro, 143–65. Amherst: University of Massachusetts Press, 1986.

————. *Within the Plantation Household: Black and White Women of the Old South.* Chapel Hill: University of North Carolina Press, 1988.

Fuller, Mary C. "Ralegh's Fugitive Gold: Reference and Deferral in *The Discoverie of Guiana.*" In *New World Encounters,* edited by Stephen Greenblatt, 218–40. Berkeley: University of California Press, 1993.

Galenson, David W. *Traders, Planters, and Slaves: Market Behavior in Early English America.* Cambridge: Cambridge University Press, 1986.

Games, Alison F. *Migration and the Origins of the English Atlantic World.* Cambridge, Mass.: Harvard University Press, 1999.

————. "Opportunity and Mobility in Early Barbados." In *The Lesser Antilles in the Age of European Expansion,* edited by Robert L. Paquette and Stanley L. Engerman, 165–81. Gainesville: University Press of Florida, 1996.

————. "'The Sanctuarye of our Rebell Negroes': The Atlantic Context of Local Resistance on Providence Island, 1630–41." *Slavery and Abolition* 19 (December 1998): 1–21.

Garland, Charles and Herbert Klein. "The Allotment of Space for Slaves Aboard Eighteenth-Century British Slave Ships." *William and Mary Quarterly* 3rd ser. 42 (April 1985): 238–48.

Gaspar, David Barry. *Bondmen and Rebels: A Study of Master-Slave Relations in Antigua with Implications for Colonial British America.* Baltimore: Johns Hopkins University Press, 1985.

————. "With a Rod of Iron: Barbados Slave Laws as a Model for Jamaica, South Carolina, and Antigua, 1661–1697." In *Crossing Boundaries: Comparative History of Black People in Diaspora,* edited by Darlene Clark Hine and Jacqueline McLeod, 343–66. Bloomington: Indiana University Press, 2001.

Gates, Henry Louis, Jr. *Figures in Black: Words, Signs, and the "Racial" Self.* New York: Oxford University Press, 1987.

————, ed. *"Race," Writing, and Difference.* Chicago: University of Chicago Press, 1986.

Geggus, David. "Sex Ratio, Age, and Ethnicity in the Atlantic Slave Trade: Data from French Shipping and Plantation Records." *Journal of African History* 30 (1989): 23–44.

Geiger, Florence Gambrill. "St. Bartholomew's Parish as Seen by its Rectors, 1713–1761." *South Carolina Historical and Genealogical Magazine* 50 (1949): 173–203.

Genovese, Eugene. *From Rebellion to Revolution: Afro-American Slave Revolts in the Making of the New World.* New York: Vintage Press, 1981.

Gilman, Sander L. *Difference and Pathology: Stereotypes of Sexuality, Race, and Madness.* Ithaca, N.Y.: Cornell University Press, 1985.

Glausser, Wayne. "Three Approaches to Locke and the Slave Trade." *Journal of the History of Ideas* 51 (April/June 1990): 199–218.

Gomez, Michael A. *Exchanging Our Country Marks: The Transformation of African Identities in the Colonial and Antebellum South.* Chapel Hill: University of North Carolina Press, 1998.

Goveia, Elsa V. *Slave Society in the British Leeward Islands at the End of the Eighteenth Century.* New Haven, Conn.: Yale University Press, 1965.

————. "The West Indian Slave Laws of the Eighteenth Century." In *Slavery in the*

New World: A Reader in Comparative History, edited by Laura Foner and Eugene Genovese, 113–37. Englewood Cliffs, N.J.: Prentice-Hall, 1969.

Gragg, Larry. "'To Procure Negroes': The English Slave Trade to Barbados, 1627–60." *Slavery and Abolition* 16 (April 1995): 65–84.

———. "Puritans in Paradise: The New England Migration to Barbados, 1640–1660." *Journal of Caribbean History* 21 (1988): 154–167.

Greenblatt, Stephen Jay. *Marvelous Possessions: The Wonder of the New World*. Chicago: University of Chicago Press, 1991.

Greene, Jack P. "Changing Identity in the British Caribbean: Barbados as a Case Study." In *Colonial Identity in the Atlantic World, 1500–1800*, edited by Nicholas Canny and Anthony Pagden, 216–66. Princeton, N.J.: Princeton University Press, 1987.

———. "Colonial South Carolina and the Caribbean Connection." *South Carolina Historical Magazine* 88 (1987): 192–210.

———. *Pursuits of Happiness: The Social Development of Early Modern British Colonies and the Formation of American Culture*. Chapel Hill: University of North Carolina Press, 1988.

———, ed. *Selling a New World: The Colonial South Carolina Promotional Pamphlets*. Columbia: University of South Carolina Press, 1989.

Gregorie, Anne King, ed. *Records of the Court of Chancery of South Carolina, 1671–1779*. Washington, D.C.: American Historical Association, 1950.

Gunkel, Alexander and Jerome Handler. "A Swiss Medical Doctor's Description of Barbados in 1661: The Account of Felix Christian Spoeri." *Journal of the Barbados Museum and Historical Society* 33 (1969).

Gutman, Herbert G. *The Black Family in Slavery and Freedom, 1750–1925*. New York: Vintage Press, 1976.

Hair, P. E. H., Adam Jones, and Robin Law, eds., *Barbot on Guinea: The Writings of Jean Barbot on West Africa, 1678–1712*. 2 vols. London: Hakluyt Society, 1992.

Hakluyt, Richard, ed. *The Principal Navigations, Voyages, Traffiques and Discoveries of the English Nation*. 12 vols. London, 1589. reprint New York: Macmillan, 1903–5.

Hall, Kim F. *Things of Darkness: Economies of Race and Gender in Early Modern England*. Ithaca, N.Y.: Cornell University Press, 1995.

Hall, Richard, ed. *Acts Passed in the Island of Barbados, 1643–1762*. London, 1844.

Handler, Jerome S. "The Barbados Slave Conspiracies of 1675 and 1692." *Journal of the Barbados Museum and Historical Society* 36 (1982): 312–33.

Handler, Jerome S. "Freedmen and Slaves in the Barbados Militia." *Journal of Caribbean History* 19 (May 1984): 1–25.

———. "Slave Revolts and Conspiracies in Seventeenth-Century Barbados." *Niewe West-Indische Gids/New West Indian Guide* 56 (1982): 5–42.

———. *The Unappropriated People: Freedmen in the Slave Society of Barbados*. Baltimore: Johns Hopkins University Press, 1974.

Handler, Jerome S. and Robert Corruccini. "Weaning Among West Indian Slaves: Historical and Bioanthropological Evidence from Barbados." *William and Mary Quarterly* 3rd ser. 43 (January 1986): 111–17.

Handler, Jerome S. and Frederick Lange. *Plantation Slavery in Barbados: An Archae-*

ological and Historical Investigation. Cambridge, Mass.: Harvard University Press, 1978.

Handler, Jerome S. and John Pohlman. "Slave Manumissions and Freedmen in seventeenth-Century Barbados." *William and Mary Quarterly* 3rd ser. 41 (July 1984): 398–400.

Harlow, Vincent T. *A History of Barbados, 1625–1685.* New York: Negro Universities Press, 1969.

———, ed. *Colonising Expeditions to the West Indies and Guiana, 1623–1667.* London: Hakluyt Society, 1925.

Hartman, Saidiya. *Scenes of Subjugation: Terror, Slavery, and Self-Making in Nineteenth-Century America.* New York: Oxford University Press, 1997.

Hatley, Tom. *The Dividing Paths: Cherokees and South Carolinians Through the Revolutionary Era.* Oxford: Oxford University Press, 1996..

Henige, David. "Measuring the Immeasurable: The Atlantic Slave Trade, West African Populations, and the Pyrrhonian Critic." *Journal of African History* 27 (1986): 296–313.

Hermndon, G. Melvin. "A Young Scotsman's Visit to South Carolina, 1770–1772." *South Carolina Historical Magazine* 85 (1984): 187–194.

Herring, William W. *Statutes at Large of Virginia,* 2 volumes, Richmond: Franklin Press, 1819–20.

Higginbotham, A. Leon, Jr. *In the Matter of Color: Race and the American Legal Process, the Colonial Period.* Oxford: Oxford University Press, 1978.

Higginbotham, Evelyn Brooks. "African-American Women's History and the Metalanguage of Race." *Signs* 17 (Winter 1992): 251–74.

Higman, Barry W. "The Slave Family and Household in the British West Indies, 1800–1834." *Journal of Interdisciplinary Studies* 6 (1975): 261–87.

———. *Slave Populations of the British Caribbean, 1807–1834.* Baltimore: Johns Hopkins University Press, 1984.

Hilton, William. "A Relation of a Discovery. . . . 1664." In *Narratives of Early Carolina. 1650–1708,* edited by Alexander S. Salley, Jr. New York: Barnes and Noble, 1953.

Hogendorn, Jan. "Economic Modeling of Price Differences in the Slave Trade Between the Central Sudan and the Coast." *Slavery and Abolition* 17 (1996): 209–22.

Hollander, Anne. *Seeing Through Clothes.* New York: Viking Press, 1975.

Holt, Thomas. "Marking: Race, Race-Making, and the Writing of History." *American Historical Review* 100 (February 1995): 1–20.

hooks, bell. *Ain't I A Woman: Black Women and Feminism.* Boston: South End Press, 1981.

Hughes, Ronald G. "Barbadian Sugar Plantations 1640–1846." unpublished paper, Department of History, University of the West Indies, Cave Hill, Barbados, 1977/78.

Hulme, Peter. *Colonial Encounters: Europe and the Native Caribbean 1492–1797.* London: Methuen, 1986.

Hyrne, Edward and Elizabeth Hyrne. "Family Letters, 1701–10." In *The Colonial South Carolina Scene: Contemporary Views, 1697–1774,* edited by H. Roy Merrens, 17–29. Columbia: University of South Carolina Press, 1977.

Ingersoll, Thomas N. "Free Blacks in a Slave Society: New Orleans, 1718–1812." *William and Mary Quarterly* 3rd ser. 48 (1991): 173–200.

Jacobi, Keith P., Della Collins Cook, Robert S. Corruccini, and Jerome S. Handler. "Congenital Syphilis in the Past: Slaves at Newton Plantation, Barbados, West Indies." *American Journal of Physical Anthropology* 89 (1992): 145–58.

Jobson, Richard. *The Golden Trade or a Discovery of the River Gambra . . . by Richard Jobson.* 1628. Reprint Amsterdam: Theatrum Orbis Terrarum; New York: Da Capo Press, 1968.

Johnson, Michael P. "Runaway Slaves and the Slave Communities in South Carolina, 1799–1880." *William and Mary Quarterly* 3rd ser. 38 (July 1981): 418–41.

———. "Smothered Slave Infants: Were Slave Mothers at Fault?" *Journal of Southern Studies* 47 (November 1984): 493–520.

Jones, Adam. "Decompiling Dapper: A Preliminary Search for Evidence." *History in Africa* 17 (1990): 171–209.

Jones, George Fenwick. "John Martin Bolzius' Trip to Charleston, Oct 1742." *South Carolina Historical Magazine* 82 (1981): 87–110.

Jones, Jacqueline. "Race, Sex, and Self-Evident Truths: The Status of Slave Women during the Era of the American Revolution." In *Women in the Age of the American Revolution*, edited by Ronald Hoffman and Peter J. Albert, 293–337. Charlottesville: University Press of Virginia, 1989.

Jordan, Winthrop. *White over Black: American Attitudes Toward the Negro, 1550–1812.* Chapel Hill: University of North Carolina Press, 1968.

Jordanova, Ludmilla. "Interrogating the Concept of Reproduction in the Eighteenth Century." In *Conceiving the New World Order: The Global Politics of Reproduction*, ed. Faye Ginsburg and Rayna Rapp. Berkeley: University of California Press, 1995.

Joyner, Charles. *Down by the Riverside.* Urbana: University of Illinois Press, 1984.

Karlson, Carol F. *The Devil in the Shape of a Woman: Witchcraft in Colonial New England.* New York: W.W. Norton, 1989.

Keim, C. Ray. "Primogeniture and Entail in Colonial Virginia," *William and Mary Quarterly* 3rd ser. 25 (October 1968): 545–86.

Kiple, Kenneth F. *The Caribbean Slave: A Biological History.* Cambridge: Cambridge University Press, 1984.

Kiple, Kenneth F. and Virginia H. Kiple. "Slave Child Mortality: Some Nutritional Answers to a Perennial Puzzle." *Journal of Social History* 10 (1977): 284–309.

Kiple, Kenneth F. and C. Ornelas Kriemhild. "After the Encounter: Disease and Demographics in the Lesser Antilles." In *The Lesser Antilles in the Age of European Expansion*, edited by Robert L. Paquette and Stanley L. Engerman. Gainesville: University Press of Florida, 1996.

Klein, Herbert S. and Stanley L. Engerman. "Fertility Differentials Between Slaves in the United States and the British West Indies: A Note on Lactation Practices and Their Possible Implications." *William and Mary Quarterly* 3rd ser. 35 (1978): 357–74.

Klein, Herbert S., Stanley L. Engerman, Robin Haines, and Ralph Shlomowitz. "Transoceanic Mortality: The Slave Trade in Comparative Perspective." *William and Mary Quarterly* 3rd ser. 58 (2001): 93–118.

Klein, Martin. "Women and Slavery in the Western Sudan." In *Women and Slavery in Africa*, edited by Claire Robertson and Martin Klein, 67–92. Madison: University of Wisconsin Press, 1983.

Klepp, Susan E. "Colds, Worms, and Hysteria: Menstrual Regulation in Eighteenth-Century America." In *Regulating Menstruation: Beliefs, Practices, and Interpretations*, edited by Edienne Van de Walle and Elisha P. Renne, 22–38. Chicago: University of Chicago Press, 2001.

———. "Lost, Hidden, Obstructed, and Repressed: Contraception and Abortive Technology in the Early Delaware Valley." In *Early American Technology: Making and Doing Things from the Colonial Era to 1850*, edited by Judith A. McGraw, 68–113. Chapel Hill: University of North Carolina Press, 1994.

———. "Revolutionary Bodies: Women and the Fertility Transition in the Mid-Atlantic Region, 1760–1820." *Journal of American History* 85 (December 1998): 910–45.

Klingberg, Frank J., ed. *The Carolina Chronicle of Dr. Francis LeJau, 1706–1717.* Berkeley: University of California Press, 1956.

Knight, Franklin. "How to Compare Slavery Systems." In *Readings in Caribbean History and Economics: An Introduction to the Region*, edited by Roberta Max Delson, 65–85. New York: Gordon and Breache Science Publications, 1981.

Kopytoff, Igor and Suzanne Miers, "Introduction: African 'Slavery' as an Institution of Marginality." In *Slavery in Africa: Historical and Anthropological Perspectives*, edited by Suzanne Miers and Igor Kopytoff, 3–81. Madison: University of Wisconsin Press, 1977.

Kulikoff, Allan. "The Origins of Afro-American Society in Tidewater Maryland and Virginia, 1700–1790." *William and Mary Quarterly* 3rd ser. 35 (1978): 226–59.

———. "A 'Prolifick People': Black Population Growth in the Chesapeake Colonies, 1700–1790." *Southern Studies* 16 (Winter 1977): 391–428.

———. *Tobacco and Slaves: The Development of Southern Cultures in the Chesapeake, 1680–1800.* Chapel Hill: University of North Carolina Press, 1986.

Labat, Pere. *The Memoirs of Pere Laba,t 1693–1705.* Translated by John Eaden. London: Constable, 1931.

Ladner, Joyce. *Tomorrow's Tomorrow: The Black Woman.* New York: Doubleday, 1971.

Landers, Jane. "Gracia Real de Santa Theresa de Mose: A Free Black Town in Spanish Colonial Florida." *American Historical Review* 95 (1990): 9–30.

Law, Robin. "Dahomey and the Slave Trade: Reflections on the Historiography of the Rise of Dahomey." *Journal African History* 27 (1986): 237–67.

———. *The Slave Coast of West Africa, 1550–1750: The Impact of the Atlantic Slave Trade on an African Society.* Oxford: Clarendon Press, 1991.

Lawton, Thomas O. "Captain William Lawton: 18th Century Planter of Edisto." *South Carolina Historical Magazine* 60 (1959): 86–93.

Lazarus-Black, Mindie. *Legitimate Acts and Illegal Encounters: Law and society in Antigua and Barbuda.* Washington, D.C.: Smithsonian Institution Press, 1994.

Lee, Jean Butenhoff. "Land and Labor: Parental Bequest Practices in Charles County, Maryland 1732–83." In *Colonial Chesapeake Society*, edited by Lois

Green Carr, Phillip D. Morgan, and Jean B. Russo, 306–41. Chapel Hill: University of North Carolina Press, 1988.

Lee, Jean Butenhoff. "The Problem of Slave Community in the Eighteenth-Century Chesapeake." *William and Mary Quarterly* 3rd ser. 43 (July 1986): 333–61.

Lerner, Gerda, ed. *Black Women in White America: A Documentary History.* New York: Pantheon Books, 1972.

Lesser, Charles H. *South Carolina Begins: The Records of a Proprietary Colony, 1663–1721.* Columbia: South Carolina Department of Archives and History, 1995.

Ligon, Richard. *A True and Exact History of the Island of Barbados.* London, 1657.

Little, Thomas J. "The South Carolina Slave Laws Reconsidered." *South Carolina Historical Magazine* 94 (1993): 86–101.

Littlefield, Daniel C. "Charleston and Internal Slave Redistribution." *South Carolina Historical Magazine* 87 (1986): 93–105.

Littlefield, Daniel C. "Plantations, Paternalism and Profitability: Factors Affecting African Demography in the Old British Empire." *Journal of Southern History* 47 (1981): 167–82.

———. *Rice and Slaves: Ethnicity and the Slave Trade in Colonial South Carolina.* Baton Rouge: Louisiana University Press, 1981.

———. "The Slave Trade to Colonial South Carolina: A Profile." *South Carolina Historical Magazine* 91 (April 1990): 68–99.

Linebaugh, Peter and Marcus Rediker. *The Many-Headed Hydra: Sailors, Slaves, Commoners, and the Hidden History of the Revolutionary Atlantic.* Boston: Beacon Press, 2000.

Loewald, Klaus G,. Beverly Starika, and Paul S. Taylor, eds. "Johann Martin Bolzius Answers a Questionnaire on Carolina and Georgia." *William and Mary Quarterly* 3rd ser. 14 (1957): 218–22.

———. "Johann Martin Bolzius Answers a Questionnaire on Carolina and Georgia: Pt II." *William and Mary Quarterly* 3rd ser. 15 (1958): 228–52.

Lok, John. "The Voyage of M. John Lok to Guinea. . . . 1554." In *Principal Navigations and Voyages*, edited by Richard Hakluyt, 6: 154–76. London, 1659. Reprint, New York: Macmillan, 1903–5.

Lovejoy, Paul. "The Impact of the Atlantic Slave Trade on Africa: A Review of the Literature." *Journal of African History* (1989): 365–97.

Manning, Patrick. *Slavery and African Life: Occidental, Oriental and African Slave Trades.* Cambridge: Cambridge University Press, 1990.

Martensen, Robert. "The Transformation of Eve: Women's Bodies, Medicine, and Culture in early modern England." In *Sexual Knowledge, Sexual Science: The History of Attitudes to Sexuality*, edited by Roy Porter and Mikulas Teich, 107–33. Cambridge: Cambridge University Press, 1994.

Martin, Joel. "Southeastern Indians and the English Trade in Skins and Slaves." In *The Forgotten Centuries: Indians and Europeans in the American South, 1512–1704*, edited by Charles Hudson and Carmen Chaves Tesser, 304–26. Athens: University of Georgia Press, 1994.

Mason, Peter. *Deconstructing America: Representations of the Other.* New York: Routledge, 1990.

Mathews, Maurice. "A Contemporary View of Carolina in 1680." *South Carolina Historical Magazine* 55 (1954): 153–59.

Mathurin, Lucille. "A Historical Study of Women in Jamaica from 1655 to 1844." Ph.D. dissertation, University of the West Indies, Jamaica, 1974.

McClaren, Angus. *A History of Contraception: From Antiquity to the Present Day.* Oxford: Basil Davidson, 1990.

McCord, David J., ed. *Statutes at Large of South Carolina.* 7 vols. Columbia, South Carolina: A. S. Johnston, 1840.

McCrady, Edward. *The History of South Carolina Under the Proprietary Government, 1670–1715.* New York: Macmillan, 1901.

Meaders, Daniel E. "South Carolina Fugitives as Viewed Through Local Colonial Newspapers With Emphasis on Runaway Notices, 1732–1801." *Journal of Negro History* 40 (1975): 288–319.

Menard, Russell R. "The Africanization of the Lowcountry Labor Force." In *Race and Family in the Colonial South*, edited by Winthrop Jordan and Shelia Skemp, 81–108. Jackson: University Press of Mississippi, 1987.

Menard, Russell R. "The Maryland Slave Population, 1658–1730: A Demographic Profile of Blacks in Four Counties." *William and Mary Quarterly* 3rd ser. 32 (1975): 29–54.

Merrell, James H. "'The Customes of Our Countrey': Indians and Colonists in Early America." In *Strangers Within the Realm*, edited by Bernard Bailyn and Edmund Morgan, 117–56. Chapel Hill: University of North Carolina, 1991.

Merrell, James H. *The Indians' New World: Catawbas and Their Neighbors from European Contact Through the Era of Removal.* New York: W.W. Norton, 1989.

Merrell, James H. "'Our Bond of Peace': Patterns of Intercultural Exchange in the Carolina Piedmont, 1650–1750." In *Powhatan's Mantle: Indians in the Colonial Southeast*, edited by Peter H. Wood, Gregory Waselkov, and M. Thomas Hatley, 198–223. Lincoln: University of Nebraska Press, 1989.

Miller, Joseph C. "Mortality in the Atlantic Slave Trade: Statistical Evidence on Causality." *Journal of Interdisciplinary History* 11 (Autumn 1991): 317–29.

Mintz, Sidney and Richard Price. *An Anthropological Approach to the Afro-American Past: A Caribbean Perspective.* Philadelphia: Institute for the Study of Human Issues, 1976.

Moitt, Bernard. "Slave Women and Resistance in the French Caribbean." In *More Than Chattel: Black Women and Slavery in the Americas*, edited by David Barry Gaspar and Darlene Clark Hine, 239–58. Bloomington: Indiana University Press, 1996.

———. *Women and Slavery in the French Antilles, 1635–1848.* Bloomington: Indiana University Press, 2001.

———. "Women, Work and Resistance in the French Caribbean During Slavery, 1700–1848." In *Engendering History: Caribbean Women in Historical Perspective*, edited by Bridget Brereton, Verene Shepard, and Barbara Bailey, 155–75. New York: St. Martin's Press, 1995.

Montrose, Louis. "The Work of Gender in the Discourse of Discovery." *Representations* 33 (Winter 1991): 1–41.

Morgan, Edmund S. *American Slavery, American Freedom: The Ordeal of Colonial Virginia*. New York: W.W. Norton, 1975.

Morgan, Jennifer L. "Some Could Suckle over Their Shoulder; Male Travelers, Female Bodies and the Gendering of Racial Ideology, 1500–1770." *William and Mary Quarterly* 3rd ser. 54 (January): 167–92.

Morgan, Philip D. "Black Life in Eighteenth-Century Charleston." *Perspectives in American History*. New Series. Cambridge: Cambridge University Press, 1984.

————. "British Encounters with Africans and African Americans Circa 1600–1780." In *Strangers Within the Realm: Cultural Margins of the First British Empire*, edited by Bernard Bailyn and Philip D. Morgan, 157–219. Chapel Hill: University of North Carolina Press, 1991

————. "Colonial South Carolina Runaways: Their Significance for Slave Culture." *Slavery and Abolition* 6 (December 1985): 57–78.

————. "The Cultural Implications of the Atlantic Slave Trade: African Regional Origins, American Destinations and New World Developments." *Slavery and Abolition* 18 (1997): 122–45.

————. *Slave Counterpoint: Black Culture in the Eighteenth-Century Chesapeake and Lowcountry*. Chapel Hill: University of North Carolina Press, 1998.

————. "Work and Culture: The Task System and the World of Lowcountry Blacks, 1700–1880." *William and Mary Quarterly* 3rd ser. 39 (1982): 563–99.

Morrison, Toni. *Playing in the Dark: Whiteness and the Literary Imagination*. Cambridge, Mass.: Harvard University Press, 1992.

Morrissey, Marietta. *Slave Women in the New World: Gender Stratification in the Caribbean*. Lawrence: University of Kansas Press, 1988.

————. "Women's Work, Family Formation, and Reproduction Among Caribbean Slaves." *Review: Journal of the Fernand Braudel Center for the Study of Economies, Historical Systems, and Civilization* 9 (Winter 1986): 339–67.

Muller, Wilhelm Johann. "Wilhelm Johann Muller's Description of the Fetu Country, 1662–9." In *German Sources for West African History, 1599–1669*, edited by Adam Jones, 132–359. Wiesbaden: Franz Steiner, 1983.

Mullin, Gerald W. *Flight and Rebellion: Slave Resistance in Eighteenth Century Virginia*. London: Oxford University Press, 1972.

Mullin, Michael. *Africa in America: Slave Acculturation and Resistance in the American South and the British Caribbean, 1736–1831*. Urbana: University of Illinois Press, 1992.

————. "Women and the Comparative Study of American Negro Slavery." *Slavery and Abolition* 6 (1985): 25–40.

Nwokeji, G. Ugo. African Conceptions of Gender and the Slave Traffic. *The William and Mary Quarterly* 3rd ser. 58 (2001): 47–68.

Nyendael, David van. "A Description of Rio Formosa or. . . . Benin, 1 September 1702" in William Bosman, *A New and Accurate Description of the Coast of Guinea*. 1704. First English edition, London, 1705; fourth English edition, London: Frank Cass, 1967.

Ogilby, John. *Africa*. London, 1670.

Oliver, Vere Langford, ed. *Caribbeana: Being Miscellaneous Papers Relating to the*

History, Genealogy, Topography, and Antiquities of the British West Indies. 6 vols. London: Michell, Huges and Clark, 1910–19.

Olwell, Robert. *Masters, Slaves, and Subjects: The Culture of Power in the South Carolina Low Country, 1740–90.* Ithaca, N.Y.: Cornell University Press, 1998.

———. "'To Speak the Real Truth': Investigating a Slave Conspiracy in Colonial South Carolina." Document prepared from "A Journal of the Proceedings of His Majestys Honorable Council of South Carolina, From the 20th day of December 1748 To the 16th Day of December 1749," by James Bullock C[lerk of the] C[ouncil]; from a microfilm at the Library of Congress, originals held at the South Carolina Department of Archives and History, Columbia South Carolina, and the British Public Record Office, Kew, London.

Oruene, Taiwo. "Magical Powers of Twins in the Socio-Religious Beliefs of the Yoruba." *Folklore* 96 (1985): 208–16.

Otto, John and Nain Anderson. "The Origins of Southern Cattle-Grazing: A Problem in West Indian History." *Journal of Caribbean History* 21 (1988): 138–53.

Owens, Leslie H. "The African in the Garden: Reflections About New World Slavery and Its Lifelines." In *The State of Afro-American History: Past, Present, and Future,* edited by Darlene Clark Hine, 25–35. Baton Rouge: Louisiana State University Press, 1986.

Park, Katherine and Lorraine J. Daston. "Unnatural Conceptions: The Study of Monsters in Sixteenth and Seventeenth Century France and England." *Past and Present* 92 (1981): 21–54.

Patterson, Orlando. *Slavery and Social Death: A Comparative Study.* Cambridge, Mass.: Harvard University Press, 1982.

Phillips, Anthony DeV. "The Parliament of Barbados, 1639–1989." *Journal of the Barbados Museum and Historical Society* 38 (1990): 422–52.

Pinckney, Elise, ed. *The Letterbook of Eliza Lucas Pinckney, 1739–1762.* Columbia: University of South Carolina Press, 1997.

Pliny the Elder. *Natural History.* Translated by H. Rackham. Cambridge, Mass.: Harvard University Press, 1915.

Puckrein, Gary A. *Little England: Plantation Society and Anglo-Barbadian Politics, 1627–1700.* New York: New York University Press, 1984.

Purkiss, Diane. "Women's Stories of Witchcraft in Early Modern England: The House, the Body, the Child." *Gender and History* 7 (1995): 408–32.

Purrey, John. "A Description of the Province of South Carolina," in *Tracts and Other Papers. . . . of the Colonies of North America.* Vol. 2, edited by Peter Force. Washington D.C., 1838.

Ravenstein, E. G., ed. *The Strange Adventures of Andrew Battel.* London: Hakluyt Society, 1801.

Richardson, David. "Shipboard Revolts, African Authority, and the Atlantic Slave Trade." *William and Mary Quarterly* 3rd ser. 58 (2001): 69–92.

Richardson, David. "Slave Exports from West and West-Central Africa, 1700–1810: New Estimates of Volume and Distribution." *Journal of African History* (1989): 1–22.

Riddle, John. *Contraception and Abortion from the Ancient World to the Renaissance.* Cambridge, Mass.: Harvard University Press, 1992.

Roberts, Dorothy. *Killing the Black Body: Race, Reproduction, and the Meaning of Liberty*. New York: Vintage Books, 1997.

Robertson, Claire and Martin Klein. "Women's Importance in African Slave Systems." In *Women and Slavery in Africa*, edited by Claire Robertson and Martin Klein, 3–29. Madison: University of Wisconsin Press, 1983.

Rodney, Walter. *A History of the Upper Guinea Coast, 1545–1800*. London: Oxford University Press, 1970.

Roper, Lyndal. *Oedipus and the Devil: Witchcraft, Sexuality and Religion in Early Modern Europe*. London: Routledge, 1994.

Rosengarten, Dale. *Row upon Row: Sea Grass Baskets of the South Carolina Lowcountry*. Columbia: University of South Carolina and McKissick Museum, 1986.

Ruddick, Sara. "Thinking Mothers/Conceiving Birth." In *Representations of Motherhood*, edited by Margaret Honey, Donna Bassin, and Meryle Mahrer Kaplan. New Haven, Conn.: Yale University Press, 1994.

Sainsbury, W. Noel, ed. *The Calendar of State Papers, Colonial Series*. London, 1889.

Salley, A. S., ed. *Journal of the Commons House of Assembly of South Carolina, November 15 1726–May 11 1726/7*. Columbia: Historical Commission of South Carolina, 1946.

———, ed. *Warrants for Lands in South Carolina, 1672–1711*. Columbia: University of South Carolina Press, 1973.

Salmon, Marylynn. "The Cultural Significance of Breastfeeding and Infant Care in Early Modern England and America." *Journal of Social History* 28 (Winter 1994): 247–70.

Sanders, Joanne McCree, ed. *Barbados Records: Baptisms, 1637–1800*. Baltimore: Genealogical Publishing Co., 1984.

Scarry, Elaine. *The Body in Pain: The Making and Unmaking of the World*. New York: Oxford University Press, 1985.

Schiebinger, Londa. *Nature's Body: Gender in the Making of Modern Science*. Boston, Beacon Press, 1993.

———. "Why Mammals Are Called Mammals: Gender Politics in Eighteenth-Century Natural History." *American Historical Review* 98 (April 1993): 382–411.

Schoenmaeckers, R., I. H. Shah, R. Lesthaeghe, and O. Tambashe. "The Child-Spacing Tradition and the Post-Partum Taboo in Tropical Africa." In *Child-Spacing in Tropical Africa: Traditions and Change*, edited by Hilary Page and Ron Lesthaeghe, 25–72. London: Academic Press, 1981.

Schwalm, Leslie A. *A Hard Fight for We: Women's Transition from Slavery to Freedom in South Carolina*. Urbana: University of Illinois Press, 1997.

Scott, Joan. "The Evidence of Experience." *Critical Inquiry* 17 (Summer, 1991): 773–97.

Scott, Julius S. "The Common Wind: Currents of Afro-American Communication in the Era of the Haitian revolution. Ph.D. dissertation, Duke University, 1986.

Shatzman, Aaron M. *Servants Into Planters: The Origins of an American Image: Land Acquisition and Status Mobility in 17th-Century South Carolina*. New York: Garland Publishing, 1989.

Shaw, Stephanie. "Mothering Under Slavery In the Antebellum South." In *Mother-*

ing: *Ideology, Experience, and Agency*, edited by Evelyn Nakano Glenn, Grace Chang, and Linda Rennie Forrey, 237–58. New York: Routledge, 1994.

Sheridan, Richard. *Doctors and Slaves: A Medical and Demographic History of Slavery in the British West Indies, 1680–1843*. Cambridge: Cambridge University Press, 1985.

Sheridan, Richard. *Sugar and Slavery: An Economic History of the British West Indies*. Baltimore: Johns Hopkins University Press, 1973.

Silver, Timothy. *A New Face on the Countryside: Indians, Colonists, and Slaves in South Atlantic Forests, 1500–1800*. Cambridge: Cambridge University Press, 1990.

Simson, Rennie. "The Afro-American Female: The Historical Context of the Construction of Sexual Identity." In *Powers of Desire: The Politics of Sexuality*, edited by Ann Sintow, Christine Stansell, and Sharon Thompson, 229–36. New York: Monthly Review Press, 1983.

Sirmans, M. Eugene. *Colonial South Carolina: A Political History, 1663–1763*. Chapel Hill: University of North Carolina Press, 1966.

Sirmans, M. Eugene. "The Legal Status of the Slave in South Carolina, 1670–1740." *Journal of Southern History* 28 (November 1962): 462–73.

Smyth, William D. "Travellers in South Carolina in the Early Eighteenth Century." *South Carolina Historical Magazine* 79 (1978): 113–25.

Snyder, Terri L. "'As If There Was Not Master or Woman in the Land': Gender, Dependency, and Household Violence in Virginia, 1646–1720." In *Over the Threshold: Intimate Violence in Early America*, edited by Christine Daniels and Michael V. Kennedy. New York: Routledge, 1999.

Sobel, Mechal. "The Revolution in Selves: Black and White Inner Aliens." In *Through a Glass Darkly: Reflections on Personal Identity in Early America*, ed. Ronald Hoffman, Mechal Sobel, and Fredrika J. Teute, 163–205. Chapel Hill: University of North Carolina Press, 1997.

———. *Trabelin' On: The Slave Journey to an Afro-Baptist Faith*. 1979. Reprint Princeton, N.J.: Princeton University Press, 1988.

South, Stanley. *Exploratory Archaeology at the site of 1670–1680 Charles Towne on Albemarle Point in South Carolina*. Columbia: Institute of Archeology and Anthropology, University of South Carolina, 1969.

Spear, Jennifer. "Whiteness" and the Purity of Blood: Race, Sexuality, and Social Order in Colonial Louisiana. Ph.D. diss., University of Minnesota, 1999.

Spruill, Julia Cherry. *Women's Life and Work in the Southern Colonies*. 1938. Reprint New York: W.W. Norton, 1972

Staves, Susan. "Resentment or Resignation? Dividing the Spoils Among Daughters and Younger Sons." In *Early Modern Conceptions of Property*, edited by John Brewer and Susan Staves, 194–218. New York: Routledge, 1995.

Steckel, Richard and Richard Jensen. "New Evidence on the Causes of Slave and Crew Mortality in the Atlantic Slave Trade." *Journal of Economic History* 46 (March 1986): 57–77.

Stedman, John Gabriel. *Narrative of a Five Years Expedition Against the Revolted Negroes of Surinam: Transcribed . . . from the Original 1790 Manuscript*. Ed.

Richard Price and Sally Price. Baltimore: Johns Hopkins University Press, 1988.

Sturtz, Linda L. "Spanish Moss and Aprons: European Responses to Gender Ambiguity in the Exploration and Colonization of South-Eastern North America." *Seventeenth Century* 11 (Spring 1996): 125–40.

Suleiman, Ayuba. "Ayuba Suleiman Diall of Bondu." In *Africa Remembered: Narratives by West Africans from the Era of the Slave Trade*, edited by Philip Curtin. Madison: University of Wisconsin Press, 1967.

TePaske, John J. "The Fugitive Slave: Intercolonial Rivalry and Spanish Slave Policy, 1687–1764." In *Eighteenth-Century Florida and Its Borderlands*, edited by Samuel Proctor, 1–12. Gainseville: The University Presses of Florida, 1975.

Thompson, Robert Farris. *Flash of the Spirit: African and Afro-American Art and Philosophy*. New York: Random House, 1983.

Thornton, John K. *Africa and Africans in the Making of the Atlantic World, 1400–1680*. Cambridge: Cambridge University Press, 1992.

———. "African Dimensions of the Stono Rebellion." *American Historical Review* 96 (October 1991): 1101–13.

———. "On the Trail of VooDoo: African Christianity in Africa and the Americas." *Americas* 44 (January 1988): 261–78.

———. "Sexual Demography: The Impact of the Slave Trade on Family Structure." In *Women and Slavery in Africa*, edited by Claire Robertson and Martin Klein. Madison: University of Wisconsin Press, 1983.

Towrson, William. "The first Voyage made by Master William Towrson Marchent of London to the coast of Guinea with 2 ships, in the yeere 1555." In *Principal Navigations and Voyages*, edited by Richard Hakluyt, 6: 177–251. London, 1659. Reprint New York: Macmillan, 1903–5.

Tryon, Thomas. *Friendly Advice to the Gentlemen-Planters of the East and West Indies*. London, 1684.

Ulsheimer, Andreas Josua. "Andreas Josua Ulsheimer's Voyage of 1603–4." In *German Sources for West African History, 1599–1669*, edited by Adam Jones, 18–44. Weisbaden: Steiner, 1983.

Whistler, Henry. "Extracts from Henry Whistler's Journal of the West India Expedition, 1654." In *The Narrative of General Venables*, edited by C. H. Firth. New York: Longmans, 1900.

Walsh, Lorena S. *From Calabar to Carter's Grove: The History of a Virginia Slave Community*. Charlottesville: University Press of Virginia, 1997.

Ward, J. R. *British West Indian Slavery, 1750–1834: The Process of Amelioration*. Oxford: Clarendon Press, 1988.

Waterhouse, Richard. *A New World Gentry: The Making of a Merchant and Planter Class in South Carolina, 1670–1770*. New York: Garland, 1989.

Watson, Alan. *Slave Law in the Americas*. Athens: University of Georgia Press, 1989.

Webber, Mabel L. "The First Governor Moore and His Children. *South Carolina Historical and Genealogical Magazine* 37 (1936): 1–23.

———. "Presentment of the Grand Jury, March 1733/34." *South Carolina Historical and Genealogical Magazine* 25 (1924): 193–6.

Weir, Robert M. *Colonial South Carolina, A History*. New York: KTO Press, 1983.

Westbury, Susan. "Analyzing a Regional Slave Trade: The West Indies and Virginia, 1698–1775." *Slavery and Abolition* 7 (December 1986): 241–56.

White, Deborah Gray. *Ar'n't I a Woman? Female Slaves in the Plantation South*. New York: W.W. Norton, 1985.

Wilson, Samuel. *An Account of the Province of Carolina*. London, 1682. In *Narratives of Early Carolina, 1650–1708*, edited by Alexander Salley. New York: Charles Scribner's Sons, 1911.

Windley, Lathan A., ed. *Runaway Slave Advertisements: A Documentary History from the 1730s to 1790s*. Westport, Conn.: Greenwood Press, 1983.

Wood, Betty. *Slavery in Colonial Georgia, 1730–1775*. Athens: University of Georgia Press, 1984.

Wood, Betty. *Women's Work, Men's Work: The Informal Slave Economies of Lowcountry Georgia*. Athens: University of Georgia Press, 1995.

Wood, Peter H. *Black Majority: Negroes in Colonial South Carolina, from 1670 through the Stono Rebellion*. New York: W.W. Norton, 1974.

———. "More like a Negro Country: Demographic Patterns in Colonial South Carolina. 1700–1740." In *Race and Slavery in the Western Hemisphere: Quantitative Studies*, edited by Stanley Engerman and Eugene Genovese, 131–72. Princeton, N.J.: Princeton University Press, 1975.

Index

Abortifacients: African, 114; American, 114
Adornment in Africa, 64
Africa, ethnicity, 120, 142, 184, 190; Akan, 175; Allada, 64; Angolan, 159, 190; Coromantee, 120, 121, 175; Dongo, 29; Fon, 64; Fula, 154; Fulbie, 28; Gaga, 29; Igbo, 64; Mandinka, 28, 63, 67, 154; Wolof, 61, 154
Africa, image of, 25
African retentions, 108
Africanus, Leo, 29
Allada, 59
Angola, 29
Arda, 52
Artisans, enslaved: male, 96, 146, 149, 168; women barred from, 169
Atkins, John, 41
Azurara, Gomes, 24

Barbados, 45, 48, 53, 74, 76, 78, 81, 84, 96, 108, 115, 148, 151, 168, 183; and Carolina, 124, 125, 127, 152
Barbados Conspiracy of 1675, 183–84
Barbados Conspiracy of 1692, 185, 187
Barbot, John, 41
Battell, Andrew, 29
Beckles, Hilary, 187
Benzoni, Girolamo, 19, 20
Bermuda, 76
Bight of Benin, 57, 59, 66
Bight of Biafra, 51, 57, 60
Birth rates: among enslaved women, 36, 70, 82, 131, 141, 185; among white settlers, 70, 131
Black militias, 171
Breast-feeding: African women in Africa, 66, 67; African women in America, 138, 181; as birth control, 66; English women, 36, 66; Native American women, 21; over the shoulder, 31, 34, 35, 41, 42
Breasts, 46, 47; sagging, 21, 27, 31, 42, 49
Brown, Kathleen, 93

Brun, Samuel, 62
de Bry, Theodor, 21, 22
Bucher, Benadette, 21, 22
Burton, Robert, 35

Callabar River, 51, 53, 62
Cannibalism, 19, 22, 30, 40
Cape Verde, 13, 14, 46, 47
Carney, Judith, 164
Cattlepens, 126, 152, 154, 157
Childbirth, 36, 66, 84, 12, 134, 141, 142, 149, 185; among white women, 75, 76; as breeding, 18, 77, 80, 82, 86, 99, 128; as connection between women, 134, 157; as evidence of acculturation, 108; as evidence of savagery, 30, 40, 66, 68, 105; as resistance, 113, 132, 167, 168; as separation from other women, 134; without pain, 18, 40, 45, 48, 65; withholding, 113, 129. *See also* Creolization
Children, 103, 108, 109, 116, 130, 134, 135, 141, 157
Christianity, 173
Columbus, Christopher, 18
Craton, Michael, 148
Creolization, 107, 108, 125, 142, 143, 169; and childbearing, 108, 119, 120, 121, 140; and resistance, 185, 187; and social control, 171, 173, 184, 185, 188

Dahomey, 59
Domestic work, 145, 148, 151, 156, 159
Domesticity, 148, 151
Dunn, Richard S., 88

Eden, Richard, 17
Eltis, David, 81, 199

Falconbridge, Anna, 46
Family life, 86, 115, 130, 132, 141
Female circumcision, 65
Fertility control, 113

Fertility rates, 111, 119, 135, 148, 149; and disease, 111, 114; of white women, 111
Fieldwork, 120, 145, 146, 147, 157
Fischer, Kirsten, 105
Florida, 146
French Guiana, 150

Gambia River, 28, 47, 67
Georgia, 145, 160
Gold Coast, 57, 58, 63, 64, 67

Hakluyt, Richard, 25, 26
Hall, Kim 14, 15
Hartman, Saidiya, 40, 109
Herbert, Thomas, 31
Herodotus, 16
Hottentot, 31, 41, 47

Increase, 19, 81, 83, 85, 89, 90, 91, 92, 97, 99, 129, 137, 138, 139, 140
Indentured servitude, 73, 74, 76, 78, 124, 149, 152
Infanticide, 178
Informants, 176, 177
Inheritance: enslaved couples as, 84, 85, 86, 88, 91, 97, 98, 101, 102, 105, 137, 139; enslaved women as, 79, 83, 90, 97, 98, 99, 101; and slaveownership, 70, 71, 83, 102
Interracial contact, 87, 122, 156, 192–95; legislation limiting, 71, 72
Islam, 64

Jamaica, 148, 149
Jobson, Richard, 28, 46, 48

Landgrants, South Carolina, 92, 152, 154
Laurens, Henry 105
Lawson, John 75, 113
LeJau, Francis, 130
Legal codes: and slavery, 72, 73, 93, 109, 167, 169, 174, 188–89; and women's work, 73, 7
Ligon, Richard, 13, 14, 15, 46, 47, 48
Lok, John, 27
Long, Edward, 46, 47

Mandeville, John, 16
Manumission, 80, 98, 125, 128
de Marees, Pieter, 30, 31
Market places: in Africa, 62; in Charlestown, 159, 177
Marriage: in Africa, 64; among enslaved

women and men, 84, 86, 102, 175, 193; as tool for investment, 124; as tool for pacification, 95, 110
Martinique, 75
Martyr, Peter, 27
Maryland, 71, 72
Merian, Maria, 113
Monetary value of enslaved women versus men, 89, 134
Monstrosity, 15, 16, 21, 23, 28, 41, 68
Montserrat, 135, 137
Morgan, Edmund, 196
Morgan, Phillip, 86, 104
Mortality rates, 110
Motherhood, 23, 24, 25, 27, 67, 113, 115, 119, 135, 139, 141, 167, 181, 186, 194
Muller, Wilhelm, 62

Nairne, Thomas, 145, 172
Naming patterns, 120
Native Americans: as instigators of violence, 183; military conflict with, 77, 4, 171; mortality of, 110; as slaves, 77, 128, 153; trade with, 77, 156
Nevis, 85, 112
Nicholls, Michael, 86
North Carolina, 100
Nudity, 14, 29, 33, 34, 35

Ogilby, John, 35

Painter, Nell, 199
Parenting, 25, 109, 114, 122, 128, 142, 149, 191
Population, enslaved versus free, 87, 94, 96, 115, 131, 157, 158, 170, 171, 174
Purchas, Samuel, 29

Racial ideology, 13
Ralegh, Walter, 20
Rebelliousness and gender, 94, 95, 96
Reproduction: as ideology, 56, 65, 68, 79, 80, 81, 110, 144, 173; as expectation of slaveowners, 84, 85, 100; and production, 122, 144, 154, 189
Reproductive potential, 91, 92, 103
Rice cultivation, 95, 100, 134, 161, 162, 163; tools of 155, 157, 161
Royal Africa Company, 42, 45, 54, 55, 58, 59, 87
Runaways, 178, 179, 181, 182, 189

St. Augustine, Florida, 178, 179, 181
St. Christopher, 135, 137, 151
St. Domingue, 150
Scarry, Elaine, 47
Schwalm, Leslie, 161
Senegambia, 54, 57, 59, 60, 63, 64, 66, 154, 161, 162
Separation: of mothers and children, 123, 133, 134, 139, 141; of couples, 123, 133, 134, 138, 139, 141
Sex as tool of white population increase, 74, 75
Sex ratios: among enslaved, 51, 83, 84, 85, 87, 94, 112, 115, 135, 136, 138, 150, 151; among white settlers, 74; in slave trade, 50, 63, 145; on plantations, 147–48, 150, 151
Sierra Leone, 54, 66, 161
Slave ships: *Arthur*, 51, 52, 107; *Hannah*, 52
Slave trade: children in, 104; demography of, 50; mortality in, 53; purchasing patterns in, 51; provisioning of, 52; sex ratios in, 53, 56, 57, 58, 59, 60, 63, 145; to Carolina, 127, 157
Slave trading forts, 54, 55, 62
Slaveowners' inventories, 104, 135, 136
Slaveowners' wills, 69, 70, 71, 78, 85, 87, 90, 96, 100, 102, 128, 129, 135, 136
Slaveownership and American identity, 73
Smith, William, 42, 45
Snelgrave, William, 41, 42
Society for the Propagation of the Gospel, 130
South Carolina, 60, 71, 75, 87, 92, 142, 152, 158, 169, 187
Spoeri, Felix, 35, 49, 174

Steckel, Richard, 111
Stono Rebellion, 140, 188
Sugar cultivation, 78, 82, 96, 146, 149, 150

Tobacco cultivation, 80
Towrson, William, 27
Travel narratives, 12, 15, 72

Upper Guinea Coast, 61, 63

Van Nyendael, David, 60
Vespucci, Amerigo, 17, 19
Villaut, Nicolas, 35
Virginia, 71, 72, 73, 86, 94, 95, 168

Walsh, Lorena, 81
Wheeler, Charles, 45
Wheeler, Roxann, 40
Whydah, 45
Wilson, Samuel, 75
Women: as animals, 80, 87, 105; as majority of workers on plantations, 147, 148, 149
Women's work: agricultural in Africa, 62, 164; agricultural in Americas, 69, 126, 146, 147, 148, 149, 153; markets in Africa, 62; markets in Americas, 160, 177; as laundresses, 159, 187; as childminders for whites, 132, 176; white women in Americas, 73, 74
Wood, Peter H., 125, 131, 199

Yamasee War, 94

Acknowledgments

There is something about acknowledgment pages that I have always loved; perhaps because seeing the network that sustains the work of writing helps to give the lie to its isolation. For even though it is ultimately just a pile of pages, a purple pen, and me, many people and institutions allowed me to shut out all the other parts of my life in order to find the focus and the energy necessary to complete this project.

My formal life as a student was bracketed by Adrienne Lash Jones at Oberlin College and my Ph.D. advisor, Julius S. Scott, at Duke University. When I was a college junior, Adrienne Jones introduced me to the idea of African American women's history, and provided me with a model of academic grace that I continue to emulate. Julius Scott opened up the black Atlantic and did so with a rigor and commitment to the power of the written word that I continue to strive for. They both taught me essential and difficult lessons about integrity and the relationship between my work and myself. I am quite grateful for their presence in my academic life and hope that my work reflects their considerable influence.

At Duke University, I was quite fortunate to have the opportunity to study and interact with an extraordinary faculty that included William Chafe, David Barry Gaspar, Henry Louis Gates, Jr., Monica Greene, Nancy Hewitt, Julius Scott, and Peter Wood. In particular, Peter Wood's work has been enormously influential. He taught me that demography held radical truths and was nothing to be scared of. Despite moments of terror, I continue to know that he was absolutely right. Herman Bennett, Matthew Countryman, Ann Farnsworth, Kirsten Fischer, Christina Greene, Deborah Montgomerie, Celia Naylor-Ojurongbe, Andrew Neather, Stephanie Smallwood, Faith Smith, Timothy Tyson, Lisa Waller, and Jocelyn Zivin were all part of an environment at Duke that encouraged the kind of intellectual risk-taking that is the foundation of this project. In Baltimore, Antoinette Burton taught me that continuing to do so is my only option. Since leaving North Carolina for northern climes, good fortune has followed me in the community of friends and colleagues in which my life and work takes shape. I find myself in a family of formidable intellects; my grandmother Ethel "Maymette" Carter, my parents John and Claudia Morgan, and my brother Zachary R. Morgan have always challenged me—both to get a word in edgewise and to do the work that I love. My friends are enormously supportive of the kind of work I do, and I cannot imagine undertaking this project without the love and kindness of such a beloved circle. Thank you to Steven Amsterdam, Barbara Balliet, Peter Bergman, Cheryl Clarke, Kristen Goldmansour, Adib Goldmansour, Mary Esther Malloy-Hopwood, Sharon Frances Moore, Robert Reid-Pharr, Lisa Waller, Sidney Whelan, and Keith Yazmir.

Once released from the confines of graduate school, I couldn't have found a setting more supportive than the departments of History and Women's and Gender Studies at Rutgers University. My colleagues at Rutgers have supported this project in many ways. The interdisciplinary context of the Department of Women's and Gender Studies has been invaluable, I am particularly grateful for the support and engagement of Barbara Balliet, Ethel Brooks, Harriet Davidson, Joanne Givand, Mary Hawkesworth, Jasbir Puar, and Johanna Regulska. The Department of History has been a most collegial academic home. Nancy Hewitt tailed me from Durham and pushed and prodded with a combination of tenacity and gentleness that is unparalleled, I owe her a great deal. Paul Clemens, John Gillis, Temma Kaplan, Steven Lawson, and Bonnie Smith offered important intellectual support. I arrived at Rutgers as Mia Bay and Deborah Gray White inaugurated the Black Atlantic Project at the Rutgers Center for Historical Analysis; the two years of lively discussion and probing intellectual work at the center were extraordinary. It gives me particular pleasure to finish this book while Deborah Gray White is my department Chair. When I was nineteen years old, I caught a glimpse of Deborah at the 1985 meeting of the Association for the Study of African Life and History in Cleveland, Ohio. She gave me my first glimpse of the pure joy and triumph of writing and publishing the history of African American women. What a delight it is for me now to offer up a contribution to a field that she inaugurated.

I appreciate the good will of folks at the University of Pennsylvania Press. Kathleen Brown's engagement with this project was above and beyond anything I expected from a series editor. I have benefited tremendously from her comments, conversation, and queries. Robert Lockhart has been patient and insistent in just the right balance. I owe a tremendous debt to Kate Babbitt, whose superlative editing skills have certainly saved me from myriad errors and confusions; those that remain are, of course, entirely my own responsibility.

Over the course of the many years I have worked on this project, I have benefitted from support and encouragement from librarians and archivists; in particular those at the Barbados Archives, the South Carolina Department of Archives and History (where Charles Lesser was invaluable), and the South Carolina Historical Society. In Barbados, Marie-Claire Evelyn rescued me at a desperate final research hour.

I have also benefited from the comments and critical eye of many colleagues and friends: Barbara Balliet, Mia Bay, Toby Ditz, Shelly Eversley, Daphne LaMonthe, Mary Gossy, Robert Reid-Pharr, Stephanie Smallwood, and Tim Tyson have read chapters; Ira Berlin, Sharon Block, Peter Bergman, Antoinette Burton, Christopher Brown, Kathleen Brown, Paul Clemens, Kirsten Fischer, Nancy Hewitt, and Tera Hunter have read and commented on the manuscript in its entirety. Venturing into work that crosses both disciplinary and geographical boundaries has been a challenge, I am very grateful for the signposts and landmarks, both obvious and subtle, to which these readers have called my attention.

An earlier version of Chapter 1 appeared as "Some Could Suckle over Their Shoulder": Male Travelers, Female Bodies, and the Gendering of Racial Ideology, 1500–1770," *William and Mary Quarterly* 54 (January 1997): 167–92. Reprinted by permission of the Omohundro Institute of Early American History and Culture.

Neither of my children has ever known me *not* to be working toward the completion of this project. I appreciated Carl's presence throughout more than he can know; and I trust that Emma (who queried in the final stages that "this book is taking a long time, can I help mama?") will perhaps understand in the future how profoundly she too helped all along.

This book is for their father.